PE

THE BACC

EURIPIDES, the youngest of the three great Athenian playwrights, was born around 485 BC of a family of good standing. He first competed in the dramatic festivals in 455 BC, coming only third; his record of success in the tragic competitions is lower than that of either Aeschylus or Sophocles. There is a tradition that he was unpopular, even a recluse; we are told that he composed poetry in a cave by the sea, near Salamis. What is clear from contemporary evidence, however, is that audiences were fascinated by his innovative and often disturbing dramas. His work was controversial already in his lifetime, and he himself was regarded as a 'clever' poet, associated with philosophers and other intellectuals. Towards the end of his life he went to live at the court of Archelaus, king of Macedon. It was during his time there that he wrote what many consider his greatest work, the *Bacchae*. When news of his death reached Athens in early 406 BC, Sophocles appeared publicly in mourning for him. Euripides is thought to have written about ninety-two plays, of which seventeen tragedies and one satyr-play known to be his survive; the other play which is attributed to him, the *Rhesus*, may in fact be by a later hand.

JOHN DAVIE was born in Glasgow in 1950, and was educated at the High School of Glasgow, Glasgow University and Balliol College, Oxford, where he wrote a thesis on Greek tragedy. From 1975 to 1984 he taught Classics at Harrow, before moving to St Paul's School to become Head of Classics, where he still teaches. He is the author of a number of articles on classical subjects and a member of the Hellenic Society's and the Roman Society's Visiting Panel of Lecturers. He divides his time between London and Oxford, where he teaches Classics to undergraduates at Balliol College.

DR RICHARD RUTHERFORD was born in Edinburgh in 1956, and was educated at Robert Gordon's College, Aberdeen and at Worcester College, Oxford. Since 1982 he has been Tutor in Greek and Latin Literature at Christ Church, Oxford. He is the author of a number of books and articles on classical authors, including a commentary on books 19 and 20 of Homer's *Odyssey* (1992), *The Art of Plato: Ten Essays in Platonic Interpretation* (1995) and *Classical Literature: A Concise History* (2005).

EURIPIDES

THE BACCHAE AND OTHER PLAYS

Translated by JOHN DAVIE,
with an introduction and notes by RICHARD RUTHERFORD

PENGUIN BOOKS

PENGUIN BOOKS

Published by the Penguin Group
Penguin Books Ltd, 80 Strand, London WC2R ORL, England
Penguin Group (USA) Inc., 375 Hudson Street, New York, New York 10014, USA
Penguin Group (Canada), 90 Eglinton Avenue East, Suite 700, Toronto, Ontario, Canada M4P 2Y3
(a division of Pearson Penguin Canada Inc.)
Penguin Ireland, 25 St Stephen's Green, Dublin 2, Ireland (a division of Penguin Books Ltd)
Penguin Group (Australia), 250 Camberwell Road, Camberwell, Victoria 3124, Australia
(a division of Pearson Australia Group Pty Ltd)
Penguin Books India Pvt Ltd, 11, Community Centre, Panchsheel Park, New Delhi – 110 017, India
Penguin Books (NZ), cnr Airborne and Rosedale Roads, Albany, Auckland 1310, New Zealand
(a division of Pearson New Zealand Ltd)
Penguin Books (South Africa) (Pty) Ltd, 24 Sturdee Avenue, Rosebank, Johannesburg 2196, South Africa

Penguin Books Ltd, Registered Offices: 80 Strand, London WC2R ORL, England

www.penguin.com

This translation first published, 2005

033

Translation copyright © John Davie, 2005
Introduction and editorial material copyright © Richard Rutherford, 2005
All rights reserved

The moral right of the translator and editor has been asserted

Set in 10/12.25 pt PostScript Monotype Bembo
Typeset by Rowland Phototypesetting Ltd, Bury St Edmunds, Suffolk
Printed and bound in Great Britain by Clays Ltd, Elcograf S.p.A.

ISBN–13: 978–0–14044–726–2

www.greenpenguin.co.uk

CONTENTS

GENERAL INTRODUCTION

'I portray men as they should be, but Euripides portrays them as they are.'
(Sophocles, quoted by Aristotle, *Poetics*, ch. 25, 1460b33–4)

'Whatever other defects of organization he may have, Euripides is the most intensely tragic of all the poets.' (Aristotle, *Poetics*, ch. 14, 1453a28–30)

'I am really amazed that the scholarly nobility does not comprehend his virtues, that they rank him below his predecessors, in line with that high-toned tradition which the clown Aristophanes brought into currency . . . Has any nation ever produced a dramatist who would deserve to hand him his slippers?'
(Goethe, *Diaries*, 22 Nov. 1831)

'What were you thinking of, overweening Euripides, when you hoped to press myth, then in its last agony, into your service? It died under your violent hands . . . Though you hunted all the passions up from their couch and conjured them into your circle, though you pointed and burnished a sophistic dialectic for the speeches of your heroes, they have only counterfeit passions and speak counterfeit speeches.' (Nietzsche, *The Birth of Tragedy*, ch. 10)

I

Already in his own lifetime Euripides was a controversial figure. Daring in his theatrical innovations, superbly eloquent and articulate in the rhetoric which he gave to his characters, closely in touch with the intellectual life of his time, he has stimulated and shocked audiences and readers not only through the unexpected twists and turns of his plots, but also by the alarming immorality of many of his characters. But before exploring these and other aspects of his work in more detail, we must briefly put him in context, by giving an outline of the earlier history of the Athenian genre of tragedy, and the work of Aeschylus, his great predecessor, and of Sophocles, his older contemporary.

Unlike epic poetry, which was a traditional form familiar throughout the Greek world, tragedy was a relatively new invention in the fifth century BC, and one which was particularly Athenian. Its origins and early development are obscure: if, as Aristotle believed, it originated in a form of choral song, the 'dithyramb', a song in honour of the god Dionysus, then it had already been transformed before the time of Aeschylus. Ancient tradition held that contests between tragic playwrights had become an established part of the festival known as the City Dionysia (held in March) some time in the 530s, and that the key figure of these early days was a dramatist called Thespis. Our earliest surviving tragedy is Aeschylus' *Persians*, performed in 472, a full sixty years later. The dramas which have survived span the rest of the fifth century, a period of intense political activity and social and intellectual change. Hence generalizations even about the extant dramas will be dangerous, and we must always bear in mind that we have only the tip of the iceberg.

The Athenian tragedies were performed in the open air, in a theatre enormous by modern standards: some experts believe that it could have contained more than 14,000 people, as it certainly could after reconstruction in the fourth century.[1] This large audience was probably composed mainly of men (it is likely that women could attend, but probable that not many did so). Those attending paid for admission, but the price was low, probably less than half a labourer's daily wage; in the fourth century even this charge was paid for out of public subsidies. The stage-arrangements were sparse: a building set behind the main area where the actors moved would represent a palace or other such building according to the needs of the play. Perhaps on a lower level (though the layout is much disputed) was the open area called the *orchestra* ('dancing-space'), in which the chorus stood or danced. The events were presented as happening out of doors, theatrically necessary but also more natural in Mediterranean life. Entrances along passages on either side of the theatre were loosely conceived as leading to different destinations – country or city, army camp or seashore, depending on the plot. Actors were all male (even for female parts), normally Athenian citizens; all wore masks and dignified formal dress; speaking actors were almost invariably limited to three in number, but could take on different roles during the play by changing costume and mask offstage. Stage equipment and props were few; the action was largely stylized, even static, with the more violent action conceived as taking place offstage, then being reported to the actors, often in a long narrative speech. All plays were in verse, partly spoken and partly sung; although Euripides made several strides towards more 'realistic' drama, the effect of a Greek tragedy in his time would still have been to move the audience to a distant world, where great figures of the mythical past fought and disputed over momentous issues.

Every Greek tragedy had a chorus, a team of twelve or fifteen singers representing the community or some other body concerned with the events of the drama. It may be that originally tragedy consisted wholly of choral songs; if so, the key innovation, whether Thespis or another was responsible, must have been the introduction of an actor who engaged in dialogue with the chorus, who could withdraw and take part in events offstage, then return to inform them of developments. Aeschylus is said to have introduced a second actor, Sophocles a third. There the tragedians stopped, though as the century passed the three actors were often expected to play more roles, and 'mute' actors (domestic slaves, attendants or soldiers) were permitted. Different sections of the drama were formally distinct: a substantial choral song normally divided major sections of the play (it is common to use the modern term 'acts'); but formal variation is found even within a single scene. Actors might address one another in long formalized speeches ('rhesis'), or in more fast-moving dialogue: the tragedians were especially fond of fast-moving line-by-line exchanges ('stichomythia'), and later in the century, especially in Euripides, this might be given still greater rapidity by dividing successive lines between characters. As we shall see, actors often move from one stylistic register to another, shifting from speech to recitative to full-scale song; in earlier tragedy they tend to sing together with or in response to the chorus, but later the actors sing solos or 'monodies'.[2] In general, the importance of the actors and the size of their role in the play increased, while that of the chorus declined; but in the work of the three great tragedians the chorus were never unimportant, and their songs or 'choral odes' do far more than fill in time or allow an interval: these odes comment on the action, react to it and ponder its significance, placing it in a larger perspective, chronological and religious. Some of the finest poetry in Greek tragedy comes in the choral odes.

We tend to think of the theatre as a recreation, and one which is available more or less any night of the year. The position in ancient Athens was quite different. Drama was part of a civic occasion, the festival of Dionysus. Although the city held many religious festivals, tragedies were performed only at a few, and at fixed points in the year. It was not possible for a dramatist to stage anything he liked at any time; he had to apply to the proper authorities and be 'granted a chorus', given permission to compete and financial support (it is true, however, that we also have evidence for theatrical activities in rural Attica, where procedure was perhaps less formal than at the great civic festivals). In the earliest times the dramatist would also play a part in his plays, though Sophocles is said to have given this up because his voice was weak. Still more important, the author was also the producer, working together with his actors and choruses and training them. At the City Dionysia three tragedians would compete for the prize every year; each of them would present three tragedies – sometimes but not necessarily a connected 'trilogy'. Aeschylus favoured these trilogies (as his masterpiece, the *Oresteia*, illustrates), but they seem to have gone out of fashion after his death, and the overwhelming majority of surviving tragedies are self-contained dramas. After that each competing dramatist would also put on a 'satyr-play'. This last was a wild and fantastic tailpiece, usually shorter than a tragedy: it always had a chorus of satyrs, the bestial entourage of Dionysus, and usually treated mythological themes in a burlesque and bawdy way. The only complete example to survive is Euripides' *Cyclops*, an amusing take-off of the story told in Homer's *Odyssey* about the hero's encounter with the one-eyed monster.

What of the content of the tragedies? Perhaps the most significant fact is that the subjects are almost always mythological.[3] The only surviving exception is Aeschylus' *Persians*, though we know of a few others in the early period. The *Persians* commemorates the victory of the Greeks in the recent war against Xerxes, king of Persia, and in particular the battle of Salamis, which had taken place only eight years earlier. But this exception in a way proves the rule, for the play is not set in Greece, but at the Persian court, presenting the subject from the Persian viewpoint. Nor is it mere jingoism: the theme is almost mythologized, raised to a grander and more heroic plane. No individual Greek is named or singled out for praise: the emphasis falls rather on the arrogant folly of a deluded king, who has led his people to defeat. There is, as always in tragedy, a supernatural element: the ghost of Xerxes' father, summoned back to earth, pronounces stern judgement on his son's rash ambition. In the rest of the tragic corpus, the dramatists use myth to distance their stories in time, and so give them universality. Instead of setting their actors the task of impersonating living generals or politicians confronting contemporary crises, the tragedians, like Homer, show us men and women who are remote from us in their circumstances, yet vividly like us and real in their hopes, fears and desires.

Secondly, Greek tragedy is civic in emphasis: its plots, that is, deal with kings and rulers, disputes and dilemmas which have vital implications for the state as a whole. If Oedipus cannot find the murderer of Laius, the plague which is already devastating Thebes will destroy it. If Odysseus and Neoptolemus cannot recover Philoctetes and his bow, Troy will not fall. Consequently tragedy normally deals with men and women of high status – monarchs and royal families, tyrants and mighty heroes. Characters of lower rank generally have smaller parts. As we shall see, however, this is one area in which Euripides showed himself an innovator: 'I made tragedy more democratic,' he is made to say in the satirical treatment of tragedy in Aristophanes' *Frogs*, produced after his death.

Thirdly, complementing and often conflicting with the political dimension, the family is regularly the focus for tragic action. Part of the lasting power of Greek drama lies in the vividness with which it presents extreme love and (still more) intense hatred within the family: matricide, parricide, fratricide, adultery and jealousy, even incest and other forbidden passions. Duty to family and duty to the state may come into conflict: can Agamemnon bring himself to abandon the expedition against Troy, or must he take the terrible decision to sacrifice his daughter for a fair wind? Loyalty to kin is central to *Antigone*; conflicting obligations to different members of the family create many of the dilemmas in the *Oresteia*. The list could easily be extended.

Fourthly, there is the religious aspect. We know too little of early tragedy to confirm or deny the theory that it concentrated mainly on the myths of Dionysus, in whose honour the plays were performed; but by Aeschylus' time the scope has obviously broadened. But no Greek tragedy is secular. Although the dramatists normally focus on the actions and sufferings of human beings, the gods are always present in the background. In early tragedy they figure quite frequently on stage as characters (as in Aeschylus' *Eumenides*). Sophocles seems to have been much more restrained in this, while Euripides normally confines them to the prologue (where they do not usually meet any mortal characters), or to the conclusion of a play, where a god may appear on a higher level, above the stage-building. Sometimes this seems to be a matter of the god standing on the roof of the building, but more spectacular still was the use of a crane-like device to allow the divinity the power of flight. From this remote position of authority the god would declare his will, *ex machina* as the phrase has it, intervening to resolve or at least impose a conclusion upon the events on earth.

Even when gods do not appear, they are frequently invoked, addressed in prayer, called to witness an oath, sometimes questioned or challenged. With the awesome powers of Olympus watching and influencing events, human affairs gain a larger significance: these are not trivial wars or petty crimes, if they attract divine attention and even retribution. Yet because the humans often seem helpless pawns or puppets in the divine game, the greatness of the heroes can seem sadly insignificant, and their proud boasts or ambitions may often be ironically overturned or frustrated. The wiser players on the tragic stage sometimes draw this pessimistic conclusion. 'I see we are but phantoms, all we who live, or fleeting shadows,' says Odysseus in Sophocles' *Ajax* (125–6); or as the chorus sing in *Oedipus the King*, after the horrible truth is out: 'Alas ye generations of men, how close to nothingness do I count your life. Where in the world is the mortal who wins more of happiness than just the illusion, and after the semblance, the falling away? With your example, your fate before my eyes, yours, unhappy Oedipus, I count no man happy' (1186–96).

One last general point should be made. Greek tragedy was intended for performance: although texts undoubtedly circulated, the primary concern was production in the theatre.[4] It is important to try to reconstruct the stage movements, the points at which characters enter and exit, observe one another, come into physical contact, pass objects to another person, and so forth. Major questions of interpretation may hinge on these seemingly small-scale puzzles: to take an example from the plays in the first volume of this series, does Hippolytus ever address Phaedra or not? It all depends on how we envisage the staging, and relate it to the words, of a particular scene (*Hippolytus* 601–68, esp. 651 ff.). Another striking instance is the uncertainty over the later part of the *Andromache*: in the original performance, the character Andromache either appeared in the final scene or she did not. Since she speaks no words in that scene, the text gives us no guidance; but her mute appearance, recalling to the audience her previous suffering and the miseries of Troy, would modify the effect of the end of the play, in which so much is made of the death of Neoptolemus, one of the sackers of Troy.

Moreover, the tragic performance involved music and dancing by the chorus, of which we can recover next to nothing – a few descriptions in ancient prose authors, a handful of papyri with musical annotation, and pictures of dramatic productions on vases do not get us very far. To compare our situation with that of an opera-lover confined to studying a libretto would be unfair to the tragedians, for the spoken dialogue of tragedy is far richer and more significant, demands far more attention from the audience, than the interludes between songs in opera. But we should not forget that, particularly in the choruses and the other lyrics, we have lost what the original cast and audience would have regarded as a vital part of the production.[5]

II

To try to sum up the work of Aeschylus and Sophocles in a few paragraphs is to risk pure banality.[6] The attempt must be made, however, if we are to see Euripides in relation to his great predecessors. Seven complete tragedies attributed to Aeschylus survive, including his monumental trilogy, the *Oresteia* (*Agamemnon, Libation-Bearers, Eumenides*). One of the others, *Prometheus Bound*, has recently been subject to close critical scrutiny, and on the basis of this analysis many authoritative judges think it spurious; but if so, its author shares something of Aeschylus' grandeur of conception and magnificence of language. As already explained, Aeschylus tended to use the trilogy form, which permitted him, as in the *Oresteia* and in the series of which the *Seven against Thebes* is the third, to trace the history of a family through several generations, showing how the sins of the elders are re-enacted or paid for by their descendants. Inherited guilt, ancestral curses, persecuting Furies, vendetta and religious pollution – concepts such as these permeate the world of Aeschylean tragedy, a world of dark powers and evil crimes, in which humans must pray and hope for justice and retribution from the gods, but may pray in vain, or find that the gods are slow to respond. Austere in its characterization, eloquent yet exotic in its polysyllabic style, dominated by long and complex choral songs, his drama often seems to belong to a much older world. Yet this is only one side of a complex artist; Aeschylus, born in the sixth century BC, is also the poet of democratic Athens, deeply concerned with its ideals of reasoned discussion and decision-making. By the end of the fifth century BC he was established as a classic (his plays were re-performed in recognition of this), though he could also be regarded as remote and difficult. Aristophanes' *Frogs*, which dramatizes Dionysus' quest in the underworld for a great poet to bring back to life, presents Aeschylus as a symbol of the good old days, but also as a composer of grandiose and incomprehensible lyrics. In the next century, Aristotle in the *Poetics* uses examples from Sophocles and Euripides far more than from Aeschylus.

To sum up Aeschylus as a poet of archaic grandeur would, however, be quite misleading. He is capable of much lighter and even humorous passages: particularly memorable are the sentimental reminiscences of Orestes' nurse in the *Libation-Bearers*, or the complaints of the herald in the *Agamemnon* about the awful time the common soldiers had at Troy (it is significant that both of these are lower-class types; the great tragic figures are not allowed these more chatty interludes). More important, in his presentation of the doom-laden world of the heroic age he not only shows us horrific events and catastrophe, but also allows his characters to work towards a difficult resolution. In Aeschylean tragedy there is a strong emphasis on the power of the gods, particularly the will of Zeus, who oversees human lives and may bring blessings as well as destruction. Not all the dilemmas faced by Aeschylus' characters are insoluble, although the final outcome may be preceded by further hard choices or disasters. The city of Thebes is saved from invasion, but only through the death of Eteocles, its king. Above all, in the *Oresteia*, the one trilogy which we can study as a magnificently unified whole, Aeschylus dramatizes the contrast between a darker world of vendetta and savage intrafamilial conflict and a society in which the rule of law has an important place, where argument and persuasion may prove superior to hatred and violence. It is a society which mirrors or idealizes his own: the refugee Argive Orestes, pursued by the monstrous Furies, finds sanctuary in a mythical Athens where Athena presides over an archetypal law-court. In this trilogy, although the suffering and crimes of the past are not forgotten, the final emphasis is on the enlightened justice of the present, and the reconciliation of opposed factions among the gods promises prosperity in the future. Aeschylus as a boy had seen the overthrow of the Athenian tyrants; he had fought at Marathon, and in his later years saw the transformation of his city into a democracy and the centre of an empire. It is no surprise that ideals of political debate and civic harmony are prominent in his work; but in view of the darker side discussed above, it would be facile to label him an optimist, either about human nature or about human society. The tragic power of his dramas is not diminished by his central recognition that something positive may, in the end, emerge after or out of suffering.

Whereas Aeschylus' characters (*Prometheus* apart) are above all members of a family or of a larger community, Sophocles tends to focus on individuals set apart from their society or at odds with those who care for them: Ajax, Antigone, Electra, Philoctetes, the aged Oedipus. With him, more than with the other two tragedians, it makes sense to speak of tragic heroes and heroines. Again we have only seven plays, selected in late antiquity for school study, and we know that this represents less than a tenth of his output; moreover, those we have are mostly impossible to date. Obviously generalizations must be surrounded with cautious qualifications, but we can recognize a number of other differences from Aeschylus (to whom he nevertheless owed much). The abandonment of trilogy form has already been mentioned. The role of the chorus is somewhat reduced, though some of the odes which reflect on human achievement and its smallness in relation to the timeless power of the gods have a poetic splendour to match almost anything in Aeschylus. The characters have more depth and subtlety: as an anonymous ancient biographer said of Sophocles, 'He knows how to arrange the action with such a sense of timing that he creates an entire character out of a mere half-line or a single expression.' Partly because he makes more varied use of the third actor, Sophocles constructs scenes which involve more shifts of attention, more realistic and sophisticated interplay between characters, than we can easily find in Aeschylus. Another difference is in the religious atmosphere. Aeschylus regularly brought the gods on stage and allowed them to converse with humans (the Furies, Athena and Apollo in *Eumenides*, Aphrodite in the lost third play of the *Suppliants* trilogy); Sophocles does so only rarely, and even then the gap between man and god is emphasized: Athena is remote and haughty with Odysseus in *Ajax*, Heracles commanding and superhuman in *Philoctetes*; both are probably out of reach, above the human level. In general, the gods do not communicate plainly or unambiguously with mortals: oracles and prophecies offer mysterious and misleading insights, and even Oedipus, the most intelligent of men, can find that his whole life has been lived on completely false assumptions. The limitations of human knowledge allow ample scope for dramatic irony, where the audience understand the double meanings or the deeper truths behind the superficial sense of the words. Central to Sophoclean tragedy is the gap between reality and appearance, understanding and illusion; his characters often discern the truth about their circumstances, or themselves, only when it is too late to avert disaster.

Sophocles has sometimes been seen as a particularly 'pious' writer or thinker. In part this results from a very partial reading of certain selected passages which have been taken to express the poet's own opinions (always a dangerous method); in part it derives from information about his involvement in Athenian religious life, for instance the cult of Asclepius. But within his plays, although the power of the gods is beyond question, and those who doubt that power or reject their oracles are swiftly refuted, it is hard to see any straightforward scheme of divine *justice* at work. Divine action is characterized as enigmatic and obscure. There is an order in the world, as is shown by the fulfilment of oracles; but the pattern is often too elusive for men to grasp. The gods are not indifferent to humanity: they punish Creon in *Antigone*, they grant a home and honour to Oedipus at the end of his life (*Oedipus at Colonus*). But there are also mysteries which remain unanswered: why does Antigone have to die? Why did Philoctetes suffer agonies in isolation on Lemnos for nine years? Any open-minded reader of these plays will acknowledge that Sophocles does not give us a simple or uniform account of human life or of mankind's relation to the gods and fate. Had he done so, the plays would probably not have remained so hauntingly powerful over two and a half millennia.

Sophocles is justly regarded as the greatest master of formal structure – no mere mechanical technique, but a vital aspect of his art. The development of each scene, in each play, is beautifully paced; the contrasts of style and mood between successive scenes, or between one scene and the choral song which follows, are achieved with seemingly effortless brilliance. These skills are combined with deep understanding of character in the scenes between Neoptolemus and Philoctetes, with mastery of tension and irony in the advancing quest which will lead Oedipus to self-discovery. On a more minute level of style, *Oedipus the King* also shows his subtlety of technique in the exchange which culminates in the revelation of the hero's identity (1173–6): here each line is divided between Oedipus and the herdsman whom he is questioning, and as the truth becomes plainer Oedipus' questions become shorter and more faltering, the servant's responses fuller and more desperate. This flexible handling of dialogue form is only one small example of the complete command Sophocles has over his medium. Appalling hatred and unbearable loss are expressed in formal verse of wonderful lucidity and sharpness; only rarely do the eloquent lines dissolve into incoherent cries of pain, as they do when Philoctetes is overcome by his repulsive wound.

III

We turn now to our main subject, the third of the great tragedians. It is far too commonly supposed that Euripides comes 'after' Sophocles, and this can easily lead to a simplifying formula which sees Aeschylus as primitive, Euripides as decadent, and Sophocles as the apex of perfection in between. In fact although Euripides was clearly younger, he and Sophocles were competing together, often against one another, for most of their lives, and Sophocles died within a year of his rival. Both were very much younger than Aeschylus, though they will certainly have seen some of his later productions. Sophocles in fact competed against Aeschylus with his first production, in 468 BC, and won; Euripides first put on a tetralogy in 455 BC with a less satisfactory result, coming third. We do not know his competitors on that occasion. From that point on Euripides was constantly in the public eye, putting on a total of around ninety plays up to his death in 406 BC (his last plays, including the *Bacchae*, were produced posthumously).

We know very little about his life, and what comes down from antiquity is often unreliable (a great deal seems to be derived from the comic treatment of the dramatist by Aristophanes).[7] There is a long-standing tradition that he was unpopular and unsuccessful in his career. We are told that he was melancholy, thoughtful and severe, that he hated laughter and women, that he lived in a cave looking out to the sea from Salamis, that he had a substantial library. None of this amounts to much more than doubtful anecdote. A more concrete statement, which probably rests on inscriptional evidence, is that he won the first prize only four times (once posthumously) in his whole career. This sounds more dramatic than it is, since prizes would be awarded to the tetralogy of plays as a whole: in other words, sixteen out of about ninety plays were winners. Even with this reservation, however, there remains a contrast with the other two tragedians: Aeschylus and Sophocles were each victorious with over half their plays. We should not attach too much importance to the figure about his victories, for it is clear that he was repeatedly granted a chorus, and that the Athenians enjoyed and were fascinated by his work. The constant parodies and references to his plays in Aristophanes' comedies are not only satirical criticism but a kind of tribute to a playwright whose work he obviously knew intimately and whose significance was beyond question.

We happen to have more plays by Euripides than by the other two tragedians put together: the complete total is nineteen, but that includes the satyr-play *Cyclops* and also *Rhesus*, a play widely thought to be a fourth-century BC imitation. This larger figure is partly accidental, the results of the hazards of transmission through the ages, but partly reflects the popularity of Euripides in the educational tradition – his language is easier, his speeches were more suitable for aspiring orators to study, and his plays, with their heady mixture of intellectual and emotional appeal, might be found more immediately accessible.[8] We can also put fairly firm dates on a good many of the plays, because of information which survives in copies of the original inscriptions recording victories in the contests and citing the names of annual magistrates of Athens. Where external evidence for dating is lacking, the date of a play can be determined within limits by 'stylometry', that is, the statistical analysis of the poet's changing linguistic and metrical habits, using the firmly dated plays as a framework.[9] This means not only that we can say something about Euripides' development as a poet, but also that it is possible to identify, or at least speculate about, passages which touch on or allude to Athenian politics and other contemporary events. This is naturally most tempting with plays such as the *Children of Heracles* and the *Suppliant Women*, which are set in Athens and present a mythological image of the Athenians as benefactors of others. But there are many other passages which, without naming Athens, use the language of contemporary politics or ideology. A good example comes in *Orestes*, in which a detailed account of a meeting of the assembly of Argive citizens includes lines which remind the reader of historical and rhetorical texts of the period – of the historian Thucydides' portrayal of Athenian demagogues, for example (*Orestes* 866–952, especially 902–16). Although the importance of this approach has sometimes been exaggerated, and the tragedies are not windows on to history, it is a mistake to rule out such allusions on principle.[10]

None of the plays we possess in entirety is from the earliest stage of Euripides' career; the first, *Alcestis*, was produced in 438 BC, when he was already in his forties. The great majority of surviving plays come from the last three decades of the fifth century BC, the period of the great war between Athens and Sparta, a time in which the cultural and political prominence of Athens was still conspicuous but no longer unchallenged, and by the end of the period increasingly under threat. Euripides did not live to see the defeat of Athens, but several of his later plays suggest growing pessimism about political and military leadership, about civic deliberation, and about the conduct of the victors in wartime. These are not novel themes, in poetry or in life, but they have an added resonance in the light of fifth-century BC history.

The sheer range and variety of Euripides' plays is extraordinary.[11] Perhaps if we had as many of Aeschylus' or Sophocles' plays they would seem equally difficult to categorize; but it is tempting to see Euripides as particularly innovative and trend-setting. Like Sophocles, he seems to have worked mainly on sequences of self-contained plays, though it looks as if the *Trojan Women* was the third of a trilogy concerning the Trojan war from its origins to its conclusion. Unlike Sophocles, he does not generally take a single heroic figure to form the focus of a play – only *Medea* easily fits this pattern. There is a strong tendency to divide the play between major characters: thus in *Alcestis* the heroine gives way to Heracles, the sufferer to the doer; in *Hippolytus* Phaedra dominates the first half of the play, Hippolytus the second; in the *Bacchae* the action is polarized, with the mortal Pentheus and the disguised god Dionysus in conflict throughout. Other plays extend this experimentation to the overall structure. Thus in *Andromache* we begin, as we might expect, with the widow of Hector in difficulties, but as the action advances Andromache is forgotten and other events follow, with different characters taking the limelight. In the *Trojan Women* the continuous presence of Hecabe, the grieving queen of Troy, seems to mark her out as the 'heroine', or at least the principal sufferer, but she is a figure who can achieve nothing. As the play unfolds we are shown a series of scenes which embody the suffering and ruin accompanying the fall of Troy, a sequence which adds up only to further misery. Other plays multiply characters and divide our attention still more: *Helen* has eight human characters with full speaking parts, *Orestes* nine, the *Phoenician Women* eleven.

The plays of Euripides, although they still work within the traditional range of myths, do not generally dramatize heroic initiatives and triumphant achievements. His are tragedies of suffering rather than of action (*Medea* again is a special case, a partial exception). Phaedra, Andromache, Hecabe, the Trojan women, the chorus of mothers in the *Suppliant Women*, the guilt-ravaged Orestes, are all presented as victims, whether of war or other persecution, human folly or divine antagonism. Even when they do attempt to take the initiative, to assert themselves through action, the consequences are rarely presented positively. Phaedra's efforts to preserve her good name bring about Hippolytus' death without achieving her objective; Electra and Orestes in *Electra* destroy their mother, but with psychologically devastating results for themselves; in *Orestes*, the young man's matricide makes him an outcast, and his efforts to take revenge on his mother's sister Helen are first frustrated, then turned to near-farce. Even when Euripides is reworking material which had been treated grimly enough by Aeschylus, he regularly gives his own version a new twist. The brutal sacrifice of Iphigenia at Aulis, so that the Greek fleet may sail for Troy, was presented by Aeschylus in an unforgettable choral song as a terrible necessity, an agonizing decision reluctantly taken by Agamemnon, and one which will have momentous consequences. In Euripides' version, *Iphigenia at Aulis*, Agamemnon and Menelaus chop and change, other members of the expedition seem to have more authority than the leaders have, Iphigenia herself changes her mind, and, most disturbing of all, there is the offstage presence of the army, an uncontrollable mob of soldiers panting for blood. *Iphigenia at Aulis* is a fast-moving and constantly attention-grabbing play, but one in which the high seriousness of the Aeschylean ode is dissipated, and the tragic sacrifice becomes wasteful self-deception. As A. P. Burnett put it: 'In these plays the poet shows men scaled for comedy trying to live in a world still ruled by the gods of tragedy.'[12]

Some of the ways in which Euripides made old subjects new have already been mentioned. This practice was not simply a perverse desire on his part to alter tradition. Between 480 and 430 BC some 500 tragedies would have been staged; a middle-aged man in his audience might have seen over two hundred.[13] The Athenians, like any audience, enjoyed innovation: indeed, originality and novelty were at a premium in the second half of the fifth century BC, as new ideas and new literary styles made their appearance in Athens. Euripides was in part responding to audience demand (though it is only fair to add that a sizeable portion of his audience would be more conservative, and that Sophocles clearly did not feel the need to innovate so ostentatiously). By the middle stage of Euripides' career Aeschylus looked archaic: in his *Electra*, the younger tragedian unmistakably parodies a recognition-scene from Aeschylus' *Libation-Bearers*, in which the discovery of a lock of hair at Agamemnon's tomb was taken as evidence of Orestes' return (513ff.). It is interesting to note that the grounds for criticism are improbability, lack of realism and violation of common sense. Aeschylus and his audience had been above such concerns; by Euripides' time it was more natural to apply to tragedy at least some of the standards of everyday life.[14] Nevertheless, the parody is two-edged: it turns out that the Euripidean Electra's scepticism is misguided, and the deduction from the Aeschylean token remains valid. The allusion to Aeschylus need not be merely dismissive.

Innovation can also be observed in the composition of Euripides' plots. It is natural for us to think of the myths as fixed and organized, as they are in the modern summaries which we find in handbooks; but in fact the fluidity of the legends is surprising, and the tragedians already found variations in the epic and lyric accounts which they inherited. Euripides often uses less familiar versions of myths, or combines stories normally kept apart. Although the loss of so much earlier literature makes firm assertions dangerous, it seems likely that he is modifying the legend in making Medea kill her own children deliberately (in an earlier version it was the Corinthians who took their revenge upon her offspring). In the legends of Heracles it was normally held that the hero's labours were a kind of penance for killing his children in a fit of insanity. Euripides reverses the sequence, making Heracles return home to his family triumphant after his labours are ended – then, the crowning horror, madness and slaughter follow. In his *Helen* he adopts the bizarre version of the lyric poet Stesichorus, which made Helen a prisoner in Egypt throughout the Trojan War, while Greek and Trojan armies fought for ten years over a phantom. The unexpected becomes the rule, in both plot and characterization: women behave manfully, slaves show nobility and virtue, barbarians express civilized sentiments.

Even when he is closer to the traditional versions, he often introduces new characters or explores the implications of legends with a fresh eye: thus in *Orestes* Menelaus, Tyndareus, Hermione and Orestes' friend Pylades all have prominent roles, and the effect is quite different from earlier versions of this myth. Characterization can also be modified: in Aeschylus' *Seven against Thebes*, Eteocles, king of Thebes, is a noble figure, though labouring under a curse; in Euripides' *Phoenician Women*, he becomes a power-crazed tyrant. In the *Electra* of Euripides it is even possible to sympathize with Clytemnestra and Aegisthus, the murderers of Agamemnon. Sharp changes of direction and unexpected shifts of personality are also common: in *Andromache*, Hermione at first seems a cruel and malicious princess, but later becomes a sympathetic victim. In *Medea*, the heroine vacillates throughout much of the play: loving mother or merciless avenger, which side of her character is to prevail? Aristotle in his *Poetics* (ch. 15) found fault with these startling reversals of character, singling out *Iphigenia at Aulis* for criticism: 'the girl who pleads for her life is quite different from the later one', he complains, referring to the scene where Iphigenia, after earlier begging for mercy, resolves to sacrifice herself in the name of Greece. Euripides also plays variations on his own earlier work: our extant *Hippolytus* is a second version, in which the portrayal of Phaedra is made more sympathetic and her character more complex.[15]

In some ways Euripides can be seen as a more self-consciously literary dramatist than his fellow tragedians. It is not accidental that it was he who was said to have a large library. He seems regularly to modify the conventions of his genre and adapt the work of his pre-decessors, sometimes even drawing attention to the changes he has made. The parody of the Aeschylean recognition-scene has already been cited; similarly, later in *Electra*, the trapping and killing of Clytemnestra within the hovel in which Electra and her husband have their home is a re-enactment of the killing-scenes within the palace of Agamemnon in Aeschylus' trilogy: humbler setting, unheroic characters, dubious morality all work together. In *Helen*, the heroine proposes that they contrive an escape by pretending Menelaus is dead and mourning him. Is that the best you can do?, asks Menelaus; 'there's a certain old-hat quality in the proposal' (1056). The point is that the trick has been tried often before in tragedy: the character is given the critic's fastidiousness. Aeschylus and Sophocles are also experienced in reshaping and adapting traditional motifs, but Euripides goes far beyond them in playing with conventions and exploiting the spectator's awareness of the dramatic situation. While shocked and moved by the events on stage, we are nevertheless frequently reminded that this is 'only' a play.[16]

As the example from *Helen* just quoted suggests, Euripides' plays are not devoid of lighter, humorous touches. Indeed, his wide repertoire includes not only starkly 'tragic' plays in the stricter sense, such as *Medea*, but also dramas which are harder to categorize. *Alcestis*, with its fairy-tale plot and happy resolution, seems to belong to a kinder and less threatening world than most tragedies. Later plays, notably *Iphigenia among the Taurians* and especially *Helen*, have often been classed as tragi-comedies. In both plays, after many misfortunes, the principal characters are reunited in a far-off setting (Helen is held captive in Egypt, Iphigenia in the Crimea), recognize one another after many false steps, and plan a successful escape back to Greece, outwitting their barbarian opponents. Hair-breadth escapes and cliff-hanging moments are common, as when Iphigenia is about to sacrifice her unrecognized brother to the goddess Artemis. We know that similar scenes occurred in lost plays by Euripides: in *Cresphontes*, a mother is on the point of killing her son with an axe, but the danger is averted, the potential tragedy dissipated.

There is much here which looks back to the *Odyssey*, with its complex plot full of deceptions and recognitions. Moroever, plays of this kind also look forward to later comedy, the types of plot favoured by Menander, Terence and eventually Shakespeare (not to mention Oscar Wilde).[17] These plays are sometimes called escapist, misguidedly; there remains a strong sense of suffering and waste in the past, and they undoubtedly still qualify as tragedies. But they do show the versatile Euripides experimenting with new types of play, and these experiments are accompanied by a lighter and more ironic tone, providing a very different kind of pleasure from the cathartic experience provided by the *Oresteia* or *Oedipus*. Euripides is plainly interested in variations of tone, juxtaposing scenes of very different emotional intensity. A 'comic' element may be found even in much grimmer plays, but there it is often used to reinforce the seriousness of the rest of the action. The self-pity and bad temper of the downtrodden Electra, for example, provide some humour as we sympathize with her husband, the long-suffering farmer; but their conversation also contributes to our understanding of Electra's tortured psyche. Far more macabre is the delusion of Heracles, who believes he is journeying to Mycenae, arriving there, punishing Eurystheus – when all the time he is in his own home, slaughtering his sons. The effect is intensely powerful: this madness would be funny if it were not so horrible.

In reading a plain text, and still more a translation, of Euripides it is easy to overlook the formal and musical aspects of the dramas. Here too we can see that he went beyond the earlier conventions of the genre, in ways which were exciting to the audiences, but also often controversial. Greek tragedy is broadly divisible into spoken verse and sung verse: the former is the medium in which the actors converse with one another or with the chorus-leader, the latter is most commonly found in the songs of the chorus. Already in Aeschylus there are plenty of exceptions: actors can sing solo parts or participate in lyric dialogue. In *Agamemnon*, the prophetess Cassandra voices her god-given insight in emotional song, to the bewilderment of the chorus; still more wild and agitated are the lyric utterances of Io, tormented by pain, in *Prometheus*. But Euripides seems to go further in giving his actors lyric passages, often highly emotional and linguistically rich (no doubt these were also striking in their musical accompaniment). The solo passages, arias or 'monodies', are often virtuoso pieces, and must have made huge demands on an actor: examples are rarer in the earlier plays, but there are several in *Hippolytus*. From the later plays the most memorable examples include Creusa's lament for the child she exposed years ago and now believes dead, the ecstatic suicide-song of Evadne, and (as in Aeschylus) the prophetic raving of Cassandra (*Ion* 859–922, *Suppliant Women* 990ff., and *Trojan Women* 308ff.). In the *Orestes* of 408 BC we find the prize example, a *tour-de-force* narrative of the attempt on Helen's life, sung by a Phrygian eunuch in a state of extreme panic, exotically foreign in its linguistic and rhythmical looseness, and no doubt accompanied by violent gestures and mime. The brilliant lyric parody in Aristophanes' *Frogs* (1309–63), which lifts lines from *Orestes* and elsewhere, shows how extraordinary audiences found his style in these arias. Other formal features of the drama would take too long to illustrate, but the general impression is of sharper and more prosaic or argumentative dialogue style combined with a more self-consciously 'poetic', decorative, image-laden, almost romantic style in lyrics.[18]

Several other aspects of Euripides' work can be illuminated by Aristophanes' *Frogs*, in which Aeschylus and Euripides compete against one another in the underworld. Although it is unsafe to use this play to establish Aristophanes' own aesthetic position, it is first-rate evidence for at least some of the things in Euripidean drama which made most impression on contemporary audiences. In the *Frogs*, Euripides is made to boast that

as soon as the play began I had everyone hard at work: no one standing idle. Women and slaves, master, young woman, aged crone – they all talked . . . It was Democracy in action . . . I taught them subtle rules they could apply; how to turn a phrase neatly. I taught them to see, to observe, to interpret; to twist, to contrive; to suspect the worst, take nothing at its face value . . . I wrote about familiar things, things the audience knew about . . . The public have learnt from me how to think, how to run their own households, to ask 'Why is this so? What do we mean by that?' (*Frogs* 948–79, tr. D. Barrett)

In Euripidean drama others besides kings and heroes play major roles; a large number of plays are named after, and focused on, female characters. Indeed, it has been pointed out that most of Euripides' *thinkers* are women: certainly Creon, Jason and Aegeus are easily out-classed by Medea, and in both the *Trojan Women* and *Helen* Menelaus is inferior to his quick-witted wife.[19] Lower-class characters are more prominent and more influential: the Nurse in *Hippolytus* is a perfect example. In *Electra*, the downtrodden princess is married to a mere farmer, who respects her in her adversity, and has not slept with her. The farmer comes from a noble family now impoverished; his low status is contrasted with his honourable behaviour, but the latter still has to be explained by his noble birth. In both *Hecabe* and the *Trojan Women*, the decent herald Talthybius is sympathetic to the captive women, and shocked at the misdeeds of his social superiors. Mention should also be made of the many messengers in Euripides, several of whom are vividly and sympathetically characterized.

The other point which the passage in the *Frogs* emphasizes is the way these characters talk. Here we come close to one of the central aspects of Euripides' work, his fascination with argument, ideas and rhetoric. In the later fifth century BC professional teachers were instructing young men, in Athens and elsewhere, in the art of rhetoric, which in a small-scale democratic society could justly be seen as the key to political success. Types of argument were collected, methods of refutation categorized. It was possible, one of these experts claimed, 'to make the worse case defeat the better'. Euripides gives his characters the inventiveness and articulacy which these teachers sought to impart. This is particularly clear in the so-called *agon* ('contest' or 'debate'), at least one example of which can be found in most of his plays. The *agon* is a scene in which two (occasionally more) characters express their antagonism in long, highly argumentative and sometimes ingenious speeches: rhetorical skill is combined with energetic emotion. Examples are Jason versus Medea, Theseus versus Hippolytus, Helen versus Hecabe (*Medea, Hippolytus, Trojan Women* respectively). These scenes sharpen our understanding of the issues, and often challenge us to adjudicate between the parties involved. There is rarely a clear winner, either on the arguments or under the prevailing circumstances in the play: often considerations of power and self-interest matter more than who is in the right. As a result, tragic conflict-scenes seldom lead to a resolution, but tend rather to heighten the antagonism of those involved.[20]

Perhaps all drama suggests larger issues beyond the particular experiences enacted on stage, but Euripides' plays articulate these more abstract and universal concerns to an unusual degree. Although the characters on stage are not mere types – what could be called typical about Medea or Heracles? – their situations and dilemmas often suggest larger questions, more general themes and problems inherent in human life and society. When does justice become revenge, even savagery? Can human reason overcome passion? Should right and wrong be invoked in inter-state politics, or is expediency the only realistic criterion? These questions are not left implicit: the characters themselves raise them, in generalizing comments which are often given special prominence at the opening of a speech. The audience, like the characters, must often have been uncertain which side was in the right, and their attitude would naturally change as the drama unfolded. Many, perhaps most, Athenian theatre-goers would also have served as jurors in the law-courts (Athenian juries were much larger than those in modern trials, numbering as many as 500 citizens); many would also have voted on proposals in the democratic assembly. They were used to moral and verbal contests, real and fictional, public and private, forensic and literary. Indeed, Athenians were notorious for their addiction to debate: the contemporary historian Thucydides makes a politician call them 'spectators at speeches', a telling paradox.[21] It is no coincidence that this 'agonistic' aspect of Athenian society is so vividly reflected in the dramas. Euripides may have taught the audience to be glib and clever, but he was responding to a development already well advanced.

Perhaps no question has been as prominent in criticism as the nature of Euripides' beliefs, his philosophy. This may seem strange: why should we expect a dramatist to adopt a philosophic position, still less to maintain it from play to play? The reason that this issue seems to many people particularly important is that Euripides frequently introduces abstract ideas or theoretical arguments, sometimes drawing attention to the oddity of his character's language or thought. In the *Suppliant Women*, the Athenian Theseus and the Theban herald argue at length about the relative merits of democratic and monarchic government (399–456). Even if we allow that Theseus, the favourite hero of Athens, is no ordinary monarch, the anachronism involved in placing such a debate in the heroic age is obvious. In *Hippolytus*, Phaedra discourses on the power of passion and how it can overwhelm the mind's good resolutions: her calmness and the abstract tone of her words seem strange after her earlier frenzy. More striking still are the many passages in which characters question the nature, or the very existence, of the Olympian gods. In the *Trojan Women*, Hecabe, in need of inspiration in the *agon*, prays as follows:

O you who give the earth support and are by it supported, whoever you are, power beyond our knowledge, Zeus, be you stern law of nature or intelligence in man, to you I make my prayers; for you direct in the way of justice all mortal affairs, moving with noiseless tread. (884–8)

These lines echo both traditional prayer-formulae and contemporary science; they involve contradictory conceptions of the supreme deity; they even hint at the theory that gods are merely externalizations of human impulses. Little wonder that Menelaus remarks in response 'What's this? You have a novel way of praying to the gods!'

In passages of this kind Euripides plainly shows his familiarity with the philosophic or metaphysical teachings of a number of thinkers: Anaxagoras, Protagoras, Gorgias and other figures known to us particularly through the writings of Plato and Aristotle. Influence from philosophy or abstract prose has occasionally been detected in Aeschylus and Sophocles, but any such cases in their work are rare and unobtrusive; with Euripides we are dealing with something new. This introduction of modern ideas coheres with his general tendency to make the characters of myth less remote and majestic, more like ordinary mortals with human weaknesses. Unsettling and bizarre these passages may seem, but they are clearly meant to surprise and stimulate: it would be absurd to suppose that Euripides did not realize what he was doing, or that he was incapable of keeping his intellectual interests out of his tragedies.[22]

Ancient anecdote claimed that Protagoras, an agnostic thinker, gave readings from his work in Euripides' house, and that Socrates helped him write his plays. Although these stories are rightly now recognized as fictions, the frequency with which Euripides introduces philosophic or religious reflections still needs explanation. An influential tradition of criticism has maintained that Euripides was a disciple of one or other of these thinkers, and that his dramas represent a concerted endeavour to open his countrymen's eyes to the moral defects of men and gods as represented in the traditional myths. In the earlier part of the fifth century BC, the lyric poet Pindar had questioned a myth which told of divine cannibalism, and in the fourth century Plato was to censor epic and tragedy in the name of morality. The myths were also criticized by Euripides' contemporaries on grounds of rationality and probability: how could sensible people take seriously stories of three-headed hounds of Hades, or other monstrous creatures? There is, then, no reason to doubt that Euripides could have seen reasons to be sceptical about some of the myths: he makes Helen doubt whether she was really born from a swan's egg, and Iphigenia question whether any deity could conceivably demand human sacrifice (*Helen* 18, 259, *Iphigenia among the Taurians* 380–91).

It is much less plausible to suppose that he was urging total scepticism about the gods or the supernatural, and proposing some alternative philosophical or humanist view in their place. It is difficult for the modern student to appreciate how different Greek religious thought and practice were from the Judaeo-Christian tradition.[23] There was no creed, no sacred books, no central priestly establishment. The city performed its sacrifices and paid honour to the gods, as had always been done; sometimes new gods were admitted to the pantheon; but cult was not the same as myth, and it was well known that myths contradicted one another and that poets made up many stories – many lies, as the Athenian Solon once said. To express doubts about one particular myth did not shake the foundations of religion. Outright atheism was rare and freakish. The more open-minded attitude of the great traveller Herodotus may have been commoner: he declared that all men were equally knowledgeable about the divine.[24]

Certainly there are serious difficulties in treating Euripides as an unbeliever on the evidence of his plays. This is not simply because, alongside the more questioning attitudes in the passages quoted, we

find many speakers expressing profound faith and devotion, and choral
odes which invoke the Olympians in magnificent poetry: one could
always argue (though with some circularity) that these characters pos-
sessed only partial or erroneous insights into religion. More important
is the fact that without the existence of the gods the plays simply do
not work. How is Medea to escape if the sun-god, her grandfather,
does not send his chariot to rescue her? How will Theseus' curse
destroy his son if Poseidon is a mere fiction? How will the plot of
Alcestis even begin to work unless death is something more than natural,
unless there is a personified being against whom Heracles can do battle?
A full discussion would also have to consider the numerous scenes in
which gods appear at the end of plays to bring events under control:
here, rationalizing interpretations truncate the dramas.

But if Euripides the 'anti-clerical' atheist cannot stand, neither can
he simply be forced into the straitjacket of 'traditional' piety, even if
that piety is defined in terms flexible and sophisticated enough to
include Aeschylus and Sophocles.[25] There remains overwhelming evi-
dence that Euripides, in this as in other respects, was an innovator: just
as he introduces new and often unfamiliar characters into traditional
myths, or views familiar tragic situations from unexpected angles, so
he combines traditional mythical and theatrical conventions about the
gods with disturbing new conceptions and challenging ideas. Some-
times the contradictions become acute and paradoxical, as in a notori-
ously baffling passage of *Heracles*. In this play Heracles, son of Zeus by
the mortal woman Alcmena, has been brought to his knees by the
goddess Hera, who persecutes him because she resents Zeus' adulteries.
Theseus, befriending Heracles and seeking to comfort him, refers at
one point to the immorality of the gods, whereupon Heracles bursts
into a passionate rejection of this concept:

I do not believe that the gods love where it is wrong for them to do so, or
that they bind one another – I have never thought it right to believe this, nor
shall I ever believe that one has been master of another. For god, if he is truly
a god, needs nothing. These are merely the wretched tales of bards.

(*Heracles* 1340–46)

This outburst comes near to rejecting the very premisses that underlie the play and Heracles' own experiences within it. Is Euripides showing us something about Heracles' psychology? Insisting, in Plato's manner, on the moral inadequacy of the myths? Alluding to the poetic and fictional quality of his own play? Or all of these at once, and more? The passage, and the issues it raises, is likely to remain controversial.[26]

Although all such labels are bound to oversimplify a many-sided artist like Euripides, we may find more valuable than 'atheist' the term proposed by E. R. Dodds, one of the most gifted interpreters of Greek literature of the last century, who dubbed Euripides 'the irrationalist'.[27] By this Dodds meant that Euripides was interested and impressed by the achievements of human reason, not least in the fields of rhetorical argument and philosophic theory, but in the end felt that they were inadequate both as explanatory tools and as instruments to enable mankind to deal with the world. Reason versus passion, order versus chaos, persuasion versus violence – these antitheses are present in all Greek tragedy, but Euripides seems more pessimistic about the limits of man's capacity to control either himself or society.[28] The demoralizing and brutalizing effects of a prolonged war surely play a part in the development of his outlook: the *Suppliant Women*, *Hecabe* and the *Trojan Women*, or a decade later the *Phoenician Women* and *Iphigenia at Aulis*, all dramatize the suffering and callousness which war makes possible or inevitable. Even *Helen*, for all its playful irony and lightness of touch, implies a bleak and pessimistic view of human action: the Trojan War, far from being a glorious achievement, was fought for a phantom; and although Menelaus and Helen are finally reunited, that partial success cannot compensate for the countless lives thrown away on the plains of Troy.

On this reading, Euripides does not assert the independence of man from divine authority; he is neither an agnostic nor a humanist. Rather, he acknowledges that there are forces in the world which mankind cannot understand or control. They may sometimes be described in the language of traditional religion, or referred to by the names and titles of the Olympians, though even then he often suggests some new dimension: 'she's no goddess, then, the Cyprian, but something greater', cries the Nurse when she learns of Phaedra's desire (*Hippolytus*

359–60). At other times he will make his characters speak of nature, or necessity, or chance: as Talthybius asks in *Hecabe*, 'O Zeus, what am I to say? Do you watch over men or are we fools, blind fools to believe this, and is it chance that oversees all man's endeavours?' (488–91). Or again, a speaker may throw out the suggestion that 'it is all in the mind': 'when you saw him your mind *became* the goddess. All the indiscretions of mortals pass for Aphrodite . . .' (*Trojan Women* 988–9). The supernatural, however it is defined, embraces those things which are beyond human grasp. The author of the following speech, again from *Hippolytus*, may not have been a conventional Greek thinker, but he understood how to communicate religious longing.

It's nothing but pain, this life of ours; we're born to suffer and there's no end to it. If anything more precious than life does exist, it's wrapped in darkness, hidden behind clouds. We're fools in love – it's plain enough – clinging to this glitter here on earth because we don't know any other life and haven't seen what lies below. (*Hippolytus* 189–96)

To discuss the poet's philosophical outlook at such length risks placing undue emphasis on Euripides the intellectual. Although the plays include passages which are clearly meant to provoke reflection, and some of these stand out conspicuously in context, they are not the whole of the dramas; they may not even be the most significant parts. The scholar in the study, the student trying to put together an essay, may lose touch with the experience of the audience in the theatre. They would have been in no doubt that tragedy was first and foremost about extreme emotion and intense suffering. When Aristotle wrote that Euripides was the most intensely tragic of the poets, he meant that he was the one who most powerfully evoked pity and fear, which Aristotle classically defined as the supremely tragic emotions. No account of the genre can be adequate which fails to give due prominence to this aspect.[29] On every side we meet grief and anger, joy and disillusionment, love and hate, jealousy and malice. The long-drawn-out parting of Admetus from his dying wife; the desperation and degradation of Hecabe, nursing the body of her murdered son; the collective grief of the mothers of the Seven against Thebes, or of the captive women at Troy; Creusa's passionate outburst against Apollo, fraught with painful recollection of the moment when the god had his way with her, and in the wake of those memories, grief for her lost child; the madly deluded delight of deranged Cassandra; the hymn of hate with which the Bacchants call down Dionysus' vengeance upon Pentheus – the list is virtually endless. Ancient descriptions of the theatrical audience make clear that their reaction was not merely cerebral but strongly responsive to the claims made on them emotionally by the characters on stage.[30] Different parts of the play give different pleasures and stimulate the theatre-goer in a variety of ways: the fast-moving stichomythic exchanges challenge their quickness of wit, the rhetorical displays delight their intellect, but the many passages of solo or communal lamentation appeal to a deep human desire to feel with and for the sufferer even when the cause of suffering does not affect oneself – even, indeed, when the suffering is fictitious. All of this is part of the paradox of tragedy, already theorized by Gorgias well before Aristotle.

How does this relate to questions concerning Euripides and his gods? Perhaps chiefly as a reminder that theological speculation or religious propaganda are not the business of a tragedian. Religion in tragic drama is not identical with religion in contemporary Greek life; nor, however, can the two be firmly distinguished.[31] Tragedy enhances and enlarges common experience in order to achieve its effects: human atrocities such as infanticide or self-blinding or devouring the flesh of one's own children are happily rare in normal life but far more frequent in tragedy; and just as human guilt and suffering is made more terrible and painful, so the gods are used and introduced in such a way as to aid in the creation of the dark and sinister world of tragic myth (comedy portrays a kinder pantheon, less firmly set on avenging insults to their honour). The picture is not simple or uniform: in some plays the gods are kind and bring about a happy ending after misfortune (though rarely without some cause for grief and regret); but in others wrongdoers may be punished, but the undeserving suffer equally terrible fates, and the gods allow or deliberately bring this to pass (Antigone in Sophocles' play; Jocasta and Antigone in the *Phoenician Women*, Iphigenia in the *Iphigenia at Aulis*). Divine justice may seem arbitrary: Orestes is acquitted and restored to honour, but Neoptolemus is to be struck down. The ways of the gods are inscrutable: occasionally, however, the veil may be lifted, and we are not meant to like what we see.

Many of these points – the gods as threatening powers well suited to tragedy, the centrality of human response to suffering, and the ultimate impenetrability of the Olympian design – are highlighted with particular clarity in the closing scene of the *Bacchae*, in which Cadmus, the head of the family, appeals to Dionysus for clemency, but the god dismisses his plea.

CADMUS Dionysus, we beseech you, we have done wrong!

DIONYSUS Too late you came to know me; when you should have, you did not.

CADMUS This we acknowledge; but you come upon us with a hand too heavy.

DIONYSUS Yes, for I, a god born, was treated by you with contempt.

CADMUS Gods should not be like mortals in temper.

DIONYSUS Long ago my father Zeus gave his consent to this.

(Bacchae 1344–9)★

The will of the god is not to be resisted, but it can still be questioned and challenged. Protests are only human. Tragedy provokes complex reactions: as a human audience watching fellow humans suffer, we are bound to sympathize with Cadmus even if we accept that the god has a right to receive worship. If our only response to the death of Pentheus were to say 'impiety has been justly punished', the tragedy would have failed to have its proper effect.

★Up to this point the text of this Introduction closely follows the version printed in earlier volumes of the present translation. In those earlier volumes the remainder of this section concentrated on the *Bacchae*, but since that play is treated in more detail elsewhere, this section has been recast. Section IV is entirely new.

IV

The last plays of Euripides come from the final years of the Peloponne-
sian War between Athens and Sparta, though the poet did not live to
see his city's final defeat. The *Phoenician Women* is not precisely datable,
but was probably produced in 410 or 409 BC. The *Orestes* is firmly
dated to 408 BC. The poet died in the year 407–6 BC and the *Bacchae*
and *Iphigenia at Aulis*, together with the lost *Alcmaeon*, were put on stage
posthumously, by the poet's son, presumably at the first opportunity, in
405 BC: this group of plays won first prize. The controversy over the
authorship of the *Rhesus* has already been mentioned, and is discussed
further in the Preface to that play. In my view, as in that of the majority
of critics, it is unlikely to be the work of Euripides, but if it is
authentically his, its date is quite uncertain. In what follows I concen-
trate on the first four plays.

Euripides' exact date of birth is not certain: ancient authorities offer
485 and 480 BC. In either case he would have been in his seventies
when he composed the plays in this volume.* Ancient biographers
report that in the final years of his life Euripides accepted an invitation
to leave Athens and take up residence at the court of Macedon; whether
or not we believe this, it is certain that he composed, probably at this
late date, a play in honour of the Macedonian royal house, entitled
Archelaus, which dealt with the mythical origins of the family and paid
indirect tribute to the living monarch of that name. Traditionally this
departure from Athens has been seen as Euripides' final gesture of
indignation at the unkind reception of his dramas by the Athenian
public. A more plausible motive may be the desire to find a comfortable
home in his declining years rather than remaining in a city hard pressed
by war. It is hard to suppose that the playwright would not have been
present as director and manager of the *Orestes*, in many ways his most
daring drama to date. Probably his emigration was shortly after the

*By a gruesome error I stated in volume 3, p. xxxvi that Euripides would have been in
his late fifties or older in 410 BC; this should have said his seventies. I apologize to any
reader who may have been misled by an oversight which will, I trust, be corrected in
later editions of the volume.

festival of 408 BC, in which case he may have been resident in Macedonia for less than two years.[32]

This is not the place in which to recapitulate the dark tale of the final years of the war: only a few key points need be mentioned here.[33] The disastrous conclusion of the Athenian expedition to Sicily had been a significant blow to morale, and prompted a wave of rebellions among Athens' subject allies, but the imperial city made a swift recovery. The remaining years of the war were dominated by three major factors. The first was internal revolution: the democratic government was temporarily overthrown in 411 BC, and a narrower establishment held power for almost a year. Thucydides gives a vivid picture of the atmosphere of terror and distrust which prevailed in the city during this period (see especially 8.66, 70, 74.3): although the new government was swiftly ousted, the democratic consensus had been exposed as seriously flawed, and the anxiety created by this episode must have been slow to fade. Second, the major power of Persia was once more extending its influence into the activities of the Greek states. Athens and Sparta both hoped to win Persian support in order to win the war, but both were reluctant to make the concessions which the Persian king's representatives might demand. In the end Sparta was to reach a lasting agreement with Persia and this proved decisive. Third, there was dissension among the Athenian leadership, not only about how best to conduct the war but on whether it should be continued at all. Many among the governing class had been exiled or executed in the aftermath of the 411 BC revolution; some who had not been punished were nevertheless in eclipse; others who continued to wield power had no clear policy or concentrated more on securing their own position; the most charismatic and controversial figure, Alcibiades, was recalled from disgrace in 407 BC after conspicuous successes, only to be removed from office once more after a single failure. Athens continued to defy expectations by winning fresh victories, but the tide had turned. By the time Euripides left Athens there can have been few who felt optimistic about the city's chances of winning the war, still fewer who expected that she could continue to hold the position of authority she had retained since the mid-century domination of the Aegean.

Greek tragic drama is not allegorical (readings which try to see Pericles or Alcibiades behind individual mythical characters are not persuasive), but the genre is strongly influenced in a more general way by contemporary events.[34] Most obvious are the scathing generalizations about war, politics, personal ambitions, governments and demagogues: although some of these are commonplaces of popular morality, they seem to acquire an added edge in the later plays of Euripides. More important is the way in which the plays dramatize individuals who are incapable of achieving the goals they desire in the public arena. The moderation of Polyneices is more attractive than the shameless ambition of Eteocles, but both are flawed, and neither survives. In the *Orestes*, the 'hero' is first sick and helpless, then besieged by powerful antagonists, then pleads a hopeless and unpersuasive case in a hostile assembly; when he takes to violence in self-defence, his efforts are no more effective, despite his vicious intentions. Positive values are found to be undependable (Menelaus ignores his nephew's claims upon him), or are subverted (Pylades' devoted friendship leads him to propose conspiracy and murder). In the *Iphigenia*, Agamemnon is a pitiful and vacillating figure, unable to resist outside forces, cast down by every setback, and finally yielding to a necessity which he might have resisted more successfully earlier. Despite the overconfident rhetoric of the principals, none of the agents in these plays has much capacity to influence events. In both the *Orestes* and the *Iphigenia* the dramatist makes us aware of the frightening presence offstage of a powerful mob – the Argive citizens in the former, the Greek army in the latter. There is violence waiting to be unleashed, violence which could crush the individual leaders. For all its differences, the *Bacchae* shows some of the same pattern (including the offstage violence, no longer potential but actual, and there made still more terrible by being the work of female hands, and done in a state of insanity). In that play Pentheus is out of his depth from the start: there is indeed a single character who can and does control the action effectively, but that authoritative figure is not human, and has little concern for what humans think of his decisions.

Despite his advancing years, Euripides shows no sign of failing powers. In the *Phoenician Women* and the *Orestes* we see a number of tendencies in his work reaching their most extreme point: in some respects the *Iphigenia*, a problematic case because of the problems of multiple authorship, sustains this trend, while the *Bacchae* represents a turning-back. The plays in general are becoming longer, the plots more complicated. In the first of the plays we find a great diversity of characters and shifting of focus: from Jocasta, Eteocles and Polyneices we turn to Creon, Teiresias and Menoeceus; Antigone, introduced early on, becomes a central figure towards the end; Oedipus makes a cameo appearance; the play has no 'hero' or central figure, but dramatizes the sickened state of unhappy Thebes, saved from destruction but still bedevilled by the misfortunes of the past. The *Orestes* and the *Bacchae* are more sharply focused on the actions and reactions of the protagonist, but as we have seen neither Orestes nor Pentheus is in control of events. Perhaps only in the *Iphigenia* is a heroic action freely chosen and in some sense admirable: but there is good reason to question the justification for the princess's self-sacrifice, and the evidence of the play itself gives us little cause for confidence that the Trojan war will be a glorious affair.

These dramas also take further Euripidean patterns in the choice and handling of the chorus: he persistently selects not elder statesmen or soldiers or citizens of the community, but figures who are in some way marginal: women, foreigners, slaves, unable to influence events but compelled to witness and bear witness to them (the *Rhesus*, with its chorus of male soldiers, stands firmly apart here). There is no place in these plays in which the chorus debate with, advise or successfully persuade the actors, as the chorus of the *Antigone* influenced the misguided monarch Creon. Even their traditional involvement in conspiracies planned on stage in their presence goes no further than a perfunctory assumption that they will observe conventional discretion and keep the actors' plans secret. In several of these plays Euripides seems to be experimenting with and enhancing another aspect of the chorus's traditional role, as narrators of the mythical past: while inactive in the present, they extend the audience's understanding of the background. It is true that in the *Bacchae* the chorus of Asian Bacchants are given something of their traditional prominence in the tragic experience: they are the companions of the god, the defenders of his cult, the singers of his praises, and they stand or fall with him. But although they enlarge our apprehension of the meaning of Dionysus, they themselves play no active part in the drama. It is appropriate that they do not even share the audience's awareness of the identity of the disguised Dionysus, but assume he is merely the god's priest.

The influence of Aeschylus seems particularly strong upon a number of these plays: the *Phoenician Women* is a reworking of the older poet's *Seven against Thebes*, the *Orestes* of the second and third plays of the *Oresteia*. The *Iphigenia* certainly makes some use of the classic narrative of the sacrifice in the *Agamemnon*, though other sources may be lost. The *Bacchae* returns to what was surely a prominent (some would say the central) myth of early tragedy, the triumph of Dionysus over his adversaries: Aeschylus had written many plays on this theme, and some direct echoes can be detected (*Bacchae* 453, 726, and notes 42 and 64). But often it is the novelty of Euripides' handling of the tradition that is most striking. Famous scenes in epic or early tragedy are introduced in novel forms: Antigone on the walls of Thebes recalls Helen on the walls of Troy in *Iliad* 3; the lyric description of the Greek ships in the *Iphigenia* is an abridged version of the long catalogue in *Iliad* 2. Myths from other contexts are allusively introduced: the death of Actaeon in the *Bacchae*, the future passing of Oedipus at Colonus in the *Phoenician Women*, the trial of the Danaids in the *Orestes*. Equally, Euripides may reject the opportunity to do the traditional thing, as being too obvious: Eteocles declines to list his champions, since time is short (*Phoenician Women* 751–2, and note 36); Aeschylus' majestic invocation of Agamemnon's ghost is compressed to a mere ten lines of perfunctory trimeters (*Orestes* 1231–9); Pylades does not break silence with momentous words but declines to speak, out of dramatic necessity (*Orestes* 1591–2).

Equally obvious is the poet's continuing readiness to exploit and develop the forms and modes of tragedy. Already in earlier plays he had begun to make more use of the trochaic tetrameter, a longer but more rapid line than the normal metre for spoken verse, the iambic trimeter. Long disused, it becomes prominent in Euripides' work from the *Heracles* onwards, often for scenes of excited but slightly informal or racy style, sometimes to accompany agitated action and violent emotion. It is most frequent in the *Orestes* and the *Iphigenia*. The messenger speeches multiply: four feature in the *Phoenician Women*, two each from different messengers! The *agon* or rhetorical conflict had already been put to novel use in the *Helen*, produced in 412 BC: there, Menelaus and Helen both make speeches, but pleading the same case, and Theonoe's response is one of ready acquiescence. In the *Phoenician Women* we again have a three-cornered *agon*, but this time much more antagonistic: Polyneices and Eteocles both speak their minds with aggressive frankness, and Jocasta's effort at peace-making proves futile. The *Orestes* again has a three-party *agon*, with Tyndareus at first addressing Menelaus because he cannot bear to speak directly to Orestes. Formally distinct conventions are combined or blended: in the *Iphigenia*, an apparent *agon* turns into a supplication-scene; in the *Orestes*, the Phrygian sings a messenger-speech in exotic lyric verses. The singing actor plays a prominent role in most of these plays: besides a monody from Jocasta, a lyric exchange between Antigone and her father probably concludes the authentic portion of the *Phoenician Women*; a monody by Electra follows a choral lamentation in the *Orestes*; in the *Iphigenia* the heroine takes over the choral role with a song that performs some of the functions that a choral ode might have in an earlier drama (1283ff.). There is a tendency for these monodies to become looser in structure and less easily defined in metrical terms. None of those just mentioned has strophic form (i.e. they are not constructed in stanzas); hence the movement and length of the arias are less predictable, the form freer of restraints. This 'astrophic' tendency also infects the choral odes themselves, in Euripides himself and his imitators (very briefly *Bacchae* 1153–64; *Iphigenia at Aulis* 1510ff.)[35] These lyric patterns cannot be unconnected with the known or conjectured developments in musical technique at the time, the so-called 'New Music': much is obscure, but it would seem that performers were now allowing themselves a wider range of notes and sharper changes between musical modes and styles.[36]

To some extent the *Bacchae* reverses many of these tendencies, returning to a more austere form. The play is shorter than most of the other late dramas (this remains true even when one takes some account of missing portions of the *Bacchae*'s text and interpolations in the others). The plot is more tightly constructed, proceeding in linear fashion and concentrating on the central antagonism between Pentheus and Dionysus. The number of characters is smaller than in the other late plays (particularly if one discounts anonymous characters such as messengers). The choral role is considerably larger, and its contributions are more significant: despite their character as Asiatic Bacchants, the poetic lyricism of the choral songs is less exotic, their moralizing commentary more traditional; the metre most frequently used, ionics, seems to have associations with religious cult songs. The play lacks an *agon*; the actors do not indulge in song (apart from Agaue, who is not permitted a full-scale monody); the messenger-speeches, while still characteristically vivid, are kept within bounds and closely related to one another and to the central plot-line. All of these factors seem to result from the choice of a deeply traditional subject; they reinforce the unmatched intensity and power of this supreme tragic drama.

When the news of Euripides' death reached Athens in 406 BC, Sophocles is said to have dressed his chorus in mourning and appeared in this style of dress at the *proagon*, the public occasion on which dramatists presented themselves prior to the theatrical contests (*Life of Euripides* 3.11–14 = T1.20 Kovacs). In the following year Aristophanes put on his *Frogs*, the last of several plays in which he had included Euripides as a character (the others were *Acharnians* and *Women at the Thesmophoria*). Although the play makes persistent fun of the dead playwright and concludes with his defeat in the contest with Aeschylus, we should not allow the anarchic humour to blind us to the fact that this dramatization of such a confrontation is itself a tribute to the standing of Euripides. Already the canon is forming: Aeschylus, Sophocles and Euripides are the three great tragedians (the dismissal of lesser rivals in a quick, contemptuous exchange early in the play is telling testimony: lines 83–102).

Recent discussions have shown that older critics were too swift in accepting that tragedy, or the authentic tragic spirit, died with the fall of Athens soon after Sophocles' death: even the surviving literary evidence should have been sufficient to show that the genre continued to thrive in the next century, although no complete play survives (unless we count the *Rhesus* as a fourth-century BC product).[37] Historical and epigraphic study, combined with a sharper examination of the evidence from non-dramatic allusions to tragedy, demonstrates the widespread fascination with tragedy well beyond Athens.[38] It remains true that no later Greek dramatist matched the stature of the great three. We know of the establishment as soon as 386 BC of an additional contest at the City Dionysia (perhaps also at the Lenaea) in which an 'old tragedy', one of the classics, was revived; and later in the fourth century BC the performance of one of the old dramas as a prelude to a presentation of new plays became standard. Our evidence is fragmentary, but in 341 BC Euripides' *Iphigenia* (we do not know which play) was reperformed, in 340 BC the *Orestes*, in 339 BC another of his plays, the title of which is not preserved. It is difficult to deny that this practice acknowledges the existence of a canon of classics, even if we allow that the canon is not necessarily closed.[39]

Not always honoured as he deserved in life, Euripides was pre-eminent after his death.[40] Aeschylus seems to have become less popular after the fifth century BC: Aristotle in the *Poetics* mentions him far less often than Sophocles and Euripides, and we know of few revivals of his work. But although Aristotle more than once compares Sophocles and Euripides to the latter's disadvantage, he quotes examples as often from Euripides' *Iphigenia among the Taurians* as from Sophocles' *Oedipus the King*, and acknowledges the younger dramatist's supremacy at the arousing of pity and fear. That Euripides was widely read is amply attested by the evidence of the papyri from Egypt,[41] which have proved a treasure trove for the recovery of portions of plays lost from the manuscript tradition: the *Erechtheus*, *Hypsipyle*, *Cretans*, *Phaethon* and *Telephus* are among those which can now be reconstructed with some clarity.[42] His influence extended far beyond the tragic genre: his recognition dramas such as the *Ion* and the *Helen*, with their bitter-sweet reunions and use of tokens or keepsakes for identification, profoundly shaped the development of New Comedy. The incomplete sentence from the *Life of Euripides* by Satyrus shrewdly defines the line of descent: (a few words are lost at the start, presumably referring to relationships of loyalty or antagonism) '. . . towards wife, and father towards son, and servant towards master, and also the whole business of vicissitudes, raping of young women, substitutions of children, recognition by means of rings and necklaces. For these are of course the main elements of the New Comedy, and Euripides brought them to perfection, though Homer was his forerunner.'[43] The tradition runs on through Menander's Latin imitators, Plautus and Terence; it continues in Shakespeare and Goldoni, Molière and Wilde. The cradle and the tokens it contains in Euripides' *Ion*, by means of which the foundling is identified, are the distant predecessors of Miss Prism's capacious handbag in *The Importance of Being Earnest*.

No less potent is the legacy of the darker side of Euripides' work – the agonies of indecision and guilty conscience, the horror of manic violence unleashed, the cruel rhetoric of tyrant and oppressor, the constant refrain of the female mourner voicing the grief of family or community. To recount in full the influence of Euripidean tragedy in antiquity would be to summarize much of ancient literary history. Descriptions of the followers of Dionysus and of the intense euphoria of the Bacchic experience could not but be indebted to the unforgettable representation of the god's entourage in the *Bacchae*. Hellenistic and Roman tragedy drew above all on Euripidean models; in particular, they followed the lead of those widely read plays, the *Phoenician Women* and the *Orestes*. Senecan tragedy constantly develops Euripidean themes and motifs; Statius' epic *Thebaid* elaborates the plots of several of his plays.[44] It is not only the higher genres such as tragedy itself, epic and high lyric that pay him tribute. The introspective, painfully emotional yet rhetorically adept speeches of Euripidean heroines (above all Medea) have a deep impact on all later representations of inner conflict: the soliloquies of Menander's characters are no less under his spell than the love-sick women of Ovid's *Heroides* and *Metamorphoses*, to say nothing of Catullus.[45] It is no accident that the rhetorical teacher Quintilian gives extended treatment to Euripides in his catalogue of the authors whom the orator in training should study: here the aspiring speaker could find not only epigrammatic quotations and moralizing tags but guidance on construction, technique and argumentative ingenuity.[46] Many more plays by Euripides survived into the Byzantine era than by the other two great tragedians, whose work was found too difficult or inaccessible; commentators annotated his work more fully, anthologists extracted improving selections, literary critics acclaimed his intelligence and skilled use of language.[47] The critic known as Longinus, author of the essay *On the Sublime*, declares that the poet devotes most effort to creating a tragic effect with two passions – madness and love (15.3); he quotes with deep admiration the madness-scene from the *Orestes*, and shows a fine appreciation of Euripides' capacity to visualize grand and extraordinary events (the chariot-ride of Phaethon, the ecstasy of nature itself in the *Bacchae*); but he also enthuses concerning the poet's skill in achieving pathetic effect through great simplicity of words and word-order:

Thus Heracles says after the killing of the children:
'I'm full of troubles, there's no room for more.'
This is a very ordinary remark, but it has become sublime, as the situation demands. If you rearrange it, it will become apparent that it is in the composition, not in the sense, that Euripides' greatness appears.   (40.3)

Even philosophers turned to Euripides for illustrations: the conclusion of Medea's monologue became a classic example for the Stoic analysis of the opposition between reason and passion.[48]

To pay proper tribute to a great poet requires a great poet. The fourth book of Virgil's *Aeneid*, in which the Latin writer recounts the passion, desertion and death of Dido, includes many elements drawn from the tragic tradition – the sister-confidante, the old nurse, the extended monologues, the long-premeditated suicide are among them.[49] In one memorable passage Virgil describes Dido's wretched dreams as her misery drives her close to madness: the simile he uses to dignify and expand on her experience unmistakably pays homage to two Euripidean masterpieces.

As mad Pentheus observes the ranks of the Eumenides, and sees a twin sun and a double Thebes revealing themselves, or as when, driven from the stage, Agamemnon's son Orestes flees his mother, armed as she is with torches and black snakes, while the avenging Furies sit upon the threshold.[50]

By comparing her sufferings to those of Euripides' classic characters, Virgil gives Dido herself the status of a tragic queen. Similarly in the underworld she is found amid the company of ghosts from heroic Greek myth, figures such as Phaedra and Pasiphae, many of whom also featured in Euripidean plays.

There can be no question here of following the fortunes of Euripides' reputation through the centuries to the modern era.[51] It is sufficient to say that he is probably admired more today than at any time since antiquity, whether as a theatrical innovator, as an experimenter with almost postmodern willingness to shift the genre's boundaries, as a composer of challenging rhetoric, as a dramatist of the horrors of war, or as a champion of human values in the face of a corrupt society and an unfeeling universe. Whatever future changes may occur in the evaluation of different plays, and however varied the assessments of Euripides in relation to his fellow dramatists, it is unlikely that a time will ever come at which his name is forgotten or his works leave audiences unmoved.

NOTES

1. On the festivals and theatrical conditions, see above all A. W. Pickard-Cambridge, *Dramatic Festivals of Athens* (2nd edn Oxford 1968); E. Csapo and W. J. Slater, *The Context of Ancient Drama* (Michigan 1995); more briefly E. Simon, *The Ancient Theatre* (Eng. tr., London and New York 1982), pp. 1–33; O. Taplin, *Greek Tragedy in Action* (London 1978), ch. 2. A readable account of the theatrical context is provided by R. Rehm, *Greek Tragic Theatre* (London 1992). See also J. R. Green, *Theatre in Ancient Greek Society* (London 1994).

2. Some but not all of these formal devices can be shown to a limited extent in English, but they are inevitably eroded in a prose version. The formal structures and variations of the genre are discussed in detail by most commentators: an important synthesis is the collection of essays edited by W. Jens, *Die Bauformen der griechischen Tragödie* (Munich 1971). Some are more briefly described by M. Heath, *The Poetics of Greek Tragedy* (London 1987), ch. 4, 'The Tragic Text'.

3. For an excellent discussion of the types of myths favoured, see B. M. W. Knox, *Word and Action: Essays on the Ancient Theatre* (Baltimore 1979), ch. 1.

4. O. Taplin, *The Stagecraft of Aeschylus* (Oxford 1977); D. Bain, *Actors and Audience* (Oxford 1977); D. Mastronarde, *Contact and Discontinuity* (London 1979); M. Halleran, *Stagecraft in Euripides* (London and Sydney 1985); R. Rehm, *Greek Tragic Theatre*. Despite the powerful impact of these studies, they have not gone unchallenged. For a variety of criticisms see D. Wiles, 'Reading Greek Performance', *Greece and Rome* 34 (1987), pp. 136ff.; S. Goldhill, 'Reading Performance Criticism', *Greece and Rome* 34 (1987), pp. 45–59, reprinted in I. McAuslan and P. Walcot (eds.), *Greek Tragedy* (*Greece and Rome Studies* 2, Oxford 1993), pp. 1–11. A thoughtful and stimulating reply by Taplin, 'Opening Performances: Closing Texts?' *Essays in Criticism* 45 (1995), pp. 93–120.

5. See M. L. West, *Ancient Greek Music* (Oxford 1992). On dance, see A. W. Pickard-Cambridge, *Dramatic Festivals of Athens*, ch. 5; S. Lonsdale, *Dance and Ritual Play in Greek Religion* (Baltimore and London 1993).

6. For fuller essays, see R. P. Winnington-Ingram and P. E. Easterling in *The Cambridge History of Classical Literature*, vol. 1, ed. P. E. Easterling and B. M. W. Knox (Cambridge 1985; paperback 1989); also the pamphlets by S. Ireland and R. Buxton in the *Greece and Rome New Surveys* series (Oxford).

7. D. Kovacs, *Euripidea* (*Mnemosyne* Suppl. 132, 1994) collects the ancient evidence for the poet's life, reputation and reception in antiquity. Since he is particularly concerned to show how much is derived from comedy, he quotes and translates long extracts from Aristophanes' *Women at the Thesmophoria* and *Frogs*. S. Scullion, 'Euripides and Macedon, or The Silence of the *Frogs*', *Classical Quarterly* 53 (2003), pp. 389–400, maintains that the dates given in the ancient sources for Euripides' birth rest purely on guesswork: the only firm chronological limits are imposed by the attested dates of his plays, which make any birth-date prior to about 476 BC feasible. The year 476 BC itself, however, would make him only twenty or twenty-one when he first produced a play: a birth-date in the 480s BC remains plausible.

8. Revivals of older tragedies became a regular feature at the festivals from 386 BC onwards: see A. W. Pickard-Cambridge, *Dramatic Festivals of Athens*, pp. 99–100. Euripides' plays were frequently chosen. For the possibility of performances outside Athens already in the fifth century BC, see P. E. Easterling, 'Euripides Outside Athens: A Speculative Note' *Illinois Classical Studies* 19 (1994), pp. 1–8. See also note 38.

9. This work is highly technical, but the essentials can be gleaned from A. M. Dale's introduction to her commentary on *Helen* (Oxford 1967), pp. xxiv–xxviii. More recent work includes M. J. Cropp and G. Fick, *Resolutions and Chronology in Euripides: the Fragmentary Tragedies* (*Bulletin of the Institute of Classical Studies* Suppl. 43, 1985).

10. See further G. Zuntz, *The Political Plays of Euripides* (Manchester 1955), chs. 1–3, esp. pp. 78–81. Some more recent approaches, which all seek in different ways to put tragedy in an Athenian context, can be found in the collections *Nothing to Do with Dionysus?*, ed. J. Winkler and F. Zeitlin (Princeton 1990); *Tragedy, Comedy and the Polis*, ed. A. Sommerstein et al. (Bari 1993); and *Greek Tragedy and the Historian*, ed. C. B. R. Pelling (Oxford 1997). Some of the strengths and weaknesses of these approaches are discussed by J. Griffin, 'The Social Function of Greek Tragedy', *Classical Quarterly* 48 (1998), pp. 39–61; contrast the responses by R. Seaford, 'The Social Function of Attic Tragedy: A Response to Jasper Griffin', *Classical Quarterly* 50 (2000), pp. 30–44, and S. Goldhill, 'Civic Ideology and the Problem of Difference: The Politics of Aeschylean Tragedy Once Again', *Journal of Hellenic Studies* 130 (2000), pp. 34–56. For a historian's intervention in the debate see P. J. Rhodes, 'Nothing to Do with Democracy: Athenian Drama and the *Polis*', *Journal of Hellenic Studies* 133 (2003), pp. 104–19.

11. For a very valuable survey of the range of his œuvre, which lays proper emphasis on the abundant evidence from the fragmentary plays and the dangers of overconfident generalization, see D. J. Mastronarde, 'Euripidean Tragedy and Genre: the Terminology and its Problems', in *Euripides and Tragic Theatre in the Late Fifth Century*, ed. M. Cropp, K. Lee and D. Sansone (Illinois 2000), pp. 23–39.

12. From the jacket blurb of *Catastrophe Survived* (Oxford 1973).

13. I draw here on R. P. Winnington-Ingram, 'Euripides, *Poietes Sophos* [Intellectual Poet]', *Arethusa* 2 (1969), pp. 127–42. His points are further developed by W. G. Arnott, 'Euripides and the Unexpected', in I. McAuslan and P. Walcot, *Greek Tragedy*, pp. 138–52.

14. In Aristophanes' *Clouds*, originally produced in 423 BC, the rebellious Pheidippides is asked by his father to sing a passage of Aeschylus, and scoffs at the idea, dismissing the older poet as a bombastic and incoherent ranter. When asked to produce a modern alternative, he shocks his father by reciting a passage from Euripides' *Aeolus* defending the merits of incest!

15. This is the usual view, found for instance in the standard commentaries of Barrett and Halleran and restated in our first volume, but J. Gibert, 'Euripides' *Hippolytus* Plays', *Classical Quarterly* 47 (1997), pp. 85–97, has shown reason to question the consensus, and his scepticism is developed further, with new arguments, by G. O. Hutchinson, 'Euripides' Other *Hippolytus*', in *Zeitschrift für Papyrologie und Epigraphik* 149 (2004), pp. 15–28.

16. An influential statement of the view that self-conscious reference to the theatre (sometimes described as 'breaking the dramatic illusion') was non-existent in the Greek tragic tradition was that of D. Bain, 'Audience Address in Greek Tragedy', *Classical Quarterly* 25 (1975), pp. 13–25 and *Actors and*

Audience (Oxford 1977), pp. 208–10. O. Taplin, *The Stagecraft of Aeschylus*, pp. 129–34, adopted a similar position, but his fuller account of the matter in 1986 made some concessions as regards late Euripides ('Fifth-century Tragedy and Comedy: a *Sunkrisis*', *Journal of Hellenic Studies* 106 (1986), pp. 163–74), and more recent work by Taplin and others has gone still further: see S. Goldhill, *Reading Greek Tragedy* (Cambridge 1986), esp. ch. 10; P. Wilson and O. Taplin, *Proceedings of the Cambridge Philological Society* new series 39 (1995), pp. 169–80, esp. pp. 169–70.

17. B. M. W. Knox, *Word and Action*, pp. 250–74 ('Euripidean Comedy'). For an important new study of these plays, see M. Wright, *Euripides' Escape-Tragedies* (Oxford 2005).

18. Good summary, with further references, in C. Collard, *Euripides* (*Greece and Rome New Surveys* 14, Oxford 1981), pp. 20–29.

19. The reference to Euripides' thinkers comes from E. R. Dodds' essay 'Euripides the Irrationalist', *Classical Review* 43 (1929), pp. 87–104, reprinted in his collection *The Ancient Concept of Progress and Other Essays* (Oxford 1973), pp. 78–91. On women in Athenian literature and society, see further J. Gould, 'Law, Custom and Myth: Aspects of the Social Position of Women in Classical Athens', *Journal of Hellenic Studies* 100 (1980), pp. 38–59, reprinted in Gould, *Myth, Ritual, Memory and Exchange* (Oxford 2001), pp. 112–57; S. Goldhill, *Reading Greek Tragedy*, ch. 5; and the essays in A. Powell (ed.), *Euripides, Women and Sexuality* (London 1990).

20. For a very helpful essay on this side of Euripides, see C. Collard, 'Formal Debates in Euripidean Drama', in I. McAuslan and P. Walcot, *Greek Tragedy*, pp. 153–66; also M. Lloyd, *The Agon in Euripides* (Oxford 1992).

21. Thucydides iii, 38, 4. It is particularly striking that the word translated as 'spectator' is the regular term for a member of the theatrical audience.

22. A. N. Michelini, *Euripides and the Tragic Tradition* (Madison, Wisconsin and London 1987), part 1, gives a well-documented history of the debate over Euripides' views. A seminal work is G. Murray's short book *Euripides and His Age* (London 1913), but although highly readable this is now very dated.

23. See the useful collection of essays edited by P. E. Easterling and J. V. Muir, *Greek Religion and Society* (Cambridge 1985), esp. J. Gould's contribution, 'On Making Sense of Greek Religion' (pp. 1–33; reprinted in Gould, *Myth, Ritual, Memory and Exchange*, pp. 203–34).

24. Herodotus ii, 3, 2. On this subject in general, J. Mikalson, *Athenian Popular Religion* (Chapel Hill 1983) and *Honor Thy Gods* (Chapel Hill and London 1991) are valuable collections of material, but tend to draw too firm a line between what happens in life and what appears in literature.

25. Protests against the cruelty and injustice of the gods are found also in the earlier dramatists: note especially Thetis' angry accusations of Apollo, who falsely promised her happiness on her wedding day, but subsequently slew her son Achilles (Aeschylus, fragment 350 Radt, translated as fragment 189 in the Loeb Aeschylus); also Sophocles, *Women of Trachis*, 1264ff.

26. T. C. W. Stinton, *Proceedings of the Cambridge Philological Society*, new series 22 (1976), pp. 60–89; reprinted in Stinton, *Collected Papers on Greek Tragedy* (Oxford 1990), pp. 236–64; H. Yunis, *A New Creed: Fundamental Religious Beliefs in the Athenian Polis and Euripidean Drama* (Göttingen 1988), esp. pp. 155–71.

27. E. R. Dodds, 'Euripides the Irrationalist' (see note 19).

28. Classic (over-)statement, in K. Reinhardt, 'Die Sinneskreise bei Euripides', in *Tradition und Geist* (Göttingen 1960), now available in English as 'The Intellectual Crisis in Euripides', in J. Mossman (ed.), *Euripides* (Oxford 2002), pp. 16–46.

29. For valuable comments on these points see J. Griffin, 'The Social Function of Greek Tragedy', pp. 54–61; the earlier, polemical part of this paper is less rewarding.

30. Cf. Gorgias, fragment B11.8–14 Diels-Kranz (also fragment B23); Plato, *Ion* 535 b–e (reactions to a rhapsode's performance of Homer); *Philebus* 48a (tragedy); Plutarch, *Moralia* 998e. Many relevant passages on Greek responses to poetry are discussed by M. Heath, *The Poetics of Greek Tragedy* (1987), pp. 5–17, 32–5, 38–47, S. Halliwell, *Aristotle's Poetics* (London 1986), ch. 1; and also by Griffin, 'The Social Function of Greek Tragedy'.

31. On these matters I have been helped above all by repeated reading of R. Parker's indispensable paper 'Gods Cruel and Kind: Tragic and Civic Theology', in C. B. R. Pelling (ed.), *Greek Tragedy and the Historian* (Oxford 1997), pp. 143–60.

32. S. Scullion, 'Euripides and Macedon', pp. 389–400, argues that Euripides' sojourn and death at the Macedonian court are fictions spun by Hellenistic biographers.

33. The main ancient sources are Thucydides, book 8, and Xenophon, *Hellenica* (translated in Penguin as 'A History of My Times'), books 1 and 2. For a detailed modern narrative see D. Kagan, *The Fall of the Athenian Empire* (Cornell 1987); shorter treatments by A. Andrewes in *Cambridge Ancient History* (2nd edn) vol. 5 (Cambridge 1992), pp. 464–98, or S. Hornblower, *The Greek World 479–323 BC* (3rd edn London 2002), pp. 181–3.

34. Another way in which contemporary trends have been thought to influence tragedy concerns the *Bacchae*. Many interpreters have seen the hostile reception of Dionysus in Thebes as in some way reflecting Athenian unease at the worship of new deities from foreign parts (e.g. the Thracian goddess Bendis, or Sabazios): see e.g. E. R. Dodds, in his commentary on the *Bacchae* (2nd edn Oxford 1960), pp. xxii–xxv; H. S. Versnel, *Inconsistencies in Greek and Roman Religion I: Ter Unus* (Leiden 1990), pp. 100–189. For criticism of this approach, arguing that the 'new gods' were neither new nor controversial, see R. Parker, *Athenian Religion: a History* (Oxford 1996), ch. 9. W. Allan, in a valuable paper entitled 'Religious Syncretism: the New Gods of Greek Tragedy', forthcoming in *Harvard Studies in Classical Philology*, shows that all references in tragic drama to 'new gods' are dramatically justified in context, and require no explanation from outside the play.

35. Astrophic choral odes are however commoner in some of the earlier dramas. For a full tabulation see G. Rode in *Die Bauformen der griechischen Tragödie*, pp. 85–6.

36. See esp. M. L. West, *Ancient Greek Music* (Oxford 1992), pp. 350–55; E. Csapo, 'Later Euripidean Music', in *Euripides and Tragic Theatre in the Late Fifth Century* (Illinois 2000), pp. 399–426. P. Murray and P. Wilson (eds.), *Music and the Muses* (Oxford 2004) is an important collection of papers: again see esp. E. Csapo's contribution, 'The Politics of the New Music', pp. 207–48.

37. E.g. P. E. Easterling, 'The End of an Era? Tragedy in the Fourth Century' in *Tragedy, Comedy and the Polis*, ed. A. Sommerstein et al. (1993), pp. 559–69.

38. See e.g. O. Taplin, 'Spreading the Word through Performance', in S. Goldhill and R. Osborne (eds.), *Performance Culture and Athenian Democracy* (Cambridge 1999), pp. 33–57; M. Revermann, 'Euripides, Tragedy and Macedon: Some Conditions of Reception', in *Euripides and Tragic Theatre*, ed. M. Cropp et al., pp. 451–67; W. Allan, 'Euripides in Megale Hellas: Some Aspects of the Early Reception of Tragedy', *Greece and Rome* 48 (2001), pp. 76–86.

39. See further P. E. Easterling, 'From Repertoire to Canon', in her *Cambridge Companion to Greek Tragedy* (Cambridge 1977), pp. 211–27.

40. For a masterly survey (in German) see H. Funke, 'Euripides', *Jahrbuch für Antiken und Christentum* 8/9 (1965–6), pp. 233–79. See also R. Garland, *Surviving Greek Tragedy* (London 2004).

41. Figures are derivable from R. Pack, *The Greek and Latin Literary Texts from Greco-Roman Egypt* (2nd edn Ann Arbor 1965); more up to date is J. Krüger, *Oxyrhynchos in der Kaiserzeit* (Frankfurt am Main 1990). More briefly see R. Garland, *Surviving Greek Tragedy*, pp. 52–3.

42. Very valuable treatment (including translations) in C. Collard, M. Cropp, K. Lee and J. Gibert, *Euripides: Fragmentary Plays I–II* (Warminster 1997–2004).

43. Satyrus, *Life of Euripides* (third century BC), fragment 29.7 Arrighetti (= Kovacs, *Euripidea* T4.11, pp. 18–20). See further B. M. W. Knox, 'Euripidean Comedy', in *Word and Action*, pp. 250–74 (whose translation of Satyrus I largely borrow); R. Hunter, *The New Comedy of Greece and Rome* (Cambridge 1985), ch. 5.

44. R. Tarrant, 'Senecan Drama and Its Antecedents', *Harvard Studies in Classical Philology* 82 (1978), pp. 213–63, somewhat modified in later publications. On Statius' sources see D. Vessey, *Statius and the Thebaid* (Cambridge 1973), pp. 67–71.

45. G. Williams, *Tradition and Originality in Roman Poetry* (Oxford 1968), pp. 461ff.

46. Quintilian, *Education of an Orator*, 10.1.67–8; like Satyrus, he remarks on Menander's debt to him.

47. E.g. Dio Chrysostom's essay comparing the three tragedians' treatments of the Philoctetes myth (*Oration* 52); see esp. 11–14. See further W. Schmid and O. Stählin, *Geschichte der griechischen Literatur* (Munich 1929–48), i, 3, pp. 823–38.

48. D. J. Mastronarde in his commentary on *Medea* (Cambridge 2002), lines 1078–80.

49. See further P. Hardie, 'Virgil and Tragedy', in C. Martindale (ed.), *The Cambridge Companion to Virgil* (Cambridge 1997), pp. 312–26.

50. Virgil, *Aeneid*, 4.469–72, alluding to *Bacchae*, 918–19 and *Orestes*, 255ff. The same scene in *Orestes*, as we have seen, aroused the admiration of Longinus.

51. For works which give access to most aspects of this history see P. E. Easterling, *Companion* (especially the essays by P. Burian and F. Macintosh); H. Flashar, *Inszenierung der Antike* (Munich 1991); M. McDonald, *Ancient Sun, Modern Light* (Columbia 1992); H. Foley, 'Twentieth-century Performance and Adaptation of Euripides', in *Euripides and Tragic Theatre*, ed. M. Cropp et al., pp. 1–13; E. Hall et al. (eds.), *Dionysus Since 69* (Oxford 2004); R. Garland, *Surviving Greek Tragedy*.

CHRONOLOGICAL TABLE

As explained in the Introduction, not all of the plays of Euripides (and fewer still of Sophocles) can be firmly dated. This table shows all of the extant Greek tragedies for which we have fairly certain dates, and also lists most of Aristophanes' surviving comedies and some major historical events to put them in context. Conjectural dates are given with question-marks, and are usually fixed by analysis of metrical technique: they may well be three or four years out either way.

Year BC

c. 535-2	Thespis competes in first tragic competition		
		490	Darius' invasion of Greece
		480-79	Xerxes' invasion
472	Aeschylus' *Persians*		
468	Sophocles' first victory, on his first attempt		
467	Aesch. *Laius, Oedipus, Seven against Thebes, Sphinx*		
463?	Aesch. *Suppliants, Aigyptioi, Danaids, Amymone*	c. 462	Radical democracy established at Athens

458	Aesch. *Agamemnon, Libation-Bearers, Eumenides, Proteus*		
456	Death of Aeschylus		
455	Euripides' first competition; third prize		
438	Eur. *Alcestis*		
431	Eur. *Medea*	431	War begins between Athens and Sparta
c. 430?	Eur. *The Children of Heracles*	430	Great Plague of Athens
		429	Death of Pericles
428	Eur. *Hippolytus* (surviving version)		
		427	Aristophanes' first play (now lost)
425?	Eur. *Andromache*	425	Arist. *Acharnians*
		424	Arist. *Knights*
pre-423?	Eur. *Hecabe*		
423?	Eur. *Suppliant Women*	423	Arist. *Clouds* (original version)
		422	Arist. *Wasps*
		421	Arist. *Peace*; death of Cleon; peace of Nicias
c. 417–415	Eur. *Heracles, Electra*	416	Athenian massacre at Melos
415	Eur. *Trojan Women*		

	414	Arist. *Birds*
	413	Athenian expedition to Sicily ends in disaster
pre-412?	Eur. *Ion, Iphigenia among the Taurians*	
412	Eur. *Helen*	
412 or later?	Eur. *Cyclops* (satyr-play)	
	411	Arist. *Lysistrata, Women at the Thesmophoria* Oligarchic revolution at Athens
c. 409?	Eur. *Phoenician Women*	
409	Soph. *Philoctetes*	
408	Eur. *Orestes*	
406–405	Death of Euripides in Macedonia; death of Sophocles	
after 406	Eur. *Iphigenia at Aulis, Bacchae* (posthumously produced)	
	405	Arist. *Frogs*
	404	End of war, with Athens defeated
401	Soph. *Oedipus at Colonus* (post-humously produced)	
	399	Execution of Socrates

NOTE ON THE TEXT

We have no manuscripts in Euripides' hand, or going back anywhere near his own time. If we had, they would be difficult to decipher, and would lack many aids which the modern reader takes for granted: stage directions, punctuation, clear indications of change of speaker, regular divisions between lines and even between words. In fact, although some parts of his plays, mostly short extracts, survive in papyri from the earliest centuries AD, our complete manuscripts of the plays translated in this volume go back no further than the tenth century. Moreover, the textual evidence for the various plays differs greatly in quantity. Three plays were especially popular in later antiquity, namely *Hecabe*, the *Phoenician Women* and *Orestes* (the so-called 'Byzantine triad'). These survive in more than 200 manuscripts, and modern editions of the last two rest on a selection of a significant number of these. The opposite situation prevails with *Bacchae* and *Iphigenia at Aulis*. Here we are essentially dependent on a single primary manuscript of the early fourteenth century, known as L (short for Laurentianus 32.2); in the case of the *Bacchae* L fails us after line 755, and recourse must be had to another manuscript of the same period known as P (Palatinus Gr. 287), whose relation to L is debated. A slightly larger range of manuscripts offers independent evidence for *Rhesus*. Papyrus fragments survive for all five plays in this volume: again most numerous are those for the *Phoenician Women* and the *Orestes*, reflecting the popularity of these two.

This situation is not unusual in the history of classical authors. No ancient dramatist's work survives in his own hand: in all cases we are dealing with a text transmitted by one route or several, and copied many times over. In an age which knew nothing of the printing-press, far less the Xerox machine, all copying had to be done by hand, every copy in a sense a new version. The opportunities for corruption of the text – that is, the introduction of error – were numerous. The reasons for such corruption include simple miscopying or misunderstanding by the scribe, omission or addition of passages by actors in later productions, efforts to improve the text by readers who felt, rightly or wrongly, that it must be corrupt, accidental inclusion of marginal notes or quotations from other plays, and very occasionally bowdlerization of 'unsuitable' passages. Problems of this kind were already recognized in antiquity: efforts were made to stabilize the texts of the tragedians in fourth-century BC Athens, and the ancient commentaries or 'scholia' to some of Euripides' plays make frequent comments on textual matters, for instance remarking that a line is 'not to be found' in some of their early manuscripts, now lost to us. In the same way, when a modern scholar produces an edition of a Euripidean play, there are many places where he or she must decide between different versions given in different manuscripts. Sometimes the choice will be easy: one version may be unmetrical, ungrammatical or meaningless. But often the decision may be more difficult, and in many cases it is clear that no manuscript preserves the lines in question in the correct form. Hence the editor must either reconstruct Euripides' authentic text by 'conjecture', or indicate that the passage is insolubly corrupt, a conclusion normally signalled by printing daggers ('obeli') on either side of the perplexing passage.

A translator is in a slightly more fortunate position than an editor. The editor must make a decision what to print at every point, and uncertainty may prevail as to the exact wording even when the overall sense is fairly clear. In this translation James Diggle's excellent Oxford Classical Text has normally been followed. When he has marked a word or phrase as probably or certainly corrupt, we have usually adopted a conjectural reading, whether made by him or by a previous editor, even though we often agree that there can be no certainty that this is what Euripides actually wrote. In cases where the corruption is more extensive, we have tried to give a probable idea of the train of thought. These problems arise particularly in choral and other lyric passages, where the language is less close to everyday speech, and where unusual metre and dialect often misled copyists.

Many of the smaller problems involving variations of words or uncertainty over phrasing will be unlikely to cause difficulties to users of this translation. More noticeable are the occasional places where it seems that something has dropped out of the text; usually this can be explained by the accidents of miscopying or by damage to some of the manuscripts from which our texts descend. Scholars refer to a gap of this kind as a *lacuna*. The most important example of this in the plays translated here occurs in the closing scenes of the *Bacchae*. Here we are dependent on manuscript P, but there are two points at which the text of P's source was evidently defective: we have lost a passage of uncertain length after line 1300 and another, probably longer section after 1329 (see the Notes on these lines). Besides this, there are other passages where a lacuna has been detected or suspected: *Bacchae* 652 and 1036 are certain examples, 200 and 843 highly probable. It is also possible, though by no means certain, that an initial prologue has been lost at the start of the *Rhesus*.

A much more serious problem which affects criticism of Euripides is that of interpolation. This is the term used to describe the inclusion of alien material in the original text, expanding and elaborating on the author's words. Sometimes the new material betrays itself by its very unsuitability to the context, and we may suppose that it has been included by accident (for instance, parallels from other plays were sometimes copied out in the margin, then found their way into the text in subsequent copies). Sometimes lines may be present in one manuscript but omitted in others: if they seem superfluous in themselves, they may well be a later addition. Sometimes a speech may seem unnecessarily wordy, and we may suspect without feeling certain that it has been expanded; here textual criticism merges with literary judgement. It has often been suggested that some passages in the plays have been 'padded out' by actors seeking to improve their parts: although this phenomenon has probably been exaggerated, it would be a mistake to rule it out altogether. One speech which has fallen under suspicion on these grounds is Medea's famous soliloquy as she wavers over the killing of her children (*Medea* 1019–80: the boldest critics would excise all of 1056–80). In the translation our normal policy is to follow Diggle's text, and therefore we normally omit passages which he brands as interpolated. Already in volume 1 of this translation, we made an exception for this speech of Medea, because the speech is so distinguished and the case remains controversial.

In the last plays of Euripides, however, there are special problems, which vary from play to play. In the *Orestes*, *Bacchae* and *Rhesus* (in the last of these the issue seldom arises) we have continued our former practice, but upon occasion have been more inclusive than Diggle. In particular we retain, though with cautionary comments in the Notes, a few passages in *Orestes* and *Bacchae* where his determination to excise the irrelevant may be thought to have gone too far (especially *Orestes* 895–7, 904–13, *Bacchae* 199–203). In the *Phoenician Women* it is widely held that extensive passages have been added or altered by later hands: scholars are in general agreement that the last 150 lines or so of the play are spurious, but there is little consensus on earlier parts of the drama. Under these circumstances we have presented the reader with a translation of most of the text, including the conclusion, while continuing to exclude shorter passages of one or two lines which seem to mar the sense or to be clearly intrusive. This may seem inconsistent, but it at least offers those using this volume a version which could be performed as a whole. Many specific difficulties are discussed further in the Notes.

The most recalcitrant case is the *Iphigenia at Aulis*. It is clear from ancient testimony that this play was posthumously produced, and it seems certain that Euripides did not finish it. Probably the greater part was complete, but there has been some additional material included at the beginning and elsewhere, either for the first performance or in the next century. At a later stage the ending has been tampered with: one hypothesis is that the original ending was lost and replaced, but by a greatly inferior composer, whose intervention is betrayed by metrical and linguistic blunders. In these circumstances to provide a version consisting only of certainly Euripidean material is hardly possible, and to do so would mean truncating the play. We therefore present a translation of the entire text, despite the manifest inconsistencies of plot, style and dramatic technique. (See further the Preface and Notes to this play.)

These complications should not deter the student or general reader. The text of Euripides is much better preserved than that of Aeschylus, and the magisterial Oxford edition of James Diggle has placed it on a much firmer foundation. Knowledge of the nature of the textual tradition helps the modern reader to understand why certain difficulties occur, but despite the depredations of the centuries, Euripides' authentic text survives in great part, and whether in the original or in translation will long continue to exercise a fascination on reader and audience.

FURTHER READING

Introductory

C. Collard, *Euripides* (*Greece and Rome New Surveys* 14, 1981), p. 3. A good one-page summary with bibliography.

D. J. Mastronarde, *Euripides, Phoenissae* (Cambridge 1994), introduction part vi (pp. 39–49), 'The Problem of Interpolation'.

L. D. Reynolds and N. G. Wilson, *Scribes and Scholars: A Guide to the Transmission of Greek and Latin Literature* (3rd edn Oxford 1991). A wide-ranging and authoritative introduction to the problems involved in the recovery and editing of ancient texts.

M. L. West, *Textual Criticism and Editorial Technique* (Stuttgart 1973), part 1.

Advanced

W. S. Barrett, *Euripides: Hippolytus* (Oxford 1964), pp. 45–84. A detailed account, requiring some knowledge of Greek and technical terms.

J. Diggle, *The Textual Tradition of Euripides' Orestes* (Oxford 1994). Not for the beginner.

R. Hamilton, 'Objective Evidence for Actors' Interpolations in Greek Tragedies', *Greek Roman and Byzantine Studies* 15 (1974), pp. 387–402.

M. W. Haslam, 'Interpolation in the *Phoenissae*: Papyrus Evidence', *Classical Quarterly* 26 (1976), pp. 4–10.

D. L. Page, *Actors' Interpolations in Greek Tragedy* (Oxford 1934).

M. D. Reeve, 'Interpolations in Greek Tragedy', *Greek Roman and Byzantine*

Studies 13 (1972), pp. 247–65 (general principles), 451–74 (*Phoenician Women*); ibid. 14 (1973), pp. 145–71.

M. L. West, 'Tragica V', *Bulletin of the Institute of Classical Studies* 28 (1981), pp. 61–78, esp. pp. 73–6 (on the end of the *Iphigenia at Aulis*).

G. Zuntz, *An Enquiry into the Transmission of the Plays of Euripides* (Cambridge 1965): Important but highly technical.

TRANSLATOR'S NOTE

A new translation of an author as great as Euripides needs little justification, perhaps, but it may be useful to point out certain respects in which this translation differs from those of the late Philip Vellacott which Penguin published in four volumes between 1953 and 1972. In these, for the most part, the translation was deliberately broken up into verse-like lines, creating a certain stateliness that reflected the dignity of the original but often resulted in the kind of English which could only exist on the printed page. My aim has been to produce a version that conforms far more to how people speak, and for this the medium of continuous prose was essential.

A further consequence of the earlier approach is that all the characters speak the same form of stylized English, whether they are princes or slaves. By adopting continuous prose I have tried to achieve a tone that is more relaxed, less stylized and less close to the Greek word-order, while remaining true to the original. There is a wider range of tones and moods in recognition of the fact that, for all the uniformity of the Greek, not every character maintains a wholly dignified register of speech. Some employ a more colloquial and fast-moving style, even verging on the humorous (for example the Old Woman in *Helen*), others require a more dignified style because they are arrogant or demented or divine.

In the lyric passages, especially the choral odes, I have aimed at a certain archaic formality of language in recognition of their emotional or religious content, but the overriding concern has been to let the freshness and beauty of the poetry come through to the reader as directly as possible. These elements of song in Euripides' work were much admired by his contemporaries and by later generations, and here, if anywhere, the translator's responsibility weighs particularly heavily.

In order to mark more clearly the distinction between spoken and sung parts in the plays, all lyric sections have been put in italics and where appropriate separated more distinctly from what was spoken. The areas chiefly affected are the choral odes. Passages of doubtful origin and speculative insertions to fill lacunae in the original text are enclosed in square brackets.

Euripides is intensely interested in human nature in all its different forms and a modern translation must therefore try to take some account of the richness of his character portrayal and psychological insight. It is this belief that underpins my attempt throughout these plays to find and express variety of tone; I have tried to think of the words as being spoken by real persons rather than literary creations, remembering the remark attributed to Sophocles that, whereas in his plays he showed men 'as they should be', Euripides showed them 'as they are'.

This said, it remains true that the language of Attic tragedy, even in the case of the modernizing Euripides, was never that spoken in the streets of Athens in the poet's day. As with Homeric epic, it is essentially a literary creation that aims predominantly at a certain grandeur in keeping with the dignity of its subject-matter. This inevitability imposes limits on how natural a style should be attempted by a translator. However modern Euripidean tragedy may seem compared with that of Aeschylus and Sophocles, its language was still sufficiently grand for Aristophanes to parody it relentlessly in his comedies as high flown and pompous.

As with the previous volumes, I have not attempted to produce an entirely modern idiom in these translations; the overall tone remains, I hope, essentially dignified, as Greek tragedy demands, and I have tried hard to be faithful to the original both in letter and in spirit, taking heart from the excellent prose translation of Virgil's *Aeneid* for Penguin Classics by Professor David West, and the sensible remarks he makes on translating poetry into prose in his own introduction to that book.

No dramatist of any age can be content to live solely within the confines of the printed page, and it is gratifying that my translations of

Trojan Women, *Bacchae* and *Hippolytus* have been used for performances on the London stage. I hope that other plays in these versions may catch the eye of modern producers and that the reader who comes fresh to Euripides in this volume may feel that his voice deserves to be heard more in the modern theatre.

My warmest thanks go, as ever, to my splendid collaborator Dr Richard Rutherford of Christ Church, Oxford, not only for his introductory essay, prefaces and notes, but also for his generosity in casting a scholarly eye over my manuscripts and rescuing me several times from 'translationese'. I am particularly grateful for his input to this last volume of the plays, with all their difficulties of text and interpretation. Any remaining infelicities are to be laid firmly at my door. I am also grateful to Professor David Kovacs, translator of Euripides for the Loeb Classical Library, for sharing his thoughts with me on the problems and pleasures of translating this elusive author; to Professor Robert Fagles of Princeton, translator of Aeschylus and Sophocles for Penguin Classics, whose generous remarks on the first volume were much appreciated by a comparative novice in the art of translation; and to Pat Easterling, Regius Professor Emeritus of Greek at Cambridge, for her encouragement and advice in the early stages. For advice on specific points Dr Rutherford and I are grateful to Professors S. Halliwell and P. J. Parsons, Dr W. Allan and Dr S. Scullion. I must not forget my students at St Paul's School, who have played their part in sharpening my focus on the plays and several times made me think again. With this volume all the nineteen surviving plays have been translated, in a project that began in 1994 – *kamatos eukamatos*.

Finally, I would like to dedicate this book to my late mother, Janet Davie, best of all possible parents.

J.N.D.

PHOENICIAN
WOMEN

PREFACE TO
PHOENICIAN WOMEN

About half of Euripides' surviving works deal with the Trojan war or its aftermath (in *Iphigenia in Aulis* the prelude). By contrast the mythology of the Theban wars and the house of Oedipus is thinly represented. The *Bacchae* is indeed set at Thebes, but deals with earlier events; the *Suppliant Women* treats the issue of the burial of the seven warriors who attack Thebes, but largely from an Athenian perspective: Theseus intervenes to ensure that justice is done. Though the fragmentary evidence shows that the legends of Thebes formed the subject of several other plays (Euripides, like Sophocles, wrote an *Oedipus* and an *Antigone*), only in the *Phoenician Women* do we find a full-blown Theban drama.

Just as the *Orestes* inevitably looks back to the Oresteian trilogy of Aeschylus, so the *Phoenician Women* is significantly indebted to the Aeschylean trilogy which culminated in the *Seven against Thebes*. The first two plays of that trilogy were the *Laius* and the *Oedipus*: the names make clear enough that the older dramatist followed the disastrous progress of three successive generations of the Theban royal house. The surviving play focuses on the figure of Eteocles, defending his city against invaders supporting his brother Polyneices; the play reaches its climax when Eteocles resolves to confront his brother in battle, and the two men slay one another. Aeschylus' treatment was majestic and slow-moving: hundreds of lines of the *Seven* are devoted to the herald's report of the names and appearance of the attacking warriors, and Eteocles' responses (cf. *Phoenician Women* 748–52 and note 37). The action of the Aeschylean play is concentrated, the cast-list small; Oedipus and Jocasta appear to be dead, and in the authentic sections there is no reference to any female offspring. All of this is changed in the

Euripidean version: although a single self-contained play, it embraces a variety of related but independently effective scenes, and (through the choral odes) extends the audience's perspective through much of the mythic history of Thebes.

The myths were flexible. There is a natural tendency for the modern reader to give priority to the surviving versions, but even these are various, and the dramatists were largely free to choose among the diverse traditions, often adding or elaborating. According to the *Iliad* Oedipus died and was buried at Thebes, whereas tragedy (especially Sophocles) normally assumes that he will be sent into exile when the truth is discovered: Euripides provides a composite version, in which Oedipus lives on at Thebes, resentful and blind, but is finally sent into exile by Creon in an effort to purify the state. In the *Odyssey* Oedipus' wife (there called Epicaste, not Jocasta) is said to have killed herself, but in the lyric poetry of Stesichorus she survives and appears to have remonstrated with her sons in a scene which presumably formed the model for the three-way debate in Euripides' play. As for Antigone and Ismene, the two daughters of Oedipus, they may not have featured prominently in the legend before Sophocles' famous play (Ismene is indeed never very prominent). Even after Sophocles, their fates could vary: in Euripides' lost *Antigone*, the heroine was married to Haemon, the son of Creon, bore his child, and cooperated with him to bury her brother, rather than acting in splendid isolation: it is even possible that divine intervention saved her from martyrdom. Characterization can also be modified: in Aeschylus' play Eteocles was a sympathetic figure, defender of Thebes in a time of crisis, noble though doomed to die: there is no suggestion that he has wronged his brother or cheated him of his inheritance. By contrast in Euripides' play he cares for nothing but keeping the throne, and is eager to come face to face with his brother in combat: although Polyneices' determination to attack his native city is condemned by Jocasta, it is clear that his cause is regarded as just even by those who will suffer if he conquers (154–5, 258–60, 467, 508).

The scope of the play is large, and has been extended further by later additions (see below). There is no 'hero' – Eteocles appears only in two scenes, Polyneices only in one. The family group, especially the triad of the two sons and their mother, form a central part of the dramatic structure: Jocasta tries to reconcile the brothers by insisting on a truce and time for debate, but fails: the *agon*, as usual, only intensifies conflict. Later she again tries to intervene, this time through action rather than words, by hurrying to the battlefield and seeking to prevent the final fratricide: again her efforts end in failure, and her own suicide swiftly follows. In contrast with the accursed royal house is the family of Creon, Jocasta's brother. The subplot of Creon, Teiresias and Menoeceus, which culminates in Menoeceus' self-sacrificial suicide to save Thebes from destruction, is probably Euripides' own invention (it is a story-pattern he particularly favours; see note 49). The heroic nobility of Menoeceus is powerfully opposed to the self-destructive ambition of the warring brothers. Yet although Menoeceus' sacrifice saves the city, it shatters Creon. Finally there is Antigone. Although some have supposed her entire part a later addition, there is no good reason to doubt that she played a part in Euripides' design, and it also seems likely that Oedipus' cameo appearance is authentic: the duet of lamentation near the close of the play is certainly a powerful moment, and may well have formed the finale of Euripides' original version.

It is clear, however, that the text has been supplemented or interfered with, probably in the fourth century BC. Problems were already detected by ancient scholars, whose comments survive in the scholia or annotations which accompany the play in some manuscripts. The issue was fully examined in the nineteenth century, but as was the fashion in that period, suspicion went too far. A more cautious approach is now prevalent. In the past critics often excised passages which they regarded as unnecessary (the scene involving Antigone and the old servant on the roof early in the play is a good example); but the fact that a scene is not strictly indispensable does not make it spurious. Another notable argument concerns the characterization of Polyneices: efforts have sometimes been made to remove lines which show him to be more self-interested, less patriotic and virtuous, than the critic would prefer (for an example see note 21). But if we find both Polyneices and Eteocles lacking in tragic greatness, that is exactly what we might expect of this playwright, especially in his later œuvre.

Elsewhere it has been supposed that certain scenes have been 'padded out' to increase a particular actor's role, or to provide supplementary information (as with the catalogue of the *Seven* at 1104–40). But the most substantial and by far the most important doubts concern the conclusion of the play. It is almost universally agreed that the ending has been modified in order to connect the play with the well-known stories of Antigone burying her brother and Oedipus dying in Athens, as dramatized by Sophocles. But the adaptation has been crudely done: as the scholia comment, how can Antigone bury Polyneices (1657) if she is to accompany her father into exile (1679) (scholia, note on 1692)? There are other doubtful features, and it seems probable that the genuine text ends at line 1581. Bolder critics would excise extensive earlier portions too (e.g. 1308–34, 1338–53, to eliminate the reappearance of Creon). In this translation the ending has been included, but some further cautionary remarks will be found in the Notes.

These problems should not interfere with the reader's appreciation of the bulk of the play. Euripides' conception and structure are still clearly discernible, even if the ending has been extended or altered. Like other Greek tragedies, the *Phoenician Women* has a particular character of its own: the poet is concerned not only to present a sequence of events but to create a certain atmosphere. The play is rich in allusion to Theban place-names and traditions: in the so-called Teichoskopia ('Viewing from the Walls') scene alone, we find references to Dirce's spring, the tomb of Zethus, Amphion's walls, the tomb of Niobe's children. More important is the account of the mythic history of Thebes in the successive choral odes, which evoke a world of monstrous crime, chthonic forces, perversion, doom and hatred. Teiresias' warnings also contribute to our sense of the race as plagued by misfortune arising from the wrath of the gods. Some have seen this as an expression of anti-Theban sentiment; more subtly, it has been suggested that the representation of Thebes, in this and other dramas, is a kind of crystallization of all that Athens is not, a dark contrast to Athenian light. This works better with the *Suppliant Women*, where Athens is prominent; here she is not. It is better to see the dark world of the play as the product of Euripides' powerful poetic imagination at work on the fertile mythical traditions.

The poet's vision continues to find expression in the traditional dramatic forms, but as in the *Orestes*, they are expanded and developed in novel ways. The *agon* involves an exchange of three speeches rather than two (Jocasta makes a vain attempt to persuade both the antagonists), and proceeds to a racy dialogue in trochaic tetrameters, full of interruptions and interjections: the effect is more naturalistic than normal stichomythic dialogues. There is a massive increase of the narrative element: while almost all tragedies have one messenger speech, the *Phoenician Women* includes four, amounting to almost 300 lines. As always, the drama includes a chorus, but an unexpected one. Whereas the chorus of the *Seven against Thebes* consisted of women of Thebes itself, the Euripidean chorus are slave-women from Tyre, en route to Delphi: Euripides seems to go out of his way to emphasize their marginality. Although distantly related to the people of Thebes, and embroiled in the conflict which threatens the city, they stand apart from the action, commentators rather than confidantes. The choral odes, though often rather loosely linked to the action of adjacent scenes, are connected with one another thematically: together they provide a 'history' of Thebes and its myths, though highly allusive and unchronological. This historical or mythographic tendency extends beyond the choral contribution: the play as a whole includes a host of cross-references to other strands of legend and indeed other plays (thus Teiresias alludes to the episode Euripides had dramatized some years earlier in the *Erechtheus*: see 852ff. and note 47). By this stage in the century mythology was becoming more systematic, a familiar though still fluid structure of genealogy and relationships: handbooks summarizing and codifying the legends had begun to appear. Euripides is aware of this tendency and makes use of it, though for poetic ends. To this extent the interpolator responsible for the present conclusion was continuing, though less skilfully, the authentic practice of his model.

The *Phoenician Women* is not a modern favourite. Extended lamentation and narration of battles is not much to modern taste; the legendary background of the Theban conflict is less familiar to the average reader than the war of Troy; the characters are unsympathetic or passive or both. But anyone who wants to understand ancient reception of tragedy needs to come to terms with the fact that this play, together with

Hecabe and *Orestes*, was one of Euripides' most popular dramas; while anyone considering the impact of Greek drama on Latin literature cannot do better than begin from the influence of this play on Seneca's tragedies (not only his *Phoenician Women* but his *Oedipus*), and still more on Statius' magnificently macabre *Thebaid*. When the imitators are figures of such importance, the model deserves closer attention, and the reader who comes to the Euripidean original with an open mind will not find it lacking in dramatic power.

CHARACTERS

JOCASTA, *mother and wife of Oedipus*
SERVANT, *old tutor of Antigone*
ANTIGONE, *daughter of Oedipus and Jocasta*
CHORUS *of captive women from Phoenicia*
POLYNEICES, *son of Oedipus and Jocasta, exiled by Eteocles*
ETEOCLES, *brother of Polyneices, ruling in Thebes*
CREON, *brother of Jocasta*
TEIRESIAS, *a blind prophet*
MENOECEUS, *son of Creon*
MESSENGER
SECOND MESSENGER
OEDIPUS, *son of Laius and Jocasta, former king of Thebes*

[*The scene is the royal palace at Thebes.* JOCASTA *enters from the palace. She wears black and her hair is close-cropped in sign of mourning.*]

JOCASTA:[1] O Sun, whirling[2] on your flames with swift steeds, what a curse it brought, the beam you aimed at Thebes that day when Cadmus came to this land, leaving Phoenicia's sea-swept country!

He took to wife Harmonia, the Cyprian's child, and in time became the father of Polydorus, whose son, men say, was Labdacus, the father of Laius.

I am the daughter of Menoeceus, and Creon is my brother, born of the same mother. Jocasta is what men call me, the name given by my father, and Laius took me as his wife.

When many years of wedlock with me had brought him no children in these halls, he went and questioned Phoebus, asking for his own sake and mine, that male offspring might bless his house.

But the god replied: 'O king of Thebes of the noble horses, do not sow your seed for children against the gods' will; for if you father a son, he will kill you, your own issue, and all your house shall wade through blood.'[3] Yet he gave way to passion and, succumbing to Bacchus' power, fathered a child on me.

And when the babe was born, recognizing his offence and remembering the saying of the god, he gave the infant to herdsmen to expose in Hera's meadow on Cithaeron's uplands, after piercing his ankles through with iron spikes, causing Greece to call him Oedipus – Swell-Foot.

But the men who tended Polybus' horses found the child and, carrying him to the home of their mistress, placed him in her arms. She suckled the fruit of my own womb's sore labour and persuaded her lord that the child was her own. 30 When he was grown to manhood and his cheeks were a burnished gold, my son, either making the discovery himself or informed by someone else, made the journey to Phoebus' dwelling, in order to learn his parents' identity. Now Laius, my husband, also was going there, eager to learn if the child he had exposed was no longer living. They met, the pair of them, at the same place, where the road divides for Phocis. The driver of Laius' carriage shouted out an order: 'Off the road with you, stranger! Make way for a king!' Oedipus in his 40 pride carried on walking and made no reply. The horses' hooves dashed against his ankles, drawing blood. And then (why should I describe what happened beyond the grim event?) the son killed his father and, taking the carriage, presented it to Polybus who had raised him.

When the Sphinx was ravaging our city, and my husband no longer lived, Creon my brother issued a proclamation that, if any man should read the riddle of that sorceress-maid, he would win my hand in marriage. Now, strangely it happened that Oedipus, my son, read the song of the Sphinx (which led 50 to his receiving the throne as his reward) and, poor wretch, all-unknowing took to wife his own mother, while she who shared his bed shared also his ignorance. To my son I bore two male children, Eteocles and Polyneices the famous and mighty, and two daughters. The one her father called Ismene, the other, the elder, I called Antigone.

But when he learned that his wife and mother were one, Oedipus, having endured the worst of suffering, brought fear- 60 ful ruin on his own eyes, drenching them in blood with golden brooch-pins.[4]

Now, when my sons had reached bearded manhood, they kept their father concealed behind closed doors, so that his fate, needing much subtlety of thought to explain away, might be forgotten. He is alive inside the house, but distracted by his fortunes he has hurled most impious curses at his sons, that they should divide this house with whetted swords.[5]

The pair of them feared that, if they lived together, the gods would bring these curses to fulfilment, and so they entered into an agreement: Polyneices, the younger, should go first into voluntary exile from Thebes, while Eteocles should remain and wield the sceptre here, then alternately they should rule for one year. But once Eteocles was firmly established in his royal office, he would not vacate the throne, and thrust Polyneices away from this land in banishment.

To Argos went Polyneices, and taking to wife Adrastus' daughter, he has mustered a strong force of spearsmen and brought them here. To these very walls with their seven gates has he come, demanding his father's sceptre and a share in the land. Seeking to prevent strife, I have persuaded one son to meet the other under truce before they resort to fighting. The messenger I have sent says that he will come.

O Zeus, dwelling in the shining folds of heaven, save us, grant reconciliation to my sons! Wise as you are, you should not leave the same mortal to languish for ever in misery!

[JOCASTA *goes back into the palace. The old tutor of Antigone appears on the roof of the palace, followed by* ANTIGONE, *who climbs a ladder behind the stage-building.*[6]]

SERVANT: Antigone, glorious flower of your father's house, since your mother has let you leave the women's quarters for the highest part of the palace, as you had begged, to view the army of Argos, stay there while I scan the pathway, in case some Theban appears walking down there, and we incur criticism – no matter for me, a servant, but you are royal.[7] When I know this, I will tell you all I saw and heard from the men of Argos,[8] the time I went to your brother with offering of a truce, passing from here to there, and back again from him. [*He looks around from the top of the roof.*] No, no Theban is approaching the palace. Climb up these old cedar steps and look over the plain, along the waters of Ismenus, past Dirce's spring to that great gathering of the enemy.

ANTIGONE: *Stretch, yes stretch out an old hand to a young one, helping me to climb up off this ladder.*

SERVANT: There you are, my girl; grasp it! You have got here in good time: the Argive army's on the move, as it happens; they're dividing companies, one from the other.

ANTIGONE: *O Lady Hecate, child of Leto, how all the plain flashes with bronze!*

SERVANT: Yes, for this is no feeble army Polyneices has brought to Thebes, with the thunder of many horses and countless weapons.

ANTIGONE: *Are the gates secure, the brass-clamped bolts fixed true in the walls that Amphion fashioned of stone?*

SERVANT: Never fear: all is safe inside the city.

ANTIGONE: *Who is the man with the white helmet-crest, who marches at the head of their army, lifting high on his shoulder his shield of bronze?*

SERVANT: A captain, my lady.

ANTIGONE: *Who is he and what is his family? Tell me, old man, what is his name?*

SERVANT: He boasts of Mycenaean birth, and dwells by Lerna's streams. He is king Hippomedon.

ANTIGONE: *Ah, what a proud and terrible sight he makes! He is like an earthborn giant, star-bright, as in pictures, not resembling one of mortal birth!*

SERVANT: Do you not see the man, a captain, now crossing Dirce's stream?

ANTIGONE: *How strange and new the fashion of his armour shows! Who is he?*

SERVANT: He is Tydeus, son of Oeneus, and the battle-fire of Aetolia lives in his breast.

ANTIGONE: *Old friend, is he the man who wedded the sister of*

Polyneices' wife? How foreign his equipment appears, half-barbarian!

SERVANT: Yes, my child, all men of Aetolia carry shields, and
140   their skill in throwing the javelin is unequalled.

ANTIGONE: *And you, old fellow, how do you know all this so
well?*

SERVANT: I saw the devices on their shields and remembered
them, that time I went to your brother with the offering of a
truce. Having noted them, I know the men who wear those
arms.

ANTIGONE: *Who is he who passes by the tomb of Zethus with his
locks flowing, that young warrior with the savage expression on his
face, a captain, to judge from the troops surging behind him in full
armour?*

150   SERVANT: He is Parthenopaeus, son of Atalanta.

ANTIGONE: *Well, I pray that Artemis who ranges the mountains
with her mother may destroy him, felling him with her bow, for
coming to lay waste to my city.*

SERVANT: That's my prayer too, my child! But they come to
Thebes with justice on their side; and I fear the gods may see
the truth of their cause.

ANTIGONE: *Where is he, the man born of the same mother as myself,
to a fate of so much suffering? O my good old friend, tell me, where
is Polyneices?*

SERVANT: He stands next to Adrastus, near the tomb of Niobe's
160   seven maiden daughters. Do you see?

ANTIGONE: I see, though not clearly, I see the outline of his
figure and likeness of his chest. *If only I could fly, a wind-swept
cloud, through the air to my brother, and fling my arms at last around
his beloved neck, the wretched exile!*

*See how he shines out in his armour of gold, old man, blazing
like the shafts of the rising sun!*

SERVANT: He shall come here under truce to the palace, to fill
170   your heart with joy.

ANTIGONE: *That man there, old fellow, who is he, the one who
stands holding the reins of his white horses?*

SERVANT: He is the prophet Amphiaraus,[9] my lady, and at his side are victims for sacrifice, whose blood will slake the earth's thirst.

ANTIGONE: *O daughter of Helios with his gleaming belt, Selene, orb of shining gold, how calm and restrained his use of the goad as he drives on his team, tapping each of them in turn! Where is the man who hurls arrogant threats at this city, Capaneus?*

SERVANT: There he is, measuring the walls from top to bottom, calculating where to place his scaling ladders.   180

ANTIGONE: *O Nemesis, o you loud-rumbling thunderclaps of Zeus and flaming radiance of his lightning, yours is the power to put the proud utterances of a boastful tongue to sleep! This is the man who claimed his spear would capture the women of Thebes and deliver them up to the daughters of Mycenae, to Lerna's trident, enslaving them to the spring Poseidon made for love of Amymone. Never, never, o Lady Artemis, golden-haired child of Zeus, may I endure   190 the yoke of slavery!*

SERVANT: My child, return to the palace and stay in the cover of your women's quarters, as you have realized your heart's desire and seen all you wished to see. For, now that confusion has entered Thebes, a crowd of women is advancing on the palace. Women are prone to finding fault, and once they find slight pretexts for talk, they import others in plenty. It gives women some kind of pleasure to say nothing good of each   200 other.[10]

[ANTIGONE *goes down the ladder, followed by the old tutor. The chorus of female prisoners from Phoenicia enter the orchestra.*]

CHORUS [Strophe I]: *Leaving the sea that washes Tyre, I have come from the Phoenician isle*[11] *as the finest offering to Loxias, to serve as a slave to Phoebus*[12] *in his halls, where under the crags of Parnassus covered with shafts of snow he has made his dwelling. Over Ionian seas I sailed, sped by the oar, while Zephyrus' chariot traversed the unharvested plains*[13] *that flow round Sicily, his breath filling the*   210 *heavens with loveliest sound.*

[Antistrophe I:] *Chosen for Loxias as the fairest blossom of my city, I came to Cadmus' land, sent here to the towers of Laius, to the*

15

towers which belong to the kin of the glorious sons of Agenor.[14] *Like*
220 *statues fashioned in gold I have become a handmaiden dedicated to*
Phoebus. But Castalia's waters still wait for me to wash in Phoebus'
service the hair that is my maidenhood's splendour.

[Epode:] *O rock that flashes with the gleam of Bacchic torches*
above the twin-peaked summit that Dionysus haunts, and you, vine,
that daily put forth shoots and offer up the fruitful cluster of your
230 *grapes; o holy cavern of the serpent, and you, mountain heights where*
the nymphs keep watch, and sacred mount scattered with shafts of
snow, may I forsake Dirce and, free from fear, honour the god,
celebrating the immortals in whirling dance, where Phoebus has his
vaulted home at earth's navel![15]

[Strophe 2:] *But now I see before these walls Ares has come in*
240 *fury, kindling blood to fire this city – oh, heaven forbid! Griefs are*
shared by kinsfolk, and Phoenicia's land will suffer too, if this city of
seven towers meets any suffering. Oh, it is true, shared is the blood,
shared the children of horn-wearing Io! I share in this tribulation.

[Antistrophe 2:] *Around the city a dense cloud of shields blazes*
250 *in token of bloody battle to come; this shall Ares soon know, if he*
brings upon the sons of Oedipus the suffering that comes from the
Furies. O Pelasgian Argos, I fear your might, and the hand of
heaven! For the son who makes his armed assault upon this house is
260 *entering a contest where his cause is just.*

[POLYNEICES *enters and approaches the palace doors cautiously.*]
POLYNEICES: All too easily the gatekeepers' bolts have wel-
comed me inside the walls. And so I fear that, having me in
their net, my captors won't let me escape without the cost
of blood. That's why I must look all around me, staring
now this way now that, for fear of some trickery. This sword
that arms my hand will give me the assurance of desperate
courage.

Ha! Who goes there? Or it just a sound that alarms me?
270 Everything seems frightening to men on a risky venture, as
soon as they set foot in enemy territory. I put trust in my
mother, who persuaded me to come here under truce, and

yet I do not. But help is close at hand (near by I see the altar-hearth);[16] the house is not deserted. Come, let me return my sword to its dark scabbard and question these women who stand beside the palace.

Foreign women, tell me, from what homeland have you come here to a Greek house?

CHORUS-LEADER: Phoenicia is the land that nurtured me, and   280 Agenor's sons' sons sent me here to honour Phoebus as the first-fruits won by their spears. The famous son of Oedipus was about to send me to the holy oracle and hearth of Loxias, when the men of Argos came in arms against the city. But tell me in turn, sir, who you are, that you have come to the seven-gated battlements that guard the land of Thebes?

POLYNEICES: My father is Oedipus, son of Laius, and Jocasta, Menoeceus' child, is my mother; the people of Thebes call me Polyneices.   290

CHORUS: *O kinsman of Agenor's sons, my royal masters who sent me here in exile, low on bended knee I fall to do you honour, my lord, respecting the custom of my homeland. You have come at last to the land of your fathers!*

Ho! Mistress, royal mistress, come quickly from the palace, fling wide its gates!

Do you hear, lady, who gave this man birth? Why are you slow to cross the high-roofed threshold to clasp your son in your arms?   300

[JOCASTA *enters from the palace and sings a monody of welcome.*[17]]
JOCASTA: *Maidens of Phoenicia, hearing your cries, I drag my tottering steps here on these old feet.* [She catches sight of Polyneices:] *O my son, at last, after days past number I see your face! Come to your mother's breast and hold me in your embrace, stoop to place your cheek on mine, your hair close to mine, your dark locks casting their shadow over my neck! Oh, oh, at last you appear, past hope, past imagining, for*   310 *your mother to embrace! What should I say to you? How can I recapture the delight of old in every way with hands and words, in the joyful intricacies of the dance, circling now this way, now that?*

O child, you left your father's halls deserted, when a brother's shameless crime sent you into exile, yearned for by your loved ones,
320 *yearned for by Thebes! Therefore have I shorn my white hair in sorrow, abandoning it to grief, and wear no more my robes of white, my son, exchanging them for these dark rags.*

But in the palace the blind old man constantly strives to master his tearful longing for the pair of like feather who were severed from the
330 *yoke of family love. He hastens to take his own life with bloody sword or noose slung over rafters, groaning in distress at the curses he levelled at his sons. With persistent cries of anguish he hides away in darkness. But you, my child, I hear, are already wedded; yours is the pleasure of fathering offspring in a foreign house and you cherish*
340 *a foreign kinship. This is a curse on your mother and the son of Laius of old, the plague of an alien marriage! I did not kindle for you the flaming torch customary at weddings, as befits a blessed mother; Ismenus was denied the glory of providing his water for your nuptials, while throughout the city of the Thebans no word was spoken*
350 *to greet your bride. I curse these woes, whether caused by the sword or Strife or your father or the gods' will that has staged its revelry in the house of Oedipus! For on my head has fallen the anguish of these sorrows.*

CHORUS-LEADER: Offspring exert a strange power over women, won as they are at the cost of painful labour; yes, all womankind love their children.[18]

POLYNEICES: Mother, I have shown both sense and folly in coming among my enemies. Yet all men are bound to love the land of their birth. The man who disagrees with this is
360 indulging in rhetoric; his thoughts tend elsewhere.

With such misgiving did I come, so much a prey to fear that some treacherous act of my brother's might cause my death, that I made my way through the town sword in hand and looking all around me. One thing has given me heart, the truce and your own pledge that brought me safe within these ancestral walls. Many a tear I shed as I came, when after so long a time I saw the temples and altars of the gods, the exercise spaces where I received my training, and Dirce's

spring. Banished unjustly from these, I now inhabit a foreign
city, and tears flow constantly from my eyes.   370

   But enough – grief ever produces fresh grief – I see you
have your head shorn and wear clothes of mourning. Oh,
mother, my sufferings are to be pitied! How terrible a thing
it is when family members become enemies and there is little
hope of reconciliation! What is my old father doing inside the
palace, with darkness instead of light in his eyes,[19] and what
my two sisters? Do they lament my banishment, poor girls?

JOCASTA: Cruelly is some god destroying the family of Oedi-
   pus. So it began: I gave birth against the laws of decency, and   380
   your father wrongly married me and made you. But what is
   to be done? The will of heaven must be endured. But how to
   ask what I want to know without causing you any pain, that
   is my dilemma. And yet I long to be satisfied.

POLYNEICES: No, ask your question; leave no desire unfulfilled.
   Your wishes are also what my own heart desires, mother.

JOCASTA: Then first I ask you what I long to know: what is it
   like to lose one's native land? Is it a grievous loss?

POLYNEICES: Most grievous; more so in deed than in word.

JOCASTA: What is its nature? What is it that causes an exile
   distress?   390

POLYNEICES: One thing above all else: he is denied freedom
   of speech.

JOCASTA: That's a slave's condition you describe, not speaking
   one's thoughts!

POLYNEICES: A man has to bear the senseless acts of his rulers.

JOCASTA: What pain, to share in the folly of fools!

POLYNEICES: But to avoid harm one must deny instinct and
   practise servitude.

JOCASTA: Hopes, they say, give sustenance to exiles.

POLYNEICES: Hopes look with eyes that are fair but their
   promise is for the future.

JOCASTA: Does time not expose their emptiness?

POLYNEICES: They have a certain charm that makes foul
   weather seem fair.

JOCASTA: How did you find food before marriage gave you
400   security?

POLYNEICES: Sometimes I had enough each day, sometimes I
had not.

JOCASTA: Had you no help from friends and former guests of
your father?

POLYNEICES: Enjoy good fortune: friends disappear once pros-
perity goes.

JOCASTA: Did your noble birth not raise you to high estate?

POLYNEICES: Poverty is a curse; nobility did not feed me.

JOCASTA: A man's homeland, it seems, is his most precious
possession.

POLYNEICES: You could not even say how precious.

JOCASTA: How did you come to Argos? What was your
intention?

POLYNEICES: Adrastus had received a certain oracle from
Loxias.

JOCASTA: What kind of oracle? What are you saying? I cannot
410   fathom.

POLYNEICES: He said that Adrastus' daughters should wed a
boar and a lion.[20]

JOCASTA: What did you have to do with beasts' names, my
son?

POLYNEICES: I do not know; the god called me to my fate.

JOCASTA: Wise is the god; how did you win your bride?

POLYNEICES: It was night; I came to the entrance of Adrastus'
palace.

JOCASTA: Looking for a place to rest, as wandering exiles do?

POLYNEICES: Yes, and then it was that another man, also an
exile, arrived.

JOCASTA: Who was he? How wretched must he, too, have
been!

POLYNEICES: Tydeus, the son, men say, of Oineus.

JOCASTA: Why did Adrastus liken the pair of you to wild
420   beasts?

POLYNEICES: Because we fought over a bed for the night.

JOCASTA: Then the son of Talaus understood the oracle's meaning?

POLYNEICES: Yes, and gave the two of us his two daughters!

JOCASTA: And is your marriage a happy or unhappy one?

POLYNEICES: To this day I have no fault to find in my wife.

JOCASTA: How did you persuade the army to follow you here?

POLYNEICES: To his two sons-in-law Adrastus swore this oath: he would bring both of us back from exile to our homelands, and first myself. Many chieftains of the Danaans and Mycenaeans are here, rendering me a kindness that is distressing but necessary to me, as it is my native city I march against. I call the gods as my witnesses that unwillingly I raised the spear against relatives all too willing to fight. Now, mother, with you rests the power to cancel these ills, by reconciling kinsmen of one parent and ridding yourself, myself and all Thebes of these troubles. It is an old, old saying but nonetheless I will repeat it: 'Wealth is honoured most by men and has the greatest influence in human affairs.' For this have I come here, with countless spears at my back; for a nobleman without wealth counts for nothing.[21]

CHORUS-LEADER: And here comes Eteocles for this reconciliation. Jocasta, as their mother the task is yours to speak the words that will bring your children to harmony once more.

[ETEOCLES *enters with a retinue of servants.*]

ETEOCLES: Mother, here I am;[22] I have come in deference to your wishes. What is to be done? Let someone explain. For I have stopped my work of marshalling round the walls the tight cordon of defence for Thebes, to hear your mediation, for which you have persuaded me to allow this man inside our walls under truce.

JOCASTA: Enough, Eteocles! Justice is not the result of haste; measured words achieve most in the eyes of wise men. Curb that fearsome glare and those stormy outbursts! It is no Gorgon's severed head you are looking at; this is your brother you see before you!

And you, Polyneices, for your part turn your face on your

brother; if you look him in the eye, you will speak and hear his words more reasonably. I want to give you both some

460 wise advice: when a man comes to meet a friend with whom he has quarrelled and looks him in the eye, he should consider only the reason for their meeting and forget all earlier grievances. You should speak first, Polyneices my son; for you have come with an army of Danaus' sons, unjustly treated, as you claim. May some god be the judge and reconcile your differences!

POLYNEICES: Truth is simple by nature in the telling, and

470 justice needs no cunning gloss of sophistries. It has a right measure of its own; but the argument that is unjust is sick in nature, and so needs the medicine of clever words. I had regard for my share and this man's in our father's house, as I wanted to escape the curses that Oedipus uttered once against us. Willingly I quitted this land, allowing him for one year's cycle to rule Thebes, so that I myself might rule in turn, claiming my share, and not clash with him in spiteful enmity,

480 doing and suffering wrong, as now has happened.

He gave his seal of approval to this and his oath in the name of the gods; but not one of his promises has he fulfilled, instead enjoying for himself the kingship and my share in the inheritance.

Even now I am prepared to take what is mine and send away my army from this land, to take my house and live in it in turn, and then for the same space of time to yield it to him once more, and not to lay waste my homeland or set against these battlements scaling-ladders for assault. This I will attempt

490 to do, if I fail to have justice. I call upon the gods to witness this – that, though acting in all respects justly, I am being robbed of my homeland unjustly, most impiously. These various points, Mother, I have stated as they stand, not entangled in fine words, and, in the eyes of men both wise and simple, my case, I think, is just.

CHORUS-LEADER: I grant we were not reared in the land of Greece but it seems to me your words are full of sense.

22

ETEOCLES: If all men agreed on what constituted honour and
wisdom, the world would be free of contentious argument.   500
But as it is, nothing is like or equal on earth, except in name;
but this naming is not reality.[23] Mother, I will disguise nothing
in what I say: I would go to where the stars or sun have their
risings, I'd go beneath the earth, if only I could, in order to
possess the greatest of the gods, Tyranny. This is what is
precious, mother, and I have no wish to yield it to another,
when I might keep it for myself. It is cowardice to forfeit
what is greater and accept what is less. Besides, I count it a
disgrace that this man should achieve his ambition by coming   510
here in arms and sacking our land. This would prove a
reproach to Thebes, if fear of Mycenaean spears should make
me resign the sceptre that is mine for him to wield! He had
no right to seek arbitration by coming here in arms; reasoned
discussion can achieve all that can be effected by enemy
swords. If he consents to live in this land on other terms, he
may. But what I hold I shall not willingly resign. When I have
the opportunity to rule, shall I ever be a servant of this man?   520

   Therefore come fire, come sword, harness your horses and
fill the plain with chariots! I will not yield my throne to him!
If it is ever right to do wrong, then for a throne's sake is
wrong most right! In all else should a man fear the gods.[24]

CHORUS-LEADER: Ignoble actions should not win praise. This
is not noble reasoning but an offence to justice.

JOCASTA: Eteocles, my son, not everything about old age is
bad; experience can sometimes speak more wisely than youth.   530
Why do you set your heart, my boy, on Ambition, the worst
of gods? Do not! She is a goddess who despises justice. Many
are the prosperous homes and cities she enters, leaving when
her worshippers are ruined. And she is the one you honour
in your madness! A nobler course, my child, is to honour
Equality,[25] who constantly binds friends to friends, cities to
cities, allies to allies. Equality is mankind's natural law, while
the less is always enemy of the more, and ushers in the day of
hate. Equality established measures and weights for men,   540

23

and apportioned number. The sightless eye of night and light of the sun pace equally through the year's cycle, and neither of them resents giving way to the other. The sun, then, and night serve proportion; will you not consent to having an equal share in your own home? Will you not give this man his due? Where is justice then? Why do you give excessive honour to Tyranny, that injustice you call happiness, and rate
550   it so highly? Is it a precious thing, to be the focus of all eyes? No, it is empty! Do you want to have in your home as many troubles as possessions? What is 'more'? Nothing but a word. Sufficient means are enough to satisfy men of sense. Mortals do not possess their wealth as personal property; we are merely stewards of what the gods bestow; whenever they wish, they take it back again. Prosperity is not constant but lasts for a day.

Come, if I put two propositions before you and ask: 'Do
560   you want to be king of your city or its saviour?' will your reply be, 'King'? But if this man is victorious and the spears of Argos master those of Cadmus' men, you will see this city of the Thebans brought low, you will see many of its daughters taken prisoner and brutally raped by enemy soldiers. Then this wealth you seek to own will prove costly indeed to Thebes, yet you remain ambitious. So much I say to you.

Now, Polyneices, my words are for you. It was a foolish kindness that Adrastus did you, and a thoughtless journey you
570   made, coming here to sack this city. Consider, if you conquer this land – and heaven forbid you should – how in the name of the gods will you set up trophies of victory to Zeus,[26] how, too, will you begin the sacrifice for destroying your homeland, or inscribe the spoils by Inachus' stream? 'Having destroyed by fire this city of Thebes, Polyneices dedicated these shields to the gods.' O my son, never pray to win such glory as this from the lips of fellow Greeks! But if you are defeated and his side triumphs, how will you return to Argos, leaving thousands behind dead?

580   This is what will be said: 'What a cursed betrothal you

24

made, Adrastus! How we have been destroyed by one girl's marriage!' You risk incurring two evils, my child: to lose Argos and Thebes, stumbling in mid-enterprise. Subdue your excessive desires, both of you, subdue them, I say! When two fools meet, complete disaster is the result!

CHORUS-LEADER: O you gods, avert these woes, I pray, and let the sons of Oedipus reach agreement!

ETEOCLES: Mother, the contest is no longer one of words.[27] Time spent here is idly wasted and all for nothing is this goodwill of yours. We cannot reach agreement except on the terms stated, that I should wield the sceptre and be king of   590 this land. Spare me, then, your tedious admonitions and leave me alone! [*Turning to* POLYNEICES:] And you, sir, get yourself clear of these walls or prepare to die!

POLYNEICES: And who will kill me? Who is so hard to wound that he can plunge his murderous sword into me and not win the same reward?

ETEOCLES: He stands near, not far off; do you see these hands of mine?

POLYNEICES: I do; how cowardly wealth makes a man, as he shamefully clings to life!

ETEOCLES: And yet you have brought an army to face a man with no stomach for battle?

POLYNEICES: Yes; the general who avoids risk is better than the one who courts it.

ETEOCLES: You are a boaster, trusting to the truce that saves you from death!   600

POLYNEICES: And saves you also! A second time I ask for the sceptre and my share in Thebes!

ETEOCLES: You ask in vain; I will live in the house that is mine.

POLYNEICES: With more than your share?

ETEOCLES: Yes; get out of the country!

POLYNEICES: O altars of my ancestral gods . . .

ETEOCLES: – that you are here to sack!

POLYNEICES: . . . hear me . . .

ETEOCLES: Who would hear you pray – the man who has brought an army against your homeland?

POLYNEICES: . . . and you dwellings of our gods, riders of the white horses . . .[28]

ETEOCLES: – who hate you!

POLYNEICES: . . . I am being driven from my country . . .

ETEOCLES: Yes; you came to drive me from it!

POLYNEICES: . . . unjustly, you gods!

ETEOCLES: Call upon the gods at Mycenae, not here!

POLYNEICES: You are the gods' enemy . . .

ETEOCLES: . . . but not my country's enemy, as you are!

POLYNEICES: . . . in driving me away without my proper share.

610   ETEOCLES: And I will take your life besides!

POLYNEICES: O Father, do you hear how I am treated?

ETEOCLES: He also hears what actions you are taking.

POLYNEICES: And you, Mother?

ETEOCLES: It is sacrilege for you to speak our mother's name!

POLYNEICES: O Thebes!

ETEOCLES: Go back to Argos and call on Lerna's waters!

POLYNEICES: I will go, do not trouble yourself; but thank you, Mother.

ETEOCLES: Leave this land!

POLYNEICES: I do leave it; but allow me to see my father.

ETEOCLES: Your request is denied!

POLYNEICES: Well then, my young sisters.

ETEOCLES: You will never see them again.

POLYNEICES: O sisters!

ETEOCLES: Why do you call on them, when you are their bitter enemy?

POLYNEICES: Mother, farewell!

JOCASTA: You see how marvellously well I fare, child!

POLYNEICES: I am your son no longer.

JOCASTA: I was born for sorrows past number!

POLYNEICES: Yes, for this man treats me with contempt.

620   ETEOCLES: Contempt is what I have had from you!

POLYNEICES: Where will you take your stance before the gates?[29]

ETEOCLES: Why do you ask me this?

POLYNEICES: I will station myself opposite in order to kill you.

ETEOCLES: I, too, long for this encounter!

JOCASTA: Oh, I cannot bear it! What will you do, my sons?

ETEOCLES: The event will show.

JOCASTA: Shun, o shun your father's curses![30]

POLYNEICES: Let the whole house go to ruin! Soon enough my sword shall be red with blood and leave its idleness. I call to witness the gods and the land that reared me that, dishonoured and pitifully wronged, I am being driven from this land, as if I were a slave and not as much the son of Oedipus as this man. And if, Thebes, any harm befalls you, blame not me but him! For I came unwillingly, and unwillingly am I driven away.   630

And to you, Apollo, Lord of the Highways, and to your shrine, farewell! Farewell, you friends of my youth! Farewell, altars of the gods, rich in sacrifice! I do not know if I shall ever again address you. Not yet asleep are the hopes in which I trust, that with heaven's aid I will kill this man and take control of this Theban land.

[POLYNEICES *departs to rejoin his army.*]

ETEOCLES: Away with you from my country! Truly did my father show divine foreknowledge when he named you Polyneices, 'man of much strife',[31] since strife is what you are.

[JOCASTA *returns to the palace.* ETEOCLES *and attendants remain on stage.*]

CHORUS [Strophe]: *From Tyre to this land came Cadmus,*[32] *where a calf unbroken to the yoke sank to its four knees before him, fulfilling*   640 *the oracle, where the divine word bade him take for his place of dwelling the wheat-bearing plains where the gushing stream of the lovely river waters Dirce's green pastures, rich land for the plough. Here did his mother in union with Zeus bring forth the Roaring One,*[33] *and the twisting ivy in blessing at once covered his infant*   650 *form, encircling him in the shade of its green tendrils, for maidens and*

27

women of Thebes to honour in the Bacchic dance with shouts of 'evoe!'

[Antistrophe:] *Here was the gory serpent of Ares that kept a cruel vigil, surveying with eyes that flashed everywhere the watery fountains*
660 *and streams that mirrored the green banks. Cadmus came to fetch lustral water and killed it, hurling a rock with mighty monster-slaying arm at the beast's blood-stained head. And at the bidding of Pallas, motherless goddess, he cast its teeth into the fertile furrows of the*
670 *earth. Then from the surface of its soil the earth sent up the sight of armed men whom bloody conflict, iron-tempered, united once more with their mother, earth, soaking with their blood the soil that had shown them to the air's sunlit breezes.*

[Epode:] *To you also I call, Epaphus,[34] child of Zeus, scion long since of our first mother, Io, to you I call with foreign cries, ah, with*
680 *foreign prayers! Come, come to this land! Your descendants founded this city and it is in the keeping of the twin-named goddesses, Persephone and Demeter, beloved deity, ruler of all things, and of Earth, nurse of all things. O send the fire-bearing goddesses, defend this land! All things are easy to the gods.*

ETEOCLES [*to an attendant*]: You, there, go and bring Creon,
690 son of Menoeceus,[35] brother of my mother Jocasta! Tell him I wish to confer with him on matters that touch my own interest and the city's before we go to battle and take our place among the spears. But here he is, releasing your feet from their toil; I see him approaching my palace.

[CREON *enters.*]

CREON: Much ground have I covered in my eagerness to see you, Eteocles, my royal lord; indeed this hunt for you took me round all the gates and guards of Cadmus' town.

700 ETEOCLES: I too wanted to see you, Creon; when I met Poly-neices to parley with him, I found little scope for agreement.

CREON: I heard he has great designs on Thebes, trusting to his kinship with Adrastus and that man's army. But we must leave this in the gods' hands; I am here to tell you of a serious obstacle in our path.

28

ETEOCLES: What kind of obstacle? I do not understand your meaning.

CREON: We have an Argive soldier as a prisoner.

ETEOCLES: And what news does he have of developments on their side?

CREON: He says the Argive army is about to throw a cordon of warriors round the city and towers of Thebes.   710

ETEOCLES: Then Cadmus' men must meet them in the field!

CREON: Where? Does your lack of years keep you from seeing what you should?

ETEOCLES: Beyond the trenches there, that's where we should fight them, wasting no time!

CREON: Thebes has few troops, but they have many.

ETEOCLES: I know them; their boldness is confined to words.

CREON: Argos has a great name among Greeks.

ETEOCLES: Never fear; I will soon fill the plain with their blood.

CREON: I hope so; but I foresee much effort to achieve this.

ETEOCLES: And so I won't keep my men penned inside these walls.   720

CREON: Well, victory lies entirely in good counsel.

ETEOCLES: Is your counsel, then, that I should take a different path?

CREON: Any path, rather than hazard everything on one throw.

ETEOCLES: What if we attack them by night and lay some ambush?

CREON: Only if you get back here in safety, should you fail.

ETEOCLES: Night evens the odds but gives an advantage to daring.

CREON: The darkness of night can spell disaster if things go wrong.

ETEOCLES: Then should I launch my attack when they are at supper?

CREON: You would create some panic, but it's victory you need.

ETEOCLES: Dirce's waters are deep to ford when they retreat.   730

CREON: Nothing is better than taking sound precautions.

ETEOCLES: What if we ride the Argive army down with a cavalry charge?

CREON: There too their troops are fenced round with chariots.

ETEOCLES: What, then, shall I do? Hand over the city to the enemy?

CREON: Certainly not! Consider the matter: you are a man of sense.

ETEOCLES: Well, what counsel is more sensible?

CREON: It's said they have seven warriors, I have heard . . .

ETEOCLES: What orders have they been given? That isn't a strong force!

CREON: Each has been assigned a company to lead against our seven gates.[36]

ETEOCLES: What, then, should we do? I won't wait for counsels of indecision.

CREON: You must choose seven warriors to meet them at the gates.

ETEOCLES: Commanding companies or as single combatants?

CREON: Companies, once you have selected the bravest men.

ETEOCLES: I understand; to repel attempts to scale our walls.

CREON: Assign them adjutants; one man does not see everything.

ETEOCLES: Chosen for their courage or good judgement?

CREON: For both; the one without the other has no value.

ETEOCLES: And so I shall; I will go to our seven towers and station captains at the gates, as you advise, seven men of mine to match seven of the enemy. It would be a costly waste of time to tell the name of each, with our foes encamped under our very walls.[37] No, I'm on my way; we must not let our hands be idle. I pray that I come face to face with my brother, clash with him in battle and kill him with my spear! But if I meet with any misfortune,[38] your task is to see to the marriage of my sister, Antigone, and your son, Haemon. Now, as I leave, I confirm their recent pledge of betrothal. You are her mother's brother; why need I speak at length? Give her the care she deserves, for your sake and mine. When my father put out his eyes, he incurred the charge of self-inflicted folly.

740

750

760

I have no praise for him, and by his curses, if it happens, he will kill us.

There is one thing we have yet to do; we must learn from the prophet Teiresias[39] if he has any oracular advice to bestow. I shall send your son Menoeceus, who bears your father's name, Creon, to bring Teiresias here. He will be glad to come 770 to speak to you, but I have criticized his mantic art to his face before now and so have earned his resentment. I give this command to you, Creon, and to the city: if my powers prevail, the corpse of Polyneices is never to be buried in this land of Thebes, and anyone who does so is to die, even if related by blood. So much have I said to you; now I speak to my servants: bring out my weapons and protective armour, so I may set out now for the trial of might that awaits me, with justice at 780 my side bringing victory. I pray to Precaution,[40] most serviceable of deities, that she keep this city safe.

[ETEOCLES *leaves with attendants.* CREON *remains on stage.*]

CHORUS [Strophe]: *O Ares, bringer of much suffering, why are you so possessed with blood and death, so out of tune with the festivals of the Roaring One?*[41] *Not for the dances where the young in their virgin beauty wear garlands do you toss your locks, singing a song to the flute's breath as the Graces lead the dance, but with armed warriors you breathe into the Argive host a lust for the blood of Thebes,* 790 *dancing before your followers a savage dance graced by no music. You do not whirl amid the frenzy of fawnskin and thyrsus but stand in your chariot behind your bridled team of four with clattering hooves, as you rush to Ismenus' stream with charging steeds, breathing hard upon the Argives, and marshalling in bronze along our walls of stone that armed, shield-bearing host of revellers to oppose the sons of the Sown Men. A fearsome goddess, truly, is Strife, who has devised these sufferings for the kings of our land.* 800

[Antistrophe:] *O glen of holy leaves, haunt of many beasts, o eye of Artemis, Cithaeron*[42] *nurturer of snows, never should you have fostered the one exposed to die, offspring of Jocasta, Oedipus, cast out of his home a babe, and marked by pins of gold. I wish the*

31

winged maid, that monster of the mountain, the Sphinx, had not
come bringing grief to this land with her unmusical song, she who,
810   sent by Hades below the earth to ravage the land of the Cadmeans,
once swooped with four-taloned feet on our walls and carried off the
sons of Cadmus into the trackless light of the upper air. But now
fresh discord, misbegotten by the gods, grows between the sons of
Oedipus in their house and in their city. What is shameful is never
in its nature honourable; those sons their mother bore against all
custom bring pollution on their sire, for she entered the bed of one
who shared her blood.

[Epode:] *You brought to birth,*[43] *o Earth, of old you brought to
birth, as once I heard tell, yes, I heard it from foreign lips in my own
home, the race that sprang from the teeth of the crimson-crested ser-*
820   *pent, eater of beast, which brought both shame and glory to Thebes.
And in time past the great gods came to Harmonia's nuptials,*[44] *and
to the sound of Amphion's lyre-strings*[45] *high rose the walls of Thebes,
high its towers, on the land between the two rivers, where Dirce pours
her waters before Ismenus into the plain and makes it green. And Io,
our horned ancestress, became the mother of kings from the line of
Cadmus. This city, which has known so many blessings from one*
830   *generation to another, now stands where Ares' finest garlands may be
gained.*[46]

[TEIRESIAS *enters, guided by his daughter, with* MENOECEUS
at his side.]

TEIRESIAS: Lead on, daughter; you are the eyes to my blind
feet, as a star is to sailors. Here on even ground set my feet
and go first, in case I stumble; your father has lost his strength.
Keep safe in your pure young hands these oracular tablets I
took, when I had noted the signs from the birds at the holy
840   seat where I divine what is to be. Tell me, young Menoeceus,
son of Creon, how long a journey remains for us before we
find your father in the city. My knees ache, and with this long
trek I have scarcely strength to continue.

CREON: Take heart! You are near your friends, Teiresias, and
soon can drop anchor. Give him support, my son; old men

and children too young to fly the nest both like to wait for
another's hand to steady them.

TEIRESIAS: Very well; here we are. Now, why this eager sum-
mons, Creon?

CREON: I have not forgotten; but put behind you the weariness
of your journey: gather your strength and get back your
breath.   850

TEIRESIAS: Well, I am tired; yesterday I travelled here from the
land of Erechtheus' sons.[47] There, too, a war was being waged,
against Eumolpus' spearsmen, and Cecrops' folk were the
victors, thanks to me. This golden crown you see me wear-
ing is my reward, the first fruits from the spoils the enemy
yielded.

CREON: I count your crown of triumph as a good omen. For,
as you know, we are engulfed by the spears of Danaus' sons,
and Thebes faces a great contest. Eteocles our king has already   860
gone in full armour to face the might of Mycenae, and he has
ordered me to discover from you what is our best means of
saving the city.

TEIRESIAS: Had Eteocles put this question, I should have sealed
my lips and withheld my oracles. But to you, since you wish
to learn, I will speak. For this land, Creon, has long been sick,
ever since Laius in defiance of the gods fathered a son, the
wretch Oedipus, who became his mother's husband.

   The bloody ruin of his eyes has been contrived by the gods   870
as a warning to Greece. Oedipus' sons, wishing to cast a veil
at last over this shame, supposing they could outrun the gods,
foolishly erred; denying their father either exile or privileges,
they turned the man from anguish to rage: racked with illness
and their contempt, he vented terrible curses upon them.
What did I not do, what words of advice did I not offer the
sons of Oedipus, only to earn their hatred?

   They are near to death, Creon, each at the hands of his
brother. Many men shall fall and lie, one corpse upon another   880
in mingled carnage, Argive and Cadmean together, bringing
bitter lamentation to the land of Thebes. You also, poor city,

33

are reduced to rubble, if no one heeds my words. It would be best if none of Oedipus' brood should inhabit this land as citizens, far less as kings, for they are accursed and will bring destruction on Thebes.

890 But since evil outweighs good in this case, there remains one other path to deliverance. But to divulge this brings harm to me and pain to those whom destiny allows to bring the city healing salvation; therefore I shall leave. Farewell. I am but one among many and will suffer, if I must, what is to be; there is no alternative.[48]

[*He turns to leave.*]

CREON: Wait a moment, old man!

TEIRESIAS: Take your hands off me!

CREON: Stay; what makes you leave in such haste?

TEIRESIAS: Fortune is leaving you, Creon, not I.

CREON: Tell me how the city and its people are to be saved.

TEIRESIAS: You desire this knowledge now, but soon you will not.

900 CREON: How can I not want to save the land of my forefathers?

TEIRESIAS: Then you wish to hear? You insist?

CREON: Yes; what could I be more eager to know?

TEIRESIAS: Then you will hear my oracles. But first I want to know this clearly: where is Menoeceus, who guided me here?

CREON: He is not far away; there beside you, in fact.

TEIRESIAS: He must leave, and get far from my prophecies.

CREON: He is my true son and will not divulge what he should keep secret.

TEIRESIAS: Then do you want me to tell you in his presence?

CREON: Yes; he will delight in hearing how Thebes can be
910 saved.

TEIRESIAS: Then hear the tenor of my prophecies. You must sacrifice Menoeceus here[49] for his country's good, your own son, as you yourself demand to know fate.

CREON: What are you saying? What have you just said, old man?

TEIRESIAS: You must carry out what the god has revealed.

34

CREON: You have spoken much evil in few words!

TEIRESIAS: For you, yes, but for your country my words bring great deliverance.

CREON: I did not hear! I did not listen! Thebes, farewell!

TEIRESIAS: This man is no longer the same; he turns away. 920

CREON: Goodbye – go away! I have no need for your oracles!

TEIRESIAS: Has truth perished because of your ill fortune?

CREON: Oh, I beg you by your knees,[50] by your grey hairs!

TEIRESIAS: Why do you stoop as a suppliant to me? Respect evils that are past all remedy.

CREON: Say no more! Do not speak of this to the city!

TEIRESIAS: You order me to do wrong; I will not keep silent.

CREON: What will you do to me? Will you kill my son?

TEIRESIAS: That task will fall to others; my office is to speak out.

CREON: What has caused this curse to light on me and my child?

TEIRESIAS: In that lair where the earth-born serpent guarded 930 the streams of Dirce he must be slain and give his crimson blood as a libation to the earth. For Ares nurses ancient anger against Cadmus, who killed his serpent born of earth, and seeks vengeance. If you do this, you and your people shall have Ares as your ally.

If the land receives fruit for fruit and mortal blood for blood, you will have the goodwill of Earth, who once sent up the golden-helmed crop of Sown Men. One must die from this race, one born a child from the seed of the serpent's teeth. 940 You are the last in our city of the Sown Men's line, you and your sons, whose blood is pure on mother's and father's side. Haemon's coming marriage bars him from slaughter, for he is not a virgin. Although he is as yet unwed, he is still betrothed.[51]

But this young fellow's life is committed to the city; his death would deliver from harm his ancestral land. Pain and sorrow he will bring to Adrastus and the Argives as they return home, their eyes veiled with death's blackness, but glory to 950 Thebes. Choose one of these two fates; save either your son or your city. Now you have heard all I have to tell.

35

Guide me back home, daughter. The man who practises the art of divination is a fool: if the signs he reads spell misfortune, he earns the hatred of those to whom he prophesies, and if pity prompts him to spare them the truth, he betrays the gods' trust. Only Phoebus ought to speak oracles to men, as he fears no one.

[TEIRESIAS *slowly leaves the stage, led by his daughter.* MENOECEUS *remains standing motionless.*]

CHORUS-LEADER: Creon, why are you silent? Why do you
960   not utter a word? This shocks me no less than you!

CREON: What could any man say? It's clear what my answer should be: never shall I become so desperate as to offer my son in sacrifice for Thebes. The life of every man is filled with love of his children, and no one would consent to his own son's death. Let no man praise my patriotism as he spills the blood of my children! But I myself, for I have reached the prime of life, am ready to die to save my country.[52] Go,
970   child, before all Thebes hears the news, ignore the reckless prophecies of seers and get away, escape from this land at once! For he will go to the captains at the seven gates and tell his tale to the commanders and men in authority there. If we act and forestall him, you are safe; if you delay, we are lost and you die.

MENOECEUS: Where should I run – to what city, which friend?

CREON: As far from this land as your steps can take you!

MENOECEUS: You tell me and I'll do what you say – that's the right course!

CREON: Go beyond Delphi . . .

980 MENOECEUS: Where should I go, Father?

CREON: To the land of Aetolia.

MENOECEUS: And where after that?

CREON: To Thesprotia.

MENOECEUS: To Dodona's holy shrine of prophecy?

CREON: Yes.

MENOECEUS: How will this give me protection?

CREON: The god will be your guide.

MENOECEUS: What shall I have for money?

CREON: I will give you gold.

MENOECEUS: Thank you, Father. Now hurry! I will go to your sister, Jocasta, who first nursed me at her breast when I was robbed of my mother and left a lonely orphan. When I have made my farewells, I shall leave and save my life. Come, lose no time! Don't let your concern delay you! 990

[CREON *leaves in haste.* MENOECEUS *turns to address the* CHORUS.]

Women, how well have I stilled my father's fears by lying to achieve my end! He seeks to rob Thebes of its fate by aiding my escape and so to make a coward of me. In this an old man might be pardoned but no such pardon would be mine, if I betrayed the city that gave me birth. So that you may know, I mean to go and save the city by dying for this land. Think of the shame, if men without compulsion of oracles or of gods shall stand shield to shield and face death unflinchingly, 1000 fighting before these towers for their homeland, while I, having betrayed father, brother and my own city, shall quit the land like a coward, and earn men's contempt wherever I live!

No, by Zeus who dwells among the stars, by bloodstained Ares who established as kings of this land the Sown Men who once sprang from the ground! I shall go and take my stand on the ramparts' heights, and there, over the deep and dark dwelling of the serpent where the prophet prescribed, I shall sacrifice myself and so set my country free. My mind is made 1010 up. I go to offer for the city my own life, a gift that honours Thebes indeed, and I shall rid this land of its sickness. If only every man would take all the good he can muster, and lay it at his country's feet, then fewer evils would beset the people of our cities and henceforth prosperity would bless them![53]

[MENOECEUS *leaves.*]

CHORUS [Strophe]: *You came, you came, winged creature,[54] offspring of Earth and Echidna that dwells below ground, to prey upon the* 1020

37

sons of Cadmus, you bringer of death and lamentation untold, savage monster, half brute, half maid, with roving wings and talons red with raw victims. You snatched our young men from Dirce's banks, chanting your hideous dirge over them, bringing a murderous Fury, bringing bloody anguish upon this land. Blood was his trade, the god who brought this to pass! Moans of mothers, moans of maidens filled the groaning homes. Cries of woe, dirges of woe echoed from one house to another, passing through the city. Like thunder-peals were their cries of sorrow and pain, each time the winged maiden made another man vanish from Thebes.

[Antistrophe:] In time he came, sent by Pytho's priestess to this land of Thebes, Oedipus the wretched, a joy to our eyes in that hour but a grief in days to come. For in the triumph of that riddle solved, in a marriage accursed, poor man, he took to wife his mother and so defiled the city. Through blood he passed into polluted strife, striking down his own children, wretched man, with curses.

Praise we give him, praise, the youth who goes to his death to protect this land of his fathers, leaving grief for Creon but winning for the seven-towered portals of Thebes a crown of victory. May we be mothers to such a child! May we be so blessed in sons, dear Pallas, who accomplished the bloody death of the serpent, slain by hurling of stones. You fired Cadmus with zeal for the deed, whence some heaven-sent doom has rushed upon this land and laid her bare!

[A MESSENGER enters[55] and starts to pound on the palace doors.]

MESSENGER: Hey there! Who keeps watch at the palace gates? Open up! Bring Jocasta from the palace! Hey, inside there! You're slow to come but answer my call anyway! Hear me, renowned wife of Oedipus, come out and leave inside your tearful cries of sorrow!

[JOCASTA comes out of the palace.]

JOCASTA: O my friend, my friend, you haven't brought news of Eteocles' death, have you? You always marched beside his shield, guarding him from enemy weapons! Is my boy dead or alive? Tell me!

MESSENGER: Alive, have no fear, to free you from this terror.

38

JOCASTA: And the circuit of walls with their seven towers – still secure?

MESSENGER: They stand unbroken; there has been no sack of Thebes.

JOCASTA: Were they in danger from the Argive spears?   1080

MESSENGER: They came to the brink itself; but Mycenae's spears proved no match for the fighting spirit of Cadmus' sons.

JOCASTA: Tell me one thing, in heaven's name: have you any news of Polyneices? This too concerns me – if he sees the light of day!

MESSENGER: Up to this point they live, the pair of your sons!

JOCASTA: Oh, the gods' blessings on you! How did you force the Argives' spears back from the gates when you were confined within the towers? Tell me, so I may go into the palace and delight the blind old man with the news his city is saved!

MESSENGER: When Creon's son, who gave his life for his country, had taken his stand on the high tower and thrust the   1090
black-hafted sword through his throat to save the land,[56] your son assigned seven companies and seven captains to each of the seven gates, to ward off the Argive spears, and he stationed horsemen in reserve to cover horsemen, and infantry to cover shieldbearers, so that, where the defences failed, help from spearsmen would not be far away. From the soaring towers we saw the army of the Argives with their white shields leaving Teumessus, and as they neared the trench they broke   1100
into a run and closed in on the city of Cadmus. Battle cries and trumpets sounded together, from their side and from our men on the walls.

And first to lead his troops[57] against the Neistian Gate, bristling as they were with serried ranks of shields, was Parthenopaeus, son of the huntress. In the middle of his shield he had the emblem of his house, Atalanta subduing the Aetolian bear with her far-darting arrows. Against the Proetean Gate came Amphiaraus the seer, with sacrificial victims in his chariot. He displayed no proud blazon but was   1110

39

soberly armed with weapons free of emblems. King Hippome-
don advanced on the Ogygian Gate with a sign at the centre
of his shield: this was the monster that sees all,[58] with eyes
spangling his whole frame, some wide open as they watched
stars at their rising, others sealed as other stars set, as we could
see afterwards, once the king had died. Tydeus took his stand
at the Homoloidan Gate, his shield decorated by the pelt of a
1120 lion with bristling mane – a veritable Titan Prometheus,[59]
wielding in his right hand a torch, so as to fire the city. Your
own Polyneices was leading the attack at the Crenaean Gate.
On his shield the young mares of Potniae leaped and fled in
panic – beneath the shield-handle they cunningly spun round
on pivots from inside, so they seemed truly possessed by fury.
Capaneus with a heart as ready as the war god's for the fray
was leading his company against the Electran Gate. On his
1130 iron-backed shield's surface was an earth-born giant carrying
on his shoulders an entire city that he had levered from its
foundations with crowbars, a hint to us of the fate in store for
our city. At the seventh gate was Adrastus, and on his left arm
he carried a shield filled with a hundred painted serpents, the
proud Argive boast of the hydra. And from the midst of our
walls these serpents were snatching the children of Cadmus in
their jaws. All this I was able to see in detail as I passed from
one company commander to another, carrying the pass-
1140 word.[60]

At first we pressed our own attack with arrows and javelins
hurled from thongs, with slingshots and crashing stones. When
the battle was turning in our favour, Tydeus and your son
suddenly shouted out: 'Sons of Danaus' sons, before their
missiles tear us to pieces, make haste, you light-armed troops,
you horsemen and charioteers, attack the gates in one body
with all your strength!' When they heard this cry, not one of
them held back; they fell in large numbers, blood pouring
from their heads, while on our side many were to be seen
1150 tumbling to the ground before the walls, like divers, drenching
the thirsty soil with streams of blood.

Then Atalanta's son, no Argive but an Arcadian, flung
himself at the gates like a whirlwind, calling for pickaxes and
torches, intent on razing the city to the ground. But his furious
assault was checked by the sea-god's son, Periclymenus, who
flung on his head a great stone, a coping-stone from the
battlements, vast as a cartload. He shattered his blond head,
crushing the bones that knit it together, and dyed red with
blood cheeks already flushed the colour of wine. A lifeless   1160
corpse shall he return to his mother the archer-maid, daughter
of Maenalus. And your son, when he saw all was well at this
gate, passed on to the others, and I followed in his steps. I saw
Tydeus with his shield-bearers pressed round him as they
hurled their Aetolian javelins at the high, roofless towers, so
the defenders quit the clifflike ramparts in panic. But your son
rallied them again, like a hunter his hounds, and made them
once more man the battlements. We pressed on to other gates,   1170
having saved this one from falling to the enemy.

But how can I describe the fury of Capaneus' attack?[61]
On he came with high-necked scaling-ladder in his hands,
boasting that not even Zeus' holy thunderbolt would stop
him from destroying the city from its highest towers. As he
uttered these words the stones were raining down on him, so
coiling himself under his shield he started his climb, passing
from one polished rung of the ladder to the next. And just as
his head rose above the coping of the ramparts, Zeus struck   1180
him with his lightning. The earth resounded with the crack,
filling everyone with terror. Off the ladder he was hurled; his
limbs were split apart, scattering everywhere like sling-shot:
to the sky his hair, to the earth his blood, while round and
round spun his arms and legs like Ixion's on his wheel; to
earth he fell, a corpse sacrificed in fire. When Adrastus saw
that Zeus was his army's enemy, he drew his troops back from
the trench.

Our men, too, had seen the favourable sign from Zeus, and
they began to charge out – chariots, horsemen, infantry – and   1190
to thrust their spears straight into the heart of the Argive

ranks. It was chaos everywhere: men were leaping or tumbling down from chariot-rails, wheels flew upwards, axles were piled on top of axles, corpses on corpses, indiscriminately. Well, for this day we've put a stop to their attempts to undermine our walls; but it is up to the gods to determine if this land will be as fortunate in the days to come.

CHORUS-LEADER: It's a fine thing to gain victory, and if the gods intend even better fortune for us, may I share in their blessing!

JOCASTA: Fortune and the gods have shown us favour, for my sons are alive and Thebes has escaped destruction. But Creon, it seems, poor man, has reaped the harvest of the shameful marriage I made with Oedipus. He has lost his son, to the good fortune of the city but the bitter pain of his own heart. But resume your report, please: what are these two sons of mine planning to do now?

MESSENGER: Let the future take care of itself; up until now you have enjoyed good fortune.

JOCASTA: Your words make me suspicious: I must not ignore the future.

MESSENGER: Surely you cannot wish for more than your sons' safety?

JOCASTA: I can wish to hear if my good fortune will continue in the days to come.

MESSENGER: Let me go; your son is without his armour-bearer now.

JOCASTA: You are concealing some terrible news, hiding it from the light of day!

MESSENGER: I will not tell you bad news after good.

JOCASTA: But you must, unless you fly up into the heavens and vanish!

MESSENGER: Ah, why would you not let me give my good news and leave, instead of telling this tale of woe?[62] Your two sons are bent on action that is headstrong and shameful: they mean to fight it out before both armies in single combat. They have spoken to Argives and Cadmeans together words that

should never have been uttered. Eteocles began, standing on
a high tower, after ordering his herald to require silence from
the armies. 'Commanders of the land of Greece,' he said,
'noblest of Danaan warriors here assembled, and you people
of Cadmus, do not squander your lives for Polyneices' sake or
mine. I myself will spare you this danger by fighting my
brother in single combat. If I kill him, I will be sole ruler of 1230
my house, but if I lose, I will resign it to him alone. And you,
men of Argos, do not give up your lives here but abandon
this quarrel and return to your homes; enough soldiers of the
Sown Men have fallen in death.' This is what he said, and
Polyneices, your son, rushed out from the ranks with praise
for his words.

All the Argives and the citizens of Cadmus roared their
approval of this proposal, thinking it a just one. On the ground
between the two armies the commanders made a truce on
these terms and swore oaths that they would abide by it. 1240
Already the two young men, old Oedipus' sons, were sheath-
ing their bodies in bronze armour, as friends assisted them –
the noblest of the Sown Men's line helped the champion of
Thebes, and the foremost men of Danaus' people his oppon-
ent. There they stood, a resplendent pair in the sunlight,
neither showing paleness in his features, longing to cast their
spears at one another. Friends on both sides were coming
forward from all around to encourage them, speaking words
like these: 'Polyneices, you have the chance to set up a statue
of Zeus as a trophy and bring Argos glory!' And, in turn, for 1250
Eteocles to hear: 'Now you fight for your city, now you can
triumph and make the crown your own!' These were the
words they spoke, as they urged them on to fight. Priests
began sacrificing sheep[63] and studying the way the victims
burned, watching the tips of the flames, whether the bladders
burst, or the flames flickered damply, and how high the blaze
rose, signifying either victory or defeat for either side. But if
you possess some remedy – wise words or enchanters' spells –
go, prevent your sons from entering this fearful contest.[64] 1260

43

Great is the danger and terrible the prize. If you lose your two sons this day, tears will be your lot.

JOCASTA [*turning to face the palace doors*]: Antigone, come out here, my child, in front of the palace! The gods have willed that you should no more take part in dancing or other maiden pleasures; rather you must join your mother in preventing your two noble brothers, bent on death, from dying at each other's hands.

[ANTIGONE *comes out of the palace in answer to her mother's call.*]

1270 ANTIGONE: Mother dear, what fresh terror are you proclaiming to friends in front of the palace here?

JOCASTA: O my daughter, your brothers' lives are close to ruin!

ANTIGONE: What do you mean?

JOCASTA: They have decided to fight one another, spear against spear.

ANTIGONE: Oh, what pain! Mother, what are you trying to say?

JOCASTA: Nothing to cause you joy. Come with me now.

ANTIGONE: And leave the other young women here in the house? Where are we going?

JOCASTA: To the army.

ANTIGONE: I feel embarrassed before a crowd.

JOCASTA: Shame does not become you now.

ANTIGONE: What is it I am to do?

JOCASTA: Bring your brothers' feuding to an end.

ANTIGONE: How, Mother?

JOCASTA: Falling to your knees with me and begging them. Now you lead the way to the ground separating the armies.
1280 There is no time for delay! Hurry, hurry, Daughter!

If I reach my sons before their spears clash, my life is saved. If they die, I shall share their deaths and lie beside them!

[JOCASTA *and* ANTIGONE, *led by the* MESSENGER, *leave in haste.*]

CHORUS [Strophe]: *Ah, ah, my heart trembles, trembles with horror! Through my flesh steals pity, pity for the wretched mother. Which of her two sons shall pierce*[65] *– oh, how this pains me, Zeus and Earth! – his brother's neck and make the blood run, shall pierce* 1290 *his brother's soul, hacking through his shield with bloody stroke? Oh, misery, misery, which one shall I cry over in grief as dead and gone?*

[Antistrophe:] *O earth, o earth, two wild beasts, two murderous souls with brandished spear shall soon slaughter a foe that is fallen, fallen! Wretches, ever to think of fighting in single combat! In accents* 1300 *of my Asian homeland will I raise a mournful cry and pay the dead the doleful tribute of my tears. Fate stands near, and death is close at hand. The sword shall decide what is to be. This slaughter is fated but accursed, and the Furies drive it on.*

Yet here I see Creon[66] coming with clouded brow towards the palace; I will bring these lamentations to an end.

[CREON *enters slowly with bowed head.*]

CREON: Oh, agony! What am I to do? Shall I shed tears of mourning for myself, or for the city, enveloped as it is in mist 1310 thick enough to consign it to Acheron? My son has died for his country and is no more. He has won a noble name but one that fills me with torment. Just now I have taken him from the serpent's steep lair and brought him forth, self-slain, in these arms – oh, what misery! My whole house cries out. I have come, an old man, in search of my sister, old Jocasta, so she may wash my boy who lives no more and lay out his remains. He who yet lives should show piety to the nether god by honouring the dead. 1320

CHORUS-LEADER: Your sister has left the palace, Creon, and young Antigone her child went with her.

CREON: Where to? With what object? Tell me!

CHORUS-LEADER: She heard that her sons were about to fight it out with the spear in single combat for the throne of Thebes.

CREON: What's that you say? I was so taken up with my dear son's dead body that I did not know this.

CHORUS-LEADER: Your sister has been gone a long time. I
think the deadly struggle between the sons of Oedipus is
1330 already over, Creon.

[*A* MESSENGER *enters from the battlefield.*]

CREON: Oh no, here I see the sign, a messenger who arrives
with eyes and features veiled in sadness. He will announce all
that has happened.

SECOND MESSENGER: How miserable I am – what words can
I utter, what lamentation?

CHORUS-LEADER: We are ruined; this is no cheerful prelude
to your speech!

MESSENGER: How miserable – I say it a second time. Great is
the burden of sorrow I bear.

CREON: It adds to other woes that have fallen upon our heads.
What is your news?

MESSENGER: Your sister's sons are no longer alive, Creon.

1340 CREON: No, no! These are heavy griefs you tell of, for myself
and the citizens of Thebes. O house of Oedipus,[67] did you
hear, two sons slain in the same calamity?

CHORUS-LEADER: Enough to make it weep, if it had feelings.

CREON: Oh, this fate crushes me with its terrible weight!

MESSENGER: If only you knew the suffering that comes after
this!

CREON: How could it be more ill-starred than this?

MESSENGER: Your sister is dead together with her two sons.

1350 CHORUS-LEADER: *Raise the lament, oh raise it, and with white
arms rain down blows on your heads!*

CREON: O my poor Jocasta, what an end to your marriage and
your life you suffered because of the Sphinx's riddle!

CHORUS-LEADER: How did the two sons spill each other's
blood as they competed in fulfilment of Oedipus' curse? Tell
me.

MESSENGER: The success our people had before the towers you
know already; the circling walls are not so far away. Once
they had put on their bronze armour, the warrior sons of old
1360 Oedipus came into the centre of the space between the two

46

armies and there they stood, ready to test each other's courage
in combat with the spear, man to man.

Polyneices, gazing towards Argos, uttered this prayer: 'Lady
Hera, I belong to you, since I took Adrastus' daughter as my
wife, and I live in your land. Grant that I may kill my brother
and let me soak my hostile hand in his blood, triumphant!' A
garland of shame he prayed to win, to kill his brother. This
terrible prayer caused many men to weep. They looked at   1370
one another, exchanging glances. But Eteocles, looking at
the temple of Pallas of the golden shield, spoke this prayer:
'Daughter of Zeus, grant that this spear of mine may fly from
my arm and pierce in triumph the chest of my brother, killing
the one who came to sack my native land!'

Now, when the beacon was lit – a signal, like the blast of
Etruscan trumpet,[68] for the bloody fight to start – they charged
at one another most terribly. Like wild boars whetting their
savage jaws they closed, their beards wet with slaver. Then   1380
with spears they rushed in, but crouched beneath the rims of
their shields, so the blades might be deflected without harm.
If one of them saw the other's eye peering over the rim, he
thrust his spear at his face, trying to wound him first. But they
kept their eyes so carefully behind the protecting shields that
spears were thrust to no effect. Such fear had supporters for
their champion that more sweat ran from them than from the
combatants.

But Eteocles brushed to one side a stone that got in the
way of his foot, and in doing so exposed a limb outside his   1390
shield. Polyneices, seeing the opportunity for delivering a
spear-thrust, struck it with his weapon: the Argive spear
pierced Eteocles' thigh, drawing a roar of triumph from all
the Danaan troops.

But seeing his enemy's shoulder exposed in this effort,
Eteocles, the first wounded, drove his own spear into Poly-
neices' chest, and gave the citizens of Cadmus something to
cheer. But the spear-head snapped. Helpless now, he began
to retreat, step by step. Then, taking hold of a lump of marble,   1400

he hurled it and broke his brother's spear in half. The battle was now evenly poised, as both men had lost their spears. Next they grabbed their sword-hilts and moved to the same ground. They clashed with shields and, locked together, raised a loud din of conflict.

Then Eteocles thought of a trick he had learned while sojourning in Thessaly and employed it: disengaging from the struggle, he moved his left foot back behind the shield, taking care to guard his belly, and stepping out with his right foot he drove his sword through Polyneices' navel, clean through to his backbone. The poor man bent double, his ribs and stomach coming together, and fell, gushing blood. Eteocles, thinking the victory his, the battle won, threw his sword on to the ground and began stripping off his brother's armour, his attention on this task, and no longer thinking of any danger to himself. This proved his undoing: Polyneices, though barely breathing, was still alive, and had kept his sword in that terrible fall; now, with a great effort, he plunged it into Eteocles' liver, he who had been the first to fall. So both men lie where they fell, next to each other, their teeth gripping the earth, the kingdom yet undivided between them.

CHORUS-LEADER: What a pitiful tale! O Oedipus, how I groan for your sufferings! It seems a god has fulfilled those curses you uttered.

MESSENGER: Hear now the sorrows that followed on these. When her two sons had fallen and were breathing their last, at that moment their mother, poor lady, came up all breathless, her maiden daughter at her side, and, seeing the pair bleeding with mortal wounds, she cried out in grief: 'O my sons, I came running to your aid, but here I am, too late now!' She sank to her knees and began to weep for her children, groaning as she lamented the long hours of nurturing them at her breast, while her comrade in sorrow, their sister, cried out: 'O my dearest brothers, supporters of our mother in old age, traitors to my marriage!'[69] King Eteocles, heaving a deep sigh, heard

48

his mother's cry, and, stretching out a bloodstained hand, he
did not utter any words but spoke to her with tears from his
eyes, showing his love.   1440

Polyneices was still breathing, and, when he saw his sister
and old mother, he spoke these words: 'Our lives are over,
Mother. I pity you and my sister here, and my brother, now
a corpse. My friend became my enemy, but the bond between
us remained. Give me burial, Mother, and you too, sister, in
the land of my forebears, and calm the anger of the city,
so that I may gain as much of my father's land as I require,
even if my inheritance is lost. Seal my eyes with your hand,   1450
mother' – he put her hand on his eyes himself – 'and fare-
well to you both; darkness now enfolds me.' At this both men
breathed out their wretched lives as one. But when their
mother had witnessed this sad end, in her agony she seized a
sword from the dead and committed an atrocious act: thrusting
the blade straight through her neck,[70] she fell between the
sons she loved so well, and lies there now, embracing both in
death.

The troops sprang to their feet and began to quarrel, our   1460
side claiming victory for my master, theirs for his adversary.
The commanders, too, were in dispute. Some were saying
that Polyneices had struck first with his spear, others that,
since both had died, there was no victory.

While this was going on, Antigone withdrew from the
scene of battle and the troops rushed to arms.[71] Through some
happy foresight the men of Thebes had been sitting next to
their weapons, and we immediately attacked the Argives,
before they had time to strap on their armour. Not one of
them stood his ground. They swarmed all over the plain in   1470
retreat, falling before our spears, so that the ground ran with
the blood of their innumerable dead. When the field was ours,
some of us set up a statue of Zeus as a trophy, others stripped
the Argive corpses of shields and sent them as spoils inside the
city walls. Others still are with Antigone, carrying the

bodies of the dead here for their families to mourn. For the people of Thebes some of this day's clashes have ended in utmost joy, others in extreme sorrow.

[*Exit* MESSENGER.]

1480 CHORUS: *No more a mere tale for the ear is the miserable fortune of this house; soon at the palace door can be seen three corpses of those who fell in common death, receiving the lot of a life in darkness.*

[ANTIGONE *enters, accompanied by soldiers bearing the corpses of* JOCASTA, POLYNEICES *and* ETEOCLES. *As the soldiers lay the bodies down and form a guard of honour beside them, Antigone begins to sing and dance a dirge for her loved ones.*]

ANTIGONE: *Not masking the ruddy glow of my tender cheeks or feeling a maiden's shame at the crimson beneath these eyes, my blushing face, I am swept along, a bacchant of the dead, as, casting* 1490 *the diadem from my hair, I drop the soft folds of this saffron dress, and conduct these corpses with many a groan.*

Oh, the pain, the pity! O Polyneices, your name proved true,[72] and Thebes now counts the cost! Your strife – no, not strife but killing on killing – has destroyed the house of Oedipus, in terrible blood, in grim blood finding its resolution. O house, o house,[73] what song, 1500 *what music of lament can I summon to my tears, my tears?*

These bodies of three kindred I bring, a mother and her sons, joyful to a Fury's heart! Before now did she bring ruin on Oedipus' house, that day his wisdom solved the riddling Sphinx's song, past men's wit to solve, and sealed her lips in death. Ah, what agony I feel!

What woman of Greece or foreign lands, who else among the 1510 *nobles of early days has endured such unstinted sorrow out of all the griefs of human bloodshed? Oh, poor soul that I am, how I cry out! What bird, high on the leafy branch of an oak or pine, with her cries of a mother robbed of her chicks matches my song of sorrow? Oh, woe, woe! With cries of pain I mourn for those who lie here, I whose* 1520 *life henceforth will be an endless libation of tears shed in solitude.*

Whose body shall I first grace with the offering of hair shorn from

my head? Shall I throw it on my mother's twin breasts, with their
milk now gone, or on my dead brothers' mortal wounds?

  Ah, woe! Leave your house, old Father, with your sightless eyes,   1530
and show, Oedipus, your piteous age, you who have cast a misty
darkness on your eyes and live still inside the palace your long-drawn-
out life. Do you hear me, you who wander through the halls on aged
feet or lie, miserable, on your bed?

  [The doors of the palace open and OEDIPUS appears. Slowly, he
  makes his way forward, tapping the ground with a stick.]

OEDIPUS: Why have you called me out into the light, girl, bedridden
as I am, and guiding these blind feet with a stick? Out from my dark   1540
chamber your pitiful tears have roused me, a grey phantom, thin as
air, a corpse from the nether world, a winged dream.

ANTIGONE: The news you shall learn, father, is calamitous; no more
do your sons see the daylight, no more your wife, who ever toiled,
Father – oh, unbearable! – to help that stick guide your blind steps
on their way.   1550

OEDIPUS: No, no! What suffering I bear! I groan, I cry out for all
these ills! What manner of fate caused three souls to quit the light of
day? Speak, child!

ANTIGONE: These words I say are not to find fault with you nor
spoken with malice; they cause me pain: your own spirit of vengeance,
laden with sword and fire and wicked conflict, swooped upon your
sons – oh, the horror of it, Father!

OEDIPUS: Ah, no!

ANTIGONE: Why do you groan at this now?   1560

OEDIPUS: I was their father.

ANTIGONE: Your path has been a painful one; but what if you had
those bright eyes that once were yours, and could see the sun's chariot
and team, see these bodies of the dead?

OEDIPUS: My children's pitiful end is clear; but what manner of fate,
child, caused my unhappy wife to die?

ANTIGONE: No one was unaware of her tears and cries of woe. She
showed her breast to her sons, showed it in suppliant appeal. She
found her sons at the Electran gate in a meadow of lotus flowers   1570
thrusting savagely at one another with their spears. Their mother

51

found them, wounded yet fighting still, like lions in their lairs, and saw the crimson libation of blood, already cold, that Ares makes and Hades accepts. Seizing the sword of hammered bronze from the dead, she plunged it in her own flesh and, in bitter grief for her sons, she fell on their corpses. The god who brings this to pass has this day,
1580 *father, piled every woe upon our house.*[74]

CHORUS-LEADER: This day has initiated a tide of suffering for the house of Oedipus. May our lives be blessed with happier fortune![75]

CREON: Cease now from lamentation, for it is time to think of burial. Listen, Oedipus, to these words. Sovereignty over this land was given to me by your son, Eteocles, when he gave your daughter, Antigone, in wedlock to Haemon, together with a dowry. I will not, therefore, permit you to continue living in this land. For Teiresias' words were clearly spoken:
1590 the city would never prosper while you inhabited this land. Come, take your leave;[76] I say this not to insult you or because I wish you harm, but in fear that your avenging spirit may cause some blight to fasten on Thebes.

OEDIPUS: O fate, how you marked me out from my very birth for wretchedness and suffering, more than any other mortal man! Why, even unborn, before I entered the light from my mother's womb, Apollo told Laius in an oracle that I would become my father's murderer. Oh, what misery is mine!
1600 When I was born, the father who made me tried to kill me, thinking me his natural enemy; he was fated to die at my hands. He exposed me, a baby thirsting for the breast, as food for beasts, a pitiful morsel. But there I was saved – Cithaeron should be cast into the bottomless pit of Tartarus for failing to destroy me! No, some god granted that I should serve Polybus as my master.[77] I killed my own father through heaven's perversity and bedded my poor mother, then fathered sons
1610 who were my brothers and destroyed them, inflicting on my sons the curse I had inherited from Laius. I was not born so lacking in sense that I cannot discern a god's hand at work in these acts I devised against my eyes and my sons' lives.

Very well; what, then, must I do, miserable creature that I am? Who will accompany me and serve as guide to my sightless steps? This woman who has died? She would, if she were living, I have no doubt. This handsome pair of sons? I have no sons. Am I still young enough to make a living for myself? How? Why, Creon, are you killing me so ruthlessly? You will be killing me, if you banish me from this land. Not that I will show myself so base as to wind my arms round your knees;[78] I will not prove traitor to my onetime noble birth, even if I am to suffer for this.   1620

CREON: I welcome your refusal to touch my knees; and I on my side cannot allow you to live in this land.

As for these dead men, the one must be carried now into the house, but the other, who came with strangers to sack this city, his home, the dead Polyneices, throw him out, unburied, beyond the borders of this land. To all Cadmus' people this proclamation shall be made: whoever is caught either placing a wreath on this corpse or covering it with earth, shall have death for his reward. It is to be left alone,[79] without grace of tears or burial, as food for birds. And you, Antigone, end your dirges for these three dead and go inside the palace. Conduct yourself as a young maid should, as you wait for the coming day, when you will enter Haemon's bed.   1630

ANTIGONE: O Father, what manner of suffering do we wretches lie in! I groan for you more than for the dead. It is not that some of your hardships are painful, others less so; you were born to misery all the days of your life. [Turning to Creon:] But I have a question for you, my newly royal lord: why do you treat my father here so insultingly by sending him away from this land? Why do you make laws against a wretched corpse?   1640

CREON: This was Eteocles' decision, not my own.

ANTIGONE: A foolish one, and you are a fool for giving it your approval!

CREON: How so? Is it not right to carry out orders once issued?

ANTIGONE: No, not if they are wicked and spoken in malice.

1650 CREON: Well, is it not right that this man be given to the dogs?

ANTIGONE: The 'right' you bring to bear on him has no basis in custom.

CREON: It has, if he was no enemy of Thebes yet behaved towards her as an enemy.

ANTIGONE: Did he not pay for this with his life?

CREON: Let him now pay also with his burial.

ANTIGONE: What was his offence in coming to claim his share in the land?

CREON: This man shall not have burial, let me assure you!

ANTIGONE: I shall bury him, even if Thebes forbids it.

CREON: Then you shall bury yourself too, next to his corpse.

ANTIGONE: When there is a bond between them, it is glorious for two to be buried together.

1660 CREON [to soldiers]: Take hold of her! Carry her into the palace!

[ANTIGONE throws herself on POLYNEICES' corpse.]

ANTIGONE: No! I will not let this dead man go!

CREON: Your wishes, young woman, run counter to the god's decree.

ANTIGONE: This, too, has been decreed: do not treat the dead with contempt.

CREON: No one, I say, shall pile moist dust round this man.

ANTIGONE: Oh, yes, Creon! I beg you by his mother Jocasta here!

CREON: You waste your effort; you will not gain your wish.

ANTIGONE: Well, give me leave to wash his corpse.

CREON: This is also forbidden to Thebes' citizens.

ANTIGONE: Then let me bandage his cruel wounds!

1670 CREON: You shall in no way do honour to this corpse.

ANTIGONE: O my dearest brother! Your lips at least I'll press with mine!

CREON: This lamentation will not cast a shadow over your marriage.

ANTIGONE: What? I am to marry your son? Never, while I live!

54

CREON: You have no alternative whatever; how will you avoid the marriage?

ANTIGONE: That night shall find me one of the daughters of Danaus![80]

CREON: Do you see how bold she is with her insults?

ANTIGONE: This blade be my witness, this sword I swear by!

CREON: Why are you so desperate to be rid of this marriage?

ANTIGONE: I will share exile with this most wretched of fathers.

CREON: Your character is noble but not without folly also.   1680

ANTIGONE: I will share his death as well, to make my meaning clearer to you.

CREON: Then away with you! You will not be the murderess of my son! Leave the land!

[CREON leaves,[81] accompanied by soldiers.]

OEDIPUS: O daughter, this show of spirit earns my praise!

ANTIGONE: How could I marry and leave you alone in exile, Father?

OEDIPUS: Stay and enjoy good fortune; I shall submit to my hard lot.

ANTIGONE: And who will look after you in your blindness, Father?

OEDIPUS: I shall fall where fate decides and there on the ground I shall lie.

ANTIGONE: Where is Oedipus, the glorious master of riddles?[82]

OEDIPUS: He is no more; the same day that made me prosper brought me to ruin.

ANTIGONE: Then must I, too, not share in your misfortune?   1690

OEDIPUS: Exile with a blind father brings shame to the daughter.

ANTIGONE: No, father, to a virtuous daughter, it brings renown.

OEDIPUS: Then lead me forward now, so I may touch your mother.

ANTIGONE: There, put your hand on her, dear old woman!

OEDIPUS: O my mother, my most miserable wife!

ANTIGONE: How pitiful she is, lying there, surrounded by all her woe!

OEDIPUS: Where does Eteocles lie, where Polyneices?

ANTIGONE: They lie stretched out in front of you, Father, side by side.

OEDIPUS: Put my blind hand on their wretched faces.

1700 ANTIGONE: There, hold with your hand your dead sons.

OEDIPUS: O my dear fallen sons, piteous children of a piteous father!

ANTIGONE: O Polyneices, name I love most dearly!

OEDIPUS: Now Loxias' oracle is being fulfilled, my child.[83]

ANTIGONE: In what way? Surely you won't tell me of further sorrows to come?

OEDIPUS: I am to die, an exile, in Athens.

ANTIGONE: Where? What Attic refuge will give you welcome?

OEDIPUS: Sacred Colonus, where the god of horses[84] has his dwelling. But come, assist your blind father here, since you are determined to share this exile.

[ANTIGONE and OEDIPUS now sing a dirge together.]

1710 ANTIGONE: *Forward into pitiful exile! Stretch out your dear hand, old Father; I am the escort you have, as a ship has a breeze to blow it on its way.*

OEDIPUS: *There, child, my journey is begun. Guide my feet, poor girl!*

ANTIGONE: *I do, I do, of all Thebes' maidens the most wretched.*

OEDIPUS: *Where do I place my old foot? Where carry my stick, child?*

1720 ANTIGONE: *Here, here walk with me, here, here place your foot, with the strength of a dream.*

OEDIPUS: *Ah, how wretched an exile is this, having to flee my country in old age! Oh, what terrible, terrible suffering I endure!*

ANTIGONE: *You speak of suffering, of suffering? The goddess of retribution does not see men's wickedness, far less punish their foolish crimes!*

OEDIPUS: *I am he who scaled the heights of wisdom in triumph and*
1730 *solved the virgin maid's dark riddle!*

ANTIGONE: *You hark back to the shameful time of the Sphinx? Have done with recalling successes of earlier days. The sorrowful fate awaiting you, father, is to die somewhere after enduring banishment from your native land. I shall leave behind my maiden friends and their tears of regret, and turn my back on the land of my forebears, a wanderer most unlike a maid!*

OEDIPUS: *Ah, you have a noble heart!* 1740

ANTIGONE: *Because I have shared my father's suffering, it will win me fame. I am to be pitied: both you and my brother are roughly used; he is bundled from his home, a wretched corpse unburied! But, though it means I must die for it, Father, I shall shroud him in dark earth.*[85]

OEDIPUS: *With prayers around the altar receive the honour of your fellow maids!*

ANTIGONE: *Enough of my lamentation, I am sated with my sorrows.* 1750

OEDIPUS: *Go to where the Roaring One has his trackless dwelling with his maenads on the mountain slopes.*[86]

ANTIGONE: *For the god I once dressed in the fawnskin Cadmus' daughters wear, and on those slopes I danced in Semele's holy band of worshippers, offering the gods a favour that wins no return.*

OEDIPUS: O you citizens of a land renowned,[87] look at me, Oedipus! I am he who discovered the famous riddle and achieved greatness. Unaided I destroyed the power of the murderous Sphinx, and now without honour I am hounded 1760 from my homeland, a pitiful creature! Yet why do I mourn for this and shed fruitless tears? I am mortal and so must endure the stern will of heaven.

[OEDIPUS, *with* ANTIGONE *supporting him, now moves slowly off.*]

CHORUS: *O Victory, most holy, support my life and do not cease from giving me your crown!*[88]

ORESTES

PREFACE TO *ORESTES*

The myth of Orestes killing his mother to avenge his father goes back to Homer's *Odyssey*, where it is introduced several times as a tale already well known to both the characters in the poem and the audience. Agamemnon on his triumphant return from Troy was trapped and killed by Clytemnestra and her lover Aegisthus, who subsequently assumed the throne (3.248ff., 303ff., 4.512ff.). His son Orestes, growing up in exile, returns some years later to avenge his father. Both Aegisthus and Clytemnestra are punished by death, though Homer is clearly concerned to play down the fact of matricide, which he does not actually narrate: the closest he comes to an explicit statement of Orestes' responsibility is in a reference to the young man organizing the funeral of 'his hateful mother and the weakling Aegisthus' (3.310). The burial of the usurpers has just taken place when Menelaus, after years of wandering at sea, returns to the Peloponnese with Helen (the point at which Euripides' play begins). In Homer, the gods on Olympus endorse the justice of Aegisthus' punishment (1.29ff.), and the heroic deeds of Orestes are held up as an example to Odysseus' son Telemachus (1.298ff.). It seems clear that the story as Homer presents it has no place for any negative consequences for Orestes, who inherits Agamemnon's throne.

Later versions were very different. Poets who treated the legend at full length, rather than only incidentally as in Homer, were clearly anxious to increase the emotional intensity and to heighten the moral complexity. In part this was achieved by providing a justification for Clytemnestra for hating her husband: did he not sacrifice their daughter Iphigenia at the start of the war? (Homer had ignored this story: see p. 169). Pindar in a well-known passage refers to this motive: though still glorifying Orestes' deed, he poses the dilemma about Clytemnestra: was it adulterous lust that drove her to her crime, or grief and anger at the death of her child (*Pythian Odes*, 11.15ff.)? Agamemnon could be represented in less than admirable terms: already in the *Iliad* he comments that he prefers his concubine Chryseis to his wife Clytemnestra, and in the *Odyssey* it is evident even from the brief references that he brought back Cassandra as a trophy of war (Clytemnestra kills her too). Still more important was the psychological and emotional potential of the matricide: this is a high point in all the dramas dealing with Orestes' return, and even in this play, where the deed is over, the moment at which Clytemnestra bared her breast and begged her son for mercy is repeatedly referred to.

Once the act of matricide became the heart of the tale, the question arose: what are the consequences? We do not know precisely when the poets introduced the motif of Orestes being pursued by his mother's Furies, monstrous supernatural spirits of vengeance, but it was already well established long before the tragedians took it up. The lyric poet Stesichorus (early sixth century BC) composed a poem of some length (two 'books') on Orestes, from which we have a few fragments. In that work Apollo gave Orestes a bow with which he was to defend himself against the Furies: this idea is recalled in the madness-scene of Euripides' play (267ff. and note 15). The Furies pursue and persecute Orestes from land to land; whether he found refuge and purification in Stesichorus' version, whether he was tried and acquitted in Athens in versions prior to Aeschylus' *Oresteia*, are controversial questions.

At all events, Aeschylus' great trilogy is the most important treatment of the Orestes myth, and the greatest single influence on Euripides' *Orestes*. It was exactly fifty years old (458 BC), already a well-established classic. Euripides had frequently echoed and exploited it in earlier dramas (including the *Electra* and the *Iphigenia among the Taurians*); Aristophanes' references in the *Frogs* suggest it was reasonably well known. In the second play of Aeschylus' trilogy Orestes had returned to Argos with his friend Pylades, met Electra, called upon the ghost of his dead father to aid him in his mission, and killed Aegisthus through a deception. He then faces the harder task of killing his mother: their confrontation on stage is a high point. In the final scene the chorus rejoice that the rightful heir has returned and the kingdom is freed from a tyrannical yoke. Orestes is more sombre, convinced of the justice of his cause but also seeking to justify it. At the end of the play he begins to lose control of his mind, and sees the Furies rushing at him (it is generally agreed that they were invisible to the audience). In panic and despair, he runs off stage; his exile and wanderings have begun.

In the third play, *Eumenides*, Orestes finds refuge at Delphi with Apollo, who guarantees him protection. In this play, by a bold stroke, the Furies form the chorus, and are visibly present onstage, conversing with and angrily threatening men and gods. The bulk of the play is occupied by Orestes' trial at Athens, judged by a jury of Athenian citizens; this provides an aetiology or 'charter myth' for the Athenians' homicide court, known as the Areopagus (Athena lays down its duties in the play itself). Though Apollo is present to speak in Orestes' defence, the role of Athena, Athens' patron deity, is more important: she oversees the court and ensures that both sides are treated with dignity. Orestes is tried and eventually acquitted; it is clear that he is to return to his kingdom free of guilt and suffering. The Furies are placated by Athena, who guarantees them a place in Athens, as guardians of morality. The salvation of Orestes is due to an Athenian court of mortal men, not the actions of the god Apollo: Athens trumps Delphi, in a remarkable demonstration of the patriotic aspect of Attic tragedy. How much of the action in the third play is Aeschylus' own invention is a matter of dispute.

The two Electra-plays by Sophocles and Euripides deal chiefly with the events leading up to the matricide, and only briefly with the aftermath (indeed, in Sophocles' play there appears to be no aftermath, the dramatist having reverted to the Homeric-Pindaric tradition). It is in the *Orestes* that Euripides treats at full length the sufferings of Orestes after the deed is done. Even from the brief summary of earlier versions given above, we can see that he has taken up and developed some points, dropped others, and invented a number of novel elements of his own. This of course was how the tragedians always worked: but in this case the new compound is a remarkably powerful and original concoction.

The main differences in the *Orestes* (most of which seem likely to be Euripidean contributions) are as follows. First, instead of journeying immediately into exile, Orestes remains in Argos, sick and hallucinating, in a weakened condition which at first seems close to death. Second, whereas in Aeschylus the chorus resented the rule of Aegisthus and Clytemnestra and acclaimed Orestes' deed, in Euripides' play the Argive population is repelled by his matricide and he is in danger of being condemned to death. Third, whereas in Aeschylus he was tried and acquitted in an Athenian court, in Euripides he is tried and condemned by the Argive assembly; and where Aeschylus' court seemed to embody the principles of justice and even-handedness, the speakers in the assembly are biased or suborned or self-interested: there can be no prospect of a just decision being reached in this body. Euripides also introduces added complications: as in earlier plays, he asks how these events might have affected others involved, such as Menelaus and Helen, or Clytemnestra's father, Tyndareus (a new figure on the tragic stage). Menelaus turns out to be no help, Tyndareus positively hostile: Orestes is isolated. Finally and most important, although Apollo commanded Orestes to undertake his mission, he seems now to have deserted him. While in Aeschylus we see the god comforting Orestes, sending him under escort to Athens, defying the Furies and appearing in the young man's defence, in Euripides characters repeatedly ask what Apollo can have been thinking of to order such a crime, and Orestes in particular stresses that the god has done nothing to help him in his time of need (28, 163–5, 416–20, etc.). The play might almost be entitled 'Waiting for Apollo'.

In the absence of the god, the human characters are thrown on their own resources. Orestes' attempt to defend himself to Tyndareus merely succeeds in infuriating the old man further; his efforts to enlist Menelaus' aid are a failure; his self-defence in the assembly proves futile. In the scene in which Orestes, Pylades and Electra review their situation, all seems black, and a shared suicide pact the only way out. It is at this point that Euripides begins to turn the plot in a completely new direction. Encouraged by Pylades, Orestes resolves on revenge against Menelaus and Helen; Electra contributes the chilling suggestion that they use Hermione as a hostage. From persecuted victims the trio turn into avenging marauders. The conspirators seem fired by a sinister enthusiasm for their task: although the Furies are no longer terrorizing Orestes, there is a kind of madness, that of desperation, which is infecting all three of them.

The plot-sequence can be compared with other plays of Euripides which focus on acts of revenge, especially *Medea* and *Hecabe*. There too the main character begins as a victim, winning much of the audience's sympathy, and in the end becomes a vicious avenger. We must beware of oversimplification: Orestes in the first half of this play may be pitiable but he is no innocent; and in none of these cases does the protagonist lose our sympathy entirely, but there is a clear shift, often focused on a key point in the action (here, the moment at which Pylades makes his proposal, 1097ff.). Before this point, the audience has been encouraged to sympathize with Orestes and his companions; from this point on, the plot becomes more startling, even bizarre, the characterization more negative, and the audience response more complex and contradictory.

In *Medea* and *Hecabe* the avenger executes her plans successfully: Medea kills her children, Hecabe blinds Polymestor and kills his children. In this play the conspiracy is a débâcle: the attempt to murder Helen is frustrated, for reasons at first opaque to both the actors and the audience; the best that Orestes can do is bully and humiliate a terrified Phrygian slave. The final confrontation of Menelaus and Orestes is a crowded and highly dramatic scene: Menelaus and his supporters surrounding the palace, while Orestes, Pylades, Hermione and probably Electra are on the roof, with Orestes holding a sword at Hermione's throat. There are threats to hurl down masonry on the attackers' heads; torches are lit, and Orestes prepares to burn the palace to the ground. From earlier thoughts of suicide he has moved to a grander scheme of general self-destruction and slaughter ('I shall never tire of killing evil women!', 1590). Both the house of Atreus and the mythical tradition seem about to disintegrate, when at long last Apollo intervenes.

Horace in the *Art of Poetry* said that tragedians should not introduce a god unless the 'knot' of the plot was so difficult to unravel that divine intervention was the only possible solution. This case is a paradigm example, but also serves to illustrate some of the difficulties modern audiences have with this convention. The epiphany of a god is a magificent theatrical moment; the contrast between divine knowledge and power and human confusion is obviously effective; and the 'plot' of the myth, which had seemed to be going wildly off course, is magisterially directed back (more or less) to its familiar track (though some points are quirkily different: Helen is to be a deity – prematurely; Orestes is to be tried in Athens – but by gods, not by men; Neoptolemus is to die, without ever marrying Hermione). The difficulty is that the imposition of this outcome seems almost arbitrary – so much that is different, or heading toward a different goal, has happened on the human level that Apollo's edict has a paradoxical, even a bizarre effect (particularly when Orestes is told to marry Hermione, 'at whose throat you are presently holding your sword'). We are not told why Apollo chose not to appear before. We can hardly acquit Euripides of some mischief here; he pushes the *deus ex machina* convention to its absolute extreme, with the result that the final outcome seems to bear very little relation to the preceding action or the motivations and passions which brought it about. Certainly the gods have the power to do this, or whatever else they please; what such acts suggest about the relation between gods and men, or the degree to which either side understands the other, is one of the most difficult issues in the interpretation of Euripides. (Cf. General Introduction, pp. xxviii–xxxv.)

Early readers already found the *Orestes* a contradictory work: the ancient summary includes the comment: 'This is one of the dramas which is most successful on the stage, but its ethics are awful; apart from Pylades everybody is bad.' (The exception is a curious one; like Aristotle's comment that Menelaus in this play is 'unnecessarily bad in character', it suggests that the audience paid particular attention to the demands of loyalty and friendship, to the question who does or does not help Orestes in his hour of need.) In modern times interpretations have been diverse. Some see the play as a drama of intense suffering leading to moral corruption, with wide implications concerning the moral and political bankruptcy of contemporary Athens (parallels with Thucydides' *History* are frequently invoked, especially the historian's famous analysis of the psychology of internal political conflict, 3.82–3). Others prefer to emphasize the bold dramatic technique, the exciting twists and turns in the plot, the sharp epigrams and clever ripostes in the dialogue, the multiple allusions to earlier drama, or the colourful costume and exotic music of the Phrygian's scene: in this play Euripides' innovative tendencies reach their zenith. A combination of these approaches seem desirable: to emphasize that Euripides is first and foremost a dramatist does not preclude allowing that he may have had something to say – though as always with a writer of this stature, our paraphrases and critical formulae do scant justice to the intellectual and emotional challenge of this extraordinary work.

CHARACTERS

ELECTRA, *daughter of Agamemnon*
HELEN, *wife of Menelaus*
CHORUS *of women of Argos*
ORESTES, *son of Agamemnon*
MENELAUS, *brother of Agamemnon*
TYNDAREUS, *father of Clytemnestra*
PYLADES, *friend of Orestes*
MESSENGER, *an old servant of Agamemnon*
HERMIONE, *daughter of Helen*
A PHRYGIAN, *a slave attending on Helen*
APOLLO
SERVANTS *attending on Menelaus, Tyndareus and Helen*

[*The scene is the palace at Argos.* ORESTES *is lying asleep on a mat up against the palace wall.* ELECTRA *sits near his feet.*]

ELECTRA:[1] There is no tale so terrible to tell, no suffering or affliction sent by the gods, that man's nature may not have to shoulder its burden. Tantalus, whose fortune men envied (I make no judgement of his fate), the son, they say, of Zeus, hovers in the air, dreading the rock that hangs above his head.

He suffers this punishment, men say, because, when he sat at table with the gods and enjoyed honour equal with their own, a mortal with gods, he did not govern his tongue – shameful madness! This man fathered Pelops, whose son was   10
Atreus, for whom the goddess Strife carding her wool spun threads of war between him and Thyestes, his brother. Why must I retrace things that should not be told? Atreus (I pass over what happened next) fathered the glorious Agamemnon, if glorious he was, and Menelaus by a Cretan mother, Aerope. Menelaus married Helen, detested by the gods, but King Agamemnon took Clytemnestra to wife in a marriage that   20
brought renown in the eyes of all Greeks. Three daughters – Chrysothemis,[2] Iphigenia and I – and a son, Orestes, were born to him by one woman, a woman most impious, who killed her husband, ensnaring him in a net from which there was no escape. I am a maiden and cannot speak of her motives[3] without shame; I draw a veil over that for any who will to consider. There is no point in accusing Phoebus[4] of wrong-doing in urging Orestes to kill the mother who gave him birth, an act not seen as glorious by every Greek. But kill   30

69

her he did in obedience to the god, and I, so far as a woman could, shared in the murder.[5]

And so he lies here, where he has fallen on his mat, my poor Orestes, wasted by the savage illness that racks him and tormented to madness by his mother's blood. Reverence prevents me from naming the goddesses whose terrors plague him, the Kindly Ones.[6] This is the sixth day since his mother died by slaughter and her body received the purification of fire, but in this time no food has passed his lips, no water scoured his body, and, when his sickness gives him respite, wrapped inside his cloak he weeps with mind unclouded, but at other times he leaps up with flying feet from his pallet and acts like a young horse released from the yoke. It is the decree of this city of Argos[7] that no one should receive us, the matricides, under his roof or at his hearth, or give us words of welcome. This is the appointed day when the citizens of Argos will give their separate votes to determine if we two must die by stoning. There is one hope we have of not being killed: Menelaus has come to this land from Troy and occupies the harbour of Nauplion with his ship. He is anchored there off-shore, having roamed, homeless, for many a day since leaving Troy. But Helen, that cause of many deaths, he has sent ahead to our house, having waited for the night in case someone whose sons met their end at Troy should see her arriving by day and set about stoning her. Now she is inside and weeps for her sister and the misery of her house. And yet she has some consolation for her sorrows: the child she left at home when she sailed to Troy, the maiden Hermione, whom Menelaus brought from Sparta and entrusted to my mother's fostering,[8] makes her rejoice and forget her woes.

I look down the long road in case I shall see Menelaus at some point; for in every other way we ride on a weak anchor, if our safety does not come from him. A house that knows misfortune is in desperate straits.

[HELEN *emerges from the palace entrance.*]

HELEN: Maiden for all too long a day,[9] Electra, poor girl, how

do you and your brother fare? Speak to me – I shall not be
contaminated,[10] as I attribute the crime to Phoebus. And yet
I weep at Clytemnestra's death, the sister I have not set eyes
on since the day I sailed to Troy, as sail I did through a fate
of divine madness. Now left abandoned, I lament my fortune.   80

ELECTRA: Helen, why should I describe to you what you can
see with your own eyes? Here I sit, keeping sleepless watch
over a wretched corpse (for his breath is so slight I count him
a corpse); his sufferings, though, I lay to no man's charge.
But here you are, you the fortunate one and your fortunate
husband, appearing before us in our misfortune.

HELEN: How long has he been lying on his bed?

ELECTRA: Since he shed his mother's blood.

HELEN: Poor man! Poor woman – how she died!   90

ELECTRA: Such is his state that his sufferings have overwhelmed
him.

HELEN: In heaven's name, maiden, would you do something
for me?

ELECTRA: Yes, as far as I can while looking after my brother.

HELEN: Are you willing to go for me to my sister's tomb?

ELECTRA: My mother's – can you ask me this? Why?

HELEN: To take a lock of hair I have cut and drink-offerings
from me.

ELECTRA: Is it not right for you to visit the tomb of a loved
one?

HELEN: No; I am ashamed to show myself to the people of
Argos.

ELECTRA: Now, at last, you see things correctly, but the day
you left your home behind was one of shame.

HELEN: Your words are just but hardly spoken like a friend.   100

ELECTRA: What is this shame you feel at facing the Mycenaean
folk?

HELEN: I fear the fathers of those who died at Troy.

ELECTRA: Yes, it is a fearful thing to hear your name shouted
by all in Argos.

HELEN: Do me this favour now and set me free from fear!

ELECTRA: I could not look at my mother's tomb.

HELEN: But it would bring disgrace on you if slaves brought these gifts.

ELECTRA: Why do you not send your daughter Hermione?

HELEN: It looks bad if a young woman makes her way through a crowd.

ELECTRA: And yet she would be showing a child's gratitude to a parent dead.

110 HELEN: Yes, I will send my daughter; you are quite right.

Hermione, child, come out of the palace!

[HERMIONE *enters.*]

Take in your hands these drink-offerings and this hair of mine, go to Clytemnestra's tomb and pour upon it honey mixed with milk and the ruddy froth of wine. Stand on the top of the burial mound and speak these words: 'Your sister Helen presents you with these drink-offerings, because she is afraid to approach your tomb and dreads the Argive mob.'

120 Bid her look kindly on you and me, and on my husband, and on this wretched pair, ruined by the god. Promise her all the gifts to the dead that duty and the hour prescribe for me to perform for a sister. Go, my child, make haste, pour the libations on her tomb and return with all speed!

[HERMIONE *exits offstage,*[11] HELEN *re-enters the palace.*]

ELECTRA: O Nature, what a curse you are to mankind! See how she has cut off only the tips of her hair, leaving her beauty intact – the Helen of old! May the gods look on you

130 with loathing for the ruin you have brought on me, on this man, and on all of Greece!

[*The* CHORUS *of Argive women is seen approaching the palace.*]

Oh, I am so miserable! Here come my friends who will sing with my lament.[12] Soon they will waken the one who is at peace here and drown my eyes in tears, when I see my brother struck by madness. O women, good friends, approach quietly, make no noise, tread softly![13] It is kind of you to show this concern but no more, please!

[*In the lyric exchange that follows* ELECTRA *and the* CHORUS *sing their lines.*]

CHORUS [Strophe]: *Hush, hush! Lightly tread on sandal, make no noise!*   140

ELECTRA: *Over there, go over there, please, far from his bed!*
CHORUS: *See, I do as you say.*
ELECTRA: *Ah, my friend, let your voice be like the breath blown through the delicate reeds of a pipe!*
CHORUS: *See how gently I sigh as I approach his bed.*
ELECTRA: *Yes, like that! Come close, come close, approach gently, gently come! Tell me your purpose in coming here. This sleep in* 150 *which he lies was long in coming.*

CHORUS [Antistrophe]: *What is his condition? Dear friend, speak to us in turn. What news should I report?*

ELECTRA: *He is still alive, but draws his breath in short gasps.*
CHORUS: *What are you saying? Poor man!*
ELECTRA: *You will be my ruin, if you awaken his eyes from the precious boon of sleep he has won.*
CHORUS: *Poor man, how I pity him for the abominable deed heaven prompted him to do!*   160
ELECTRA: *What labours he endures! Unjust the speaker, unjust the words he uttered that day when on Themis' tripod Loxias decreed my mother's death — unnatural deed!*

CHORUS [Strophe]: *Do you see? He stirs beneath his cloak!*

ELECTRA: *Yes, you wretch, by crying out you have forced him out of his sleep!*
CHORUS: *No, I took him to be asleep still!*
ELECTRA: *Leave me, leave this house! Wend your way back with* 170 *circling steps that make no noise!*
CHORUS: *He is inclined yet to sleep.*

ELECTRA: *You are right. O Night, sovereign Lady, who bestow on long-suffering men your gift of sleep, from Erebus come forth! Come to the house of Agamemnon, on sweeping wing come! We are ruined,*
180 *ruined by our sorrows and the fate we endure!*

[To the CHORUS:*] You make a noise! Sh! Sh! Guard your lips, my friends, make no sound, keep away from his bed and let him enjoy undisturbed the boon of sleep!*

CHORUS [Antistrophe]: *Tell me, what end to this suffering can he expect?*

ELECTRA: *Death, death, what else? Not even food stirs any desire in him.*
190 CHORUS: *Then the event is all too clear!*
ELECTRA: *Phoebus has marked us down for sacrifice by decreeing that we spill a mother's blood in revenge for a father's — wretched and unnatural deed!*
CHORUS: *A just deed!*
ELECTRA: *A shameful one! O mother that gave me birth, you killed and were killed in turn, and you destroyed our father and these*
200 *children of your own blood. We are ruined, ruined, virtual corpses! This man is among the dead and, as for me, who have no part in marriage or children, the greater part of life has gone, as I wretchedly drag out my days to eternity in groans and tearful lamentation shrouded by night.*

CHORUS-LEADER: Electra, maid, you are at your brother's side, take care that he has not died without your knowledge; I am
210 distressed to see him lie there so limp.

ORESTES [*waking*]: O beloved enchantment of sleep, my ally against sickness, how precious and timely was your coming to me! O Oblivion from suffering, lady divine, how wise a goddess you are, how often invoked by those in distress! How comes it that I came here? How did I find this place? I forget, I can't recall my past thoughts.

ELECTRA: O dearest, how your falling asleep gave me joy! Should I take hold of you and lift you up?

ORESTES: Take me, yes, take hold of me, and wipe the thick
    foam from my wretched lips and eyes.   220

ELECTRA: There we are; sweet is the slavery and one that brings
    me no shame, to tend a brother with a sister's hand.

ORESTES: Come close and support me; sweep the matted hair
    from my face; my eyes see only dimly.

ELECTRA: O poor head of hair, so marred! How savage your
    looks are after so many days without washing!

ORESTES: Lay me back on the mat. When the disease of madness
    leaves me, I become nerveless, with no strength in my limbs.
        [ELECTRA *lays him down.*]

ELECTRA: There you are. When a man is ill, having a bed to
    lie on is like having a friend – it may be a place of pain but it
    is necessary to him.   230

ORESTES: Raise me up once more, shift my body round! Help-
    lessness makes patients hard to please.

ELECTRA: Do you want to set foot on the ground and take a
    step at last? Change brings pleasure in all things.

ORESTES: Yes! This has the semblance of health; and the sem-
    blance is what matters, even if it falls short of the truth.

ELECTRA: Well, listen to me now, my dearest brother, while
    the Furies allow you to think rationally.

ORESTES: You mean to tell me something new. If it is good,
    you do me a kindness; if it tends to my harm, my cup of
    sorrow is filled already.   240

ELECTRA: Menelaus, your father's brother, has returned; his
    oared ship rests at anchor in Nauplia.

ORESTES: What do you say? He has come, a light to shine on
    my woes and yours, the kinsman who owes a debt of gratitude
    to our father?

ELECTRA: He has come [*she extends her right hand to* ORESTES]
    (take this assurance of my words), bringing Helen with him
    from the walls of Troy.

ORESTES: If he'd escaped with his life alone, he would be more
    enviable; if he brings his wife as well, he comes with a cargo
    of terrible harm.

ELECTRA: The daughters Tyndareus fathered were stamped
250   with reproach and infamy throughout Greece.

ORESTES: Then do not imitate bad women – this is within your
power – and make sure these are your thoughts, not just your
words!

[*Suddenly* ORESTES' *manner changes, and he begins to jerk
about in agitation.*]

ELECTRA: Oh no – your eyes are rolling, Brother![14] You have
swiftly changed to madness, from being lately sane!

ORESTES: O Mother, I beg you, do not set on me those maidens
with gory eyes and snaky hair! There, there they are beside
me, leaping at me!

ELECTRA: Stay on your bed and do not tremble, poor man!
You see nothing of this vision you fancy is so clear to your
eye!

260   ORESTES: Phoebus, they will kill me, with their dog-faces and
gorgon-eyes, these priestesses of the dead, goddesses of terror!

ELECTRA: I will not let you go! I will hold you close to me and
stop you leaping into the abyss of sorrow!

ORESTES: Let me go! You are one of my Furies and clasp me
round the waist to cast me into Tartarus!

ELECTRA: O pity me, pity me, what help can I find, now that
the gods are numbered among my enemies?

ORESTES: Give me my horn-tipped bow,[15] gift of Loxias, with
which Apollo told me to ward off the goddesses, if they sought
270   to terrify me with their frenzy of madness. One of them shall
feel the wound, a goddess shot by mortal hand, if she does
not quit my sight! Are you not listening? Don't you see the
feathered arrows about to fly from my far-shooting bow? Aha!
Away with you now! Soar up to the heavens on your wings
and find fault with Phoebus' oracles!

Oh, what now? I am wandering without any sense, breath-
ing hard from the lungs! Where have I leaped to from this
pallet, where? For once more I see calm descending on the
stormy waves![16]

280   Sister, why do you weep with head covered by your cloak?

76

I am ashamed to make you share my suffering and to afflict a maiden with my malady. Do not waste away because of woes that are mine; you may have consented to it but the hand that spilt our mother's blood was mine. I give the blame to Loxias, who urged me to commit the accursed crime and cheered me on with words but not with deeds.

I think my father, had I asked him face to face whether I should kill my mother, would have begged me earnestly, clasping my chin,[17] never to thrust a sword through my 290
mother's throat, as this would not make him regain the light of life and would cause me to drain such a cup of woe in misery.

Uncover your head this instant, my sister, and stop weeping, though our state is wretched indeed. When you see me in despair, be physician to my irrational panic and give comfort! And when you give way to sorrow, I must be at your side and restrain you with gentle words. These are the ways of helping one another that bring honour to friends. Now, poor 300
girl, go inside the palace, lie down and give sleep to your sleepless eyes; take food and bathe yourself. For if you falter, or catch some illness through nursing me, I am ruined. You are the only helper I have, and others, as you see, have abandoned me.

ELECTRA: Never shall I leave you! With you shall I choose to live or to die. They amount to the same thing; if you die, what shall I, a woman, do? How shall I have a secure life on my own, with no brother, no father, no loved one? But if this is your wish, I must do it. But lie back on your pallet, and do 310
not be too troubled by terrors that hound you from your bed, but stay where you are. Whether a man is ill or merely imagines it, weariness of body and spirit afflict him.

[ELECTRA *goes inside and* ORESTES *lie back on his mat.*]

CHORUS [Strophe]: *O you terrible goddesses*[18] *who run on winged feet, whose lot it is to revel amid tears and lamentation where no Bacchants dance, you dark Eumenides, who ride the far-spreading* 320

77

sky seeking retribution for blood spilled, retribution for murder, on bended knee I implore, I implore you, let Agamemnon's son forget the frenzy of madness that drives him astray!

Poor man, what a pitiful task you were set, a task that, once attempted, brought you to ruin, when you accepted words chanted by Phoebus from his tripod on the sacred ground where, men say, is his innermost sanctuary at earth's navel.

[Antistrophe:] *O Zeus, what pitiable suffering, what bloody trial approaches that drives you onward, man of sorrows? Tears on tears he sends upon you, some spirit of vengeance dancing into the house and driving you into a frenzy because of your mother's blood. Tears of pitiful lamentation fall from my eyes, from my eyes! Great happiness does not remain constant among men; for a god rends it, like the sail of a fast ship, and overwhelms it in fearful disaster, as a ship is engulfed by the furious, deadly waves of the sea. For what other house deserves my honour before that of Tantalus, that derives from wedlock with gods?*[19]

But here I see the king, royal Menelaus, approaching in grand luxury[20] that proclaims to the eye his descent from the blood of one of Tantalus' line. Hail, you who sailed with ships a thousand strong to Asia's land! Prosperity is your own companion, for with heaven's blessing you have fulfilled your prayers!

[MENELAUS *enters with attendants.*]

MENELAUS: My house, I look upon you with joy now I have returned from Troy, yet the sight brings me grief as well. For never yet have I set eyes on another house so encircled by wretched woes. The unhappy end of Agamemnon was known to me, as my ship was approaching Malea; from the waves Glaucus, son of Nereus,[21] sea-god whose prophecies to mariners never fail, gave me report, speaking these words face to face before me: 'Menelaus, your brother lies dead and has received the final ablutions of his wife.' This brought floods of tears to me and my crew. But when I landed at Nauplia, expecting to clasp Orestes, Agamemnon's son, in a warm embrace, and his mother, as still enjoying good fortune, I

78

heard from a seafaring man how Tyndareus' daughter had been
foully murdered. Now tell me, young women, where he is,
Agamemnon's son, who dared to do such a terrible deed. He
was just a baby in Clytemnestra's arms that day I left my palace,
bound for Troy, so I wouldn't recognize him if I saw him.[22]

ORESTES [*from his sick-bed, behind* MENELAUS]: Here I am,
Menelaus, the Orestes you inquire about. Freely I will testify   380
to my woes. But as prelude to my supplication I clasp your
knees, fastening the leafless prayers[23] of my lips. Save me from
disaster! You have arrived in the very nick of time.

MENELAUS: Gods, what sight is this! What ghost do I see?

ORESTES: A good description; my sufferings rob me of life,
though I see the sunlight.

MENELAUS: Poor fellow, how wild you look, with matted hair!

ORESTES: It is not what you see that disfigures me but what I
have endured.

MENELAUS: Your eyes have no moisture in them – how fear-
some your stare is!

ORESTES: My body has gone; only my name remains to me.   390

MENELAUS: Ah, your appearance is ugly beyond my imagining!

ORESTES: Here I am, a wretched mother's murderer!

MENELAUS: So I have heard; spare your words; say little of that
vile act.

ORESTES: I will be sparing, though my fortune is not niggardly
with horrors!

MENELAUS: What is it that ails you? What sickness is destroying
you?

ORESTES: Awareness:[24] the knowledge that I have done a ter-
rible deed.

MENELAUS: What is your meaning? Wisdom lies in clarity, not
obscurity.

ORESTES: Grief is what chiefly is destroying me . . .

MENELAUS: A goddess to be feared indeed but still there is a
remedy against her.

ORESTES: . . . and madness, as punishment for spilling my
mother's blood.   400

MENELAUS: When did you begin to lose your senses? On what day did it start?

ORESTES: The day when I raised a grave over my wretched mother.

MENELAUS: At home or when you kept watch at her pyre?

ORESTES: Out of doors, as I waited for the gathering up of her bones.

MENELAUS: Was anyone else standing by to support you?

ORESTES: Pylades,[25] who shared in the bloodshed of my mother's killing.

MENELAUS: What kind of phantoms cause this sickness of yours?

ORESTES: I thought I saw three maidens resembling Night.

MENELAUS: I know the women you speak of but have no wish to name them.

ORESTES: Yes, they are the Dread Ones; you are wise to avoid
410   naming them.

MENELAUS: They are the ones who drive you mad with kindred blood.

ORESTES: Oh, how I fear their pursuit that hounds me in my misery!

MENELAUS: Terrible suffering afflicts those whose deeds are terrible – it is no wonder.

ORESTES: But I have a way of ending my affliction . . .

MENELAUS: Do not speak of death! That is no wise course of action.

ORESTES: Phoebus, whose order it was that I perform my mother's murder.

MENELAUS: Little understanding he showed of justice or right!

ORESTES: We are the gods' servants, whatever the gods are.

MENELAUS: And does Loxias not shield you from your torments?

ORESTES: For the moment he delays; such is the nature of the
420   gods.

MENELAUS: How long is it since your mother breathed her last?

ORESTES: Six days now; her funeral pyre is yet warm.

MENELAUS: How little delay they showed, these goddesses, in avenging your mother's blood!

ORESTES: A man does not show true wisdom in abusing loved ones.[26]

MENELAUS: What benefit is it to you that you have avenged a father?

ORESTES: None yet; but delay I count the same as inaction.

MENELAUS: What of Argos' people – how do they view you after this act?

ORESTES: They so hate me that none will speak to me.

MENELAUS: Are your hands yet cleansed of blood, as custom prescribes?

ORESTES: No; I am barred from every house I visit.   430

MENELAUS: Which citizens are seeking to banish you?

ORESTES: Oeax, who still feels hatred for my father because of what happened at Troy.[27]

MENELAUS: I understand; he wants to punish you for the spilling of Palamedes' blood.

ORESTES: And this was none of my doing; I am being ruined at third hand.

MENELAUS: What other enemies do you have? Some of Aegisthus' friends, perhaps?

ORESTES: Yes, they insult me; Argos hears them at this moment.

MENELAUS: Do the Argives let you keep Agamemnon's sceptre?

ORESTES: Hardly, seeing that they no longer want to let me live!

MENELAUS: What action have they taken? Do you have some reliable news to tell me?

ORESTES: This day shall see me condemned.   440

MENELAUS: Then why aren't you crossing the boundaries of the land to make your escape?

ORESTES: I am encircled by shields of bronze.

MENELAUS: Are these private enemies in arms or Argos' full complement of warriors?

ORESTES: It is the whole city, and they want my death; there you have it.

MENELAUS: My poor friend, you have plumbed the depths of misfortune!

ORESTES: My hope lies in you; you are my refuge from disaster. You come in prosperity to one in misery, so give part of your good fortune to one of your own family. Do not take and hoard your blessings, but take your share of troubles, too, by paying back where duty requires the services my father did to you. Friends whose friendship fails in time of trouble are friends in name, but not in deed.

450

CHORUS-LEADER: Here comes Tyndareus[28] the Spartan in cloak of black, toiling along on aged feet, his hair shorn in mourning for his daughter.

ORESTES: I am done for, Menelaus! Here comes Tyndareus towards me, and, after what I have done, he more than any other is the man whose eye I dread to meet.

460

For when I was a baby, he was the one who brought me up, showing his love in many things he did, carrying me around in his arms as 'Agamemnon's son', with Leda at his side, and honouring me no less than the Sons of Zeus. O wretched heart and soul of mine, I have made them no honourable return! What veil of darkness can I use to mask my face? What cloud can I spread before me, to escape the old man's piercing eye?

[TYNDAREUS *enters with attendants*.]

TYNDAREUS [*to* CHORUS]: Where, where can I find Menelaus, my daughter's husband? When I was pouring libations on Clytemnestra's tomb, I heard that he had come safe to Nauplia with his wife after many a year. Lead me to him! I want to approach his right hand and clasp it in welcome, seeing a loved one after so long!

470

MENELAUS: Greetings, dear old man, fellow husband with Zeus![29]

TYNDAREUS: And greetings to you, Menelaus, my kinsman!
[*seeing* ORESTES:] Ah, there he stands before the palace,[30]

the mother-killing serpent, his eyes darting lightning flames
that spread pollution, the creature I detest! Menelaus, do you   480
speak to one the gods abhor?

MENELAUS: Of course; he is the son of a man I loved.

TYNDAREUS: What! Someone of his stamp, the son of that
hero?

MENELAUS: His son; and if he knows misfortune, he deserves
our honour.

TYNDAREUS: You have forgotten what it is to be Greek, having
spent so long away from Greece!

MENELAUS: It is Greek, I say, always to honour a kinsman.

TYNDAREUS: Yes, and not to wish to override the laws.

MENELAUS: Everything that is caused by compulsion is servile
in wise men's eyes.[31]

TYNDAREUS: Make that your guiding principle if you want; I
will not accept it.

MENELAUS: Your temper together with your advanced years
does not make for wisdom.   490

TYNDAREUS: Now is the time to debate wisdom with this
man.[32] If right and wrong were clear to everyone, what man
would possess less wisdom than this one? He neither showed
regard for justice nor consulted the common law of the
Greeks.[33] When Agamemnon had breathed out his life, struck
on the head by my daughter – a deed of utter shame (never
shall I condone it) – Orestes should have prosecuted her,   500
imposed a holy blood-penalty, and expelled his mother from
the home. He would have gained, in place of disaster, a name
for wisdom, and he would have allied himself to the law and
piety. But as it is, he shares the same fate as his mother; rightly
considering her vile, he has proved viler still by committing
matricide.

This question I will put to you, Menelaus: if this man
were killed by the wife who shared his bed, and his son kills
his mother in turn, and then the son's son spills blood in
vengeance for blood spilled, just where shall the limit of   510
these horrors lie? Our early forefathers ordained this matter

well: when a man was stained with blood-guilt, they would not let him come before their eyes or cross their path, but commanded him to seek purification by means of exile, instead of seeking blood for blood. Otherwise one man, through staining his hands with the latest blood-guilt, would always make himself liable to a bloody end in turn.

What I cannot bear is a woman who despises the gods, my daughter most of all, who killed her husband; and, as for
520 Helen, your wife, never shall I praise her or even speak to her; I do not envy you your journey to the land of Troy for the sake of so false a woman. As far as my strength permits, I will stand up for the law and seek to curb this bestial and murderous impulse in men that constantly destroys both lands and cities. What possessed you in that hour, you wretch, when your mother held out her breast to you in supplication?[34] I did not witness the horror of that meeting but even now at the thought of it my old eyes melt with tears of grief. Yet
530 there is one thing that gives credence to my words: you are hated by the gods and pay the penalty for your mother's murder with your terrors and mad ravings. Why do I need to hear from other witnesses what is plain to my eyes? Be warned, then, Menelaus: do not seek to oppose the gods in your eagerness to help this man. Leave him to be stoned to death by the townsmen. My daughter has paid for her crime by dying; but she should not have died at this man's hands. In all
540 other respects my life has been blessed, but not in daughters; here I have not known good fortune.

CHORUS-LEADER: Enviable is the man who has been blessed in his children and has avoided disaster plain for all to see.

ORESTES: Sir, your years make me afraid to address you. Let your old age, that overawes my tongue, present no barrier to my speech, and I will press on my way. But for the moment
550 I dread these grey hairs of yours.

What was the right thing for me to do? Set one argument against its antithesis; my father sowed the seed of my life, your daughter gave me birth, and was only the field that received

seed from another.[35] I am unholy as one who killed his mother,
yet holy in the other sense, that I avenged my father. Your
daughter (I am ashamed to call her 'mother') in selfish and
lustful 'wedlock' took a lover. It will be my own shame I
voice when I speak of hers but I will voice it nonetheless.   560
I killed him and sacrificed my mother, a sinful act but one
that avenged my father.

As to your threat that my fate should be stoning, let me tell
you how I have benefited all Greece by my action.[36] If women
become so bold as to murder their husbands, seeking refuge
with their children and courting pity by baring their breasts,
other women will think nothing of killing their husbands for
any kind of grievance. Now by my terrible act, as you proclaim   570
it, I have done away with this practice. But justice it was that
made me hate and destroy my mother, who, when her hus-
band was absent from home and under arms, commanding
the army for all the land of Greece, betrayed him and failed
to keep his bed pure.

When she became aware of her error, she did not punish
herself but, to avoid punishment at her husband's hands,
inflicted on my father the penalty of death.

You, sir, by fathering a woman who was vile, brought ruin
upon me; it was her recklessness in robbing me of a father
that made me commit matricide. You gods – no good time, I
grant, to call on the gods, who pass judgement on murder –
had I kept silent about her behaviour and so condoned it,   580
what would the dead man have done to me?[37] Would his
hatred not have caused the Furies to drive me mad? Are there
goddesses ready to fight in support of my mother but not of
my father, who suffered a greater injustice? And what of   590
Apollo,[38] who has his seat at the earth's navel and dispenses
his oracles most sure? It was in obedience to his word that I
killed my mother. Treat him as the sinner and execute him!
His was the crime, not mine! What was I to do? Has the god
no power to acquit me of my guilt when I appeal to him?
What escape, then, can anyone have, if *he* does not protect

me from death after ordering me to do the deed? Oh, do not
600 say that this act was ill done; say rather that it turned out ill!

CHORUS-LEADER: It is always somewhat disagreeable to men
when women become involved in their fortunes.

TYNDAREUS: Since you show so little respect in your words
and will not shorten sail but rouse my heart to anger by your
reply, you will stir me all the more to urge your execution. I
610 shall reckon it as a fine bonus to the task for which I came, to
adorn my daughter's tomb. I will go to the assembly of the
Argive folk and set them on to stone you and your sister to
death – little persuasion will the city need!

She deserves death more than you,[39] for hardening your
heart against your mother, incessantly filling your ears with
words intended to deepen resentment, reporting as a scandal
what happened to Agamemnon and her adultery with
Aegisthus – may the gods of the underworld look on this with
620 loathing (for in this world too it offended the gods) – until
she set the palace ablaze with fire not of the Fire-god.

Menelaus, I say this to you, and I will be as good as my
word: if you place any value on my enmity and my connection
by marriage, do not shield this man from death, in defiance
of the gods, or else do not set foot on Spartan soil! These are
my words and note them well; do not choose friends who
flout the gods' will, while thrusting away friends who show
them more reverence.

Servants, accompany me away from this house!

[TYNDAREUS leaves with attendants.]

ORESTES: Go! I want the words I have yet to say to reach this
630 man's ears unhampered, escaping you and your old tongue!
Menelaus, why do you walk around in anxious thought,
pacing the double paths of some dilemma?

MENELAUS: Leave me alone! I am reflecting on a problem and
after what has happened I'm at a loss which way to turn.

ORESTES: Do not come to a hasty decision; listen to what I
have to say and then make your deliberations.

MENELAUS: Have your say; you are right: silence is sometimes preferable to speech, and speech sometimes to silence.

ORESTES: Then I will speak. A long speech is better than a short one and more clearly understood. 640

Give me nothing that belongs to you, Menelaus, but rather repay what you received as my father's gift. I do wrong; for this wrong's sake I ought to gain a wrong from you. For Agamemnon my father did wrong in mustering the Greeks and going to Troy: it was not his own offence but his attempt to heal the offence and wrong your wife had done. He sold 650 his life in true fashion, as friends should do for friends, toiling with shield at your side to help you win back your spouse. This is what you gained there, so now pay me back in kind, toiling for a single day, not for ten years on end, and standing at our side to win our safety.

This one kindness you should render me in return for mine to you. As for the spilling of my sister's blood that Aulis 660 claimed, I do not grudge you this; I do not ask that you kill Hermione.[40] You must have the advantage over me, when my circumstances are as they now are, and I must show forgiveness. Grant my life to my wretched father; if I die, I will leave his house without an heir. 'Impossible,' will be your reply. Just so: it is when disaster strikes that friends should help friends. When the gods are generous, what need is there of friends? Their help suffices when willingly given. Every Greek believes that you love your wife; I do not say this out of flattery to win your favour. In her name I beg you – oh, how 670 wretched I am, to what depths have I sunk! And yet, I must soldier on; it is for my whole house that I make this entreaty – o uncle, brother of my father, imagine that it is he who hears this,[41] the dead one below the earth, and his spirit that hovers above you and speaks the words I speak! You have heard my words, my claim for recompense as I hunt for salvation, a prize that all men seek, not I alone.

CHORUS-LEADER: I too, woman though I am, make my

680   humble appeal to you to help those in need; it lies in your
       power.

MENELAUS: Orestes, I have full respect for your status and I
       want to help you shoulder the burden of your woes. Indeed,
       it is right that kinsmen should aid kinsmen in clearing troubles
       from their path, if a god grants the power, taking the lives of
       enemies or sacrificing their own in death. But the power –
       this is the gift I want from the gods! I have returned with a
       single spear in hand and not one ally, a wanderer beset by
       countless troubles, and scant is the help I can count on from my
690   remaining friends. In battle we could not overcome Pelasgian
       Argos, but if we were able to prevail with soft words – this is
       the hope we have now. For when the people in angry mood
       turn to violence, it is as if one has to quench a raging fire; but
700   should one gently yield to their tension, accommodating its
       strength, and keep watch to choose the right moment, their
       storm should lose its force; and when it subsides, you would
       easily win them round to any course you please.

       I will go and try to persuade Tyndareus and the city on
       your behalf to show moderation.⁴² For the gods have no liking
       for zeal that is excessive, nor have citizens. What I must do
       (and this is the plain truth) is save you by wisdom, not by
710   defiance of those who are stronger. I would not save you by
       armed force, the hope, perhaps, you cherish: it is no easy thing
       to triumph with a single spear over the troubles that afflict
       you.

       [*Exit left, in the same direction as* TYNDAREUS *earlier.*]

ORESTES [*calling after* MENELAUS]: You contemptible creature,
       useless in championing friends except when it comes to lead-
       ing an army to win back a woman, are you turning away from
       me, shunning me? Have you forgotten Agamemnon's ties of
720   blood? O Father, you have no friends, it seems, now that
       Fortune has deserted you! Ah, I have been betrayed, no more
       have I hopes of any refuge from the Argives' penalty of death!
       For this man was my haven of safety.

       But here I see Pylades, dearest of men, approaching from

88

Phocis at a run – joyous sight! A man you can trust in trouble
is a sight more welcome than calm to a sailor.

[*Enter* PYLADES[43] *from the right side of the stage.*]

PYLADES: I came through the town with more than usual haste,
hearing that there was an assembly of the citizens and, indeed,
seeing it with my own eyes. But what does this mean? How   730
are you? What is your condition, dearest of comrades to me,
and of friends and kinsmen? You are all of these to me.

ORESTES: I am ruined, to tell you my woes in brief.

PYLADES: Then your ruin will bring mine too; friends share
each other's fortunes.

ORESTES: Menelaus has shown himself a traitor to me and to
my sister . . .

PYLADES: It is no surprise that a bad woman's husband should
prove bad.

ORESTES: As far as his debt to me is concerned, it is the same
as if he had not come.

PYLADES: Do you mean he actually has set foot in this land?

ORESTES: Yes, finally; but in no time he was convicted of
treachery towards his own kin.   740

PYLADES: And did he bring his shameless wife on his ship?

ORESTES: He did not bring her here; rather she brought him.[44]

PYLADES: Where is she, the woman who single-handedly
destroyed so many Greeks?

ORESTES: In my house, assuming it can still be called mine.

PYLADES: What appeal did you make to your father's brother?

ORESTES: That he should not stand by while my sister and I
were executed by the townsfolk.

PYLADES: In heaven's name, what did he say to this? I want to
know!

ORESTES: He was circumspect, as false friends usually are with
friends.

PYLADES: What kind of excuse was he seeking to use? This will
tell me the whole story.

ORESTES: That fellow had come, the father of those magnificent
daughters.   750

PYLADES: Tyndareus, you mean; he was full of anger against you, no doubt, because of his daughter.

ORESTES: You are right; and Menelaus chose this man as his kinsman before my father.

PYLADES: He did not dare to stand firm and help you shoulder your burden?

ORESTES: No, he was not born to wield a spear but to cut a dash among women.

PYLADES: Then you are in dire straits indeed; does it also follow that you must die?

ORESTES: It is for the citizens of Argos to cast their votes on the charge of murder.

PYLADES: What will be determined? Tell me! I am afraid!

ORESTES: Death or life; no long description for matters of some length.

PYLADES: Then leave this house and flee, taking your sister with you!

ORESTES: Don't you see? We are guarded everywhere by sen-
760   tinels.

PYLADES: I saw the streets of the city fenced off by armed men.

ORESTES: We find ourselves surrounded, like a city that endures an enemy siege.

PYLADES: Now consider my state as well; for like your own my life is at an end.

ORESTES: At whose doing? This evil will cap my own.

PYLADES: Strophius drove me from my home; my father's anger has made me an exile.

ORESTES: Was the charge he brought against you a private one or did it concern the people?

PYLADES: He claimed that I aided you in killing your mother, calling me unholy.

ORESTES: Poor man, it seems my misfortunes will bring you pain as well.

PYLADES: I am no Menelaus; I must bear these afflictions.

ORESTES: Are you not afraid that Argos may seek your death as
770   well as mine?

PYLADES: It is not those men but the land of Phocis that has the right to punish me.

ORESTES: The people are to be feared when led by unscrupulous men.

PYLADES: But when they choose honest ones, they always receive honest counsel.

ORESTES: Well, then; we must confer.

PYLADES: What is the crucial point?

ORESTES: What if I should go and tell the citizens . . .

PYLADES: That your action was just?

ORESTES: . . . avenging my father?

PYLADES: I fear they will give you a warm reception.

ORESTES: Then should I cower and meet my death in silence?

PYLADES: That would be no end for a man.

ORESTES: What should I do, then?

PYLADES: Have you any hope of life, if you stay here?

ORESTES: None.

PYLADES: And if you go, is there some prospect of escaping death?

ORESTES: It is possible, no more.

PYLADES: Then is this not preferable to staying?   780

ORESTES: Should I go, then?

PYLADES: Yes; if you die in such a way, it will be a more honourable death.

ORESTES: You are right; this way I escape the charge of cowardice.

PYLADES: More than if you stay here.

ORESTES: And my cause is just.

PYLADES: Put your trust only in what men think of this.

ORESTES: And somebody might pity me . . .

PYLADES: Your noble birth counts strongly in your favour.

ORESTES: . . . resenting my father's death.

PYLADES: All this is plain for men to see.

ORESTES: I must go; only a coward chooses death without glory.

PYLADES: Bravely spoken!

ORESTES: We shouldn't tell my sister about this, should we?
PYLADES: In heaven's name, no!
ORESTES: It would certainly result in tears.
PYLADES: And would this not be a serious omen?
ORESTES: Obviously, silence is better.
PYLADES: And you will profit by saving time.
ORESTES: There is just one stumbling block I face . . .
790 PYLADES: What is this new problem you raise now?
ORESTES: I fear the goddesses may grip me with madness.
PYLADES: But I will care for you.
ORESTES: It is unpleasant for someone to touch a sick man.
PYLADES: Not when it is my hands that are laid on you.
ORESTES: Take care you do not catch my madness!
PYLADES: Don't let *that* trouble you!
ORESTES: You will not shrink, then?
PYLADES: Shrinking is a great offence in a friend.
ORESTES: Lead on, then, pilot of my steps . . .
PYLADES: This service of care is one my heart gives freely.
ORESTES: . . . and guide me to my father's tomb!
PYLADES: What is your reason for this?
ORESTES: I intend to ask him as a suppliant to save me.
PYLADES: This is a just claim.
ORESTES: But may I not see my mother's tomb!
PYLADES: No friend was she. But hurry, or else the Argive vote
may destroy you first, and cling to me with your sick and
800 feeble frame. I will bear you through the town without shame,
paying scant attention to the rabble. Where shall I show myself
your friend, if I fail to support you in terrible misfortune?
ORESTES: That's why men say: 'Get yourself friends, not just
kin.' A man whose soul is one with your own, though he be
not kin, is a better friend for a man to have than any number
of blood-relatives.

[ORESTES *and* PYLADES *leave together.*]

CHORUS [Strophe]: *The great prosperity and prowess of the house of*
Atreus stood proud throughout Greece and by the banks of Simois;

but now their good fortune is reversed once more. So it has been ever   810
since the ancient misfortune of that house,[45] *when on Tantalus' sons*
came strife over the golden lamb, as royal children were given most
piteously to slaughter and feasting. Hence it is that trouble on trouble,
exchanging blood for blood, ever pursues the two sons of Atreus.

[Antistrophe:] *Not noble was that noble act*[46] *– to pierce a*
parent's throat with fire-forged weapon and to display to the sun's   820
brilliance a sword blackened with gore!

To do wrong and yet be right is meretricious impiety, the delusion
of wicked men. For in fear of death the daughter of Tyndareus,
miserable woman, cried out: 'Child, you dare a deed of sacrilege in
killing your mother! Do not assume a cloak of everlasting dishonour
in paying the homage due to a father!'   830

[Epode:] *What sickness is worse, what rouses greater pity or tears*
than a son's shedding on the ground his mother's blood? Having done
such a deed, he is tormented by madness, a prey for the Furies to
hunt, and panic whirls in his darting eyes, Agamemnon's son!

Wretched was that youth, when, seeing his mother's breast appear
from her gold-woven robe, he struck her down like a beast at the altar,   840
to requite his father's sufferings.

[ELECTRA *comes out of the palace.*]

ELECTRA: Women, can poor Orestes have fled from the palace
here, overcome by heaven-sent madness?

CHORUS-LEADER: He has not; he has gone before the
assembled people of Argos.

ELECTRA: Oh! What has he done? Who persuaded him?

CHORUS-LEADER: Pylades; but this messenger, it seems, will
soon tell us what was decided there about your brother.   850

[*A* MESSENGER,[47] *an elderly man, enters.*]

MESSENGER: Daughter of Agamemnon, lady Electra, hear the
sorrowful words I bring.

ELECTRA: Ah, I am ruined! Your speech is plain.

MESSENGER: It has been decided this day by vote of Argos'
people that your brother and you, poor lady, are to die.

ELECTRA: Oh no! What I expected has come, the calamity

I feared, long since wasting away with tears at the thought of
it! But what course did the trial take? What arguments put to
the Argives destroyed us and ratified our deaths? Tell me, old
man! Am I to die by stoning or the sword, gasping out my
final breath, sharing my brother's fate?

MESSENGER: It happened that I was coming inside the city gates
from the country, eager to learn the news about you and
Orestes. For I was always in the old days a loyal servant to
your father: your house nurtured me, a man of humble means
but noble in my dealings with friends. I saw a crowd making
its way to the hill and sitting down there, where men say
Danaus first gathered the folk together in common session
when he granted arbitration to Aegyptus.[48]

Seeing the assembly, I asked one of the citizens: 'What's
the news in Argos? I hope some report of an enemy hasn't
put Danaus' folk in a panic?' He replied: 'Don't you see
Orestes there coming forward to run the race for his life?'
Then I saw a sight I never looked to see, and I wish I never
had – Pylades and your brother moving forward together, the
one downcast and limp from his sickness, the other like a
brother sharing his friend's distress and ministering to his illness
with a tutor's care.

When the assembly of the Argives was full, a herald stood
up and announced: 'Who wishes to say whether Orestes
should die or not for killing his mother?' At this Talthybius[49]
rose, who had served under your father when he sacked Troy.
Always subservient to those in office, he spoke ambivalent
words, showering praise on your father but giving none to
your brother, spinning to and fro words of eulogy and censure,
saying that he was establishing a law that did little good to
parents. Constantly he threw a flatterer's glances at the friends
of Aegisthus. That's what his kind is like; heralds are always
jumping across to the side of the prosperous; the man who
has power among the citizens and holds office, that's the one
they like to cultivate.

After him royal Diomedes addressed the assembly. He

860

870

880

890

counselled that they should not kill you or your brother but rather sentence you to exile out of respect for the gods. Some roared in response that his advice was good, but others did not approve.

Then a fellow got to his feet, who let his tongue run free and was strong in impudence. He was an Argive and yet no true Argive,[50] suborned and relying on noisy bluster and the crass licence of his tongue, yet persuasive enough to bring some evil on his listeners' heads in the future. When a man of attractive speech but no sense persuades the people, it brings great harm to the city. But men who have intelligence and always give good advice bring benefit to the city, not immediately, perhaps, but in the long term. And this is how one should view the leader; for the business is the same for the public speaker as for the man who holds office. Now this fellow told us to pelt you and Orestes to death with stones, and Tyndareus prompted him as he spoke.

Another got to his feet and started to put the opposite case to his predecessor, a fellow not handsome to the eye but manly, who did not often set foot in the town or circle of the market-place. A farmer he was, one of those who are the only mainstay of the land, shrewd and eager to come to grips with words, whose life hitherto had been honest and beyond reproach. He urged us to place a wreath on the head of Orestes, Agamemnon's son, for having seen fit to avenge his father and kill a wicked woman who had forgotten the gods. Because of her actions, he said, men would no longer arm themselves and leave home to go on campaign, if those left behind were going to destroy their households from within and seduce their wives. To honest men his words seemed well chosen, and no one spoke afterwards.

Then your brother came forward and said: 'Inhabitants of Inachus' land, I acted in your cause no less than my father's when I killed my mother; for if the killing of men is to be a virtuous act for women, you should lose no time in dying, or you are bound to be slaves to women! And you will be doing the opposite of what you should be doing. For as things stand, the woman who betrayed my father's bed is dead; but if you actually kill me, that is an end of established custom, and one might as well be dead. For effrontery will not be in short supply.'

I thought he spoke well but he did not win over the crowd. That villain who urged that you and your brother should die won in the vote of hands. Wretched Orestes with difficulty prevailed on them not to execute him by stoning. He promised that with his own hand he would end his life and yours this very day.

Pylades, weeping, is now bringing him away from the assembly, and friends accompany them, shedding tears of pity. He comes to you as a sight to wound the heart, a spectacle of misery. So make ready a sword, or noose for the neck, for you must leave the light of day. Your nobility has done you no service, nor Phoebus, sitting on his Pythian tripod; it is ruin they have brought.[51]

[*The* MESSENGER *leaves. The* CHORUS *and* ELECTRA *share the lament that follows.*[52]]

CHORUS [Strophe]: *Land of Pelasgus, I take the lead in lamentation, scoring my cheeks in bloody ruin with white fingers and beating my head in honour of Persephone, fair child and goddess, who rules the dead below the earth. And let the Cyclopean land*[53] *cry out, setting shearing steel to the head,*[54] *in lament for the woes of the house. Pity, pity comes upon us for those about to die, who once were leaders of the Greek host.*

[Antistrophe:] *It is gone, yes, gone and passed away, the whole lineage of Pelops' sons, and with it the pride of a house once so blessed in fortune! The envy of the gods has destroyed it, and the vote of the citizens, whose anger demands blood.*

Ah, you tribes of mortal men, long-suffering and lamentable, see how fate comes on and cheats your hopes! In the long lapse of time different woes afflict different men in turn, and the whole of human life defies calculation.

ELECTRA: *Oh that I might come to the rock that hangs poised midway between heaven and earth suspended by golden chains, as it whirls round, a lump from Olympus' mass, that I might cry aloud in lament to aged father Tantalus, true sire of my forebears, the calamities I have seen in his house: the winged pursuit of the horses that day when Pelops raced his team of four along the seashore and hurled* 990 *Myrtilus to his death in the swell of the sea, speeding onward by Geraestus' shore where the ocean waves break in white foam. Hence it was that a curse arose, bringing much grief to my house, when that famous wonder was created, the lamb with fleece of gold, that brought ruin on Atreus rich in horses.* 1000

So it was that Strife turned round the Sun's winged chariot, changing his westward course through the sky towards the dawn with her single horse, and Zeus steered on a different course the seven pathways of the running Pleiads. And so followed the exchange of deaths for deaths, the feast to which Thyestes gave his name, and Cretan Aerope's betrayal of her marriage-bed, treacherous wife! Now the final sorrows fall on me 1010 *and my father through the calamitous necessity of this house.*[55]

[ORESTES *and* PYLADES *enter.*]

CHORUS: Here your brother comes, condemned by the vote to death, and Pylades, most loyal of all men, like a brother to him, guiding Orestes' faltering limbs and lending him support with anxious step.

ELECTRA: Oh, the pain! I mourn to see you, brother, before the tomb, before the pyre of death!

Oh, further pain! As I look at you for the last time I lose 1020 my senses!

ORESTES: Hush this womanish wailing and accept what has been decreed! Our state is pitiful but we must endure.

ELECTRA: How can I stay silent? We wretches shall never more look upon this light the god sends!

ORESTES: Don't *you* be the death of me as well! It is enough that I will be killed by Argive hands; say no more about our present troubles!

ELECTRA: Oh, Orestes, I pity you for your youth, your lot, your untimely death! You should have lived, not died! 1030

ORESTES: In heaven's name do not unman me, causing me to weep by mention of our woes!

ELECTRA: We are going to die; I cannot help lamenting our fate. All mankind grieves when a precious life is at stake.

ORESTES: This is our appointed day; we must grasp a noose to hang ourselves or prepare to use a sword.

ELECTRA: Then *you* must kill me now, brother, so that no Argive may do the deed and so bring insult on the son of Agamemnon.

ORESTES: It is enough that I have spilled my mother's blood, without killing you as well; die by your own hand in whatever
1040   way you wish.

ELECTRA: So I shall; my own sword-thrust shall not lag behind yours. But let me put my arms around your neck!

ORESTES: Enjoy that empty pleasure, if an embrace can give joy to those who have come near death.

ELECTRA: My dearest! O my beloved brother, how I delight in the name of your sister! We are one soul!

ORESTES: Oh, your words melt me! I want to answer your love with a loving embrace of my own. Why should I any longer
1050   feel shame at this,[56] wretch that I am?

[*He accepts her embrace.*]

ELECTRA: Ah, if it were right, I wish the same sword might kill us both, and a single tomb, fashioned of cedar wood, might receive the two of us!

ORESTES: This would be most welcome; but you see how we lack friends to see that we share one tomb.

ELECTRA: Did Menelaus – that coward, that traitor to my father – not speak on your behalf, did he not plead strongly against your death?

ORESTES: He did not show his face but fixed his hope upon the throne, taking care not to save his friends. But come, let us make sure we die after doing noble deeds most worthy of
1060   Agamemnon!

I will plunge a sword into my heart and show the people of Argos the nobility of my line. You, in turn, must act in imitation of my bold deed. Pylades, you must preside over our bloody contest, and once we have died, lay our bodies out properly, carry us to our father's tomb and there bury us together. Now, farewell; I go to do the deed, as you see.

PYLADES: Wait! I have one fault to find with you, that you expected me to desire life when you had died. 1070

ORESTES: But what need is there for you to die with me?

PYLADES: You ask that? What need to live without your companionship?

ORESTES: *You* did not kill your mother, as I did in my wretchedness.

PYLADES: But I shared your deed and so must bear the same consequences.

ORESTES: Return to your father, do not die with me. You have a city,[57] I have none; you have a father's house, a spacious haven of wealth. You cannot marry this ill-starred woman whom I promised to you out of respect for our friendship.

Choose another bride and have children. The marriage tie 1080 between you and me is not to be. Now, dearest and best of friends, farewell! This is not for us to enjoy, but perhaps for you; no joy shall we have once dead.

PYLADES: You have no grasp of what my intentions are. May the fruitful earth not receive my blood, no, nor the bright air of heaven, if ever I betray you, ever preserve my own life and fail you! I shared in the act of murder, I will not deny it, and planned everything for which you now face punishment. Therefore I should also share death with you 1090 and this woman; for I judge her to be my wife, as I willingly accepted her hand in marriage. What honourable words shall I speak when I go to the land of Delphi, the citadel of the Phocians, I who was your friend before your fortunes waned but, now that disaster has struck, am your friend no longer? It is unthinkable!

This woe is my concern as much as yours. Since we are going to die, let us consider together how Menelaus should share our misery.[58]

ORESTES: O my dear friend, if only I might see this before I
1100   die!

PYLADES: Then listen to my words, and delay that sword-
stroke!

ORESTES: So I shall, if it means taking vengeance on my enemy!

PYLADES [looking at the chorus]: Keep your voice down! I put
little trust in women.

ORESTES: Do not fear them; they are here as our friends.[59]

PYLADES: Let us kill Helen, and torture Menelaus with grief!

ORESTES: How? You will find me ready, if we can succeed.

PYLADES: Run a sword through her throat; she hides inside
your house now.

ORESTES: So she does; yes, and puts her seal on all my
belongings.

PYLADES: This will stop soon, once she has Hades as her
bridegroom!

1110   ORESTES: But how? She has her foreign attendants.

PYLADES: Who are they? Phrygians! None of *them* would make
me tremble!

ORESTES: Yes, the sort who are in charge of mirrors and scents!

PYLADES: What? Has she returned here with Trojan luxuries?

ORESTES: Let me tell you, Greece provides too small a house-
hold for her!

PYLADES: Slaves cannot compare with men who are free-born.

ORESTES: Yes! Let me do this deed and I have no fear of dying
twice over!

PYLADES: Nor have I, if only I gain vengeance for you!

ORESTES: Explain the business to me and make your meaning
clear.

PYLADES: We will go into the house as though to our deaths.

1120   ORESTES: So much I understand; it is the rest I fail to grasp.

PYLADES: We will shed tears before her at our lamentable
situation.

ORESTES: And make her weep, while secretly rejoicing!

PYLADES: And the pair of us will have the same feelings then
as she has!

ORESTES: How are we then going to fight this contest?

PYLADES: We shall have swords hidden here in our cloaks.

ORESTES: How shall we get rid of the attendants first?

PYLADES: We will exclude them, shutting them up in different parts of the house.

ORESTES: And we must kill anyone who doesn't hold his tongue.

PYLADES: After that the deed itself will show us how to proceed.

ORESTES: Kill Helen; I understand the sign.[60]   1130

PYLADES: You are right; and let me tell you how my plan is an honourable one. If we were drawing our swords against a more virtuous woman, the killing would be inglorious. But as it is,[61] she will be answering to the whole of Greece, whose fathers she killed, whose sons she destroyed, whose brides she robbed of their husbands. Cries of exultation shall be raised, and fires kindled to the gods, as men pray for blessings to befall you and me for having shed the blood of a wicked woman. Once you have killed this woman, you shall not hear the name of 'matricide' but lose this reproach and gain a better   1140 name, when men call you 'the killer of Helen who killed many a man'.

It is not right, not right, I say, that Menelaus should prosper, while your father and you and your sister should die, or that your mother – but enough of that subject: it is not proper to speak of – and that he should possess your house, when it was Agamemnon's spear that won him back his bride!

May I indeed no longer go on living if I fail to draw my black sword against her! So if we fail to slaughter Helen, we shall set fire to this house and then die. For one thing we shall   1150 surely achieve and then enjoy glory, having died with honour or won safety with honour.

CHORUS-LEADER: Tyndareus' daughter, who brought shame on her sex, deserves the hatred of all women.

ORESTES: Ah, there is nothing a man should value more than a firm friend, not wealth, not kingship. A multitude counts for nothing when weighed against an honourable friend. You

were the one who devised a deadly end for Aegisthus and
stood at my side in the hour of danger, and now, yet again,
1160   you show me the way to punish my enemies and stand fast
beside me. I will stop praising you, since even this, excessive
commendation, can prove irksome.

As for me, as I draw my last breath, I wish above all else to
do some harm to my enemies before I die, to repay those who
betrayed me and hear the groans of those who made me
wretched. I was born the son of Agamemnon, who was
thought worthy to rule Greece, no despot, but wielding power
such as a god might possess. I will not disgrace him by dying
1170   like a slave but will relinquish life as a free man should, and I
will have my vengeance on Menelaus. For we could count
ourselves happy if we succeeded in one aim; and, if the
unexpected should happen and we win safety from some
source, killing without being killed, most welcome would this
be. This is the outcome I wish, and it is pleasant to voice
winged words at no expense and so bring one's heart joy.

ELECTRA: Brother, I think I see a way to achieve this very
thing,[62] deliverance for you, for this man, and, thirdly, for me!

ORESTES: These words suggest a god has inspired your thoughts!
But what is the plan? I know you have never lacked intelli-
1180   gence.

ELECTRA: Listen to me now; and you too, Pylades, pay
attention.

ORESTES: Go on. What advantage is there in deferring good
news?

ELECTRA: You know Helen's daughter? Of course you do!

ORESTES: I do: Hermione, whom my mother raised.

ELECTRA: She has gone to Clytemnestra's tomb . . .

ORESTES: With what in mind? What hope are you suggesting?

ELECTRA: To pour libations at the grave on her mother's behalf.

ORESTES: Why are you saying this? How does it help us to win
safety?

ELECTRA: Seize hold of her, when she comes back, and hold
her hostage!

ORESTES: What evil will this cure for us three friends?   1190

ELECTRA: Once Helen is dead, if Menelaus tries to do some
    harm to you, to this man, or to me (this band of friends is
    one), say that you will kill Hermione. You must hold your
    drawn sword close to the girl's neck. And if Menelaus, not
    wanting his daughter killed, seeks to spare your life, let him
    have her back alive, his darling girl; but if he fails to control
    his fierce anger and seeks to kill you, then cut her maiden
    throat. He may rage and rant at first, but I think his temper   1200
    will soon subside: he is not brave or warlike in nature. This is
    the plan I offer, a wall to keep us safe from our enemies. You
    have heard it all.

ORESTES: Oh, you may have a body that suits your female sex
    but the mind you have is a man's! How you deserve to live
    rather than to die! Pylades, such is the wife you will forfeit,
    poor fellow, or, should you live, the enviable marriage you
    will make!

PYLADES: Oh, may this prize be mine and may she come to
    the city of the Phocians with lovely wedding-hymns to do
    her honour!   1210

ORESTES: How soon will Hermione return to the house? Your
    suggestions are in other respects excellent, if we succeed in
    capturing the cub of an impious father.

ELECTRA: I think she is already near the house; the time is right.

ORESTES: Good. Now, Electra my sister, wait in front of the
    house and be ready to receive the girl when she arrives. Be
    on guard in case anyone enters the house first, before the
    killing is completed, and, if so, shout a warning into the
    building – strike the doors or send a message inside. Now let   1220
    us go in and arm our hands with swords for the final contest.   1230
        O Father, who dwell in the halls of gloomy Night, your
    son Orestes calls you to come as helper![63]

ELECTRA: Oh, come, Father, if from the earth below you hear
    your children calling; it is for you that we are dying!

PYLADES: O Agamemnon, my father's close kinsman, listen to
    my prayers also and save your children!

ORESTES: I killed my mother . . .

ELECTRA: And my hand gripped the sword . . .

PYLADES: And my voice urged them on and removed their scruples.

ORESTES: . . . in your cause, Father.

ELECTRA: . . . and I did not betray you!

PYLADES: When you hear their shameful condition will you not protect your children?

ORESTES: I pour for you the libation of my tears.

ELECTRA: And I my cries of sorrow!

1240 PYLADES: Enough! Let us proceed to the task. If prayers, like javelins, can pierce below the earth, he hears. O Zeus, our ancestor, and Justice, majestic goddess, grant success to this man, to me and to this woman! Three friends we may be but one dangerous struggle awaits us, and one just cause.

[ORESTES *and* PYLADES *go into the palace.* ELECTRA *and the* CHORUS *now sing, now speak in dramatic exchange as the plan unfolds.*]

ELECTRA [Strophe]: *Women of Mycenae, my friends, highest in rank in the Pelasgian seat of the Argives –*

CHORUS: *What is it you are saying, lady? For you can still count on*
1250 *our loyalty in the city of Danaus' folk.*

ELECTRA: . . . position yourselves, some along the highway there, the rest on the other road here, to keep watch on the house.

CHORUS: *But tell me, my friend, why do you ask this service of me?*

ELECTRA: *I am afraid that someone, seeing my brother poised to do the bloody killing, will devise further woes for us.*

CHORUS-LEADER: Onward! Let us hurry! [*The* CHORUS *now divides into two, taking up the different positions as instructed.*]

SEMICHORUS 1: I will guard this road that faces the sun's rays.

1260 SEMICHORUS 2: And I this road that looks westward.

ELECTRA [*to the whole* CHORUS]: *Now turn your eyes to right and left!*

CHORUS: *We are looking from one side to another and back again, as you urge.*

ELECTRA: *Very well, then, let your eyes range all around, peering in all directions through your hair.*

SEMICHORUS 1: *Here comes someone on our path! What countryman is this who visits your palace?*   1270

ELECTRA: We are ruined, friends! He will at once reveal to our enemies the armed hunt that lurks in hiding inside!

SEMICHORUS 2: *Don't be afraid — the road is empty, my friend; there is no one there, as you thought.*

ELECTRA: *What? Can I rely on you still? Give me a report I can trust, if there is no one there in front of the palace.*

CHORUS-LEADER: No cause for alarm here; but look on your side. None of Danaus' folk is coming near to us

LEADER OF SEMICHORUS 2: Your report squares with mine; no crowd is to be seen on this side either.   1280

ELECTRA: *Very well, let me listen at the doors!*

CHORUS: *You two inside, all is quiet, so why delay in staining with red blood the sacrificial victim?*

ELECTRA: They do not hear; oh, pity me for my misery! Have their swords lost their edge in the face of beauty?[64]

CHORUS-LEADER: In no time some armed man of Argos shall rush up to the rescue and burst into the palace!   1290

ELECTRA: Keep closer watch now! This is no time for sitting still; use your eyes, you on this side, you others on that!

CHORUS: I am going up and down the road, spying everywhere.

HELEN [*screaming from inside*]:[65] Pelasgian Argos, I am being foully killed!

ELECTRA: Did you hear? The men are at their murderous work! That shriek was Helen's, I guess!

CHORUS: *O Zeus, Zeus, whose power is everlasting, come to the aid of my friends with all your might!*   1300

HELEN [*from inside*]: Menelaus, I am dying! And you are not at my side to help me!

ELECTRA AND CHORUS: *Stab her, kill her, strike her, destroy her!*[66] *Drive home at close quarters your twin swords with double edge — kill*

the woman who deserted both father and husband, who brought death
by the spear to countless Greeks who perished by that river, where
tears fell on tears for the iron shafts that hailed down by Scamander's
1310 whirling stream!

CHORUS-LEADER: Silence, keep silence! I heard the sound of
someone's steps coming along the road beside the palace!

ELECTRA: Dearest women, here comes Hermione,[67] walking
into the jaws of death! Our cries must stop, for here she
approaches, about to tumble into the meshes of our net! A
fine prey to catch she'll be, if she is caught. Compose your-
selves once more and look on calmly; don't let your colouring
betray the deed that is done! I, too, will wear a sullen look in
1320 my eye, as if I know nothing of what has been achieved.

[HERMIONE enters.]

Maiden, have you returned from garlanding Clytemnestra's
grave and pouring drink-offerings to her dead spirit?

HERMIONE: I am here, having gained her goodwill. But I felt a
pang of fear at a cry I heard from inside the house when I was
yet some distance away.

ELECTRA: Well, the fate that has befallen us does merit wailing.

HERMIONE: Oh, do not say words like that! What news do you
have to tell?

ELECTRA: This land has decided that Orestes and I must die.

HERMIONE: Oh, no! My own cousins!

1330 ELECTRA: It is fixed; necessity's yoke is upon us.

ELECTRA: Was this the cause also of the cry inside the palace?

ELECTRA: Yes; he cried out when he fell in supplication at
Helen's knees . . .

HERMIONE: Who? I know nothing more unless you tell me.

ELECTRA: . . . the wretched Orestes, begging for his life, and
for mine.

HERMIONE: So there is cause indeed for the house to ring with
cries of woe.

ELECTRA: What stronger reason would a man have for crying
out? But come, help your kin in their entreaty, falling before
your mother so blessed by the gods, that Menelaus should

106

not look on while we die. Come, you were nurtured in my
mother's arms – have pity and lighten our burden of sorrow!   1340
Come with me to face this trial, and I will lead the way. You
alone can bring us safely to our goal.

HERMIONE: See, I hurry into the house at once! As far as rests
with me, your safety is assured.

[HERMIONE *enters the palace.*]

ELECTRA: You armed friends indoors, seize your prey! Hold
her, hold her fast, put the sword at her throat and wait in
patience for Menelaus to learn his lesson, that he has found   1350
men here, not cowardly Phrygians, and has met the kind of
treatment cowards deserve.

[ELECTRA *follows* HERMIONE *into the palace.*]

CHORUS [Strophe]: *Now, now, friends, raise a din, din and shouting
before the palace, lest the murder done should strike a terrible fear in
the Argives' hearts and make them run to the royal dwelling to bring
help before I see with my own eyes Helen lying indoors in bloody
death, or hear the news from one of the servants. Some of what has
happened I know, but the rest not clearly. With justice has the*   1360
*vengeance of the gods come upon Helen; she filled all Greece with
tears for Idaean Paris' sake, that man of death and destruction, who
brought Greece to Ilium.*

CHORUS-LEADER: But there is a rumbling from the palace
doors.[68] Keep quiet! One of the Phrygians is coming out; we'll
learn from him how things stand indoors.

[*A* PHRYGIAN HOUSE-SLAVE *emerges from the palace, per-
haps running out, perhaps appearing on the roof and leaping or
jumping down, in any case in a state of extreme agitation. He
sings a monody, in a wide variety of metres, narrating the terrible
events inside.*]

PHRYGIAN: *From death by Argive sword have I escaped, climbing
over the cedar rafters of the chambers and down the Dorian triglyphs*   1370
*in my foreign slippers – gone, gone, o Earth, Earth! – running away
like the foreign slave I am!*

Ah! Where can I flee, ladies, soaring into the white air of heaven or over the sea that bull-headed Oceanus moves to and fro in his embrace as he circles the earth?

CHORUS-LEADER: What is your news, servant of Helen, you
1380 who once dwelt in Ida?

PHRYGIAN: *Ilium, Ilium – oh, misery, misery! – city of Phrygia, and you, Ida, holy and fertile mountain, in foreign tones I wail for your downfall, caused by the vision of beauty bird-born, Leda's swan-winged chick,[69] Helen the Hell-child, Hell-child, sent as a Fury to punish the shining towers Apollo raised.*

1390 *Oh, misery, misery and mourning! Unhappy land of Dardanus, where Ganymede[70] rode his horses and brought pleasure to the bed of Zeus!*

CHORUS-LEADER: Tell us plainly and directly all that happened in the house.

PHRYGIAN: *'Woe for Linus! Woe for Linus!' – the beginning of the dirge that foreigners chant – ah, misery! – in their Asian tongue, when royal blood is spilled on the earth, as iron swords do their deadly*
1400 *work! There came into the house, to tell you the whole tale exactly, two lions of Greece with double step. One was called son of the commander of the host, the other was Strophius' son, a wicked schemer of a man, like Odysseus, silent and crafty, loyal to his friends, brave in the fight and shrewd in war, a serpent craving blood. Curse him for his patient forethought, the villain!*

In they came and approached the throne of the woman whose hand
1410 *Paris the archer won, their eyes stained with tears, and grovelling, the pair of them, one on this side, one on that, and clasping her on left and right, they cast, yes, they cast suppliant hands around Helen's knees. Up leaped her Phrygian attendants, up they leaped in haste; and falling to the ground in fear, they said, one to another: 'Some*
1420 *treachery here, I fancy!' Some thought not, but others felt a cunning net was being coiled round Tyndareus' daughter by that serpent who killed his mother.*[71]

CHORUS-LEADER: Where were you at that moment? Or had you fled long since in terror?

PHRYGIAN: *In the Phrygian fashion, it happened, the Phrygian, I*

was stirring the air, the air,[72] with a round fan of feathers by the hair
of Helen, and cooling the cheeks of Helen, while she twined with her   1430
fingers the flax from her distaff and the threads trailed down to the
floor. She wanted to use this thread to embroider a purple robe she
was making from the Phrygian spoils, as a gift to adorn the tomb of
Clytemnestra. Orestes addressed the Spartan lady: 'Child of Zeus,
rise from your seat, step down here to the ground, and accompany me   1440
to the ancient altar-hearth of ancestral Pelops, to learn what news I
bring.' And on he led her, led her, while on she followed, little
divining what lay in store. But his accomplice was engaged in other
business: 'Out of the way, away with you, Phrygian cowards!' he
cried, as he shut them up in various parts of the palace, some in the
stables, others in outlying apartments, separating and disposing of   1450
them in different places, away from their mistress' side.

CHORUS-LEADER: What then happened after this?

PHRYGIAN: Mother, Mother of Ida, mighty, mighty one invoked in
prayer, what bloody suffering, what lawless wickedness did I see, did
I see in the palace of the king! From their purple-bordered cloaks
where they lay concealed they pulled out their swords and held them
as they darted glances around, Orestes this way, Pylades that, in case
someone should be there to witness. Like mountain boars they stood   1460
there facing the woman and cried out: 'You will die, you will die!
Your killer is your coward of a husband who betrayed his brother's
son to death in Argos!' Then wildly she cried, she cried: 'Oh, pity
me, pity me!' And dashing a white forearm against her breast she
struck her head with piteous blows, and was turning to flee, to flee,
in her gold sandals, when Orestes stepped forward in his Mycenaean
boots and, thrusting his fingers into her hair, he bent her neck down   1470
to her left shoulder, poised to plunge his black sword through her
throat.

CHORUS-LEADER: But where were you Phrygians in the palace
to defend her?

PHRYGIAN: The house raised a cry and we ran to help, having used
crowbars to break down the doors of the stables where we still were
imprisoned, all of us from different parts of the palace, one carrying
stones, another a bow, a third a drawn sword in his hands. But

1480   *against us came the indomitable Pylades, like Hector the Phrygian or*
triple-helmed Ajax, whom I saw, I saw at Priam's gates. We clashed
with swords, point to point. Then, yes, then it was clear to see
how much we Phrygians are inferior to Greek spearsmen in martial
prowess,[73] *as one of us took to his heels, another lay dead, a third*
was wounded, a fourth turned suppliant as a defence against death.
Men were falling, dead, some on the point of death, others prone
already. So under concealment we tried to make our escape.

1490   *Then poor Hermione entered the house, as the wretched mother*
who gave her birth lay covered in blood on the ground. They ran at
her and seized hold of her, like Bacchants without wands, who have
caught a young beast of the mountain, then turned back eagerly to
their slaughter of Zeus' daughter. But she was not to be seen – o
Zeus and Earth, Light and Night! – she had vanished from the
house, whether by black magic or wizards' spells or stolen away by
the gods.

Of what then ensued I know no more; for I had turned runaway
and was making my stealthy escape from the palace. Ah, little, little
1500 *did it profit Menelaus to win his wife back from Troy – much misery,*
much misery and suffering did she cost him!

CHORUS-LEADER: A novel tale and here we have fresh novel-
ties: I see Orestes, sword in hand, striding forth from the
palace – his passion gives his feet wings!

[ORESTES *enters from the palace doorway.*[74]]

ORESTES: Where is the fellow who escaped my sword by run-
ning out of the palace?

PHRYGIAN: O my royal lord, I prostrate myself before you! I
fall at your feet in the barbarian way!

ORESTES: This is not Ilium where we find ourselves but the
land of Argos.

PHRYGIAN: Men of sense everywhere find life a more pleasant
prospect than death!

ORESTES: You didn't shout out for Menelaus to come to the
1510   rescue, did you, now?

PHRYGIAN: No! I shouted for you to be helped! You are the
worthier man.

ORESTES: Then it was just, was it, that Tyndareus' daughter perished?[75]

PHRYGIAN: Most just – if she had had three throats for slitting!

ORESTES: You curry favour with a coward's tongue; these are not your true feelings.

PHRYGIAN: Should she not have perished, when she involved Greece and Phrygians in one shameful ruin?

ORESTES: Swear (or else I will kill you) that you're not saying this just to please me.

PHRYGIAN: I swear by my own life – the most sacred oath I could make!

ORESTES: Did the sword make all Phrygians quake like this at Troy as well?

PHRYGIAN: Take your blade away – it flashes fearful murder at such close quarters!

ORESTES: Are you afraid of turning into stone, as though you had seen a Gorgon?   1520

PHRYGIAN: No – of turning into a corpse; I don't know about a Gorgon's head!

ORESTES: You, a slave, fear Hades, who will give you freedom from misery?

PHRYGIAN: Every man, even if he is a slave, enjoys seeing the light of day.

ORESTES: You're right, and this good sense has saved your life. Off you go, into the house!

PHRYGIAN: Then you are not going to kill me?

ORESTES: You are spared.

PHRYGIAN: Now that's a welcome word in my ear!

ORESTES: But I will change my plan.

PHRYGIAN: That's less welcome news!

ORESTES: You fool – to think I would bring myself to make your throat red with blood, a creature that is neither woman nor man! I came out of the palace to stop your shouting; Argos is quick to rouse itself once the cry for help is heard.   1530

[*The* PHRYGIAN *exits at a run away from the palace.*]

As for Menelaus, I have no fear of welcoming him in range

of my sword; let him come, parading his golden curls down to his shoulders! For if he does raise a force of Argives and come against this house, seeking blood to avenge Helen's murder, and proves unwilling to save me, my sister, and Pylades, my partner in this deed, he will see his daughter and his wife both lying dead!

[ORESTES *exits into the palace.*]

CHORUS [Antistrophe]: *Oh, what fortune assails the house! Again it falls into a further terrible conflict concerning Atreus' offspring! What should we do? Take word of these happenings to the city or* 1540 *keep silent? That is the safer course, friends.*

[*Smoke and flame begin to appear above the palace.*]

Look, look, where the smoke billows skyward and sends its message from the palace front! They are kindling pinewood torches to fire the palace of Tantalus and are still bent on murder!

The gods' will determines the final outcome for mortals, and that outcome is as they choose. A mighty kind of power also is the power of vengeful spirits; this house has fallen, fallen in bloody ruin because Myrtilus fell⁷⁶ from his chariot!

But here I see Menelaus approaching the palace in haste – 1550 he must have learned what is happening here! Children of Atreus inside the house, bar the gates as quickly as you can! A prosperous man is an enemy to be feared by those in trouble, as your fortune now is low, Orestes.

[MENELAUS *enters with attendants.*]

MENELAUS: I come having heard of strange and violent deeds 1560 done by twin lions; I do not call them humans. Someone open up the house! Servants, put your shoulders to the doors here – we must rescue my daughter from the murderous hands of these men!

[ORESTES *and* PYLADES *carrying swords and torches appear above the stage, with* HERMIONE *between them;* ELECTRA *is by their side.*]

ORESTES: You there, don't lay a hand on these bolts, yes, you,

Menelaus, you tower of arrogance! Otherwise I'll crush your
head with this coping-stone, tearing up this ancient roof that
masons toiled to build! The bolts are securely held with levers   1570
and will frustrate your efforts at rescue, however vigorous.
You will not gain entry to the house!

MENELAUS: Ah, what's this? I see flaring torches and, on the
palace roof, those men at bay, manning the ramparts with my
daughter under guard, a sword held at her throat!

ORESTES: Are you here to ask questions or to listen to me?

MENELAUS: Neither; but it seems I must listen to you.

ORESTES: I intend to kill your daughter – if you want to know.

MENELAUS: You have murdered Helen – will you add blood-
shed to bloodshed?

ORESTES: If only I had succeeded in that without the gods
cheating me!   1580

MENELAUS: Do you now deny you killed her and say these
words to mock me?

ORESTES: It pains me to deny it; oh, how I wish . . .

MENELAUS: You had done what? Your words frighten me!

ORESTES: . . . I had flung that woman who polluted Greece
down to Hades' kingdom!

MENELAUS: Give me back my wife's body – let me bury her!

ORESTES: Ask her back from the gods; but I will kill your
daughter.

MENELAUS: Was the stain of her mother's blood not enough
for you?

ORESTES: I will never tire of killing wicked women.   1590

MENELAUS: And you, Pylades, do you also share his murderous
act?

ORESTES: His silence proclaims he does;[77] my words will suffice.

MENELAUS: You won't get away with this, unless you have
wings for your escape!

ORESTES: We do not intend escape; we mean to set the palace
on fire.

MENELAUS: What? You mean to destroy this house of your
fathers?

ORESTES: Yes – to keep you from possessing it, and I will sacrifice this woman as well over the flames!

MENELAUS: Then be a killer – you will feel the vengeance of my hand for this!

1598

ORESTES: Be silent then, and accept with patience the misfortune you have justly earned!

[ORESTES *raises his sword above* HERMIONE.]

MENELAUS: Oh, take your sword away from my daughter![78]

ORESTES: You are a born liar!

MENELAUS: You are going to kill my daughter?

ORESTES: But now you tell the truth!

MENELAUS: Oh, this is agony! What shall I do?

1610

ORESTES: Go to the Argives and urge them . . .

MENELAUS: What should I urge?

ORESTES: Beg the people to spare our lives.

MENELAUS: Or you will murder my child?

ORESTES: Yes.

MENELAUS: Is it just that you should live?

1600

ORESTES: Yes, and that I should rule this land besides!

MENELAUS: What land?

ORESTES: Here in Pelasgian Argos.

MENELAUS: How fitting that would be – you touching the holy vessels . . .

ORESTES: Why should I not?

MENELAUS: . . . and performing sacrifice before battle!

ORESTES: You would do so with honour, would you?

MENELAUS: Yes; my hands are not polluted.

ORESTES: But your heart is!

MENELAUS: What man would speak to you?

ORESTES: Anyone who loves his father.

MENELAUS: And what about one who honours his mother?

ORESTES: He's a lucky man!

MENELAUS: Well, you are not.

ORESTES: I agree; I hate women who are wicked.

MENELAUS: O Helen, how I pity you . . .

ORESTES: Are my sufferings not to be pitied?

MENELAUS: ... I brought you back from Troy to be a sacrifice ...

ORESTES: I wish she had been!

MENELAUS: ... and many a long, hard labour it cost me!

ORESTES: For me you endured no hardship.

MENELAUS: This treatment is outrageous!

ORESTES: You were no friend to me before.

MENELAUS: You have me in your grip.

ORESTES: You have trapped yourself by having no principles. Come, Electra, set this house on fire! And you, Pylades, truest of my friends, light up the roof and battlements here!   1620

MENELAUS: O land of Danaus' people, men who dwell in horse-rearing Argos, come, take up weapons and run to our aid! This man who has defiled himself with the blood of his own mother is seeking to live by doing violence to your whole city!

[APOLLO *appears on high,*[79] *with* HELEN *at his side.*]

APOLLO: Menelaus, your anger has too sharp an edge – curb it now! It is I who stand near and call upon you – Phoebus, son of Leto! And you, Orestes, standing guard with sword over this girl, cease, so you may hear the words I bring.

As to Helen, whom you failed to kill for all your eagerness, stirred by anger against Menelaus, I saved her from your   1630
sword, snatching her up at the bidding of my father Zeus. As the child of Zeus it is her fate to live immortal; in the distant heavens she will sit enthroned with Castor and Polydeuces, bringing safety to mariners.[80] For the gods used this woman's unequalled beauty to make Greeks and Phrygians clash in war; they caused men to die in order to rid the earth of its   1640
complement of mortals,[81] who had swollen in arrogance as in number.

So much for the destiny of Helen. You, Orestes, are fated in turn to quit the borders of this land and for the cycle of one year to dwell on Parrhasian soil, that shall be called after your name in memory of your exile there. From that place you are to journey to the city of the Athenians and submit to prosecution by the three Furies for spilling the blood of your mother in murder. On Ares' Hill gods shall sit in judgement at your trial and cast their votes most righteously; here you are destined to prevail.[82]

As for Hermione, at whose throat you hold your sword, Orestes, it is fated that you take her as your wife. The man who thinks that he will marry her, Neoptolemus,[83] shall never win her hand; he is destined to die by Delphian swords when he seeks recompense from me for the death of his father Achilles. Give Pylades your sister's hand in marriage – you promised her to him once; a life of happiness awaits him in the years to come.

And you, Menelaus, do not stand in the way of Orestes' ruling over Argos. Go to the land of Sparta and be king there, enjoying that as your wife's dowry – she has now ceased to bring you countless troubles, as she did before. As for this man's low standing with the folk of Argos, I compelled him to murder his mother and I will reconcile them to him.

ORESTES: O prophetic Loxias, then your oracles came from no false lips but were true? And yet I began to fear that I might have heard some spirit of vengeance[84] and only imagined hearing your voice. But it is a happy conclusion and I will do as you say. See, I release Hermione from sacrifice, and when her father gives his consent I'll gladly marry her!

MENELAUS: O Helen, child of Zeus, farewell! I envy you the blessed home you will have among the gods! Orestes, I betroth my daughter to you, at Phoebus' command.

Your blood is noble, as is your bride's – may she bring happiness to you, and to me who give her to you!

APOLLO: Take now the various paths I have prescribed and relinquish your strife!

MENELAUS: We must obey.

ORESTES: I agree. I call a truce, Menelaus, with what has passed between us, and likewise, Loxias, with your oracles.

APOLLO: Depart now on your journeys and pay honour to the fairest of divinities, Peace! I will convey Helen to the dwelling of Zeus, after traversing the star-bright vault of heaven, where she shall sit enthroned beside Hera and Hebe, wife of Heracles, forever receiving the tribute of men's libations and, with her brothers, sons of Tyndareus and of Zeus, ruling over the watery ocean for mariners. 1690

[APOLLO *and* HELEN *withdraw;* ORESTES, PYLADES, ELECTRA *and* HERMIONE *descend into the house;* MENE-LAUS *and his attendants march off stage. Only the* CHORUS *remain.*]

CHORUS: O Victory, most holy, support my life and do not cease from giving me your crown![85]

[*Exit.*]

BACCHAE

PREFACE TO *BACCHAE*

The *Bacchae* is in some ways the quintessential Greek tragedy, not only because of its emotional intensity and potent dramatic ironies, but because it deals with the god of the dramatic festivals. It dramatizes the vengeance of Dionysus, newly arrived in Greece, upon the hapless King Pentheus, who not only refuses to offer him worship but threatens and imprisons him and tries to hunt down his followers. The theme is traditional. Aeschylus had composed a *Pentheus*, and indeed seems to have presented a whole trilogy which dealt with Dionysus' confrontation with his opponents. This is a recurring theme in Greek mythology: a mortal defies a god, and is punished (thus in the *Iliad* Patroclus overreaches himself in battle, defying the warning of Apollo to fall back, and Apollo strikes him down; and Niobe, who boasted she had borne more children than the goddess Leto, was forced to witness Leto's children Apollo and Artemis destroying her own). Gods can work their will from afar (as does Aphrodite in *Hippolytus* or Hera in *Heracles*), but here the god not only appears in the prologue, but dominates the play, playing an active part in the events, though in disguise. Here again we have a recurring motif, that of the god who walks among men in order to test their piety. As far as we can see, it was uncommon by this date for a god to play so prominent a part in the action of a Greek tragedy: elsewhere in Euripides' work they figure in prologue or epilogue, occasionally in both, but the main part of the play focuses on the human actors. Things were different on the stage of Aeschylus, and this is one of a number of ways in which the play can be seen as 'archaic' in design.

The story patterns we have already identified in the play make it obvious that the conclusion will be the triumphant vengeance of the god and the punishment of the human transgressor: such is the nature of Greek religion, at least as presented in serious drama. But the position is complicated by the identity of the god. All Greek divinities have their terrifying aspects, but Dionysus is a particularly complex figure, hard to assess. He is a bringer of joy and celebration, but also the cause of violence and madness. Even the gift of wine is two-edged, but Dionysus is far more than the god of drinking: he is a god of inspiration and intoxication in every form. In this play he is also a god of the wild: he and his votaries are at home on the mountain-side, and the departure of the Theban women for the hills is seen by Pentheus as a threat to the political order of the male-dominated *polis*. Dionysus is represented as a new arrival in Greece, exotic, alien, sinister, yet seductive. In the play itself he and the cult he represents are seen in many different lights, none of which does full justice to the god. Does he bring salvation or chaos, ecstasy or insanity? He himself declares that he is 'most gentle to mortals', but also 'most terrible' (861).

It has often been assumed that the *Bacchae* shows us what the Greeks actually believed about Dionysus, and that Bacchic rites involving slaughter of beasts (perhaps even men) were practised in ancient Greece, if only in prehistoric times. Caution is necessary here: the play is a mythical drama, set in the distant past. The idea that Dionysus was originally a foreign god and only imported into Greek religion at a relatively late stage has been exploded by the discovery of the god's name in Linear B tablets, over 500 years before Euripides' birth (cf. note 3). Similarly the play must not be treated as a window on to Athenian reality. It is indeed important that the terrible events of the play take place in Thebes, not Athens: as often, other cities suffer horrors and experience supernatural assaults of a kind which the tragic poets refrain from inflicting on their own city, even in myth. Even in the mythical world of the play, it is made clear that Agaue and the rest of the Theban women are not 'normal' maenads, unlike the chorus: they have been driven mad by Dionysus and forced to the hills: at one point they are experiencing a wondrous closeness to nature and performing miracles, at another they are filled with supernatural strength and murderous violence. This kind of maenadism cannot correspond with any historical reality. It seems, in any case, that actual

maenadism (meaning the ecstatic worship of Dionysus by women) was
not a feature of Athenian cults of the gods, though there is clear
evidence that it did exist in Thebes – in a more moderate and regulated
form than the uncontrollable and violent frenzy of the Theban women
in the *Bacchae*. Athenian women sometimes journeyed to take part in
the Theban celebrations, but at fixed times and for a brief period, after
which they returned to their accustomed domestic lives. In short, myth
exaggerates and tragedy dramatizes: what is terrible and dangerous in
myth is orderly and ritualized in cult. Art and poetry naturally prefer
the more dramatic and exotic versions of Dionysiac ritual.

Perhaps the most memorable aspect of the play is the interaction
between Dionysus and Pentheus, whereby the king, at first blustering
defiance of the god, gradually falls under his influence and becomes
first his butt, finally his victim. The characterization of Pentheus is a
fascinating study. He could have been made a majestic but misguided
king, rather like Eteocles in Aeschylus' *Seven against Thebes* or Creon
in Sophocles' *Antigone*. Or he might have been a stock tyrant, like
Lycus in the *Heracles*, whose overthrow no spectator mourns: the play
would have been a straightforward vindication of the god. Instead we
find something typically Euripidean: a young ruler who shares some
of the features of the tyrant (aggressive outspokenness, a tendency to
bully, a refusal to listen to reason), but also one who is weak and
perhaps uncertain of himself. He repeatedly assumes that the Bacchic
rites mask some form of sexual orgy, persisting in this belief even after
the messenger has insisted on its falsehood. His taunting of Dionysus
for his good looks also has a whiff of sexuality about it. It is his secret
eagerness to see the Bacchants 'lying together in the bushes' that
Dionysus discerns and exploits. In the later scenes he is not himself –
mesmerized or maddened, for Dionysus is a god who presides over
delusion and madness – but the god's manipulation of his victim would
not be so disturbing if we did not feel that he is drawing out something
in Pentheus himself. No two readers will think exactly alike about
Pentheus' psychology; but the macabre scenes in which we witness
Dionysus attaining the dominant role, the king dressing up as a maenad,
and his excited anticipation of his triumphal return from the mountain
make an unforgettable sequence. There are a number of indications,

both within the play and in vase-paintings of the myth, that the 'standard' version may have involved Pentheus unsuccessfully attacking Dionysus and his followers at the head of an army; but the plot of the *Bacchae* involves his dressing up as a maenad in order to spy on them. The hypothesis that this is Euripides' innovation cannot be proved, but has seemed likely to many.

In the *Orestes*, as we have seen, Euripides carried his innovations of tragic form and style to unparalleled extremes: disruption of regular act divisions, play with dramatic conventions, the tour de force of the Phrygian's song, and so forth. A few years later, the *Bacchae* represents a decisive change of direction, back not only to a traditional theme famously handled by Aeschylus, but also to more austere metrical and formal practice. The play contains no sustained *agon*, unlike almost every play by this poet (the dispute between Pentheus, Cadmus and Teiresias does not have the highly rhetorical quality we find in the *agon*-scenes of the other plays in this volume). Choral odes predominate over actor-lyric: there are no monodies of the type mocked by Aristophanes, only the short lyric exchange between Agaue and the chorus, a mere thirty lines. The chorus's role is less peripheral, and their odes are long, frequent and important: they also lack the mannerisms and love of repetition which we meet so often in the *Orestes*. Some of what they sing recalls the grandeur of Aeschylean meditation on the workings of divine justice, and there are also specific imitations of Aeschylus' Dionysiac plays. The imitation of Aeschylus goes so far that Euripides even revives the refrain, virtually unknown elsewhere in his work (this may also owe something to songs performed in religious contexts). The whole play is more tightly constructed than others of this period, lacking digressions and extraneous characters. The emotions and pathos of the finale have special force because they are framed in so relatively rigid a form.

Despite the archaizing touches, the play remains very recognizably the work of Euripides. The interest in ecstatic or irrational religious cult is already attested in a well-known fragment of the *Cretans*, an early play (fr. 472), which mentions initiation, night-time feasting, eating of flesh and other exotic practices. The ode in the *Helen* invoking the Mountain Mother, Cybele, also belongs to this world: the rites of

Dionysus and Rhea/Cybele are akin, as is mentioned more than once in the *Bacchae*. Some other dramatic elements seem familiar from the poet's earlier work: the avenging god reminds us of Aphrodite's punishment of the hero of *Hippolytus*; the violence inflicted by women recalls *Medea* and *Hecuba*; the scene in which Agaue is coaxed back to sanity by Cadmus is reminiscent of the awakening of Heracles from madness; the painful parting of Agaue and Cadmus at the end of the play resembles the departure into exile of Orestes, parted from his sister in the *Electra*. But while we may readily identify certain items in the tragedian's repertoire, the ingredients do not account for the compound: the *Bacchae* retains its unique status as a drama of divine persecution and religious fanaticism.

The greatest of Euripides' dramas is naturally the most difficult to sum up. At one time it was regarded as an authentically religious drama, evidence that at the end of his life the poet had renounced the philosophic or sceptical beliefs which many had detected in his work. This position is hard to maintain: although Pentheus' defiance of the god is wrong and his punishment inevitable, the severity of divine retribution, involving the killing of a son by his mother, dismays any audience, and Cadmus at the end of the play protests that the god 'goes too far'. The prophet Teiresias does not make a very effective advocate of Dionysiac worship: in that scene we can surely see some hint of the 'sceptical' Euripides, poking fun at Teiresias' self-interested appropriation of the new god. However, the antithetical position, to see the play as an attack on Dionysus or a critique of ecstatic religion (or of the irrational in general) seems equally misguided. The play cannot be reduced to simplistic formulae like these. Even the conclusion of the sensitive study by Winnington-Ingram, that 'Euripides recognized Dionysus but hated him', seems vulnerable, not only because it looks behind the play to the playwright's supposed personal opinions, now irrecoverable, but because 'Dionysus' is made to stand for a whole medley of things, including mob emotion and unthinking collective action. Interpreters can understand the play on many levels and find within it many polarities: man versus god, culture versus nature, individual versus group, foreigner versus Greek, reason versus unreason, inhibition or repression versus self-fulfilment. Gender, sexuality and the family are also clearly significant aspects: it is the women who respond to the Dionysiac command, abandoning their homes and families; it is Agaue his mother who leads the way in the slaughter of her son. Both son and mother expect that the other will take delight in their success; the bond between them is clearly a close and intimate one. Seldom has the truth of Aristotle's precept that tragedy is most effective when played out between members of the family been so clearly demonstrated.

No single reading can exhaust this paradigmatic tragedy. From another angle, the play can be seen in metatextual terms: a play about playing parts. Cadmus and Teiresias dress up as Bacchic worshippers, a scene which does not lack humour; the same scene is echoed later in the play when Pentheus, under the sway of the god, goes as far as to don female attire and practises carrying the Bacchic thyrsus. Illusion and delusion are widely prevalent in the play: at one point Dionysus eludes his captor and leaves him struggling to bind a bull, under the impression that he has Dionysus in his power; soon afterwards the god creates a double of himself. Dionysus himself, of course, is in disguise throughout: the god of tragedy tries his hand at the typically tragic technique of ironic double-meaning (e.g. lines 498, 502, 518). In one key scene Dionysus asks the question which has perplexed theorists of tragedy: 'would you really like to see what gives you pain?' (815). Dionysus, ironic questioner and stage-manager of the action, is a double of the poet himself. The difference is that the god lacks the dramatist's compassion.

CHARACTERS

DIONYSUS (*also called Bacchus, Bromius, Evius*)
CHORUS *of Bacchants, women of Asia*
TEIRESIAS, *the blind prophet of Thebes*
CADMUS, *founder and former King of Thebes*
PENTHEUS, *King of Thebes and grandson of Cadmus*
SERVANT *of Pentheus*
FIRST MESSENGER, *a herdsman from Cithaeron*
SECOND MESSENGER, *a servant of Pentheus*
AGAUE, *mother of Pentheus and daughter of Cadmus*
Guards, attendants

[*The scene is outside the royal palace on the citadel of Thebes.
There is a tomb on stage, with smoke rising from it, and a
surrounding fence covered with ivy-shoots.*]

[*Enter* DIONYSUS.]

DIONYSUS: Newly arrived in this land of Thebes, I am
Dionysus, son of Zeus, whom Semele, child of Cadmus, once
bore, delivered by the lightning-flame.[1] I have changed my
appearance from a god's to a man's,[2] as I come to Dirce's
stream and the waters of Ismenus. And here close by the palace
I see the tomb of my mother, whose life the thunderbolt
ended, and the wreckage of her home that smoulders with
the still living flame of Zeus' fire, immortal token of Hera's
10   outrage against my mother. Cadmus has my approval: he has
consecrated this ground as holy, where his daughter may have
her tomb. But the green vine that clusters round it in a wreath
was my work. I come from Lydia's fields[3] abundant in gold,
and Phrygia's. Persia's sunny uplands have I traversed, Bactria's
walled cities and the bleak land of the Medes, rich Arabia,
too, and all of Asia that lies by the salt sea and boasts fair-
towered cities full of mingled Greeks and barbarians together.
20   Now to this city of Greeks have I come first, to make my
godhead plain for mortal men to see, now that I have set those
peoples dancing and instituted there my worship.

First in the land of Greece I have made this city of Thebes
resound to women's cries, dressing them in fawnskins and
putting the thyrsus in their hands, my ivy-bound spear. My
mother's sisters – they should have been the last ones to do

this – claimed that Dionysus was no son of Zeus. Semele, they said, had been seduced by some mortal and was attributing to Zeus the loss of her virginity – a pretence they ascribed to Cadmus. Because of this lie she had told about her lover, they announced gloatingly, Zeus had killed her. 30

For this reason I have spurred those same sisters to madness and driven them in distraction from their houses. They now have the mountain as their home and their wits have deserted them. I have made them wear the dress that suits my worship. So all the female seed of Cadmus' people, all the womenfolk, I have caused to quit their homes in frenzy. With the daughters of Cadmus in their midst they sit beneath the green firs, on rocks open to the sky. This city must learn its lesson, however reluctantly, that it lacks the blessing of my rites. I must defend 40 the cause of Semele, my mother, by showing myself to mortals as the god she bore to Zeus.

Now Cadmus has given the kingship and its powers to Pentheus, his daughter's son, who makes war on divinity in my person by thrusting me away from his sacrifices and making no mention of me in his prayers. Because of this I mean to 50 reveal myself as a true god to him and to everyone in Thebes. When I have settled matters here satisfactorily, I shall turn my steps to another land and reveal myself there. But if the people of Thebes, growing angry, take up arms and seek to drive my followers from the mountain, I shall engage them, leading my maenads into battle.[4] This is why I have assumed mortal shape and transformed myself into the likeness of a man.

[He addresses the CHORUS, who are beginning to file into the orchestra, as if in response to his will.]

Ho, my band of worshippers, you women who left Tmolus that stands guard over Lydia! I brought you from among barbarians and you have been my companions on the march and at rest. Now rouse the kettledrums native to the land of the Phrygians, the invention of Mother Rhea and myself,[5] 60 come, beat them around the palace of Pentheus here, so that Cadmus' citizens may see! I will go to where my Bacchants

are, in Cithaeron's glens, and join in their dances. [*Exit*
DIONYSUS.]

CHORUS [*chanting as they enter*]:⁶ *From Asia's land I come, forsaking
sacred Tmolus, in my eagerness to perform my joyous labours for the
Roaring One,⁷ the toil that brings no toil, crying 'Evoe'⁸ to the Lord
of Bacchants. Who is in the street? Who is in the street? Who is in*
70   *the house? Let him make way, let every man make himself wholly
pure by keeping reverent silence. For I am about to sing to Dionysus
hymns ever honoured by custom.*

[*singing:*] [Strophe:] *Blessed is the man who has the good fortune
to know the gods' mysteries, who consecrates his life and makes his
soul one with the throng, worshipping Bacchus in the mountains with
holy purifications. Observing the rites of Cybele, the Great Mother,*
80   *he whirls his thyrsus on high as, garlanded with ivy, he serves
Dionysus. On you Bacchants, on you Bacchants! Bring home the
Roaring One, god and son of god, Dionysus, from the mountains of
Phrygia to the spacious streets of Greece, bring the Roaring One!*

[Antistrophe:] *While his mother was carrying him,⁹ Zeus'*
90   *thunderbolt flew, and, in forced pains of labour she bore him, shed
untimely from her womb, and died from the stroke of the lightning.
At once Zeus, son of Cronus, stored him in a secret birth-chamber
and concealed him in his own thigh, fastening him with golden clasps,
hidden from the eyes of Hera. And when the Fates had brought round*
100   *the appointed time, he gave birth to a god with bull's horns¹⁰ and
crowned him with a garland of serpents, whence it is that maenads
entwine in their hair wild serpents they have caught.¹¹*

[Strophe:] *O Thebes, nurse of Semele, garland yourself with
ivy! Teem, teem with green, bright-berried bryony, and become true*
110   *Bacchants by wearing sprigs of oak or fir! Trim the hems of your
dappled fawnskins with white tufts of braided wool, and show rever-
ence when you wield the wand with its violence. Soon the whole land
will be dancing, when the Roaring One leads his groups of worshippers
to the mountain, to the mountain, where the female throng awaits
him, driven from their places at loom and shuttle by the madness of
Dionysus.*

[Antistrophe:] *O secret chamber of the Curetes,*[12] *sacred haunts of Crete that saw the birth of Zeus, where the Corybantes with triple* 120 *helmet devised for me in the cavern this circle of stretched hide; and in the fierce dance of ecstasy they blended its sound with the sweet-voiced breath of Phrygian flutes and placed it in the hands of Mother Rhea to beat time for the joyous cries of her worshippers; and from the goddess mother the crazed Satyrs took it for their own, and joined* 130 *it to the dances of the second-year feast that delights Dionysus.*[13]

[Epode:] *He is a delight to see*[14] *on the mountains when he leaves the running bands to fall to the ground, wearing his holy garment of fawnskin, hunting the blood of the slaughtered goat, carnivorous delight,*[15] *as he rushes on to the mountains of Phrygia, of Lydia; he* 140 *is the Roaring One, the leader of our dance. Evoe! The ground flows with milk, flows with wine, flows with the nectar of bees. The Bacchic One raises on high the pine torch, its blazing flame fragrant as fumes of Syrian frankincense, and makes it stream from his wand, as with running and dancing he spurs on the stragglers and stirs them with his call, tossing his delicate curls in the air. Among the worshippers'* 150 *cries his voice bellows: 'On you Bacchants, on you Bacchants, you pride of Tmolus that flows with gold, sing the praises of Dionysus to the booming kettledrums, celebrating with "Evoe!" the god Evius, with Phrygian crying and clamour, when the holy and melodious flute sends out its notes of holy joyfulness, fit measures as you troop to the* 160 *mountain, to the mountain!' Oh, with happy heart, then, like a filly at its mother's side as she grazes in the pasture, leaps the worshipper, gambolling on swift feet!*

[*Enter* TEIRESIAS,[16] *old and blind, in the costume of a Bacchant.*]
TEIRESIAS: Who is on duty at the gates? Call Cadmus out of the palace, Agenor's son, who left Sidon's town and founded 170 this towered city of the Thebans![17]

One of you, go and announce that Teiresias is seeking him. He himself knows my reasons for coming and the pact we made, one old man with another older still, to bind the thyrsus and wear fawnskins and crown our heads with shoots of ivy.

[Enter from the palace CADMUS, *similarly dressed.]*

CADMUS: My dear friend, for I heard and recognized your voice
inside the palace – the wise voice of a wise man! Here I am
180 ready, wearing the god's livery as you see. He is my own
daughter's child, and, so far as we have the strength, we must
exalt him to greatness. Where must I go and dance? Where
set my foot and shake this grey head? Explain to me, Teiresias,
one old man to another; you have the wisdom. Night or day
I will never tire of pounding my thyrsus on the ground; in
my pleasure I have forgotten that I am old.

TEIRESIAS: Then you feel as I do. I, too, am young again; I,
190 too, will attempt the dance.

CADMUS: Shall we not go to the mountain by carriage?[18]

TEIRESIAS: This would not be showing the same honour to the
god.

CADMUS: Shall I take you – one old man playing nursemaid to
another?

TEIRESIAS: The god will lead us there with no effort.

CADMUS: Are we the only Thebans prepared to dance for
Bacchus?

TEIRESIAS: Yes; we are alone in being of sound mind; the rest
are not.

CADMUS: We waste time delaying; take hold of my hand!

TEIRESIAS *[stretching out his hand]*: There, clasp it and make a
pair of them.

CADMUS: I am of mortal birth and so do not despise the gods.

TEIRESIAS: We do not chop logic when speaking of divinity.[19]
200 The traditions of our forefathers that we have inherited, as old
as time, shall not be overthrown by any clever argument,
though it be devised by the subtlest of wits.

CADMUS: It will be said I have no shame at my age, intending
to dance with my head bound with ivy.

TEIRESIAS: No; the god has made no distinction between
young and old, in calling them to the dance. He wishes to
receive honour from all alike and to be exalted without
exception.

CADMUS: Since you do not see this light, Teiresias, I will serve
as your interpreter now. Here comes Pentheus, Echion's son,   210
to whom I have entrusted sovereignty of Thebes. He is
hurrying towards the palace. How excited he is![20] What news
will he have to tell?

[PENTHEUS *enters in haste with attendants. He is at first un-*
aware of CADMUS *and* TEIRESIAS.[21]]

PENTHEUS: I've been out of the country, as it happens, but
tales of strange goings-on in Thebes,[22] criminal actions, have
brought me back. They say our womenfolk have left home
on a pretence of Bacchic worship, and are frolicking in the
dark mountain-glens, honouring with dances the parvenu god   220
Dionysus, whoever he may be. In the middle of their bands,
I hear, stand mixing bowls filled to the brim, and one by one
they creep off to lonely places to serve the lusts of men.[23] In
this, of course, they pretend to be inspired priestesses of their
god, but actually they rank Aphrodite above Bacchus. Some
of them I have caught, and my guards hold them fast with
tied wrists in the public gaol.[24] The rest who are still at large
I'll hunt from the mountain; I'll bind them in iron nets and
soon put an end to this pernicious revelling!   230

They say that some foreigner has arrived from the land of
Lydia, a wizard conjuror, with fragrant golden curls and the
flush of wine in his complexion. In his eyes he has the charms
of Aphrodite, and day and night he escorts young women,
luring them with the prospect of his joyous mysteries. If I
catch him inside the borders of this land, I'll cut his head off
his shoulders[25] and put a stop to his making his thyrsus ring
and shaking his locks! This is the man who says that Dionysus   240
is a god, this the man who says he was once sewn into the
thigh of Zeus, when in fact he was destroyed by the fiery
lightning bolt, he and his mother, because she falsely named
Zeus as her lover![26] Is this not monstrous, does it not merit
the hangman's noose, to commit acts of such insolence,
whoever the stranger may be?

[*He suddenly becomes aware of the two old men.*]

But here's another sight to marvel at! It's the prophet Teiresias
I see in dappled fawnskins and my own mother's father – how
250   ridiculous – playing the Bacchant, complete with wand! [*To*
      CADMUS:] Sir, I am embarrassed by the sight of you both –
so old, so foolish! Shake off that ivy! Rid your hand of the
thyrsus, Grandfather! You're the one who put him up to this,
Teiresias! You want to foist one more god as a novelty on
mankind and so to scan the flight of birds and take more fees
for burned sacrifice![27] If your grey hairs did not protect you,
260   I'd have you bound and sitting among the Bacchants for
seeking to import these pernicious rites! Where women are
concerned, when the grape gleams liquid at feasts, I say there
is nothing wholesome left in their ceremonies!

CHORUS-LEADER: What blasphemy! Stranger, have you no
      reverence for the gods, or for Cadmus who sowed the earth-
      born crop?[28] Will you disgrace the family of Echion, though
      you are his son?

TEIRESIAS: When a clever man has an honest case to make, it
      is no great task for him to speak well. You possess a fluent
      tongue, as if you were a man of sense, but your words lack
270   all judgement. The good speaker whose influence rests on
      self-assurance proves to be a bad citizen; for he lacks intel-
      ligence.[29]

This new god[30] whom you mock will achieve a greatness I
cannot describe throughout Greece. Men enjoy two great
blessings, young man: firstly, the goddess Demeter, the Earth
– call her by whichever name you will – who sustains mankind
by means of dry foods; then there is he who came afterwards,
Semele's son, who invented the liquid draught of the grape
to match her gift and introduced it to mortals. This it is that
280   puts an end to the sorrows of wretched men, when they get
their fill of the flowing vine, this that confers sleep on them
and forgetfulness of daily troubles. There is no other antidote
to suffering. He, a god himself, is poured out in honour of
the gods, so that he is the cause of man's blessings.[31]

Do you mock the notion that he was sewn into the thigh

of Zeus? I will instruct you in the truth of this. When Zeus
snatched him from the lightning flames and carried the infant
child to Olympus, Hera wanted to cast him out of heaven.   290
But Zeus devised a plan to counter this, as well a god might.
He broke off a portion of the ether that envelops the earth,
and giving this to Hera as a hostage he rescued Dionysus from
her spitefulness. But in time mortals said that Zeus' thigh was
host to the god, making up the story by the change of a word,
for he served as *hostage* once to Hera, god to goddess. And he
is a prophet, this god. For those who experience his power and
those who are touched by madness possess no small measure of
prophecy. When the god enters the body in full strength, he   300
makes men mad and gives them the gift of prophecy. He also
has assumed a certain part of Ares' functions. For when troops
are armed and standing in ranks, they are sometimes struck
with panic before lifting a spear. This, too, is a madness sent
by Dionysus.

You shall yet see him on Delphi's rocky summit,[32] bounding
across the upland with its twin peaks, brandishing and
flourishing his Bacchic wand, a mighty force throughout
Greece.

Take to heart what I say, Pentheus: don't be too sure that
force is what controls human affairs; and, if you have a thought   310
and your thought is unhealthy, do not think your folly is
wisdom. Receive the god into your land, pour libations,
worship Bacchus and garland your head! It is not for Dionysus
to force women to show chastity in the affairs of love; this lies
in their own nature. You should reflect on this: even in
performing the rites of Bacchus the woman of virtue will not
be corrupted. Don't you see how pleased you are when
crowds line the gates and the name of 'Pentheus' swells in the   320
praise of your people? He, too, I think, takes pleasure in
receiving honour.[33] Now Cadmus, whom you laugh at, and
I will wear wreaths of ivy and join in the dancing, two old grey
heads together, but dance we must. I will not be persuaded by
your words to fight against the gods. For you are mad, most

painfully mad; you can find no cure for your malady, either with drugs or without them.

CHORUS-LEADER: Old man, these words of yours bring credit to Phoebus, and in honouring the Roaring One, a mighty god, you show good sense.

CADMUS [to PENTHEUS]: My boy, it is good advice that Teiresias has given you: live with us and not beyond the bounds of convention. For you are up in the air at the moment; you have your senses but you are senseless. Even if, as you say, this god does not exist, say that he does.[34] To declare that he is Semele's child is a lie that does us credit: people will think she gave birth to a god and the honour will reflect on us, on the whole family. You recall the pitiful end of Actaeon,[35] torn apart by the ravenous hounds he had reared, because he boasted that he was a greater hunter in the mountain glades than Artemis.

Do not let this fate overtake you! [He moves towards PENTHEUS.] Come here, let me put this crown of ivy on your head; join us in giving honour to the god!

PENTHEUS [stepping back in revulsion]: Hands off! Go and play your Bacchic games, but don't smear me with your stupidity! [Turning to face TEIRESIAS:] This man, though, your instructor in folly, will answer to me! [To his attendants:] Quick, one of you, go to this fellow's seat where he watches birds, heave it up with crowbars, and turn it upside down! Throw everything there into confusion, fling his holy ribbons to the winds and breezes! This way I will cause him greater torment than anything. And you others, go through the town and track down the womanish stranger, who infects our women with his new-fangled disease and pollutes their beds. Once he is caught, bind him and bring him here to face the penalty of being stoned to death, after seeing a painful end to his revelling in Thebes. [PENTHEUS leaves, preceded by his attendants.]

TEIRESIAS: Wicked man, you do not know what you are saying. Now you are truly mad; before you had lost your head. Let us go, Cadmus, and make our prayers for him, savage though he is, and for the city, asking the god to do nothing untoward.[36] Keep me company with your staff of ivy, and try to hold me up, as I shall you. It would be shameful for two old men to fall; still, let it happen, if it must. We must serve our master, Bacchus, the son of Zeus. But I only hope that Pentheus does not bring sorrow[37] on your house, Cadmus, and prove his name true. It is not prophecy that makes me say this, but the facts; a fool speaks foolish words.

[*The two old men leave the stage.*]

CHORUS [Strophe]: *Holiness, queen among the gods! Holiness, who fly over the earth on your golden wings, do you hear these words of*   370 *Pentheus? Do you hear his unholy contempt for the Roaring One, Semele's son, the god who is first among the Blessed Ones, where fair garlands adorn delightful pleasures? These are his gifts: to make men dance together as one, to rejoice at the sound of the flute, and to*   380 *put an end to care, when the liquid gleam of the grape enters the feasts of the gods and in the ivy-wreathed feasts of men the wine-bowl casts its veil of sleep over them.*

[Antistrophe:] *The end of tongues uncurbed and lawless foolishness is unhappiness; but the life of quiet contentment and good sense survives the buffeting of the sea and keeps homes together; for though*   390 *they dwell far off in the sky, yet the heavenly ones observe the deeds of men.*

To be clever is not to be wise,[38] *and thoughts that go beyond mortal limits spell a short life. In view of this who would pursue great ambitions rather than accept his present lot? These are the ways of madmen, in my verdict, whose wits have left them.*   400

[Strophe:] *Oh, that I might come to Cyprus,*[39] *Aphrodite's isle, where dwell the Loves who cast their spell on mortal hearts, to Paphos, enriched without rain by streams of the barbarian river with its hundred mouths, and to the fairest land of Pieria, that the Muses have as their home, on the holy slope of Olympus. Oh, take me there, Roaring*   410 *One, Roaring One, god who leads your Bacchants, spirit of joy! There are the Graces, there is Desire, there your worshippers have leave to celebrate your name.*

[*Antistrophe:*] *The god, the son of Zeus, delights in feasts, and*
420 *loves Peace, bestower of wealth, goddess who nurtures young men.
Equally to rich and lowly he gives the joy of wine that knows no
grief; but he hates the man who has no care for this: by day and
blissful night to live the life of blessedness, and in true wisdom to
keep mind and understanding apart from men of excess. Whatever*
430 *humanity at large believes and makes its rule of conduct, that I would
accept.*

[*Enter a* SOLDIER *with one or more companions. They bring
with them the Lydian stranger, his arms trussed behind him, and
make straight for* PENTHEUS, *who enters from the opposite side
of the stage, with attendants.*]

SOLDIER: Here we are, Pentheus, we've caught the prey you
sent us after[40] – a successful mission! But we found this a tame
beast; he didn't turn and run from us, but surrendered his
hands willingly. He didn't turn pale, or change his ruddy
complexion, but with a smile[41] told us to bind and take him
prisoner, and he waited, making my task easy. I was ashamed,
440 and said to him, 'Stranger, it's not my idea to take you prisoner;
these are the orders of Pentheus, who sent me.'

But the Bacchants you imprisoned, the ones you seized and
put in chains in the public gaol – they're loosed and are
dancing away to the mountain-glades, calling upon Bromius
their god. Without the action of any guard the fetters were
loosed from their ankles, and the bolts let the doors swing
open untouched by mortal hand. Full of many wonders has
450 this man come here to Thebes – but what comes next is yours
to consider.

PENTHEUS: Untie his hands; now that he's in the net, he's not
quick enough to escape me. [*He turns from the soldiers to examine*
DIONYSUS.] Well, stranger, your body is not without
beauty,[42] to women's taste, at least, which is your reason for
being in Thebes. Those locks of yours are long, not a
wrestler's, then, and they ripple right down your cheek, most
alluringly. Your skin is fair, a deliberate ploy as you keep out

of the sun's rays and in the shade, using your prettiness to
hunt Aphrodite! First then tell me your birth. 460

DIONYSUS: I can tell you this without hesitation; it is easy to
answer. You know of flowery Tmolus, I take it, from hear-
say?

PENTHEUS: I do; it encloses in its embrace the town of Sardis.

DIONYSUS: That is my home, and Lydia is my native land.

PENTHEUS: How is it that you are bringing these rites to
Greece?

DIONYSUS: Dionysus himself initiated me,[43] the son of Zeus.

PENTHEUS: Is there a Zeus there who fathers new gods?[44]

DIONYSUS: No, it is the one who wedded Semele here.

PENTHEUS: Did he compel you in the hours of night or to your
face, when you were awake?

DIONYSUS: He saw me and I him, and he gave me his rites. 470

PENTHEUS: What is the nature of these rites of yours?

DIONYSUS: They are secrets that only Bacchus' initiates may
know.

PENTHEUS: What benefit do they bring to his worshippers?

DIONYSUS: You are not permitted to learn, but it is knowledge
worth having.

PENTHEUS: A false answer but a clever one, to make me want
to hear!

DIONYSUS: The god's rites hate the man who practises impiety.

PENTHEUS: This god, since you say you saw him clearly, how
did he look?

DIONYSUS: As he wished to be; *I* did not order it.

PENTHEUS: Again you sidetrack me – with a clever and mean-
ingless answer!

DIONYSUS: He who speaks wisdom to a fool will be thought a
fool himself. 480

PENTHEUS: Is this the first place you have come to with your
god?

DIONYSUS: Every one of the foreigners is dancing these rites.

PENTHEUS: That's because they have much less sense than
Greeks.[45]

DIONYSUS: In this case they have more; their customs, how-ever, differ.

PENTHEUS: Do you perform these rituals by night or in the daytime?

DIONYSUS: By night, for the most part; darkness confers sanctity.

PENTHEUS: That spells trickery and corruption for women!

DIONYSUS: In daytime also immoral behaviour is to be found.

PENTHEUS: You must be punished for your vile sophistries!

DIONYSUS: As must you for your folly and impiety towards the
490   god.

PENTHEUS: He's a bold one, our bacchant, quite the practised speaker!

DIONYSUS: Tell me what I must suffer; what terrible thing are you going to do to me?

PENTHEUS: First I'll cut off your love-locks.

DIONYSUS: My hair is sacred; I grow it in the god's honour.

PENTHEUS: Then hand over that wand you carry.

DIONYSUS: Take it from me yourself; I carry this for Dionysus.

PENTHEUS: I will put you in prison and keep you under guard.

DIONYSUS: The god himself will set me free, whenever I wish.

PENTHEUS: Yes, when you call on him, standing there among your bacchants!

DIONYSUS: This very moment he is near me and witnesses
500   what I am suffering.

PENTHEUS [looking round]: And where is he, then? I certainly don't see him!

DIONYSUS: Where I am; but you are impious yourself, and so do not see him.

PENTHEUS [to the soldiers]: Seize him! He is mocking me and Thebes!

DIONYSUS: I tell you, do not bind me – I have control of my senses and you have not.

PENTHEUS: And I say bind – my authority exceeds yours.

DIONYSUS: You do not know what your life is, or what you do, or who you are.

PENTHEUS: I am Pentheus, son of Agaue; my father was Echion.

DIONYSUS: You have a name that makes you ripe for disaster.[46]

PENTHEUS: Away with you! [*To the soldiers:*] Shut him up in the neighbouring stables, so he can peer into the darkness there! [*To* DIONYSUS, *as he is taken away:*] Dance away now!   510
As for these women you have brought with you as your partners in crime, either I'll sell them into slavery, or I'll stop their hands from beating and thumping their drums and keep them at the loom as servants.

DIONYSUS: I will go; for I do not have to suffer what is not to be. Be sure, however, that this insolence of yours will be punished by Dionysus, whose existence you deny. When you wrong me, you are leading him off to prison.[47]

[DIONYSUS *is escorted into the palace by the soldiers and attendants, followed by Pentheus.*]

CHORUS [Strophe]: *Daughter of Achelous, sovereign Dirce,*[48] *blessed*   520
maiden, for you did once receive in your springs the infant son of Zeus, when from the deathless flames Zeus his sire snatched and hid him in his thigh, crying thus: 'Come, Dithyrambus, enter this my male womb; I reveal you, O Bacchus, to Thebes, that she call you by this name!'[49] *But you, blessed Dirce, are thrusting me away when*   530
on your banks I try to join in the rites, wearing the garland with my fellow worshippers!

Why do you reject me? Why do you shun me? The day will come, yes, by the clustering joy of Dionysus' vine, the day will come when you shall take thought for the Roaring One.

[Antistrophe:] *Pentheus shows his origin from the earth, that he is sprung from the dragon of old,*[50] *he whom Echion the earthly sired – a savage monster, not a mortal man, but like some murderous giant*   540
to stand against the gods; soon he will fasten me, the Roaring One's servant, in his snares, and even now he holds my partner in the holy band inside his palace, hidden away in the darkness of its prison. Do you see this, Dionysus, son of Zeus, your prophets in conflict with   550
oppression? Come down from Olympus, lord,[51] *shaking your golden thyrsus, and crush the arrogance of this murderous man!*

[Epode:] *Where, then, on Nysa, nurse of beasts, or on Corycian peaks, Dionysus, do you wave your wand over the band of worshippers? Perhaps it is in the glades of Olympus, thickly wooded,*
560 *where once Orpheus played his lyre and gathered the trees by his music, gathered the beasts of the wild.*

O Pieria, blessed are you! The god of joy honours you, and he shall come to set you dancing in his holy rites, and over Axius'
570 *swift-flowing stream shall he lead his whirling maenads, and over father Lydias,*[52] *giver of prosperous happiness to men, who, I hear tell, makes fertile with his waters a land of noble horses.*

[*The voice of* DIONYSUS *suddenly rings out from inside the palace.*[53]]

DIONYSUS: *Ho, my Bacchants, hear, hear my voice!*

CHORUS: *What cry is this, what cry? Where does it come from, this summons to me from the Lord of Joy?*

580 DIONYSUS: *Io, io! Again I call, the son of Semele, the son of Zeus!*

CHORUS: *Io, io! Master, Master! Come to us now, to the band of your worshippers, o Roaring One, Roaring One!*

DIONYSUS: *Shake the earth's floor, o sovereign spirit of Earthquake!*

CHORUS: *Ah! Ah! Soon the house of Pentheus shall be shaken to its*
590 *fall! Dionysus is in the palace; revere him!*

SOME OF THE CHORUS: *O, we revere him!*

OTHERS: *Do you see the stone lintels there gape apart on their columns? The Roaring One is raising his cry of triumph within the palace!*

DIONYSUS: *Kindle the gleaming flame of the lightning; destroy, destroy with fire the house of Pentheus!*

[*Lightning flashes above the palace and Semele's monument.*]

CHORUS: *Ah! Ah! Do you not see flames? Do you not perceive, around Semele's holy tomb, the flame of Zeus' lightning, left long ago when he struck her with his bolt? Cast your trembling bodies*
600 *down, cast them to the ground, maenads! For our lord is making high things low, he is assaulting this house, the son of Zeus!*

[DIONYSUS, *still disguised as the Stranger, enters from the palace.*]

DIONYSUS: Women of Asia,[54] are you so stricken with fear that

you have fallen to the ground? You were aware, it seems, of
Dionysus making Pentheus' house shake. Rise up and take
heart – stop this trembling!

CHORUS-LEADER: O our greatest light in the worship we
rejoice in, what happiness to see you – we were forsaken and
alone!

DIONYSUS: Did you despair when I was taken inside to be
thrown into Pentheus' dark dungeon?   610

CHORUS-LEADER: Of course; who was there to protect me if
you should come to grief? But how did you win your freedom
after meeting with that man of sin?

DIONYSUS: I saved myself, easily and without effort.[55]

CHORUS-LEADER: Did he not tie your wrists in the bonds of
a prisoner?

DIONYSUS: That was where I made a fool of him, for he
imagined he was binding me, when in fact he neither touched
nor grasped me, but fed on hopes. He found a bull near the
stall where he was leading me to be imprisoned, and tried to
throw his ropes round this creature's knees and hooves, pant-
ing with rage and biting his lips, while sweat dripped from his   620
body.[56] I sat quietly beside him, watching. It was at that time
that Bacchus came and made the palace shake, and kindled
the fire on his mother's tomb. When Pentheus saw this, he
thought the palace was on fire, and started to rush in all
directions, giving orders to his servants to fetch water, and
every slave was busy at his task, but his labours were all for
nothing. Then, supposing that I had escaped, he gave up on
this task and, seizing his dark sword, he dashed inside the
palace. And then it was that the Roaring One fashioned, or
so I imagine – I give you my own guess here – a phantom in   630
the courtyard. And Pentheus, launching himself at this in a
rush, started stabbing at the bright air, supposing he was put-
ting me to the sword. But Bacchus did not stop at this; there
were other indignities he had in store for him. He brought
his palace crashing to the ground, and all is in ruin: Pentheus
has seen a painful end to my imprisonment. He has dropped

his sword, exhausted from his efforts; for, though a man, he
dared to fight against a god. I calmly left the palace and have
come to you, thinking no more of Pentheus.

    Soon, it seems to me (there is certainly the sound of feet
inside), he will appear in front of the gates. Whatever will he
say after this? I will receive him calmly, though he comes out
640   breathing fury. A modest and gentle temper is the mark of a
wise man.

    [PENTHEUS *enters*.]

PENTHEUS: This is outrageous! The stranger has escaped me,
the fellow who was clapped in irons a moment ago! [*He
catches sight of* DIONYSUS.] Aha! Here is the man! What's the
meaning of this? How do you come to be out here, showing
yourself before my palace gates?

DIONYSUS: Stop there! Calm that angry temper of yours!

PENTHEUS: How is it you have slipped your bonds and come
out here?

DIONYSUS: Did I not say, did you not hear, that someone
would set me free?

650 PENTHEUS: Who? The words you speak are always strange.

DIONYSUS: The one who makes the clustered vine grow for
mortals.[57]

PENTHEUS: [A shameful gift – to make men lose their senses!]

DIONYSUS: You make an insult of the gift that brings honour
to Dionysus.

PENTHEUS [*to his guards*]: Bar every gate round the circuit of
these walls!

DIONYSUS: What of that? Do gods not leap over walls as well?

PENTHEUS: Oh, you are clever, clever – except where clever-
ness is needed![58]

DIONYSUS: Where it is needed most I am clever enough. But
listen first to this man and note what he has to tell, the one
who is here from the mountain to bring you some news. I
shall stay at your side; I will not run away.

    [*A* MESSENGER *enters*.[59]]

MESSENGER: Pentheus, lord of this Theban land, I come here

from Cithaeron, where the white snow's gleaming falls never   660
relax their grip.

PENTHEUS: And what important news is it you bring?

MESSENGER: I saw the wild women, the Bacchants, whose
white limbs sped away from this land in frenzy, like spears in
flight. I am here, my lord, as I want to tell you and your
people their actions, strange, more than wonderful. Please say
if may describe these events freely to you, or if I should keep
a check on my tongue. I fear your quick temper, my lord,
your sharpness to anger and all-too-kingly manner.[60]   670

PENTHEUS: Speak; you will come to no harm from me, what-
ever your story. The more shocking your account of the
Bacchants' behaviour, the more I will punish this fellow who
taught our women these tricks.

MESSENGER: The cattle pasturing in herds were just climbing
up to the hill-country, at the time when the sun sends out his
rays to warm the earth. I saw three bands of female wor-
shippers,[61] one of which Autonoe led, the second your   680
mother, Agaue, and the third Ino. They were all sleeping, their
bodies relaxed, some resting their backs against pine-greenery,
others with their heads laid at random on the ground, amid
the oak-leaves. It was a chaste sight – they weren't, as you
say, drunk with wine and with the sound of the flute, hunting
the Cyprian in lonely places in the wood.[62]

When your mother heard the lowing of our horned herds,
she stood up in the midst of the Bacchants and cried out to
them to shake the sleep from their limbs. And, casting the   690
deep sleep from their eyes, they sprang to their feet, a marvel-
lous sight for its good order, young and old – and among
them girls as yet unwed. First they let their hair hang loose
over their shoulders and secured their fawnskins where the
bands that fastened them had loosened, and tied dappled hides
round themselves with snakes that licked their cheeks.

Some of them held in their arms young deer or wild wolf-
cubs, and offered them their white milk – all the women   700
whose breasts were still full, as they had recently given birth

145

and left their infants behind. Then they put on wreaths of ivy
and oak and flowering bryony. One of them took her thyrsus
and dashed it against a rock, causing a dewy stream of water
to spring forth. Another thrust her wand into the level soil,
and there the god made a fountain of wine spout up. Those
who desired a draught of white liquid scraped the earth with
their fingertips and were rewarded with lively jets of milk:
and from their ivy wands dripped sweet streams of honey.
Had you been there and witnessed these things, you would
have entreated with prayer the god you now criticize.

We herdsmen and shepherds came together to confer and
debate with each other. And one fellow who hung about in
town a good deal and had a ready tongue[63] addressed us all:
'You men who call these holy uplands of the mountain your
home, what do you say to hunting Pentheus' mother Agaue
from her Bacchic revels and obliging our king?' This seemed
a good plan to us, and so we set our ambush, hiding ourselves
in the leafy bushes. At the appointed time the women began
to wave their wands for the Bacchic rites, all calling together
with one voice on Bromius, offspring of Zeus, as Lord of
Cries. The whole mountain and its wild creatures were pos-
sessed by the god,[64] and their motion made all things move.

Agaue happened to run past me and I jumped out in my
eagerness to grab hold of her, deserting the place of ambush
where we had been hiding. But she cried out: 'Ho, my
fleet-footed hounds, we are being hunted by these men!
Follow me, follow, armed with thyrsus in hand!'

Now we took to our heels and escaped being torn apart by
the Bacchants, but they, with weaponless hands, attacked the
cattle that were grazing on the grass. One of them you might
have seen using her hands to wrench asunder a young heifer
with swollen udders – how the creature bellowed! Others
were rending and tearing apart full-grown cows. You might
have seen ribs or cloven hooves flung everywhere; and blood-
stained pieces hung dripping from the pine-branches. Bulls
that had been proud creatures before, with anger rising in

146

their horns, were wrestled to the ground, dragged down by the countless hands of young women. They were stripped of the flesh they wore faster than you could have closed those royal eyes of yours.

On they went, soaring like birds in flight, across the plain stretched below, that produces rich crops of corn by Asopus' stream for the folk of Thebes, and, like an invading army, they swooped on Hysiae and Erythrae on the lower foothills of Cithaeron, scattering everything and turning it upside down. They snatched children from their homes, and all that they put on their shoulders stayed there without the help of fastenings and did not fall. They carried fire on their hair and it did not burn them.

But the villagers, being plundered by the Bacchants, ran in their anger to take up arms. This was the moment when I saw that dreadful sight, my lord. No blood was drawn by their pointed spears, whether they used bronze or iron, but the Bacchants, hurling their wands from their hands, inflicted wounds and made those villagers turn and run – women routing men – surely the work of some god. Then back they went to the place they had started from, to the very springs the god had caused to well up for them, and they washed off the blood, while snakes licked clean the gory stains from their cheeks.

So welcome this god into Thebes, master, whoever he may be! He is great in many ways, but this above all they say of him, I hear, that the vine which puts an end to sorrow is his gift to men. Take away wine and there is no Cyprian any more, or any other pleasure left to man.[65]

CHORUS-LEADER: I hesitate to speak with freedom to the king but nonetheless it shall be said: no god is greater than Dionysus.

[*Exit* MESSENGER.]

PENTHEUS: Already it blazes up at our feet like fire, this Bacchic insolence, making our credit in the eyes of Greeks small indeed! This is no time to show fear. [*To one of his attendants:*] On your way! Go to the Electran Gate and tell them to

750

760

770

780

assemble[66] – all my shieldbearers, and those who ride their swift horses, all those who wield the light shield and whose hands pull the bowstring: we march against the Bacchants! It is intolerable if we are to let women treat us in this manner!

DIONYSUS: You hear my words, Pentheus,[67] but you pay no attention to them. Despite your harsh treatment of me, I say you should not take up arms against a god but be calm instead.

790 The Roaring One will not stand by while you try to clear his worshippers from the hills of joy.

PENTHEUS: Spare me your lectures![68] You have escaped from prison: try to keep your freedom – or I'll clap you in irons again!

DIONYSUS: I would sacrifice to him rather than kick against the goad in your rage, a mortal fighting against a god.

PENTHEUS: I will make him a sacrifice – of women's blood, as they deserve; I'll spread it far and wide among the glens of Cithaeron.

DIONYSUS: You will all be put to flight; and that will be a disgrace, when your shields of beaten bronze turn before the wands of Bacchants!

PENTHEUS: I am locked in combat with this stranger, but find
800 no way to throw him: in prison or out of it he will not keep silent!

DIONYSUS: My good fellow,[69] it is still possible for us to settle this matter sensibly.

PENTHEUS: What am I to do? Play servant to my own servants?

DIONYSUS: I will bring the women here – no need for conflict!

PENTHEUS: Ah, I sense a cunning trick against me now!

DIONYSUS: What kind of trick is it, if I want to *save* you by my scheme?

PENTHEUS: It's a pact you've made with them, to keep you all Bacchants for ever!

DIONYSUS: I did make a pact, have no doubt of that, but with the god.

PENTHEUS [*to his attendants*]: Bring my weapons to me here! [*To* DIONYSUS:] No more words from you! [*He turns away.*]

DIONYSUS: Ah![70] [*Pause.*] Do you want to see them,[71] huddled 810
together there on the mountain slopes?

PENTHEUS: Oh, yes! I'd give a treasury of gold for that!

DIONYSUS: Why this sudden desire for such a thing?

PENTHEUS [*recovering himself*]: I wouldn't enjoy seeing them
drunk.

DIONYSUS: And yet you'd enjoy looking at something that
distressed you?

PENTHEUS: Certainly I would, but privately, seated under the
firs.

DIONYSUS: But they will track you down, even if you get there
without their notice.

PENTHEUS: Well, then, I'll go openly; that was a good point
you made.

DIONYSUS: Should I be your guide, then? Will you attempt
the journey?

PENTHEUS: Lead me without delay! I grudge you every
moment. 820

DIONYSUS: Then put on a linen dress over your flesh.

PENTHEUS: What? Am I to give up being a man and rank as a
woman?[72]

DIONYSUS: They may kill you, if you are seen there as a man.

PENTHEUS: Another good point! What a clever fellow you
have been all the while!

DIONYSUS: Dionysus was my instructor in this wisdom.

PENTHEUS: How, then, would this advice you give me be
properly carried out?

DIONYSUS: I will come inside the palace and dress you
there.

PENTHEUS: In what dress? A woman's? I am ashamed.

DIONYSUS: Have you lost your eagerness to view the maenads?

PENTHEUS: What dress do you speak of putting on me? 830

DIONYSUS: I'll place on your head a wig with flowing hair.

PENTHEUS: What is the second item in my costume?

DIONYSUS: Robes that reach your feet; and on your brow will
be a headband.

PENTHEUS: Is there any other feature you mean to add to these?

DIONYSUS: A thyrsus in your hand and a dappled fawnskin.

PENTHEUS: I could not bring myself to put on female dress.

DIONYSUS: But you will cause bloodshed if you join battle with the Bacchants.

PENTHEUS: You are right; I must first make a reconnaissance.

DIONYSUS: That's certainly a wiser course than hunting evil by evil means.

PENTHEUS: How shall I make my way through the town with-
840   out Cadmus' folk seeing me?

DIONYSUS: We will go by deserted streets; I will be your guide.

PENTHEUS: Anything is better than being laughed at by the Bacchants.

DIONYSUS: Let us go into the palace[73] [and make the necessary preparations].

PENTHEUS: [Wait; I myself] shall consider my decision.

DIONYSUS: By all means; in any case *I* am prepared.

PENTHEUS: I think I will go in; either I'll set out with my army or I'll take your advice.[74]

> [PENTHEUS *enters the palace and* DIONYSUS *turns to address the* CHORUS.]

DIONYSUS: Women, the man is swimming into the net. He will go to the Bacchants and there he will be punished with death. Dionysus, now it is for you to act! You are not far
850   away. Let us take revenge on him! First rob him of his wits, instilling in him a light-headed fantasy. For never in his senses will he agree to put on female clothing, but once out of his mind he'll put it on. I want him to be mocked by the Thebans as he is led through their town in women's dress, after those dire threats he made earlier. I will go to dress Pentheus in the garments he will take with him to Hades' realm, when he has been slaughtered by his mother's hands. He shall learn that
860   Dionysus, son of Zeus, is by turns[75] a god most terrible and most gracious to mankind.

> [DIONYSUS *goes into the palace.*]

CHORUS [Strophe]: *Shall it ever come, the time when I tread, white-footed in ecstasy, in the night-long dances, my head flung back to the dewy air? Like a fawn at play amid the green joys of a meadow, when she has escaped the terrors of the hunt, leaping over the woven nets and cheating her watchers, while the huntsman cries out to his* 870 *coursing pack and quickens their pace. Storm-swift, with toil of hard racing, she gallops over the fields by the river, delighting in places devoid of men and in the leafy shade of the forest.*

What is wisdom? Or what heaven-sent gift is more honourable in men's eyes than to hold one's hand in triumph over the head of an enemy? Honour is ever cherished.[76] 880

[Antistrophe:] *Slow to advance, yet sure, is the might of heaven; it punishes those mortals who honour ruthlessness and, in the madness of their thoughts, do not give glory to the gods. Subtly they conceal the leisurely stride of time, as they hunt down the man who fails to honour them. For never is it right to think or act beyond what custom* 890 *has prescribed.*[77] *It is no great expense to accept that power lies with the divine – whatever the divine may be – and that what has become accepted through long ages is everlasting and grounded in nature.*

What is wisdom? Or what heaven-sent gift is more honourable in the eyes of men than to hold one's hand in triumph over the head of an enemy? Honour is ever cherished. 900

[Epode:] *Happy the man who has escaped storm at sea and found harbour; happy the man who has surmounted toils. In diverse ways one man outstrips another in prosperity and power. Countless men, besides, nourish countless hopes; some of these end in happiness for mortals, others vanish. The man whose life is happy day by day is* 910 *the one I count blessed.*

[DIONYSUS *comes out of the palace, followed by* PENTHEUS, *dressed as a Bacchant.*]

DIONYSUS: You there, eager to see what you should not – yes, it's you I mean. Pentheus, you who are bent on prying into what should remain secret, come out in front of the palace! Let me see you dressed like a woman, a maenad, a Bacchant, on your way to spy on your mother and her company!

[PENTHEUS *comes out in Bacchic dress, no longer in possession of his faculties.*] Well, you *do* look like one of the daughters of Cadmus!

PENTHEUS: Hey! I think I see two suns and two Thebes, two cities with seven gates! And you, my guide, look just like a bull, with horns growing on your head. Were you perhaps a beast all along? You certainly have become a bull now.[78]

DIONYSUS: The god accompanies us; he was hostile before, but now is in league with us; now you see what you should see.[79]

PENTHEUS [*throwing his head back in exaggerated imitation of a typical maenad*]: Well, how do I look? Do I not have the very pose of Ino, or Agaue, my mother?

DIONYSUS: I seem to see their very selves, as I look at you. [*He moves forward to adjust* PENTHEUS' *wig.*] But this lock of hair is out of position, not as I arranged it under your head-band.

PENTHEUS: I dislodged it inside, when I was shaking my hair this way and that, behaving as Bacchants do.

DIONYSUS: There, I'll put it back in place; I'm your valet now. Straighten your head!

PENTHEUS: There you are! You must be my dresser now; I am completely in your hands.[80]

DIONYSUS: Your girdle is loose, and the pleats of your dress are not hanging straight below the ankle.

PENTHEUS: I agree, at least at my right ankle. [*He looks over his shoulder at the back of his left leg.*] On this side the dress hangs straight by my ankle.

DIONYSUS: I'm sure you'll think me first among your friends, when you see what you do not expect – Bacchants behaving purely.

PENTHEUS: Shall I look more like a Bacchant if I hold the thyrsus in my right hand or in this one?

DIONYSUS: The correct hand is the right, and you should lift and ground it in time with the right foot. I am glad that you have undergone a change of mind.

PENTHEUS: Would I be able to carry on my shoulders Cithaeron
and its glens, Bacchants included?

DIONYSUS: You would, should it be your wish; before you
were not of sound mind, but now you are . . . as you should
be.

PENTHEUS: Should I carry crowbars with me or put my shoul-
der or arms under the peaks and heave them up with my bare
hands? 950

DIONYSUS: You wouldn't want to destroy the shrines of the
Nymphs and the haunts of Pan, where he plays his pipes,
would you?

PENTHEUS: Good point; force is not the way to defeat women;
I will conceal myself under the firs.

DIONYSUS: You will get all the concealment you should find
if you go to spy on maenads.

PENTHEUS: Imagine it – there they lie now, I fancy, like mating
birds in the bushes, snuggling together in the joyous nets of
love!

DIONYSUS: Isn't this the very reason for your vigilant mission?
Perhaps you will catch them unawares – [aside:] unless you
are caught first. 960

PENTHEUS: Take me through the midst of the land of Thebes;[81]
I am the only man among them to dare this deed.

DIONYSUS: You are the only one who bears the burden for this
city,[82] the only one. And so you face the trial you have
deserved. Now follow; I will escort you there safely, but
another will bring you back from there . . .

PENTHEUS: Yes, my mother!

DIONYSUS: A sight to strike every eye.

PENTHEUS: It is for this reason I go!

DIONYSUS: You shall ride home . . .

PENTHEUS: You mean to pamper me!

DIONYSUS: . . . in your mother's arms.

PENTHEUS: You really want to spoil me!

DIONYSUS: To spoil you, yes – in my own way.

PENTHEUS: I go to claim only what I deserve. 970

[PENTHEUS *begins to leave the stage.*]

DIONYSUS: You are formidable, formidable, and formidable are
the sufferings you will find there, such as will earn you renown
that towers to heaven.[83] Stretch out your hands, Agaue, and
you, her sisters, daughters of Cadmus! I bring this young man
to a great contest, whose winner shall be myself and the
Roaring One. The rest the event will show.

[DIONYSUS *follows* PENTHEUS *offstage.*]

CHORUS [Strophe]: *On, swift hounds of Madness,*[84] *on to the moun-
tain, where Cadmus' daughters are joined in worship! Rouse them*
980 *to frenzy against the one disguised in woman's clothes, who spies on
the maenads in his madness. First his mother will see him,*[85] *as he
watches from a smooth rock or crag, and will call out to the maenads:
'Who is he that has come to the mountain, my Bacchants, has come
to the mountain, tracking down the mountain-dancing daughters of
Cadmus? What creature is his mother? For he is not sprung of*
990 *women's blood; a lioness gave him birth, or Libyan Gorgons.'*

*Let Justice come for all to see, let her come sword in hand, stabbing
through the throat to his death the godless, the lawless, the unjust
man, the earth-born offspring of Echion!*

[Antistrophe:] *This man with unjust intent and lawless anger at
your rites, god of Bacchants, and your mother's, sets forth with mad*
1000 *craft and deluded spirit to master by violent means what may not be
conquered. Death will discipline his purpose.*[86] *But acceptance without
protest of what the gods decide, and to abide by the mortal lot, means
a life free of sorrow. I feel no envy of those who seek out wisdom in
moderation. But the other things are great and not hidden from view,
leading our lives ever towards beauty. May it be my aim to be reverent
and holy by day and on through the night, and, rejecting all customs*
1010 *that transgress justice, to know the gods!*

*Let Justice come for all to see, let her come sword in hand, stabbing
through the throat to his death the godless, the lawless, the unjust
man, the earth-born offspring of Echion!*

[Epode:] *Appear as bull or many-headed serpent to view, or as a
flaming lion to the eye! Come, Bacchus, beast-god, over the hunter*

of Bacchants fling with smiling face the net of death,[87] when he has   1020
fallen among the maenad herd!

[*A* MESSENGER *enters,*[88] the personal attendant of
PENTHEUS.]

MESSENGER: O house that once in earlier days was counted
happy by all Greeks, how I grieve for you, slave though I am!

CHORUS-LEADER: What is it? Do you have some news of the
Bacchants?

MESSENGER: Pentheus is dead, son of Echion, his sire.   1030

CHORUS-LEADER: [*breaking into song*]: *O Bromius, my master,
you are shown to be a mighty god!*

MESSENGER: What do you mean? Why did you say that? Do
you take pleasure in the misfortune of one who was my
master, woman?

CHORUS-LEADER: *A foreigner am I, and in barbaric strains I hail
my god; no more do I cower in fear of chains!*

MESSENGER: Do you think Thebes so lacking in men [that you
shall not be punished for this?]

CHORUS-LEADER: *Dionysus, Dionysus, not Thebes, has power
over me!*

MESSENGER: I can sympathize with you, but to rejoice in the
doing of a foul deed, there is no honour, women, in that.   1040

CHORUS-LEADER: *Tell me, speak! How did he meet his end, the
enemy of justice in his unjust mission?*

MESSENGER: When we had left behind[89] the farms of this
Theban land and crossed Asopus' waters, we started to strike
into the foothills of Cithaeron, Pentheus and I (for I was
attending my master) and the stranger who was leading the
way on our mission. First we sat down in a grassy glade,
making sure no sound came from our feet or tongues, so that
we might see without being seen. A ravine, bound with cliffs,   1050
lay there, with pines casting their shadow over the stream that
rushed through it. There the maenads were sitting, their hands
employed in pleasant tasks. Some of them were restoring to a
worn-out wand its crown of ivy locks, others, with the joy of

young mares released from the painted yoke, were singing
bacchic antiphonies. But Pentheus, wretched man, not seeing
the throng of women, spoke: 'Stranger, where we stand my
1060 eyes cannot see the maenads' mischief. But on the banks, if I
climbed into a tall pine-tree, I would get a clear view of their
shameful behaviour.'

Then my eyes saw miracles worked by the stranger. He
seized the topmost branch of a pine where it soared into the
sky, and began to force it down, down, down to the dark
earth, until it was bent round like a bow, or a rounded wheel
traced by a compass in a whirling circuit. In this way the
stranger pulled down that mountain trunk with his hands and
bent it to the ground, a feat no mortal could perform. He
1070 seated Pentheus on the branches of the pine and then he let
the stem pass through his hands until it straightened; but
gently, taking care the mount did not unseat its rider. High
into the high heavens it soared, with my master sitting on the
top. Then he saw the maenads, but not so well as they saw
him. He was just becoming visible on his lofty perch, when
the stranger no longer could be seen, and from the sky a voice
– it was Dionysus, I guess – rang out: 'Young women, I bring
you the man who makes a mockery of you and me and my
1080 rites. Punish him!' As the voice spoke these words, a flash of
awful fire appeared set between heaven and earth. Hushed
was the air, hushed the leaves of the forest glade, not a cry
from a single beast could you have heard.

But the Bacchants' ears had not clearly taken in the voice,
though they stood up and stared around them. Then he issued
a second command. When they understood the clear order of
Bacchus, Cadmus' daughters and all the Bacchants with them
1090 sped out with the swiftness of doves, and through the glade,
over its torrent and boulders they leaped, maddened with the
inspiration of the god. And when they saw my master seated
in the pine-tree, first they climbed a cliff towering opposite
and began to pelt him furiously with stones. Some used
branches of fir as javelins against him, while others hurled

their holy wands through the air at Pentheus, a cruel target to
aim at, but to no effect. For the wretched man was sitting too   1100
high for their desperate attempts, trapped in his helplessness.
In the end they used branches of oak to destroy the roots of
his tree, attempting to prise them up with crowbars not of
iron. When their efforts ended in failure, Agaue spoke: 'Come,
my maenads, form a circle and seize hold of the trunk, so we
can capture this climbing beast.[90] He must not reveal our
secret dances for the god!' Then they put their countless hands
on the pine and pulled it up from the earth. And headlong   1110
from his lofty perch to the ground below, with unending
shrieks, fell Pentheus. For he realized his fatal hour had come.
His mother was first to attack him, initiating as priestess the
bloody rite. He threw the headband from his hair, so that the
wretched Agaue might recognize him and stay her murderous
hands. Touching her cheek, he spoke these words: 'Mother,
it is I, your son, Pentheus, whom you bore in the house of
Echion! O Mother, pity me, and do not kill your son because
of my offences!'[91] But Agaue, foaming at the mouth and   1120
rolling distorted eyes, her senses gone, was in the grip of
Bacchus and deaf to his entreaties. She grabbed his left arm
below the elbow, set her foot against the doomed man's ribs
and tore out the shoulder, not by strength but by ease of hand
that was the gift of the god. Ino worked away at the other
side, tearing at his flesh, while Autonoe and the whole horde   1130
of Bacchants pressed home their attack. All was one confused
shout – he screaming with the little breath he had left, the
women yelling in triumph. One of them was carrying an arm,
another a foot, still covered by its sandal; his ribs were stripped
bare by the clawing nails, and every woman had blood on her
hands, as she tossed Pentheus' flesh in sport like a ball.[92]

His body lies scattered, part beneath the jagged rocks, part
in the green depths of the woodland – no easy thing to find.
His wretched head his mother has. She seized it in her hands,   1140
and, sticking it on the top of her holy wand, now carries it,
as if it were a mountain lion's, through the midst of Cithaeron,

leaving her sisters behind with the bands of maenads. Exulting in her ill-fated quarry, she is coming inside these city walls, calling on Bacchus as her 'fellow-huntsman', her 'comrade in the chase', 'the giver of triumph' – though what he gives her in triumph is tears!

I shall remove myself from this calamitous scene before Agaue reaches the palace. To be virtuous in one's life and show the gods reverence is the noblest course; it is also, I think, the greatest wisdom a man can possess.

1150

[*Exit* MESSENGER.]

CHORUS: *Let us dance for the Bacchic god, let us celebrate with cries the fate of Pentheus, offspring of the dragon, who donned women's clothing and took up the blessed fennel wand, weaponry of death, and had a bull to guide him to his end.*

1160   *Bacchants of Cadmus' town, famous is the song of triumph you have fashioned, but its ending is lamentation and tears. A noble contest – to clasp a child with a hand that drips with his blood!*[93]

Enough; I see Agaue, mother of Pentheus, rushing towards the palace, her eyes rolling. Give her welcome into the revelling band of the god of joy!

[AGAUE *enters,*[94] *dancing. She carries the head of* PENTHEUS *in her arms.*]

AGAUE [Strophe]: *Bacchants of Asia . . .*

CHORUS: *Why do you call on me, woman?*

AGAUE: *I bring from the mountain a curling thing, freshly cut, to the*
1170   *palace, a blessed trophy of the hunt!*

CHORUS: *I see, and will accept you as partner in the revel.*

AGAUE: *I seized him without snares, this young whelp [of a mountain lion], as you may see.*

CHORUS: *In what desolate place?*

AGAUE: *Cithaeron . . .*

CHORUS: *Cithaeron?*

AGAUE: *. . . brought him death.*

CHORUS: *Who struck the blow?*

AGAUE: *That honour fell first to me. 'Blessed Agaue', they call me in the worshipping band!*   1180

CHORUS: *Who else?*

AGAUE: *Cadmus it was . . .*

CHORUS: *Cadmus?*

AGAUE: *. . . whose daughters laid hands on this beast – but not before me, not before me! This was a happy hunting!*
    [Antistrophe:] *Share now in the feast!*[95]

CHORUS: *Share in what, you wretch?*

AGAUE [*caressing the head:*] *Young is the calf; under his crest of delicate hair the down has grown but lately on his cheek.*

CHORUS: *Yes, his hair makes him look like a beast of the wild.*

AGAUE: *The Bacchic god, a skilful huntsman, skilfully*[96] *loosed his maenads on this beast.*   1190

CHORUS: *Yes, our lord is a hunter.*

AGAUE: *Do you praise me?*

CHORUS: *I praise you.*

AGAUE: *Soon the people of Cadmus . . .*

CHORUS: *Yes, and Pentheus, your son . . .*

AGAUE: *. . . will praise his mother, for capturing this prey in lion shape.*

CHORUS: *No ordinary prey.*

AGAUE: *No ordinary killing.*

CHORUS: *Are you exultant?*

AGAUE: *Joy is mine, for I have achieved great things, great things for all to see, by this hunting!*

CHORUS-LEADER: Then, you wretch, show the citizens your spoil of victory that you have brought with you.   1200

AGAUE [*she has stopped dancing*]: You who dwell in the fair-towered city of the Theban land, come to view this prey, the beast that we daughters of Cadmus have hunted down, not with thonged javelins of Thessaly, not with nets, but with the white blades of our hands! After that should huntsmen wield spears, and get themselves useless weapons from the armourers? We with nothing but our hands caught this beast and tore apart his limbs! Where is my old father? Let him   1210 come near. And Pentheus, my son, where is he? Let him take a sturdy ladder and set it against the house, so he may climb up and nail this head to the façade – this lion's head I bring back from my hunting!

[CADMUS *now enters*[97] *with attendants who carry the ruined body of* PENTHEUS.]

CADMUS: Follow me, bearing the woeful burden that was Pentheus, follow me, servants, to the house where I am bringing this body. My search was endless and cost me much toil; in Cithaeron's glades I found him, scattered, with no two pieces
1220 on the same part of ground. I had already returned with old Teiresias from the Bacchants and was inside the city's walls when I heard news of my daughters' fearful deeds. Back I turned my steps to the mountain, to fetch home the son whom the maenads had killed. There I saw Autonoe, who once bore Actaeon to Aristaeus, and with her Ino, still stricken with madness, poor creatures, in the woodland; but the other,
1230 Agaue, I was told, was coming here on frenzied feet. What I heard was true enough; I see her now, a sight that brings no happiness.

AGAUE: Father, you may make the proudest of boasts – you have sired by far the finest daughters in the world! I mean them all, but foremost myself, who left the shuttle by the loom and have risen to higher things – hunting beasts with my hands! I bring here in my arms, as you see, this prize of my valour, to be hung on your palace roof. [*She holds out*
1240 PENTHEUS' *head.*] Here, father, take it in your hands! Exult in my hunting and invite your friends to a feast. You are blessed, blessed in such a feat performed by my hands!

CADMUS: O sorrow beyond measure – no eyes can bear the sight! Pity the hands that did the bloody deed! Fair is the sacrifice you have offered the gods that makes you invite all Thebes together with me to a feast. Oh, I grieve for these woes, first your own, and then mine! How he has destroyed us, the god, the king who is the Roaring One – justly but
1250 excessively, though he is our own kin![98]

AGAUE: How churlish a thing in men is old age, with its scowling face! If only my son were a skilful hunter, taking after his mother's ways, so as to join in hunting beasts with the young men of Thebes! But all he is capable of is opposing the gods. You must take him to task, father! Won't anyone call him here into my sight, to witness my good fortune?

CADMUS: Oh, what pain, what sorrow! If ever you come to know what you have done, you will know grief past bearing. If you remain to the end in this state, you will not deserve the name 'fortunate' but in your fancy you will have escaped misfortune. 1260

AGAUE: What cause for shame is here?[99] What is there to make one grieve?

CADMUS: First turn your eyes to yonder sky.

AGAUE: There. Why do you tell me to look at it?

CADMUS: Does it seem the same to you or changed?

AGAUE: It is brighter than before, more translucent.

CADMUS: And the excitement you felt inside you, is it still there?

AGAUE: I don't understand what you say; but I'm becoming – somehow – rational, and changing from my earlier feelings. 1270

CADMUS: Can you hear at all? Can you give clear answers?

AGAUE: Yes, for I have actually forgotten what we said a moment ago, Father.

CADMUS: Whose house was it you entered on the day of your wedding?

AGAUE: You gave me to Echion, seed of the Dragon, men say.

CADMUS: Who was the child born in his house to your husband?

AGAUE: Pentheus, born to me and his father both.

CADMUS: Well, then, whose head is it you have in your arms?

AGAUE: A lion's – or so the hunting women said.

CADMUS: Look properly now; it is a small effort to look.

AGAUE: Ah, what do I see? What is this prize I am carrying in my hands? 1280

CADMUS: Look at it closely and understand more clearly.

AGAUE: Oh, no, no! I see my greatest sorrow!

CADMUS: You don't still think it looks like a lion?

AGAUE: No, it is Pentheus' head I hold – oh, misery!

CADMUS: I shed tears for him long before you recognized him.

AGAUE: Who was his killer? How did he come into my hands?

CADMUS: O unhappy truth, how untimely your presence here!

AGAUE: Speak! My heart beats in terror at what is to come!

CADMUS: You killed him, you and your sisters.

1290 AGAUE: Where did he die? Was it at home? Where?

CADMUS: It was where Actaeon's hounds once tore him apart.

AGAUE: Why did he go to Cithaeron, this ill-fated man?

CADMUS: He went there to insult the god and your acts of worship.

AGAUE: What of us? How did we come to be there?

CADMUS: You had become mad; the whole city was in the power of Bacchus.

AGAUE: Dionysus is our destroyer; now I understand.

CADMUS: Yes, for the contempt that was shown to him; you did not regard him as a god.

AGAUE: My son's dear body – where is it, Father?

CADMUS [he gestures to the bier with Pentheus' remains]: Here I bring it – not easily discovered.

1300 AGAUE: Is it all decently arranged, limb to limb?[100]

[. . .]

What part did Pentheus have in my madness?

CADMUS: He proved himself to be like you; he did not revere the god. So Dionysus has involved all together in a single ruin, both you and this man. He has destroyed our house and me as well; having no male offspring of my own, I have seen this fruit of your womb, poor girl, most foully and wretchedly slain. O my child, through you the house had gained its sight again; it was you, my daughter's child, who held my palace
1310 together and kept our citizens in awe. No one, seeing your face, would dare insult the old man; otherwise you would make him suffer as he deserved. But now I shall be an exile from my home, dishonoured – I, Cadmus the great, who

sowed the Theban race and reaped that splendid harvest! O dearest of men (though you are alive no more, I will still number you, child, among my loved ones), never again will you touch this chin of mine with your hand and embrace me, child, calling me 'Grandfather' and saying, 'Who wrongs you, who dishonours you, sir? Who vexes your heart with his annoying ways? Tell me, so I may punish the one who wrongs you, Grandfather!' 1320

But now it is sorrow for me and misery for you, pity for your mother and misery for her sisters. If there is anyone who holds deities in contempt, let him consider this man's death and believe in the gods.[101]

CHORUS-LEADER: Your lot is painful in my sight, Cadmus, but your grandson has the justice he deserves, though it brings you pain.[102]

AGAUE: Father, you see how great is the change in my fortunes . . .[103]

[. . .]

DIONYSUS [speaking from above the stage-building]: [. . .] You will be transformed into a snake, and your spouse, becoming a beast, will take on the form of a serpent, the lady Harmonia, daughter of Ares, whom you, a mortal born, took to wife. With your spouse at your side, as the oracle of Zeus says, you will drive a cattle-drawn chariot, and, leading barbarians in a mighty host, you will sack many cities. But when they plunder the oracle of Loxias, they will win for themselves a miserable homecoming. From this Ares will save you and Harmonia, and he will transport you alive to the land of the blessed.[104] 1330

I, Dionysus, speak these words as the son of no mortal father but of Zeus. If you had possessed the sense to show wisdom, when you would not, you would have won the son of Zeus as your ally and now know happiness. 1340

CADMUS: Dionysus, we beseech you, we have done wrong![105]

DIONYSUS: Too late you came to know me; when you should have, you did not.

CADMUS: This we acknowledge; but you come upon us with a hand too heavy.

DIONYSUS: Yes, for I, a god born, was treated by you with contempt.

CADMUS: Gods should not be like mortals in temper.

DIONYSUS: Long ago my father Zeus gave his consent to this.

1350 AGAUE: Ah, it is decided, Father, our woeful exile!

DIONYSUS: Why, then, do you delay what must be?

[DIONYSUS *leaves the stage.*[106]]

CADMUS: My child, how fearful a calamity we have all come to – you, poor creature, your sisters, and my unhappy self. I shall go in my old age to share a home with barbarians, and there is yet for me the oracle's command to lead a disparate host of foreigners against Greece. The daughter of Ares, Harmonia, my wife, shall assume the form of a savage snake, while I, a snake myself, shall take her at my side, as I lead an army of spearsmen against the altars and tombs of the Greeks.

1360 There will be no end to my wretched sufferings, and no peace shall I have, even when I have made the voyage down plunging Acheron.

AGAUE [*embracing* CADMUS]: Father, I must go into exile without you to share my path![107]

CADMUS: Why do you throw your arms around me, unhappy child, as the young swan shelters the old, feeble and grey in his plumage?

AGAUE: Oh, where am I to turn, now I am banished from my country?

CADMUS: I do not know, child; your father is of little help.

AGAUE: *Farewell, my house! Farewell, city of my fathers! I am leaving*
1370 *you in misery, driven from my marital bed.*

CADMUS: *Go now, daughter, to the house of Aristaeus . . .*[108]

[. . .]

AGAUE: *I grieve for you, Father.*

CADMUS: *And I for you, child; and I weep for your sisters.*

AGAUE: *Terribly has Lord Dionysus brought this outrage upon your house!*

CADMUS: *Yes, for terrible was his treatment[109] at our hands, having his name go without honour in Thebes.*

AGAUE: *Farewell, Father!*

CADMUS: *Farewell, wretched Daughter! But you will not find it easy to fare well.*   1380

AGAUE: *Take me, friends, where I shall find the unhappy sisters who are to share my exile. Oh, to go where foul Cithaeron may not see me, nor I Cithaeron, to a place where no dedicated thyrsus may stir the memory! Let other Bacchants care for these things!*

[AGAUE *leaves the stage.* CADMUS *also leaves, in the opposite direction.*]

CHORUS: *Many are the forms taken by the plans of the gods and many the things they accomplish beyond men's hopes. What men expect does not happen; for the unexpected heaven finds a way. And*   1390 *so it has turned out here today.[110]*

[*Exit* CHORUS.]

IPHIGENIA AT
AULIS

PREFACE TO *IPHIGENIA*
AT AULIS

The name of Iphigenia is absent from Homer. In one passage he mentions three daughters of Agamemnon as still alive and marriageable in the final phase of the Trojan war: Electra, Chrysothemis and Iphianassa. The last is sometimes identified with Iphigenia in later usage, but if that was Homer's understanding, either he must be unaware of the tale that Agamemnon sacrificed his daughter at Aulis to gain a fair wind for the fleet, or he is silently rejecting it. It has often been argued that certain tales were objectionable in Homer's eyes, and that he may have deliberately avoided stories involving kin-killing: in the *Odyssey* he does mention, but guardedly and in passing, the matricide of Orestes (cf. Preface to *Orestes*, p. 61). Other poets, however, were less squeamish or more sensational: the sacrifice of Iphigenia figured in an early Greek epic known as the *Cypria*, and is mentioned frequently in Attic tragedy: both Aeschylus and Sophocles wrote plays entitled *Iphigenia*, now lost, and the sacrifice is invoked as a major part of the indictment against Agamemnon by Clytemnestra in the *Electra* plays of both Sophocles and Euripides. Above all, the prophecy of Calchas and the horror of the child-killing were recounted in an unforgettable lyric passage of Aeschylus' *Agamemnon*.

> So he was hard enough to sacrifice
> his daughter, in aid of a war
> to punish a woman
> and as first-rites for the fleet to sail.

Her entreaties and appeals to her father,
and her maiden's years – in their love for battle
the officers set this at naught;
her father after praying gave an order
for the servers to come and lift her like a goat-kid
over the altar, when she had fallen forward
about his robes to plead with all her heart;
the lips in her beautiful face
were curbed to suppress
any word making the house accursed,

violently and with a bridle's muting power.

(*Agamemnon* 224–38, tr. C. Collard)

As early as the *Cypria*, there was a tradition that Iphigenia did not die at Aulis but was miraculously rescued by Artemis, to whom she was being offered in sacrifice. According to the surviving summary of the *Cypria*, Artemis carried her off to the land of the Tauri (the modern Crimea) and made her immortal. In some versions she is replaced by a deer or a bear, beasts associated with the goddess. But in Aeschylus it is taken for granted by all, including the audience, that she died at the altar; nor would the ferocity of Clytemnestra's vengeance be easy even for her to justify were this not believed to be the case. Euripides in his earlier play *Iphigenia among the Taurians* (see volume 3 of this translation) had taken this as the premiss and dramatized the novel chain of events whereby Orestes finds his sister and brings her home. In the present play, the last which survives from his pen, he returns to the beginnings of the tale and the prelude to the Trojan war.

Aeschylus' narrative in the *Agamemnon*, though austere and selective, had made clear that Agamemnon struggled over the decision: patriotic duty (and his obligations to his brother) prevailed over natural father-feeling. Euripides develops this hint in a number of ways, characteristically exploring the emotional impact of the divine command on the different members of the family. At the start of the play the king has already sent a message summoning his daughter to Aulis, ostensibly in order for her to be married to Achilles. Agamemnon now thinks better of this, and paternal love takes first place over patriotism (the reverse of Aeschylus's sequence). But Menelaus' interests must also be taken into account: whereas Aeschylus had spoken of the two brothers acting in unison, Euripides sets them in conflict. While Agamemnon wants to call off the expedition, Menelaus is determined that it should go ahead: his motive, it seems, is purely personal, the hope of recovering Helen, although he attempts to put a fine gloss on this by high-sounding words about the glory of Greece. Further complications ensue: not only Iphigenia arrives but also Clytemnestra: how can the plan be executed with the girl's mother present? Agamemnon is in despair, and his grief-stricken speech finally moves Menelaus to a change of heart: he will help his brother and forget his worthless wife. Immediately still further problems arise: even if the two brothers are at one, how can they achieve their goal against the connivances of Calchas and Odysseus? The whole army will soon be up in arms against them and force them to sacrifice the girl. As this fast-moving plot unfolds, we glimpse political rivalries and motives of personal ambition which go well beyond the original premisses of the story.

The next scene, involving the meeting of Agamemnon with wife and daughter, is rich in the ironies of double meaning and ominous anticipation which the tragedians love. The portrait of Iphigenia is charmingly sketched: a naive, affectionate and playful girl, hardly more than a child. Clytemnestra is characterized quite differently from the more familiar representations of her in her later life, embittered and bent on vengeance: instead she is amiable and obedient. We sense that this is how the family could have been, how it ought to be. A sharper edge is evident, however, when the king tries to send her home: she will not hear of the marriage being celebrated without her presence. Euripides cleverly contrives to anticipate future tension: later, when Agamemnon's true motive emerges, there are still clearer signals of trouble ahead, when Agamemnon eventually returns from Troy (1171 ff., 1454–7).

Clytemnestra's presence and involvement in events is probably a Euripidean innovation: we recognize the technique of the dramatist who asked himself what the reaction of Admetus' father would be to his son's request that he die in his place, or how Tyndareus would have felt about his grandson murdering his daughter. Another creative device can probably be seen in the role of Achilles. As Iphigenia's alleged bridegroom, he has an obvious stake in all this: but how much did he know about Agamemnon's intentions? It is not clear how earlier writers dealt with this issue, but in Euripides Achilles is ignorant both of the marital proposal and of the underlying plan to sacrifice the girl. This ignorance makes first for comedy (the awkward encounter with an unexpected mother-in-law to be!), subsequently for angry indignation. Throughout, Euripides shows us an Achilles who is both like and unlike his Homeric prototype – like him in being honourable, straight-forward, courageous; unlike him, in that his proud outbursts become self-important expostulations, his heroic gestures ineffectual. When he first appears he is coming to convey to the commander-in-chief the discontent of his followers, the Myrmidons; later he arrives hot and bothered after being almost lynched by his rebellious men. The power of the army cows the prowess even of the greatest warrior of the *Iliad*. Although he declares his willingness to help Iphigenia repeatedly and at length, Achilles in the end achieves precisely nothing. Nor are the mother and daughter any more successful in their dual appeal to Agamemnon for mercy: the king explains that he is in the grip of necessity (Aeschylean motifs are redeployed, but here debased), and he himself now voices the patriotic arguments that had been put to him by Menelaus. 'It is not Menelaus who has turned me into a slave, my child, nor his desire that guides my actions, but Greece: to her, whether I wish it or not, I am bound to offer you in sacrifice; against this I have no power. Greece must be free, as far as you and I, my child, can bring it about; we are Greeks, and must not let foreigners use violence against our wives and carry them off' (1269–75).

Thus the stage is set, the victim must be sacrificed. This type of plot, or story-pattern, was common in Euripides. In this volume Iphigenia's role is paralleled in the *Phoenician Women* by Menoeceus, who sacrifices himself to save Thebes, at Teiresias' bidding; more usually the victim is female, as in the *Children of Heracles* (to save Athens), the fragmentary *Erechtheus* (also to save Athens) and the *Hecabe* (to placate the ghost of Achilles). It is usual for all those concerned to be at first horrified and reluctant (thus Creon, Menoeceus' father, rejects Teiresias and hopes to help his son escape), but for the victim himself or herself finally to accept the necessity and go voluntarily to the slaughter. This sequence enabled the poet to dramatize a whole gamut of emotions – ominous foreboding, terror and dismay, anger and defiance, grief before and after the death-scene, but also heroic pride and the spirit of self-sacrifice. Since the story-pattern is well established, the audience probably anticipated that Iphigenia would in the end go willingly to her death (as the myth, and ritual propriety, demanded), and she does so, voicing her decision in a speech of memorable firmness (1368 ff.), in which she too seems to subscribe to the patriotic rhetoric used by Menelaus and Agamemnon. Aristotle complained that Euripides had made her character inconsistent, but we may suspect that a striking, even extraordinary change of attitude was exactly what he wished to represent.

The difficulties of interpretation are considerable. On the one hand, we must admire Iphigenia's courage and eloquence (as does Achilles) and we need not doubt that in appropriate contexts the Athenian audiences might have responded positively to anti-barbarian rhetoric (cf. note 65); on the other, we are bound to question the value of her self-sacrifice and still more of the cause for which the Greeks are fighting. The campaign as represented in this play can hardly be seen as a crusade by virtuous Greeks against depraved barbarians: the champions of Greece are ignoble and unheroic, the crime of the Trojans consists of the abduction of one woman whom her husband admits to be of little worth. Later reshapings of the legend laid more stress on economic motives, glory, ambition, loot: there are hints of these in the Euripidean text, but more emphasis is laid on the collective sickness or passion which has inflamed the Greek forces: 'a heaven-sent affliction', is what Agamemnon calls it (411, cf. 407, 808, 1264). While we may feel confident that we are meant to admire the victims' virtue when one death saves the lives of many or preserves a city from destruction (as in several of the parallel plots), the example of the *Hecabe*, where the wholly sympathetic Polyxena is slaughtered to satisfy a resentful ghost, shows that the motif is capable of more complex uses. In this play the nobility of Iphigenia is thrown away on a cause which is important in terms of its mythical stature – the Trojan War must indeed take place — but which, as represented here, is a shabby undertaking led by weak and vacillating generals. We need not suppose that it is mere anachronism to find in ancient literature hostility to war and suspicion of arguments used to promote military ends. The poet of the *Hecabe* and the *Trojan Women* knew well enough what the cost of war was for the victims, and its brutalizing effect upon the victors.

So far we have avoided confrontation with the most intractable problems of the play, those concerning its multiple authorship (for some general comments on these issues, see the Note on the Text). The essential point is that the play was (like the *Bacchae*) produced posthumously, but (unlike the *Bacchae*) appears not to have been finished by the playwright. Nowhere else in the dramatic corpus of Greek tragedy do we find such great variety of style, tone and quality. There are parts which cannot have been written by Euripides, and other parts where it is hard to believe that he is the author. Sometimes it is a matter of additional material of clearly inferior quality being added to a text which perhaps seemed unduly short to the editor (the clearest case is the latter part of the choral entrance-song); elsewhere more than one version seems to have been combined, and it is not clear which version, if any, was in the original text (as in the prologue). There are superfluous or clumsy lines; there are passages where the text has been certainly or probably expanded. Most important, the ending of the play is certainly not Euripidean: the authentic text probably ends with Iphigenia's exit at 1509. As explained further in the Notes, the ending we have has numerous defects (including linguistic and metrical errors which cannot possibly be the work of Euripides or any competent dramatist of the fifth or fourth century BC): it must be a much later composition. There is also external evidence that a different ending (Euripides' own?) once existed, in which Artemis appeared and promised that she would rescue Iphigenia and replace her with a deer as victim.

Most of these points are objectively demonstrable; but when editors and critics get down to detail, the degree of disagreement as to which parts of the play belong to which layer of revision rapidly becomes evident, and some of the more specific arguments can seem worryingly subjective. We cannot expect to be able to peel away the newer layers

and find the original still intact: as is clear from the case of the con-
clusion, authentic or at any rate early material has been irretrievably
lost. Part of the problem lies in the need to be clear about what we
are trying to achieve: to identify Euripides' own contribution, while
admitting that the play may have been incomplete when he died? To
establish what was actually presented to the public in the first perform-
ance (perhaps a composite work by Euripides senior and junior)? Or
to produce a text which could be performed effectively today, whether
or not it corresponds closely to the original work? There are many
specific problems which are disturbing to scholars but which make
little impact on the theatre-goer or on those who read the play in
translation. After much consideration we have translated the whole
text, despite the obvious weaknesses of some parts: to present the
reader only with the portions of the play which are certainly Euripidean
would be impossible, and even if possible would leave the play trunc-
ated. In the Notes I draw attention to the most serious problems
and offer some references to more detailed discussions. By general
agreement the most suspicious portions are 1–162, 231–302, 1510–
1628: in my view none of this is likely to be Euripidean. Controversy
elsewhere takes us into more difficult territory, and detailed argument
is inappropriate here.

Despite the special problems of the play, it retains astonishing power,
and many recent productions have shown that it continues to speak to
our age. The audience which gathered in the Theatre of Dionysus in
405 BC to witness the last dramas of the dead Euripides was surely most
impressed, as we are today, by the *Bacchae*; but we need not doubt that
in the *Iphigenia at Aulis* they recognized a drama of a different kind,
also recognizably the work of the master's hand, and equally deserving
of the first prize that the great playwright had so often been denied.

CHARACTERS

AGAMEMNON, *commander of the Greek expedition and king of Argos*
OLD SERVANT *of Agamemnon*
CHORUS *of women from Chalcis in Euboea*
MENELAUS, *brother of Agamemnon and king of Sparta*
MESSENGER
CLYTEMNESTRA, *wife of Agamemnon*
IPHIGENIA, *daughter of Agamemnon and Clytemnestra*
ACHILLES, *a Greek leader, king of the Myrmidons*
SERVANTS *of Agamemnon*
FOLLOWERS *of Achilles*
BABY *Orestes*
SECOND MESSENGER

[*The scene is set in front of* AGAMEMNON*'s tent[1] in the Greek camp at Aulis. Agamemnon is seated at a makeshift table, pen and ink near at hand, fingering a message-tablet.*]

AGAMEMNON: *Old man, come out here in front of the tent![2]*

[*The* OLD MAN *emerges.*]

OLD MAN: *I'm coming. What new plan do you have, my lord Agamemnon?*

AGAMEMNON: *Hurry!*

OLD MAN: *I'm hurrying! This old age of mine stays wide awake, I tell you, and alert on my eyes.*

AGAMEMNON: *What star with blazing light is that in its course, still speeding along high in the heavens near the seven Pleiads? There is no sound either of birds or of the sea; a windless silence prevails all along the Euripus.* 10

OLD MAN: *But why do you pace restlessly outside your tent, my lord Agamemnon? All is still quiet here at Aulis and the watchmen who guard our walls do not stir. Let's go inside.*

AGAMEMNON: *I envy you, old man, and I envy those who live their lives free from danger, not winning fame or a name among men. I feel less envy for those in office.*

OLD MAN: *And yet there is honour in such a life.* 20

AGAMEMNON: *Yes, but an honour that brings danger; eminence may be pleasurable but once attained it causes grief. Sometimes the service of the gods improperly conducted overthrows a man's life, sometimes it is shattered by the diverse and peevish judgements of his fellow men.*

OLD MAN: *These sentiments in a leader I do not admire. Atreus did*

not father you to enjoy unmixed blessings, Agamemnon. You must
30 *acquaint yourself with pain as well as joy; for you are of mortal stock.*
Whether you wish it or not, this shall be the gods' will.

But you have kindled your lamp's light; you keep writing[3] on this
tablet that you still hold in your hands, then you erase the same
message again, you seal the tablet and open it once more, flinging it
40 *on the ground as tears pour freely from your eyes. Anyone would*
suppose from these signs of despair that you have lost your wits! What
troubles you? What new problem vexes you, my royal lord? Come,
share the news with me! You will be speaking to a good man worthy
of trust; I was sent by Tyndareus all those years ago as part of your
wife's dowry and a loyal attendant of the bride.

AGAMEMNON: Three daughters were born to Leda, Thestius'
50 child: Phoebe, Clytemnestra, my wife, and Helen. The young
men counted the foremost in fortune in Greece came to seek
Helen's hand in marriage. This gave rise to jealousy among
the rival suitors, and threats of dreadful action, if they did not
succeed in winning the maiden. Her father Tyndareus faced
a dilemma. Should he give her away or not? What was the
best way to handle the problem?

This was the solution he found: the suitors should swear
a mutual oath sealed by the clasping of hands, and, with
burnt-sacrifice, they should make libations and offer up this
60 solemn pledge: whoever Tyndareus' daughter should marry,
they would rally round him, if anyone ever took her from her
home and carried her off, dispossessing her husband of his
bride; they would make war on such a man and level his city,
be it Greek or foreign, by force of arms.

When they had sworn this oath (a cunning enough trick
by old Tyndareus to win them round), he gave his daughter
permission to choose one man from the suitors, wherever the
fond breezes of Aphrodite might carry her. Her choice fell on
70 the one who should never have taken her, Menelaus. Then
that man who judged the goddesses,[4] as the story goes,[5] came
from Phrygia to Sparta, florid in the style of his dress and
glittering with gold, suitably lavish trappings for a foreigner.

Finding Menelaus away from home, he seized Helen – his passion for her was fully returned – and took her off to Ida, where he kept his cattle.

Menelaus was filled with rage and rushed up and down Greece, invoking the ancient oath of Tyndareus that the wronged party should receive military aid. So the Greeks next grabbed their spears and leapt at the call to arms. They brought their weaponry to these narrow straits of Aulis where now they are encamped: ships and shields, together with a host of horses and chariots, formed their preparation. And they chose me as commander for Menelaus' sake, as I am his brother; but I wish this honour had fallen to some other man!

Once the army had been mustered and was assembled, we remained idle at Aulis, becalmed and unable to sail. As we found ourselves in this difficulty Calchas announced the divine will: we must sacrifice my own daughter Iphigenia to Artemis, who inhabits this land; if we made the sacrifice, we would have our voyage and bring the Phrygians to their knees, but if not, neither would follow.

When I heard this, I ordered Talthybius to dismiss the whole army with shrill proclamation, for never would I bring myself to kill my own daughter.

Then it was that my brother, employing every form of argument, persuaded me to dare the dreadful deed. In a folding tablet I wrote a message and sent it to my wife, telling her to send our daughter here in the belief that she would marry Achilles.

I made great play of the hero's distinction, saying that he was refusing to sail with the Greek expedition unless a bride from our house should go to his Phthia. This was the means of persuasion I used with my wife, weaving the web of a false marriage to get the girl here. Of the Greeks only we four know the true situation: Calchas, Odysseus, Menelaus and I.[6] Now I am writing a new letter in turn, having changed my thoughts afterwards from the wrong ones I had before, and it

is this one you saw me opening and sealing again, old man,
110 under cover of night. Here, take it now and make your way
to Argos! I will tell you in words the whole message that lies
hidden in the tablet's folds, for you are loyal to my wife and
to my house.

[AGAMEMNON *and the* OLD MAN *now sing in a lyric
exchange.*][7]

OLD MAN: *Speak, tell me, so my tongue may utter words in harmony
with your message.*

AGAMEMNON: *'I send you this letter in addition to my earlier one,
child of Leda. Do not send your daughter to waveless Aulis, sheltered*
120 *wingtip of Euboea. We shall postpone our daughter's wedding to
another time.'*

OLD MAN: *And if Achilles is cheated of his bride, will this not rouse
him to furious anger against you and your wife? That is certainly to
be feared. Tell me your meaning.*

AGAMEMNON: *It is the name and nothing else that Achilles provides;*[8]
he knows nothing about a marriage, or our intentions either, or my
130 *supposed desire to give my child to him in marriage, to clasp in a
bridegroom's embrace.*

OLD MAN: *This is boldness that makes me afraid, Agamemnon, my
royal lord; in order to bring your daughter here to be sacrificed by the
Greeks, you held out the promise of her marriage to the son of the
goddess.*

AGAMEMNON: *Ah, my wits deserted me! Oh, the pain! I fall into
ruin! But hasten on your way, old man; make no concessions to your
years!*

140 OLD MAN: *I hurry, king.*

AGAMEMNON: *No sitting down by shady springs or letting sleep
seduce you!*

OLD MAN: *What a thing to suggest!*

AGAMEMNON: *When you pass a place where the road divides, look
all round you, making sure no carriage on rolling wheels escapes your
eye, as it carries my girl here to the ships of the Greeks.*

OLD MAN: *Rely on me.*

AGAMEMNON: *If she has left the shelter of her home and you encounter*

her escort, turn their bridles round at once and hurry to the dwellings   150
raised by the Cyclopes.⁹

OLD MAN: *But tell me, when I give this instruction to your daughter
and wife, how will they believe me?*

AGAMEMNON: *Guard the seal on the letter you carry here. On your
way! See, the dawn already breaks with the white light of the Sun's
flaming chariot. Be the partner of my labours.*

[*The* OLD MAN *leaves.*]

*No mortal experiences happiness to the end; no one is born free   160
from sorrow.*

[AGAMEMNON *retires into his tent. The* CHORUS *enters.*¹⁰]

CHORUS [Strophe]: *I have come to the sandy shores of Aulis by the
sea, sailing through the surging waters of Euripus' narrow channel
and leaving behind my city of Chalcis, nurse of glorious Arethusa,   170
whose waters mingle with the sea. To see the Achaean army I came,
and the Achaean heroes' seafaring ships. These men, our husbands
say, with a fleet of a thousand craft are being led to Troy by fair-haired
Menelaus and noble Agamemnon. They go to reclaim Helen, whom
the herdsman Paris took from reedy Eurotas as the prize awarded by   180
Aphrodite, when at the bright fountain waters the Cyprian competed,
competed in beauty with Hera and Pallas.*

[Antistrophe:] *Through Artemis' grove rich in sacrifices I came
in haste, my cheeks crimsoned with a young girl's blush, as I wanted
to see the fortifications of the shield-bearing Greeks, the tents of the   190
warriors and their massed horses. I saw the two Ajaxes sitting together,
Oileus' son and Telamon's, crown of fame to Salamis, and Protesilaus
and Palamedes,¹¹ whom Poseidon's daughter bore, seated at the
draught-board and delighting in the many complicated moves. Diom-
edes, too, I saw, charmed by the pleasures of the discus, and beside   200
him Meriones, offspring of Ares, a marvel to mortal eyes, and also
the son of Laertes from his mountainous island, and at his side
Nireus, most handsome of the Achaeans.*

[Epode:] *And swift-running Achilles I saw, whose feet match the
wind, Thetis' son whom Cheiron trained, running a race in full
armour along the shingle by the seashore. He was competing hard   210*

against a chariot drawn by four horses, lap after lap, struggling to win the victory. The charioteer, Eumelus of Pheres' line, kept shouting. I saw his horses, beautiful animals with bridles of finely worked gold, being urged onward by his goad. The two harnessed in the middle were dappled with white hair, while the tracers on the outside, confronting the bends of the course, were bays and dappled at the ankle above the solid hoof. The son of Peleus in his armour sped along beside them, keeping alongside the rail by the chariot-wheels.

[Strophe:] To the host of ships I came, a marvellous spectacle, to satisfy a woman's eyes with the sight and taste the pleasure, honeysweet. The right wing of the fleet the Myrmidon warriors held, Phthia's men, with their fifty swift vessels. Divine Nereids stood at the sterns in images of gold, the emblem to signify the ships of Achilles.

[Antistrophe:] The Argive vessels stood near by, a like number of oared ships. These were commanded by the son of Mecisteus, whom Talaus raised as grandfather, and by Sthenelus, son of Capaneus. The next station was held by the son of Theseus with his sixty Attic ships. Their insignia that raised their sailors' spirits was the goddess Pallas in a winged chariot drawn by horses with uncloven hoof.

[Strophe:] And the naval host of the Boeotians I saw, fifty ships, wearing their ensign with pride. This was Cadmus holding a golden serpent at the curved stern. Laitus the earth-born commanded their naval force. There were vessels from the land of Phocis,[12] [. . .] and also ships from Locris equal in number to these, led by the son of Oileus, who had left the famous city of Thronium behind.

[Antistrophe:] From Cyclopean Mycenae the son of Atreus sent a hundred ships manned with crews. With him as fellow commander came his brother, kin alongside kin, so that Greece might take righteous vengeance on the one who abandoned her home to marry a foreigner. And I saw the ensign of Gerenian Nestor from Pylos, [. . .] his neighbour Alpheus, represented at the stern with bull's hooves.

Of the Aenians there were twelve ships commanded by their king, Gouneus. Near these in turn were the rulers of Elis, whom all the people called Epeians. Eurytus was their commander, and also led the white-oared warriors of Taphos, whose king was Meges. He was the son of Phyleus and had left behind the islands of Echinae shunned by mariners.

The Ajax whom Salamis reared combined his right wing with the left wing of those near his own station, making the link with his ships 290 drawn up at the end of the line, twelve of the trimmest vessels. So much I heard or saw of the naval host. Whoever engages his foreign 300 craft with them will not win a safe return home, such is the preparation of ships I saw there! But some news of the assembled army I heard at home and keep this in mind.

[MENELAUS *enters, followed by Agamemnon's* SERVANT, *from whom he has taken the letter.*]

OLD SERVANT: Menelaus, you go too far! This is an outrage!

MENELAUS: Get away! You show too much loyalty to your master.

OLD SERVANT: That's a reproach that brings me honour![13]

MENELAUS: You'll regret it, if you go too far!

OLD SERVANT: You should not have opened the letter I was carrying!

MENELAUS: And you should not have carried something that spelled ruin for every Greek!

OLD SERVANT: Argue this with others; give me back this letter!

MENELAUS: I will not release it.

OLD MAN: And I will not let it go! 310

MENELAUS: Then I'll soon give you a bloody head with my sceptre!

OLD MAN: Well, it's an honourable end to die for one's master.

MENELAUS: Let go! For a slave you talk too much!

OLD MAN: Master, we're being wronged! This man snatched your letter from my hands by force, Agamemnon, and has no wish to behave justly!

[AGAMEMNON *comes out of his tent.*]

AGAMEMNON: Ha! What is this disturbance outside my tent,[14] this angry exchange of words?

MENELAUS: My account has a better right to be heard than this fellow's.

AGAMEMNON: What has caused you to quarrel with this man, Menelaus, and to use violence?

[*The* SERVANT *goes hastily into the house.*]

320 MENELAUS: Look at me. I will begin my speech in this fashion.

AGAMEMNON: What? Do you think the son of Atreus the Unafraid is afraid to look you in the eye?

MENELAUS: Do you see this letter that serves as a vile messenger?

AGAMEMNON: I do. First of all, hand it over to me now.

MENELAUS: Not until I show its contents to all the Greeks.

AGAMEMNON: Do you mean you have broken the seal and know what you have no business to know?

MENELAUS: Yes, I opened it, and I know the wicked plan you hatched in secret. You'll be sorry for it!

AGAMEMNON: And where did you catch him? Gods, what shamelessness!

MENELAUS: I was waiting for your daughter to reach the camp from Argos.

AGAMEMNON: Why must you watch for what is my concern? Is this not effrontery?

330 MENELAUS: Because I felt the whim; I am not your slave!

AGAMEMNON: Monstrous! Shall I not be allowed to govern my own affairs?

MENELAUS: No, for your thoughts are crooked, some just now, others long since, others still to come.

AGAMEMNON: You present a fine case for dishonesty; a clever tongue breeds hatred.

MENELAUS: Yes, and an inconstant mind makes a man unjust and devious towards friends. I want to prove your guilt in this. Don't let anger turn you away from the truth and I in turn will not press my case too far. You remember the time[15] when you were ambitious to lead the Greek force to Ilium. You appeared reluctant but the desire was there in your heart. What an embarrassing spectacle you made – grasping every man by the hand and keeping your doors unlocked for any 340 citizen who wished to enter! You tried to speak to all of them, one after the other, whether they wanted it or not, and by this behaviour you made a bid for popularity against all comers. Then, once the command was won, you assumed a different manner: you no longer showed your friends the love they had before but became difficult to approach and rarely seen, as you stayed behind locked doors. A good man should not change his character when he rises in the world; no, that is the time for him to remain true to his friends, when good fortune enables him to benefit them more than ever. This is my first criticism of you, as here I first found you wanting.

Then, when you and the army of all Greece[16] came to Aulis   350
and you lacked a wind to blow you on your way, you were completely helpless; this fortune sent by the gods kept you in a state of panic, as the Greeks clamoured for the fleet to be disbanded and an end made to all their fruitless labour at Aulis. What an unhappy look you wore, how dismayed you were at the prospect of not leading a host of a thousand ships and filling the plain before Priam's city with your soldiery! You kept asking for my help: 'What shall I do? What way out can I find and where?' All this so you would not be stripped of your high office and lose your glorious name! Then, when Calchas said you had to sacrifice your daughter to Artemis at the altar for the Greeks to have their voyage, your heart leaped and readily you promised to sacrifice the girl. Of your own free will you sent to your wife, not under duress – do not   360
claim that – to have your daughter brought here under the pretext that she was to be Achilles' bride.

And then you turn about and are caught sending a different message: no longer will you be your daughter's murderer. Just so! The sky above us is the same one that witnessed your promises then. But this is the experience of countless men: they labour hard to win against obstacles, and then they fail basely. Sometimes the foolish judgement of the citizens is the cause but sometimes their fall is deserved, as they prove incapable themselves of keeping their city safe. But it is wretched Greece I weep for above all: she wishes to perform   370

185

a glorious deed, but thanks to you and your girl she will have to allow those foreign nobodies to mock her.

Oh, may I never appoint a man leader of his country or commander of its forces because of his courage! It's a good head that a city's general must have; any man who is shrewd is capable of doing the job.

CHORUS LEADER: It is a terrible thing when brothers trade insults and fight as the result of some quarrel.

AGAMEMNON: I now wish to criticize you, but not at length, not shamelessly raising my eyes too high, but in modest fashion, as you are my brother. A good man is disposed to
380 show respect. Tell me, why this fearful huffing and puffing, that makes your face flushed? Who does you wrong? What do you want? Do you yearn to have a good wife?[17] I cannot give you one: you made a poor job of governing the one you did get. Am I to be punished for your errors, when I haven't gone astray myself? It's not *my* ambition that vexes you; you long to hold a beautiful woman in your arms, throwing discretion and honour to the winds. A bad man's pleasures do not bear examination. If I made a wrong decision previously and came to my senses subsequently, does that make me a madman? You are a better candidate for that title, the man who lost a bad wife and now wants to get her back, despite
390 heaven's kindness in doing you a good turn.

Those misguided suitors swore the oath to Tyndareus in their desire for Helen's hand; but it was hope, a goddess, I think, that brought this about rather than you and your strength. Take them and lead the expedition; the folly in their hearts makes them ready enough. But divinity is not stupid: it can recognize when oaths are sworn wrongfully and under compulsion. I will not kill my own children; I will not offend against justice so that you may prosper by avenging yourself on your harlot wife, while night and day consume me with tears for my lawless deeds, my crimes against my own children!

This is my brief response to you, one that is clear and not

hard to understand. If you choose not to see good sense, so   400
be it; I shall order my own affairs well.

CHORUS-LEADER: These words strike a different note from
those you spoke before, and are welcome – sparing the life of
your child.

MENELAUS: Ah, my state is a sorry one! I have no friends, it
seems.

AGAMEMNON: You would have, if you weren't trying to ruin
your friends!

MENELAUS: How will you give me proof that your father and
mine are one?

AGAMEMNON: I want to share your sensible thoughts, not your
foolish ones.

MENELAUS: Friends should share one another's grief.

AGAMEMNON: Ask for my help when you are helping, not
harming, me.

MENELAUS: Are you not prepared to share this great task with
Greece?   410

AGAMEMNON: Greece, like you, suffers from some heaven-sent
affliction.[18]

MENELAUS: Then betray your brother and glory in your sceptre!
I shall resort to other plans, to other friends . . .

[A MESSENGER *enters in a hurry.*]

MESSENGER: King of the united Greeks, Agamemnon, I bring
you your daughter, to whom you gave the name Iphigenia in
your palace. Her mother accompanies her, the lady Clytem-
nestra, and your son Orestes. She means to give you joy at
the sight of him, after your long absence from home. But
since the journey they were on was long, they are giving cool
refreshment to their feet by a fountain's gracious waters, both   420
the ladies and their horses. We let the animals loose to graze
in a green meadow and crop the grass.

But I have run on here in advance to tell you to be ready.
The army has heard[19] – word spread fast – that your daughter
has arrived. The whole crowd is hurrying to look, eager to
set eyes on your daughter. Men of note are there, famous by

everyone's consent and the object of every eye. They are
saying: 'Is there to be a wedding or something? Does King
Agamemnon miss his daughter so much that he had the girl
brought here?' From others you would have heard this: 'They
are preparing the girl's bridal offerings for Artemis, Aulis'
queen. Who on earth will be her groom?'

Come, look to what follows now, begin the sacrificial rites
with the baskets; put garlands on your heads, and you, my
lord Menelaus, prepare the nuptials; let the flute send out its
notes in the hall, let feet pound out the dance! This day that
has dawned is a blessed one for the maid!

AGAMEMNON: Thank you; now go inside the house. The rest,
as fortune moves on its course, will be well.

[*The* MESSENGER *leaves.*]

Oh, what pain![20] What a wretch I am! What can I say?
Where begin? Necessity's harsh yoke is on my shoulders.
Destiny has stolen up on me and proved subtler by far than
my subtle plans. There is some advantage in being of humble
birth. It is easy for such men to weep and to tell the full
tale of their sorrow. The man of noble birth suffers no less
misfortune, but we have dignity to rule our lives and are the
slaves of the mob.

So I am ashamed to shed a tear but shame again afflicts my
wretched heart if I do not weep at finding myself in such a
calamitous state. So be it; what shall I say to my wife? How
shall I receive her? What looks shall I assume? She has
destroyed me by coming in the midst of troubles to see me,
uninvited. But it is natural that she accompany her daughter,
to do her office as mother of the bride and give away her
greatest treasure – where she will discover me a traitor! And
then there is the poor maiden – but why 'maiden'? Hades, it
seems, will be her bridegroom soon[21] – how I pity her! I
imagine how she will beg me as a suppliant: 'Father, will you
kill me? I hope you and anyone you love may make such a
marriage!' And Orestes will be there at her side, wailing

unintelligibly, but his meaning will be clear. He is still a baby.[22]
Oh, how I suffer! How he has destroyed me by making this
marriage to Helen – Priam's son Paris! *He* has brought all this
about!

CHORUS-LEADER: I, too, pity you, as a foreign woman must
lament the misfortunes of kings.   470

MENELAUS: Brother, give me your right hand to clasp![23]

AGAMEMNON: I give it; the victory is yours, and I am in des-
pair.

MENELAUS: I swear by Pelops, who was called my grandfather
and yours, and by our father Atreus, to speak plainly to you
and from the heart, saying nothing deceitful but what is in my
mind. When I saw you weeping, I myself felt pity and shed
tears in turn for you. I retract my earlier words and have no
wish to be cruel but rather put myself in your own position
now.   480

My advice to you is that you should neither kill your
daughter nor prefer my interest to your own; there is no
justice in you grieving, while I prosper, or in your family
dying, while mine sees the daylight. What is it I wish for? Can
I not make other choice marriages if it is wedlock I desire?
Am I to sacrifice a brother, who should be my dearest friend,
to win back Helen, a poor prize in place of one so noble? I
was a fool and rash in judgement before I examined the matter
closely and saw what it is to kill one's child. In any case I felt   490
pity for the wretched girl when I considered the blood we
share: she is to be sacrificed for the sake of my marriage! What
has your child to do with Helen?

Let the expedition be disbanded and quit Aulis. And you,
my brother, stop making your face wet with tears, and inviting
me to shed them likewise. Whatever you feel about the oracles
concerning your daughter, let them not concern me; I resign
my claims in this to you.

Have I left my earlier threats behind and undergone a
change? It is natural to feel this way: I have changed because   500

189

of love for one who has the same mother as I. Such are the ways of a man whose instincts are sound, on each occasion to adopt the best course.

CHORUS-LEADER: These are noble words, worthy of Tantalus, son of Zeus;[24] you do not disgrace your ancestors.

AGAMEMNON: I commend you, Menelaus, for the course you advise is honourable and worthy of you – it is not what I expected. Strife between brothers comes about through love or domestic ambition. I loathe this kind of kinship that brings pain to both parties. But I have reached a point where I no longer have any choice: I must bring about the bloody execution of my daughter.

MENELAUS: How so? Who will compel you to kill your child?

AGAMEMNON: The whole gathering of the Greek army.[25]

MENELAUS: Not if you send her back to Argos.

AGAMEMNON: That I might manage to do in secret but there is another issue.

MENELAUS: What do you mean? You should not be too afraid of a mob.

AGAMEMNON: Calchas will voice his oracles to the Greek army.

MENELAUS: Not if he dies first; and this is easily managed.

AGAMEMNON: The whole breed of prophets[26] is corrupted by ambition!

MENELAUS: Yes, they are good for nothing – a useless presence.

AGAMEMNON: Do you not fear another possibility that occurs to me?

MENELAUS: Unless you tell me your thought, how would I infer it?

AGAMEMNON: The son of Sisyphus[27] knows all of this.

MENELAUS: You and I have nothing to fear from Odysseus.

AGAMEMNON: He is a subtle fellow always and takes the mob's side.

MENELAUS: Yes, he is enslaved by ambition, a terrible plague.

AGAMEMNON: Can't you see him standing in the midst of the Greeks, proclaiming the oracles expounded by Calchas and saying how I promised to make the sacrifice to Artemis, then

510

520

tried to go back on my word? Won't he sweep the troops off   530
their feet and tell the Greeks to kill you and me before
butchering the girl? And if I escape to Argos, they will come
and destroy my land, razing it to the ground, Cyclopean
walls[28] and all. Such are the sorrows that weigh on me. Oh,
what misery! How helpless I am in the face of these troubles
the gods have sent!

Take care of one task for me, Menelaus: go through the
army and make sure that Clytemnestra does not learn about
our plan before I seize my child and offer her to Hades. I want   540
to achieve my horrible purpose with as few tears as possible.

And you, women, keep silence.[29]

[MENELAUS *leaves;* AGAMEMNON *goes back into his tent.*]

CHORUS [Strophe]: *Blessed are those to whom Aphrodite is gentle,*
who share in due measure in the bliss of marriage, enjoying a spirit
of calm untroubled by mad passions; for when golden-haired Eros
bends his bow with arrows twofold in charm, one is for a destiny of
happy days, the other for life's ruin. O fairest Cyprian, keep this fate   550
far from my bedchamber!

May the delights of love visit me in due measure, and my desires
be pure! May I know Aphrodite in moderation; I want none of her
rage!

[Antistrophe:] *Different are the natures of mortals, different are*
their ways; yet true goodness is always clear. Nurture and education   560
greatly contribute to virtue; for a modest spirit is itself wisdom and
has the exceptional charm whereby reflection makes one discern the
right course; then good repute confers on its possessor a glory that is
forever young. A great thing it is to pursue virtue; among women it
lies in love that is chaste and secret, whereas with men it is observing
inner discipline in its countless forms;[30] this will make a city greater.   570

[Epode:] *You came, Paris,[31] to the place where you were raised*
as a cowherd among white heifers on Ida, piping foreign notes as you
breathed on your reeds an imitation of Olympus' Phrygian flute. The
beasts were browsing, their udders swollen, that day the goddesses
came to be judged in the trial that sent you to Greece. Before Helen's   580

191

*throne of ivory you stood, sending shafts of love into her eyes as they
gazed at you, and yourself succumbing to love's distraction. Hence
came the strife, the strife with Greece that you bring with spears and
ships against the towers of Troy.*

[CLYTEMNESTRA *enters with* IPHIGENIA *and* ORESTES *in
a carriage, accompanied by servants and another carriage.*[32]]

590   *Oh, look! Great is the blessed state of the great! See the king's
daughter Iphigenia, my queen, and Tyndareus' child Clytemnestra.
How great the houses that gave them birth, how happy and lasting
the fortune they have found! The powerful and wealthy are as gods
to mortals not blessed by fortune.*

    *Let us stand near, daughters and nurslings of Chalcis, let us receive
600 the queen steadily as she steps to the ground from her carriage, with
gentle hands and kind intent; I would not have Agamemnon's glorious
child feel afraid on her new arrival. Let us not, visitors here ourselves,
give the Argive visitors cause to be disturbed or alarmed.*

CLYTEMNESTRA: This I count a favourable omen – your kind
hearts and the graciousness of your greeting. It is my hope
610 that I am here to be the bride's matron at a happy wedding.

    [*She turns to her attendants:*] Fetch the dowry gifts I bring
for the maiden from the carriage and carry them with care
into the house.

    And you, my child, leave this horse-drawn carriage, step-
ping down with tender and delicate feet.

    [*To the* CHORUS:] And you, young women, receive her
in your arms and escort her from the carriage. Someone lend
me a supporting hand, so I may leave my carriage-seat in a
graceful manner.

    Some of you stand in front of the horses' yoke; a horse's
620 eye is timorous if no one is near to soothe him. [*To Orestes'
nurse:*] And take this boy, Agamemnon's son, Orestes; he is
still just a babe. My child, do you sleep, overcome by the
carriage's movement? Wake up for your sister's wedding and
bring her luck! You will gain as kinsman a noble warrior, as
you yourself are noble, the son of Nereus' daughter, a man

like the gods. [CLYTEMNESTRA, *escorted to a seat, gestures towards the nurse.*] Sit down here, child, near my foot. And you, Iphigenia, stand next to me and let these strangers see how blessed your mother is. And here is your loving father – give him your greetings! 630

[AGAMEMNON *enters.*]

Agamemnon, my most revered lord and king, we have come in full obedience to your command.

IPHIGENIA [*running to embrace* AGAMEMNON]: Oh, don't be angry with me, mother – I want to hug my father, pressing close against him! I want to sneak up close and press against your chest, father, after all this time! How I have longed to see your face! Oh, don't be angry!

CLYTEMNESTRA: And so you should, child; of all the children I bore him you are the most devoted to your father.

IPHIGENIA: O father, what joy to see you after such a long time! 640

AGAMEMNON: Your father's joy is the same; you speak for both of us.

IPHIGENIA: Greetings! Thank you for bringing me to you, father!

AGAMEMNON: I don't know whether I deserve your thanks or not, child.

IPHIGENIA: Ah! How ill at ease you look, for one so glad to see me!

AGAMEMNON: A king and commander has many thoughts to occupy him.

IPHIGENIA: Stay with me for the present; dismiss your worries!

AGAMEMNON: I am with you for now, all of me, and nowhere else.

IPHIGENIA: Then relax that frown and put on a loving expression.

AGAMEMNON: There, I am as joyful as I feel in seeing you, my child.

IPHIGENIA: And yet there are tears in your eyes? 650

AGAMEMNON: Yes, for my absence from you is to be a long one.

IPHIGENIA: I don't understand your meaning, dearest Father, I
don't understand![33] Where do they say the Phrygians have
their home?

AGAMEMNON: Where I wish Priam's son Paris had never lived!

IPHIGENIA: It's a long voyage you are making, Father, leaving
me behind.

AGAMEMNON: You will come to the same place as your father,
daughter.[34] These sensible words of yours move me the more
to pity.

IPHIGENIA: Then I will not speak sensibly, if that will make
you happy!

AGAMEMNON [turning away from IPHIGENIA]: Ah! I have not
the strength to keep silent! [Turning back to face her:] That's my
good girl!

IPHIGENIA: Stay at home with your children, Father!

AGAMEMNON: That is my wish, but my torment is that I cannot
bring it about.

IPHIGENIA: Destruction fall on spears and Menelaus' woes!

AGAMEMNON: What is destroying me now will bring destruc-
tion on others.

660 IPHIGENIA: How long you have been away, deep in Aulis' bay!

AGAMEMNON: And even now there is something that hinders
me from starting the expedition.

IPHIGENIA: Ah, if only your honour and mine allowed me to
share your voyage!

AGAMEMNON: You, too, have a voyage still to make, one that
will make you remember your father.

IPHIGENIA: Shall I sail with my mother or make the voyage
alone?

AGAMEMNON: Alone, unaccompanied by father or mother.

IPHIGENIA: You aren't finding me another home to live in are
670 you, Father?[35]

AGAMEMNON: Enough! Girls should not know such things.

IPHIGENIA: Please hurry back from Phrygia, Father, once you
have settled matters well!

AGAMEMNON: First I must conduct a certain sacrifice here.

IPHIGENIA: Well, piety needs to be observed through holy rites.

AGAMEMNON: You will know; you will be standing near the sacred vessels.

IPHIGENIA: Shall we be dancing round the altar, Father?

AGAMEMNON: I envy you your lack of understanding; I wish I shared it! Go into the house – it harms a girl's reputation to be seen – kiss me and let me take your hand;[36] you are going to spend a long time away from your father's home.   680

Oh, dear bosom and cheeks, oh your golden hair! What a burden the Phrygians' city and Helen have proved to me! I must speak no more; my eyes grow wet with tears the moment I touch you.

Go into the house.

[IPHIGENIA *leaves*.]

I beg you to bear with me in this, child of Leda, if I show too much grief at the thought of giving away my daughter to Achilles. These leave-takings are happy but still painful to parents' hearts, when a father after all his loving care hands a child over to another house.   690

CLYTEMNESTRA: I am not so insensitive; consider that I myself will also have these feelings – so I do not criticize you – when I lead the girl out to the sound of wedding songs. But it is customary practice, and this will join with time in easing the pain. Now I know the name of the man you have betrothed our child to but I wish to learn his lineage and where he comes from.

AGAMEMNON: Aegina was the daughter of Asopus.[37]

CLYTEMNESTRA: What mortal or god joined with her in marriage?

AGAMEMNON: Zeus; he fathered Aeacus, lord of Oenone.

CLYTEMNESTRA: Which son of Aeacus inherited his home?   700

AGAMEMNON: Peleus; and Peleus won the hand of Nereus' daughter.[38]

CLYTEMNESTRA: Was she the gift of a god or did he take her in spite of the gods?

AGAMEMNON: Zeus betrothed her and gave her away as guardian.

CLYTEMNESTRA: Where did he marry her? Was it under the ocean waves?

AGAMEMNON: Where Cheiron[39] has his dwelling at the base of holy Pelion.

CLYTEMNESTRA: Where they say the race of Centaurs have their home?

AGAMEMNON: There the gods celebrated the wedding of Peleus.

CLYTEMNESTRA: Did Thetis or his father raise Achilles?

AGAMEMNON: It was Cheiron, so that he would not learn the ways of wicked men.

CLYTEMNESTRA: Ah, wise was the teacher, and also he who

710   entrusted him to a wiser head.

AGAMEMNON: Such is the man who will be your daughter's husband.

CLYTEMNESTRA: No fault can be found in him. What city of Greece is his home?

AGAMEMNON: He lives in the land of Phthia, by the river Apidanus.

CLYTEMNESTRA: And is it there he will take your daughter and mine?

AGAMEMNON: That will be for him to decide as her new lord.

CLYTEMNESTRA: Well, may they be happy! What day will the marriage be?

AGAMEMNON: When the full moon comes round.

CLYTEMNESTRA: Have you already performed the initial sacrifices to the goddess?

AGAMEMNON: I am about to; this is the business I am engaged in at present.

CLYTEMNESTRA: Then after this you will celebrate the wed-

720   ding feast?

AGAMEMNON: Yes, once I have made the sacrifice required of me to the gods.

CLYTEMNESTRA: Where shall I hold the feast for the women?

AGAMEMNON: Here, by the ships of the Greeks with their fine prows.[40]

CLYTEMNESTRA: That is good, as there is no alternative; still, may it turn out well!

AGAMEMNON: Do you know what you must do, lady? Do what I ask.

CLYTEMNESTRA: What? I am accustomed to following your orders.

AGAMEMNON: Here, where the bridegroom is, it will be my task . . .

CLYTEMNESTRA: What task will you perform that is my duty, in the mother's absence?

AGAMEMNON: . . . to give away your daughter amidst the men of Greece.

CLYTEMNESTRA: And where am *I* to be at this time?   730

AGAMEMNON: You are to return to Argos and look after your girls.

CLYTEMNESTRA: And leave my daughter? Who will raise the marriage torch?

AGAMEMNON: I will provide the torch that is fitting for this wedding.

CLYTEMNESTRA: But this is not the customary way; these things should not be looked upon as trivial!

AGAMEMNON: It is not right that you should be away from home, in the middle of a mob of soldiers.

CLYTEMNESTRA: It is right that I should give my own child in marriage – I am her mother!

AGAMEMNON: It is also right that your daughters should not be left at home alone.

CLYTEMNESTRA: They are well guarded in the security of their chambers.

AGAMEMNON: Do what I ask!

CLYTEMNESTRA: No, by the heavenly Queen of Argos![41] Go and organize matters away from home; but I will see to domestic affairs and do what must be done for a maid about   740
to be married.

197

[CLYTEMNESTRA *enters the tent with* ORESTES *and* ATTEN-
DANTS; *the carriages are removed from the stage area.*]

AGAMEMNON: Ah, I was too hasty and failed! My hope is
dashed, my plan to get rid of my wife frustrated! I make clever
plans and devise plots against those I love best, and on every
front I lose the battle! Nevertheless I will go with the priest
Calchas and together we will set in train what is pleasing to
the goddess but disastrous for me – no happy outcome for
Greece. A wise man should keep in his home a good and
750   helpful wife or not keep one at all.

[*Exit* AGAMEMNON.]

CHORUS [Strophe]: *Now to Simois and its silvery whirling waters
the assembled host of the Greeks will come with ships of war and
weaponry, to Ilium and the plain of Troy where Phoebus toiled,*[42]
where Cassandra,[43] *I hear, decked with garland of green-leafed bay,
tosses her golden locks, whenever she feels the compelling breath of the*
760   *god's prophetic power.*

[Antistrophe:] *On the battlements of Troy, around its walls the
Trojans will stand, when upon the sea, driven by the oars of fair-
prowed ships, Ares of the bronze shield draws near to Simois' chan-
nels, eager to bring back Helen, sister of the twins who dwell in*
770   *heaven, the Dioscuri, back from Priam's land to Greece, through the
spears and shields of the Achaeans, unwearying warriors.*

[Epode:] *When he has encircled Pergamum, city of the Phrygians,
and its battlements of stone with the carnage of war and has sacked
the city from its foundations, cutting off heads and severing throats,*
780   *he will bring many tears to Priam's wife and daughters.*

*And Helen, child of Zeus, shall be consumed in tears for the
husband she has lost. Never may I or my children's children know
such fearful thoughts as the Lydian women rich in gold and Trojan*
790   *wives shall have, sitting at the loom and saying to one another: 'What
man, then, will take my fine, abundant hair in his tight grip as I
weep, and pluck me from the withering flower that is my homeland?'
It is you who are to blame, offspring of the long-necked swan,*[44] *if the
story is true that Leda encountered the winged bird when Zeus*

changed his shape, or else these things are mere tales brought to men
by the writings of poets, lacking sense or reason. 800

[*Enter* ACHILLES.]

ACHILLES: Where can I find the commander of the Greeks?
Let some servant announce that the son of Peleus, Achilles, is
at his door and looking for him! Not all of us who wait here
by the Euripus are on the same footing: some who left their
homes empty and sit here by the shore are unmarried men,
others have wives and children; so wondrous a passion for this
expedition has taken hold of Greece – some god must have
inspired it. I must now state my own justification for inter-
vening: any other man who pleases will speak for himself. I 810
left the land of Pharsalus behind, and Peleus, and here I wait
by these narrow waters of the Euripus, trying to restrain my
Myrmidons. They pursue me endlessly with their questions:
'Achilles, why are we waiting? How much more time do we
still have to sit out before the voyage to Ilium? Act, if you
mean to act at all, or else lead your men back home without
waiting for the sons of Atreus to make up their minds!'

[*Enter* CLYTEMNESTRA *from the door of the tent.*[45]]

CLYTEMNESTRA: Son of Nereus' divine child, I heard your
words indoors and have come out in front of the house. 820

ACHILLES: By all that's modest, who on earth is this lady I see,
so blessed with beauty?

CLYTEMNESTRA: It is no wonder that you do not know me,
since we have never met; I applaud your respect for modesty.

ACHILLES: Who are you? Why have you come to the gathering
of the Greeks, a woman to men fenced with shields?

CLYTEMNESTRA: I am Leda's daughter, Clytemnestra is my
name, and my husband is King Agamemnon.

ACHILLES: Well answered, brief and to the point! [*He turns as*
if to go.] But it is not right that I should converse with women. 830

CLYTEMNESTRA: Wait – why do you run away? Clasp your
right hand in mine in token of a happy marriage!

ACHILLES: What are you saying? Clasp my hand in yours?

I would feel ashamed before Agamemnon, if I touched what I have no right to touch!

CLYTEMNESTRA: You have a perfect right, son of the sea-goddess, Nereus' child, as you are about to marry my daughter!

ACHILLES: What marriage is this? I am speechless, lady. Is some delusion causing you to speak so strangely?

840 CLYTEMNESTRA: It is natural for men to be embarrassed when they see new relatives and think of marriage.

ACHILLES: I have never courted your daughter, lady, and no talk of marriage has reached me from the sons of Atreus.

CLYTEMNESTRA: How can this be? You may well puzzle over my words, for your own fill me with wonder.

ACHILLES: Wonder indeed; but together we can puzzle this out. We are both equally deceived in what we say.

CLYTEMNESTRA: Am I the victim of some monstrous hoax? I am in search of a marriage that does not exist, it seems! This fills me with shame!

ACHILLES: Perhaps someone has played a trick on both of us.
850 Think nothing of it. Do not let it upset you.

CLYTEMNESTRA: Goodbye; I can no longer look you properly in the eye, now that I have been turned into a liar and humiliated.

ACHILLES: Goodbye to you also; I go to find your husband inside the house here.

[The old SERVANT of Agamemnon is heard calling out from inside.]

OLD MAN: Stranger, born of Aeacus' line, wait![46] It's you I mean, the son of the goddess, and you, Leda's daughter!

ACHILLES: Who is it that calling from behind these half-opened doors? What fear there is in his voice!

OLD MAN [peering out and half-emerging]: A slave, and little pride it gives me; fortune does not permit it.

ACHILLES: Who is your master? Not I; my property is separate from Agamemnon's.

OLD MAN: I belong to this lady who stands before the house.
860 She received me from Tyndareus, her father.

ACHILLES: Here I stand; say what reason you have for holding me back. What do you wish to say?

OLD MAN: Are the two of you quite alone at the entrance here?

ACHILLES: Speak, for we alone will hear; but come out of the king's house!

[*Enter the old* SERVANT *of Agamemnon.*]

OLD MAN: O Fortune and my own foresight, save the ones I want saved!

ACHILLES: This speech of yours keeps us waiting: you shrink from saying what you mean.

[*The* SERVANT *kneels to take hold of* CLYTEMNESTRA's *right hand.*]

CLYTEMNESTRA: You have my protection – do not hesitate if you want to tell me anything.

OLD MAN: Well, then, you know me, the kind of man I am, how loyal a servant to you and your children!

CLYTEMNESTRA: I know that for many a year you have been one of my household retainers.

OLD MAN: And that King Agamemnon received me as part of your dowry?

CLYTEMNESTRA: You accompanied me to Argos and have been mine ever since. 870

OLD MAN: It's true; and it's your interests I care about, more than your husband's.

CLYTEMNESTRA: Well, now's the time to uncover the secret message you have for me.

OLD MAN: Your daughter is going to die, and her own father with his own hand will do the deed!

CLYTEMNESTRA: What do you mean? What an abominable suggestion, old man! You have lost your senses!

OLD MAN: He means to cut the poor girl's white throat with a sword.

CLYTEMNESTRA: Oh, what misery I feel! Has my husband gone mad, then?

OLD MAN: He has his wits, except where you and your daughter are concerned; that's where sanity has left him.

CLYTEMNESTRA: But why? What angry spirit is driving him to this?

OLD MAN: An oracle, so Calchas says, so that the army may set out.

CLYTEMNESTRA: Where are they bound? O pity me, pity the one her father intends to kill!

880

OLD MAN: For the palace of Dardanus, to win back Menelaus' Helen.

CLYTEMNESTRA: Then it was fated that Iphigenia's life should be the price for Helen's return?

OLD MAN: Just so; her father is going to sacrifice your child to Artemis.

CLYTEMNESTRA: And the marriage with which he brought me from home, what was the point of that story?

OLD MAN: He wanted you to bring your child here, happy at the prospect of her becoming Achilles' bride.

CLYTEMNESTRA: O daughter, you have come to meet destruction, you and your mother also!

OLD MAN: It is pitiful, what you both have to endure; Agamemnon has contrived a monstrous act.

CLYTEMNESTRA: I am ruined! Ah, the pain! No more can I staunch the flow of these tears!

OLD MAN: If the loss of a child is matter for grief, let the tears flow.

CLYTEMNESTRA: But where do you say you learned this, old man? How did this knowledge reach you?

890

OLD MAN: I was sent on my way with a letter for you, one that concerned the earlier one he wrote.

CLYTEMNESTRA: Did it forbid me to bring my daughter to her death or reinforce the instruction?

OLD MAN: It said you should not bring her; in that hour, it happened, your husband had returned to his senses.

CLYTEMNESTRA: Then how was it that, if you had this letter, you failed to deliver it into my hands?

OLD MAN: Menelaus took it from me. He is responsible for this sorry situation.

CLYTEMNESTRA: O child of Nereus' daughter, son of Peleus, do you hear this?

ACHILLES: I hear it, and know your misery, but my own part in this vexes me indeed.

CLYTEMNESTRA: They mean to kill my daughter, and marriage to you was the trap they set!

ACHILLES: I, too, blame your husband; my anger is twofold.

CLYTEMNESTRA: It will cause me no shame to fall at your knees,[47] for I am mortal and a goddess is your mother. This is 900 no time for me to show pride, and where should I devote my energy if not for my child's sake?

Son of the goddess, champion my misfortune and hers, the maiden who was called your wife – falsely, yes, but protect us nonetheless! For you I put a garland on her hair, and I escorted her to be your bride, but now it is to the sacrificial knife I bring her. The disgrace of not defending her will fall on your head; for though you did not marry her, yet at any rate you were called the poor girl's loving husband.

By your beard, by your right hand, by your mother – it is your name has ruined me, and your name that should protect me – I have no other altar where I can seek refuge except 910 your knees, and no friend stands at my side. Agamemnon's conduct you have heard of, his cruelty and lack of any scruple. And here I have come, as you see, a woman among an army of sailors who lack discipline and have the boldness for any wicked deed, but can be of service when they will.[48] If you have the courage to offer us your protection, we are saved; if not, we are not.

CHORUS-LEADER: Motherhood is a formidable thing, and it casts a powerful spell. All mothers possess this trait in common: they will endure any labour for their children's sake.

ACHILLES: My anger rises[49] high and far. But I know how to exercise restraint in grieving at misfortune and rejoicing in 920 success. Such mortals show true judgement in their thinking: they will pass through life wisely. There are times when it is pleasant not to show too much wisdom, and times when it is helpful to have good sense. Now, I was reared in the house of Cheiron, a most pious man, and I learned to be straightforward in my dealings with people. As regards the sons of Atreus, I will obey them if their leadership is honourable; if it departs from honour, I will not obey. Here and in Troy I will keep my nature free, and do my utmost to honour Ares with my spear.

But you, lady, have been outrageously treated by those closest to you. I give you the tribute of my pity, as much as lies in a young warrior to bestow. Never, now that she has been named as mine, shall your daughter be slaughtered by her father! I will not let your husband play tricks with Achilles! My very name, though it never raised the sword, will bring death to your daughter. And your husband is the cause. My body is no longer pure, if because of me and my marriage this girl is to die, suffering a terrible, unendurable end, shamefully dishonoured past imagining.

I am, it seems, the basest of the Greeks, I am nothing, and Menelaus is a proper man; I am not Peleus' son but some fiend's, if, to please your husband, my name is to commit murder. No, by Nereus who was reared in the watery waves, sire of Thetis who gave me birth, king Agamemnon shall not lay hands on your daughter, not even a finger, so as to touch her robes! Or else Sipylus, that barbarian fortification where our generals' family has its origin, will be held in high honour, and the name of Phthia nowhere spoken on men's lips. Prophet Calchas shall rue the day he offers up his barley-cakes and lustral water! Who is he, your prophet? A man who tells a few truths and a lot of lies when he is in luck, and when he isn't, counts for nothing.

It is not for the sake of marriage that I have said this[50] – countless girls compete to have me as their husband. No, King Agamemnon has insulted me. He should have asked my permission to use my name to entrap this girl. It was my name above all as the bridegroom that persuaded Clytemnestra to give her daughter in marriage. I would have given the Greeks my name, if the voyage to Troy depended upon it; I would not have refused to further the common good of all my comrades. But, as it is, I count for nothing; the commanders do not care whether they treat me well or badly. My sword shall soon know, when I tarnish it with someone's life-blood before we ever reach the Trojans – any man who tries to take 970 your daughter from me.

Do not be troubled. You see in me a god strong to save, though I am not one; but I will yet prove to be one.

CHORUS-LEADER: Son of Peleus, your words do honour to yourself and to the goddess of the sea, a power whom we revere.

CLYTEMNESTRA: Ah, how can I praise you with words that do not exceed the mark or fall short and so lose your good-will? Good men feel a certain distaste for those who praise them, if their compliments go too far. I am ashamed to bur- 980 den you with piteous appeals when mine is a personal afflic-tion; this malady I suffer does not vex *you*. And yet it is a fine sight when a good man assists the unfortunate, far removed though he be from their problems. Pity me: my sufferings are pitiful. First, I thought I would have you as a son-in-law but I hoped in vain. Moreover, perhaps my child's death may prove an omen for your own marriage, when it comes, and you must guard against this. But your first words were well said, as were your last: if it is your wish, my child shall be 990 saved.

Do you want her to clasp your knees as a suppliant would? This does not become a maiden, but, if you so de-cide, she will come forth, with modesty and frankness in her looks. But if you will extend me the same kindness without her presence, let her stay indoors; her manner is reserved and proud. But still, as far as possible, entreaty must prevail.

ACHILLES: Do not bring your child into my sight, lady; I have no wish to be criticized by men without feeling. An army gathered from every source, untroubled by home cares, loves 1000 foul gossip and slander. In any case, whether you come as suppliants or not, it will make no difference to your success; my one supreme challenge is to save you from danger. Be sure of one thing: I will not speak falsely: if I am guilty of lying or deluding you to no purpose, may I die. But may I be spared death, if I save the girl.

CLYTEMNESTRA: May you be blessed for constantly helping those in distress!

ACHILLES: Listen to me now, so that our enterprise may prosper.

1010 CLYTEMNESTRA: Why tell me this? I must listen to you.

ACHILLES: Let us persuade her father to adopt a better frame of mind.

CLYTEMNESTRA: He is something of a coward and fears the army too much.

ACHILLES: But arguments overthrow fears.

CLYTEMNESTRA: It is a cold hope; but tell me what I must do.

ACHILLES: Beg him first not to kill the child; if he resists, you must come to me. If you succeed in your request, there is no need for me to intervene; your safety is assured. I shall be on better terms with my friend, and the army 1020 would not blame me, if I resolved this matter by deliberation rather than by force. If things are resolved well, and turn out as you and your loved ones want, you will succeed even without me.

CLYTEMNESTRA: Your words are full of sense; I must act as you think best. If, however, I fail in any of my plan, where shall I see you again? Where am I to go in my misery to find your protecting hand?

ACHILLES: I shall keep watch for you where I am most needed. We don't want you to be seen rushing distraught through the crowd of Greek soldiers. You must not disgrace the house of 1030 your ancestors. Tyndareus does not merit the abuse of men's tongues; his name is great among the Greeks.

CLYTEMNESTRA: So be it; give your orders; I must be your

servant. If the gods are intelligent,[51] then, being a just man,
you will find them gracious; if they are not, why should we
exert ourselves?

[ACHILLES *leaves;* CLYTEMNESTRA *re-enters the tent.*]

CHORUS [Strophe]: *What was the melody that Hymenaeus[52] raised
on the Libyan flute, to the strains of the dance-loving lyre and reedy
pipes, that day when the Pierian maids with lovely hair, beating time* 1040
*on the earth with gold-sandalled feet, came over Pelion to the wedding
of Peleus, where the gods held feast? With tuneful airs that echoed in
the Centaurs' mountain haunts and the woodlands of Pelion they
sang the praises of Thetis and Aeacus' son. And the scion of Dard-
anus, Phrygian Ganymede,[53] beloved darling of Zeus' couch, was* 1050
*there to draw the wine-libation from bowls in cups of gold, while
Nereus' fifty daughters celebrated the marriage in dance, whirling in
a maze of circles upon the gleaming sand.*

[Antistrophe:] *And with staffs of pine, and heads wreathed in
greenery, there came to the feast of the gods and mixing-bowl of
Bacchus the troop of mounted Centaurs. Loud was the cry they made:* 1060
*'Daughter of Nereus, the prophet who is skilled in Phoebus' lore,
Cheiron, has proclaimed that you will bear a son to be a great light
to Thessaly. He shall come to the land of Priam with the spears and
shields of his Myrmidons, to destroy that famous land by fire, and* 1070
*shall be furnished with a suit of armour for his body,[54] weaponry of
gold fashioned by Hephaestus, that he shall wear as a gift from his
goddess mother, Thetis, who gave him birth.' Then did the gods bless
the nuptials of the first of Nereus' noble daughters, and the wedding
of Peleus.*

[Epode:] *But your head, rich in lovely hair, the Greeks will* 1080
*wreathe like a flawless heifer's, a dappled beast that has come from
its rocky cave in the mountains; a human throat they will make run
red with blood. Not with a shepherd's pipe were you reared, or amid
the whistling of herdsmen, but in your mother's home, to be adorned
as a bride for one of Inachus' sons to wed!*

Where can the face of Modesty, the face of Virtue, prevail, when 1090
Godlessness holds sway, and mortals put Virtue behind them, paying

her no regard, when Lawlessness controls laws, and men make no common effort to keep heaven's anger at bay?

[CLYTEMNESTRA *enters.*]

CLYTEMNESTRA: I have come out of the house on the look-out for my husband, who has left his quarters and has been absent a long while. My poor child is in tears; all the different notes of lamentation pour from her lips, for she has heard of the death her father plans. I spoke of him and here he comes – Agamemnon approaches, who will soon be exposed for his wicked plots against his own child!

[AGAMEMNON *enters.*]

AGAMEMNON: Daughter of Leda, it is timely that I find you outside the house; I wish to tell you, away from the girl, things a bride ought not to hear.

CLYTEMNESTRA: What seems to you so urgent at this time?

AGAMEMNON: Bring the child out of the house to join her father. The lustral water is prepared and ready, and the cakes of barley to throw on the purifying fire, as are the heifers that must die for the goddess before the wedding, their nostrils spouting dark blood for Artemis.[55]

CLYTEMNESTRA [*aside, as she moves away to the door*]: Your words sound well, but your actions – I cannot bring myself to praise *them.* Daughter, come outside – you know, in any case, your father's intentions – take your brother Orestes under your cloak, child, and bring him out! [*She turns and addresses* AGAMEMNON, *as* IPHIGENIA *enters with* ORESTES:] Look, here she comes, obedient to your will! In all things now I will speak for her as well as for myself.

AGAMEMNON: Child, why do you weep? Are you no longer glad to see me? Why do you stare at the ground and keep your cloak before your eyes?

CLYTEMNESTRA: Ah! Where am I to begin my tale of woes? I may start with any one of them; first, last, middle – they're all as grim as the rest!

AGAMEMNON: What is this? How you all combine to show me faces of confusion and despair!

CLYTEMNESTRA: Answer whatever I ask you, husband, as a man of honour should.

AGAMEMNON: You need not instruct me; I am willing to be questioned! 1130

CLYTEMNESTRA: This child – your daughter, and mine – do you intend to kill her?

AGAMEMNON: Oh! What cruel words! These suspicions do you no honour!

CLYTEMNESTRA: Calm yourself; answer me that first question.

AGAMEMNON: You'll get a reasonable answer if you ask reasonable questions!

CLYTEMNESTRA: One question is all I ask you; answer this and this alone.

AGAMEMNON: O sovereign destiny, chance and my evil fate!

CLYTEMNESTRA: My evil fate as well, and this girl's – three evil fates in one!

AGAMEMNON: How are you wronged?

CLYTEMNESTRA: You ask me this? That brain of yours has little sense in it!

AGAMEMNON: I am ruined! My deception has been exposed! 1140

CLYTEMNESTRA: I know it all. I have learned what you intend to do to me; your very silence is a confession – and these sighs. Spare yourself the effort of a lengthy speech!

AGAMEMNON: See, I am silent; why should I add shamelessness to my misfortunes by telling lies?

CLYTEMNESTRA: Then listen; I shall speak plainly, no longer dealing in riddles or obfuscations.

Firstly, let me make this my first charge against you:[56] you married me against my will and took me by force, after you had killed my former husband, Tantalus. You tore my infant 1150 child rudely from my breast and dashed his brains out on your floor. The twin sons of Zeus, my brothers, rode against you in war, resplendent on their horses, but you turned suppliant and won the protection of my old father, Tyndareus. Next you gained me as your wife.

As such, I was reconciled to you, and you will testify that I was a blameless wife to you and your house; chaste in my conduct, I brought honour to your halls, so that you entered with joy and left a happy man. It's a rare catch for a man to find such a wife; to have a bad one is common enough. I gave birth to three daughters and presented you with this boy, besides; one of these you cruelly mean to take from me. And if you are asked why you intend to kill her, tell me, what will your answer be? Or must I say it for you? So that Menelaus may have Helen. A fine price to pay for a woman of no morals – one's own child! We use what we love dearly to buy what we loathe.

Come, if you go to war,[57] leaving me at home, and spend a long time away on campaign, what feelings do you suppose I will have back at home? When I go through her chambers and see them vacant, vacant every chair, and sit on my own with tears for company, chanting an endless dirge for her: 'He destroyed you, child, the father who sired you, himself and no one else the killer, and by no other man's hands. [You] were the price he paid on departure, [so as to bring Helen back] to her home.'[58] No great excuse is now needed for me and the daughters you left at home to give you the welcome back that you deserve. In heaven's name do not compel me to play the wicked wife by being wicked yourself!

Now then, when you sacrifice your child here, what prayers will you voice? What blessing will you ask of the gods as you butcher your daughter? A sorry homecoming to match the shameful way you left your home? What blessing is it right that *I* should ask for you? We would hardly be crediting the gods with intelligence if we wish murderers well! Will you embrace your children on your return to Argos? The gods would not permit it; which of your offspring will meet your eye, accepting your embrace only to be killed?

Did you give any thought to this, or were you concerned

only to parade your sceptre and play the general? You should
have made this speech to the Greeks, an honourable one:
'Men of Greece, is it your wish to sail against the land of the
Trojans? Then decide by lot whose child must die.' That
would have been an equitable solution, not that you should
select your own daughter as a victim for sacrifice and give her
to the Greeks, or that Menelaus should kill Hermione for her   1200
mother's sake, though the quarrel is his. But now it is I, the
woman who has been loyal to your bed, who am to lose my
child, while that criminal will keep her daughter in Sparta
under her roof, and be happy!

    Answer me if there is any point here I have misrepresented;
but if my words are true, then do not kill your daughter and
mine, and you will show sense.

CHORUS-LEADER: Do as she says! Honour requires that you
    join her in saving the child, Agamemnon; no one on earth
    will speak against it.   1210

IPHIGENIA: If I had the eloquence of Orpheus,[59] Father, charm-
    ing rocks to follow me at my song and bewitching with my
    words whoever I pleased, I would have taken that course. But
    as it is, I will offer the only art I possess, my tears; that *is*
    within my power. Like a suppliant's branch I press against
    your knees this body of mine that this woman bore to you;
    do not destroy me before my time! It is sweet to gaze on the
    light; do not force me to see the underworld! I was the first
    to call you father, as you first called me daughter; I was the   1220
    first to hug your knees, to give loving caresses and receive
    them in turn. These were your words at that time: 'O my
    child, shall I see you happy in some husband's home, alive
    and blooming to bring me honour?' Then I would reply, my
    hand clinging to your beard as now it clasps you, 'What state
    shall I find you in? Shall I welcome you into my home with
    loving hospitality, father, when you are old? Shall I make you
    a proper return for the effort and care you spent on my
    upbringing?'   1230

    These words I keep in my memory but you have forgotten

them; your wish is to kill me. Do not, I beg you by Pelops, by your father Atreus, by my mother here, whose former birth-pains have now returned to cause her agonies a second time! What have I to do with the marriage of Alexander and Helen? Why must I perish for his coming to Sparta, father? Look at me – give me a glance, a kiss! Let me have this at least as a memory of you when I die, if my words fail to persuade you.

1240

Brother, you may be no strong ally to your loved ones, but still, share your tears with mine, and beg our father humbly not to let your sister die! [*The child wails*.] Even infants are aware of suffering. See, Father, he does not speak but begs you just the same!

Oh, hear my appeal! Take pity on my young life! Yes, by your beard we beseech you, both loving you well, the one a fledgling still, the other full grown. I will win my case by summing it all up in one plea: the greatest joy for mortals is to look upon the light of this world; the nether world is nothing. Mad is the man who prays for death; a sorry life is better than a noble death.

1250

CHORUS-LEADER: O cruel Helen, because of you and your marriage a great trial faces the sons of Atreus and their children!

AGAMEMNON: I love my children and understand what stirs pity and what does not; otherwise I would lack all reason. It is a terrible thing for me to carry out this act, my wife, and terrible if I do not;[60] it is the same for me in either case.

[*To both* CLYTEMNESTRA *and* IPHIGENIA:] You see the size of this naval preparation, the scores of Greek warriors, armed in bronze, for whom there will be no voyage to conquer Ilium's towers and level Troy's glorious foundations, unless I sacrifice you as Calchas the prophet prescribes. A passionate desire rages in the Greek army to sail with all speed against that foreign land and to teach them not to carry off the wives of Greeks. These men will kill my young daughters in Argos, as well as you and me, if I ignore the command of the gods' oracle. It is not Menelaus who has turned me into

1260

a slave, my child, nor his desire that guides my actions, but   1270
Greece: to her, whether I wish it or not, I am bound to offer
you in sacrifice; against this I have no power. Greece must be
free, as far as you and I, my child, can bring it about; we are
Greeks and must not let foreigners use violence against our
wives and carry them off.

[*Exit* AGAMEMNON.]

[CLYTEMNESTRA *sings a short response to Agamemnon's
speech, then* IPHIGENIA *sings of her despair in a monody.*]

CLYTEMNESTRA: *O ladies, and you, my child, how wretched it
makes me to think of your death! Your father runs away, consigning
you to Hades!*

IPHIGENIA: *Pity me, mother! Fortune has descended on us both with
the same doleful strain. No more shall I see the light, no more these*   1280
rays of the sun!

Ah, ah, snow-clad glen of Phrygia,[61] *mountain haunt of Ida,
where Priam once cast out for a deadly end the tender babe he had
wrested from its mother – Paris, who was called 'Ida's child', yes,
'Ida's child' was he called in the city of the Phrygians.*[62]   1290

Would that he had never been raised as a herdsman among cattle,[63]
*that Alexander, never given a home by you beside the shining waters
where the fountains of the nymphs lie, and the meadow blooming
with fresh flowers, and roses and hyacinths for goddesses to gather!
There one day came Pallas, and the wily Cyprian, and Hera, and*   1300
*Hermes, messenger of Zeus; the Cyprian prided herself on the desire
she inspires, Pallas on her spear, and Hera on her royal union with
Lord Zeus. So to that loathsome judgement they came, to that dispute
over beauty that would bring death to me but glory to the maidens of
Greece, as Artemis accepted the sacrifice for the voyage to Ilium. But*   1310
*the man who fathered me in my misery is gone, Mother, o Mother;
he has left me alone and forsaken! Oh what a wretch am I! How
cursed, cursed was the day I set eyes on that monster, Helen! My
blood is being spilled, I perish at my father's hands – unholy the
deed, unholy the doer!*

*I wish that Aulis here had never welcomed into this anchorage the
sterns of bronze-beaked ships, the fleet to speed the army to Troy,*   1320

and that Zeus had not blown winds on the Euripus to oppose their sailing! Many and varied are the breezes he sends to mortals: some have joy in raising the sail, some sorrow, some hardship; one ship speeds from port, another's sails are furled, another waits for wind.

1330   *Born to sorrow, then, is the race of man that lives for a day, born to sorrow. Destiny is unhappiness for men to discover. Ah, great is the suffering, great the sorrow that Tyndareus' daughter brings upon the Greeks!*

CHORUS-LEADER: I pity you for the grimness of your fate; it is one that should never have befallen you.

IPHIGENIA: O Mother, my Mother,[64] I see a crowd of men approaching!

CLYTEMNESTRA: It is the son of the goddess, Achilles, my child, for whom you came here.

1340 IPHIGENIA: Open up the house, servants! I want to hide!

CLYTEMNESTRA: Why are you running away, child?

IPHIGENIA: I am ashamed to see this Achilles.

CLYTEMNESTRA: But why?

IPHIGENIA: The miserable outcome of this marriage embarrasses me.

CLYTEMNESTRA: You cannot afford such fastidiousness in your situation. Stay where you are. It is no time to stand on our dignity if we are to be saved.

[ACHILLES *enters with attendants who carry his armour.*]

ACHILLES: Poor lady, daughter of Leda . . .

CLYTEMNESTRA: Your words are true!

ACHILLES: . . . there is fearful shouting among the Greeks . . .

CLYTEMNESTRA: What shouting? Tell me!

ACHILLES: . . . about your daughter . . .

CLYTEMNESTRA: Your words are an omen of evil.

ACHILLES: . . . that she must be sacrificed.

CLYTEMNESTRA: Does no one speak against this?

ACHILLES: I myself got into some danger . . .

CLYTEMNESTRA: What danger, sir?

ACHILLES: . . . of being pelted with stones.

1350 CLYTEMNESTRA: Not for trying to save my girl?

ACHILLES: Exactly that.

CLYTEMNESTRA: Who would have dared to lay a finger on you?

ACHILLES: All the Greeks.

CLYTEMNESTRA: Were your Myrmidon warriors not there to protect you?

ACHILLES: They were the first to turn against me.

CLYTEMNESTRA: Then we are ruined indeed, my child!

ACHILLES: They called me a slave to my hopes of marriage.

CLYTEMNESTRA: And what answer did you give?

ACHILLES: That they should not kill the bride who was meant to be mine . . .

CLYTEMNESTRA: Quite right!

ACHILLES: . . . who was promised to me by her father.

CLYTEMNESTRA: The man who sent for her from Argos!

ACHILLES: But their roars beat me down.

CLYTEMNESTRA: Yes, a mob is a curse and a fearful thing.

ACHILLES: Even so, I will defend you!

CLYTEMNESTRA: You will fight, one against many?

ACHILLES: Do you see these men who bear my armour?

CLYTEMNESTRA: May your generous spirit be rewarded!

ACHILLES: I will have my reward.

CLYTEMNESTRA: Then will my child no longer be slaughtered?   1360

ACHILLES: Not with my consent.

CLYTEMNESTRA: Will someone come forward to lay hands on the girl?

ACHILLES: Men past numbering, with Odysseus at their head.

CLYTEMNESTRA: You mean the son of Sisyphus?

ACHILLES: None other.

CLYTEMNESTRA: Acting on his own initiative, or at the army's bidding?

ACHILLES: They may have chosen him, but he is willing enough!

CLYTEMNESTRA: A wicked choice – to commit murder!

ACHILLES: But I will prevent him.

CLYTEMNESTRA: Will he seize her and lead her off, though she resists?

ACHILLES: Certainly, and by her golden hair!

CLYTEMNESTRA: What am I to do when that happens?

ACHILLES: Hold on firmly to your daughter.

CLYTEMNESTRA: If that's what's needed, she shall escape the knife!

ACHILLES: Yet this is what it will come to.

IPHIGENIA: Mother, you must hear what I have to say.[65] This anger you feel against your husband, I see that it is pointless;

1370   when our task is impossible, resistance is hard indeed. It is right for us to praise the stranger for his zeal; but you must also see that his reputation with the army does not suffer, that he should not come to grief, while we gain no advantage.

Let me tell you what occurred to me, Mother, as I reflected. I am resolved to die; and I want to do so gloriously, banishing all ignoble thoughts from my mind. Come, Mother, consider it with me; see how right I am in this. All eyes in mighty Greece now turn to me. On me depend the voyage of the fleet and the destruction of the Phrygians; with me it lies to

1380   stop barbarians carrying off our women from prosperous Greece in days to come, should they make any such attempt, and to make them pay for the ruin of Helen when Paris abducted her. All this I will achieve by my death, and my fame as the liberator of Greece shall prove blessed. Again, it is not right that I should love life too much. You bore me to be the child of all Greeks, not yours alone.[66] Countless men stand armed with shields, countless with oars in hand, who will dare to do brave deeds against the enemy and to die for Greece, now that their country has been wronged; shall my

1390   one life stand in the way of all this? Where would lie the justice in this? What argument could we offer? Consider this point as well: it is not right that this man should have to fight with all the Greeks and be killed for a woman's sake. One man has greater claim to see the sunlight than ten thousand women.[67] If it is Artemis' will to take this life of mine, shall I,

a mortal, oppose the goddess? It is impossible. I give my body
to Greece. Sacrifice me, sack Troy! This will be my memorial
for many an age, this my children, my marriage, my renown!
It is natural that Greeks rule barbarians, Mother, not barbarians   1400
Greeks;[68] the one is a race of slaves, the other free men.

CHORUS-LEADER: Young woman, you have a noble heart! It
is fortune and the goddess that are at fault.

ACHILLES: Child of Agamemnon, a happy man indeed some
god meant to make me, if only I won you for my wife! I envy
Greece one such as you, and you a land like Greece. These
are fine words you have spoken, and worthy of your country;
you have given up striving against heaven's will, that over-
powers you, and have correctly judged the proper course that
necessity requires. All the more do I long to have you as my
bride now that I have seen into your soul; for you are truly   1410
noble. Look now, I want to do you service and to win you
for my house. It will cause me pain, Thetis be my witness, if
I do not fight the Greeks and save you. Consider; death is a
grim and fearful thing!

IPHIGENIA: I say this without hesitation. Tyndareus' daughter
has done enough to make men fight and kill one another for
her beauty's sake; do not die on my account, sir, or take
another's life, but allow me to save Greece, if it is in my
power.   1420

ACHILLES: Ah, noble spirit![69] I can no longer argue against you,
as this is your decision. Your sentiments are noble ones; why
should a man not admit the truth? Nevertheless you may
perhaps change your mind about this. So, to assure you of my
intentions, let me speak them now: I will go and put my
weapons near the altar, as I intend not to allow your death
but to prevent it. You may well make use of my offer when
you see the blade near your throat. I will not allow you to die
through your impetuousness. I will go with these weapons to   1430
the goddess's temple and be on the look-out for your arrival.

[*Exit* ACHILLES *and his escort.*]

IPHIGENIA: Mother, why do you weep but say nothing?

CLYTEMNESTRA: My misery gives me reason for my heart to ache.

IPHIGENIA: Enough – do not turn me into a coward! Do as I ask in this.

CLYTEMNESTRA: Then speak; *I* will do you no wrong, child!

IPHIGENIA: Then do not cut off a lock of your hair or dress yourself in black clothes.

CLYTEMNESTRA: What do you mean, child? When I have lost you?

IPHIGENIA: But you have not! I am saved, and through me
1440   you shall have glory!

CLYTEMNESTRA: In what way? Should I not mourn your passing?

IPHIGENIA: By no means: for a tomb will not be raised for me.

CLYTEMNESTRA: Is it not customary to honour the dead with a tomb?

IPHIGENIA: My memorial shall be the altar of the goddess who is daughter of Zeus.

CLYTEMNESTRA: Well, I shall do as you ask, child: you are right.

IPHIGENIA: I shall be fortunate: I shall be the benefactor of Greece.

CLYTEMNESTRA: What report should I give your sisters?

IPHIGENIA: Do not dress them either in black garments.

CLYTEMNESTRA: Is there any word of love from you I should give the girls?

IPHIGENIA: Bid them farewell; and make sure you bring up
1450   Orestes here as a man!

CLYTEMNESTRA: You look at him for the last time – hold him tight!

IPHIGENIA [*holding Orestes close*]: Darling boy, you helped your dear sister as much as you could!

CLYTEMNESTRA: Is there anything I can do in Argos to please you?

IPHIGENIA: Do not hate my father[70] – he is your husband.

CLYTEMNESTRA: A terrible course must he run because of you.

IPHIGENIA: Against his will, for the sake of Greece, he ended my life.

CLYTEMNESTRA: But he used treachery; he acted without honour and brought shame on Atreus.

IPHIGENIA: Who will come to take me there before they drag me by the hair?

CLYTEMNESTRA: I will be at your side . . .

IPHIGENIA: No, not you – that would not be right!

CLYTEMNESTRA: . . . holding on to your clothes!

IPHIGENIA: Mother, oblige me in this: stay here! This is the   1460
nobler course for me and for you. Let one of my father's attendants here escort me to Artemis' meadow, where I shall be sacrificed.

[IPHIGENIA *begins to move away from* CLYTEMNESTRA.]

CLYTEMNESTRA: O my child, are you going?

IPHIGENIA: Yes, and never shall I come back.

CLYTEMNESTRA: You will leave your mother?

IPHIGENIA: Yes, as you see; we do not deserve this.

CLYTEMNESTRA: Wait – don't abandon me!

IPHIGENIA: I forbid you to shed tears. [CLYTEMNESTRA *sinks to the ground.* IPHIGENIA *turns to the* CHORUS:] And you, young women, sing with good omen for my fortune the paean to Artemis,[71] daughter of Zeus! Let the Greeks be told to keep holy silence! Let the rites commence with the sacred baskets, and the fire blaze up with the purifying barley-meal. And let   1470
my father walk round the altar from left to right. I go to give deliverance and victory to the Greeks!

[IPHIGENIA *sings her last words and the* CHORUS *respond in song.*]

Lead me on, the sacker of cities, of Ilium and of the Phrygians! Give me garlands to hang round me and bring – here is my hair to crown – fresh water for the lustral basins! Weave in the dance round her altar, round her temple, honouring Artemis, Lady Artemis the   1480
blessed! For with the blood of my sacrifice, if it must be, will I wash away the bidding of her oracle!

O holy, holy Mother, I will not give you my own tears: at the

1490 shrine is no place for tears. Ho, young women, ho! Join with me in
singing the praise of Artemis who looks over the waters to Chalcis,
where now in the narrow anchorage of Aulis because of me the timbers
chafe with impatience. O Pelasgia, my motherland, and Mycenae,
home of my youth . . .

1500 CHORUS: Do you call on the city of Perseus, that the Cyclopes' hands
raised with toil?

IPHIGENIA: . . . you reared me to be a light to Greece; I die with no
complaint.

CHORUS: For glory will never leave you.

IPHIGENIA: I hail you, day that brings the light, and you, radiance
of Zeus – a new life, a new state will be mine!
Farewell, welcome light!

[IPHIGENIA leaves with Agamemnon's ATTENDANTS. CLY-
TEMNESTRA rises and goes inside.]

1510 CHORUS: Hail her![72] See the sacker of cities, of Ilium and of the
Phrygians, as she goes to be crowned with garlands on her head and
sprinklings of lustral water, to stain the holy goddess' altar with drops
of flowing blood, when she is killed in all her loveliness and her throat
cut! The dew-fresh water awaits you, and your father's lustral bowls,
1520 and the army of the Greeks, eager to advance on Ilium's city.

But let us celebrate the daughter of Zeus, Artemis, queen of the
gods, so that a happy destiny may ensue. O Lady revered, whose
wish it is to receive a human life in sacrifice, send the army of the
Greeks on its way to the land of the Phrygians, to the treacherous
city of Troy, and grant that Agamemnon through the might of spears
may crown Greece with supreme glory, and set upon his own brows
1530 a fame that will never die![73]

[Enter a SECOND MESSENGER.]

SECOND MESSENGER: Clytemnestra, daughter of Tyndareus,
come out of the house, so that you may hear my words!

[Enter CLYTEMNESTRA.]

CLYTEMNESTRA: I come, hearing your voice. I am afraid in

my misery and terror grips me. Are you here to bring me
news of some fresh disaster to crown the present one?

MESSENGER: I wish to tell you about your daughter – wonderful
and fearful news.

CLYTEMNESTRA: Then do not hesitate: speak at once!

MESSENGER: You shall learn it all, dear mistress, in plain terms.   1540
I shall tell it from the start, unless my memory stumbles
anywhere and disturbs my tongue in the telling.[74]

When we reached the grove of Artemis, daughter of Zeus,
with its flowery meadow, and brought your daughter to the
mustering-point of the Greek army, at once a crowd of Greeks
began to gather. When King Agamemnon saw the girl enter-
ing the grove for sacrifice, he heaved a sigh and, turning his
head away, he shed tears, holding his robe in front of his eyes.   1550
She took her position next to her father and spoke as follows:
'Father, here I am, as you asked. Willingly I give my body for
my homeland, for all the land of Greece. Let them lead me to
the altar of the goddess for sacrifice, if so it is ordained. As far
as lies in me, I wish you all success. May your spears be
crowned with victory and a safe return to your native land be
yours! Therefore let no Greek lay hands upon me: without a
word, and in good heart, I will offer up my throat.' So much   1560
she said; and all who heard marvelled at the courage and virtue
of the maiden.

Talthybius, whose office it was, stood forth and called for
silence in the army, bidding the men guard their tongues.
Then Calchas the prophet, drawing out a sharp knife from its
sheath, placed it inside the gold-studded basket, and he put a
garland on the girl's head. The son of Peleus took the basket
and, at the same time, the lustral bowl, and swiftly making a
circuit of the goddess' altar, he spoke: 'O daughter of Zeus,
slayer of wild beasts, spinner of your shining beams by kindly   1570
night,[75] accept this sacrifice that we present to you – the
army of the Greeks, together with King Agamemnon – the
undefiled blood from the throat of a fair maiden. Grant that

no harm may befall the fleet on its voyage, and that our spears may bring down in ruin the towers of Troy!' The sons of Atreus and the whole army stood there, gazing at the ground. Then the priest, taking the knife, uttered a prayer and started to examine her throat for the point to strike. Bitter anguish was filling my heart,[76] and I stood with head lowered.

Then suddenly there was a wonder to see. Every man heard distinctly the sound of the blow but, as to the girl, she disappeared – where to, no one knew. The priest cried out, and all the army echoed his shout, when they saw the unexpected portent sent by some god, past belief even for one who saw it: a deer was lying on the ground,[77] gasping, a magnificent creature beautiful to the eye, whose blood was sprinkled all over the goddess' altar. Then Calchas spoke – you can imagine with what joy: 'You kings of this united army of Greeks, do you see this victim that the goddess has laid before her altar, this deer that runs the hills? She welcomes this offering as far more to her liking than the girl, so that her altar may not be defiled by noble blood. Gladly she has accepted this sacrifice, and she grants us a favourable voyage for launching our attack on Ilium. Therefore take courage, every mariner, and march off to your ship! This is the day we must leave Aulis' hollow bay and sail over the Aegean sea.' When the entire victim had been reduced to ashes by Hephaestus' flames, he made the appropriate prayer, that the army should come home safe. Agamemnon sent me to tell you this news and to say what manner of fortune he has received from the gods, what undying renown he has won throughout Greece. I speak as one who was there and witnessed the event; your daughter has been wafted up to the gods – no doubt of it!

Forget your sorrow, then, and end your hostility toward your husband. The gods act in ways that mortals cannot foresee but they preserve those they love. This day has seen your daughter dead and alive.

CHORUS-LEADER: What joy to hear these words of the messenger! He says your child lives and dwells among the gods.

222

[CLYTEMNESTRA *and the* CHORUS *now express their emotion in lyrics, in contrast with Agamemnon's final words.*]

CLYTEMNESTRA: *My child,*[78] *which god has stolen you? How should I address you? How say that this is not some idle tale told to comfort me, to put an end to my bitter grief for you?*

CHORUS-LEADER: *Here comes King Agamemnon, with this very story to tell you.*

1620

[*Enter* AGAMEMNON.]

AGAMEMNON: Lady, our daughter's fate should make us happy; she truly shares the company of the gods. Now you must take this new-born calf of ours[79] and return home: the army looks to the voyage. Farewell; many a day it will be before I greet you again, returning from Troy. I wish you well.

[*Exit* AGAMEMNON; CLYTEMNESTRA *returns into the house silently.*]

CHORUS: *In happiness, son of Atreus, go to the land of Phrygia, and in happiness return, having won from Troy, I pray, spoils most splendid!*

RHESUS

PREFACE TO *RHESUS*

In the tenth book of the *Iliad*, often referred to as the 'Doloneia' or 'Lay of Dolon', a night-time adventure is described. Deprived of Achilles' aid on the battlefield, the Greeks are hard-pressed and despondent, while the Trojans are encamped on the plain and confident of success the next day. A council is held among the Greeks, and they agree to send out Odysseus and Diomedes as scouts to gather information and do what else they can to improve the situation. Meanwhile among the Trojans Hector also decides to send out a spy, by name Dolon (a name which suggests secrecy and guile, in Greek *dolos*). As reward for his efforts Dolon requests the gift of the magnificent horses of Achilles once the Trojans have won. In the area between the armies Dolon is intercepted by the two Greeks, who threaten him and demand information. Losing his nerve completely, Dolon pours out every detail, including news of the arrival of Rhesus, an ally of the Trojans. Diomedes kills Dolon, and the two friends proceed to enter the Trojan camp, kill Rhesus and some of his followers, then hurry back to their own side, taking with them Rhesus' horses. The goddess Athena, who regularly befriends Odysseus and Diomedes, oversees the expedition and helps them at crucial moments, though without appearing to them directly.

It is a curious coincidence that the tenth book of the *Iliad* is widely regarded as a later addition to the poem, just as the *Rhesus* is thought by many to be a spurious work wrongly ascribed to Euripides. Some of the arguments for the latter view will be mentioned below: first we should consider the drama on its own terms.

It is obvious that the basic framework of the story is similar: Trojan successes, spies on both sides, the two Greek intruders, the killing of

Rhesus, the abduction of his horses. Some of the changes that the dramatist makes are clearly the consequence of transferring the story to the stage: thus the murder of Rhesus must now be reported in a messenger speech, and the bad dream which Rhesus was having just before his death is transferred to his charioteer, because Rhesus will not live to narrate it. There are however a number of other significant differences.

First, the play is set exclusively in the Trojan camp, and seen almost entirely from the Trojan perspective. From the Greek side we see only Odysseus and Diomedes, and they appear only in two successive scenes.

Second, the connection we find in the *Doloneia* between Dolon's story and that of Rhesus is severed. In the *Iliad* Dolon told the Greek intruders about Rhesus and where to find him; in the play, Dolon departs on his mission before Rhesus' arrival, and the Greeks appear to be looking for Hector: it requires Athena's intervention in person to send them in pursuit of the Thracian king.

Third, whereas the part of Dolon has been minimized, the role of Rhesus has been greatly expanded. In the *Iliad* he is introduced only to be killed: he speaks no lines and is disposed of without difficulty, and he has no special status to warrant extended mourning. In the play he is not just another ally but a warrior of outstanding stature, welcomed by the chorus as a saviour figure, compared and even identified with Zeus and Ares (355ff., 385ff.). Athena predicts ruinous bloodshed among the Greek ranks if he lives to fight them the next day. His parentage is altered: in the drama he is the son of the River Strymon and of one of the Muses, and his mother appears at the end to mourn him. She also declares that she will be responsible for his burial, and that he will become an oracular hero, human yet also divine, uttering prophecies as a spokesman for Dionysus – no ordinary end.

It is clear that the dramatist was not simply adapting a single episode in the *Iliad*. He visibly draws on other parts of the Homeric poems (the Muse, for instance, resembles Thetis, the mother of Achilles, who regularly bemoans the imminent death of her son); similarly he has also developed other motifs from the epic and lyric tradition. A lost poem of Pindar described how Rhesus came to Troy and in a single day wrought havoc, slaughtering many Greek soldiers. In that poem

Hera and Athena inspired Odysseus and Diomedes to make their night raid specifically in order to dispose of this formidable threat to the Greek cause. This version also gave Rhesus the same parents he has in the play. The résumé of Pindar's poem makes no mention of Dolon, who is indeed irrelevant to the story as told in this form. It seems clear that the author of the Rhesus has blended elements from the Doloneia and from the version invented or inherited by Pindar. It may be only the accident of survival that makes us regard the Doloneia as his chief source.

None of this is to deny that the poet of the Rhesus made his own contribution. The characterization is probably mostly his invention. It is notable that none of the characters cuts a very impressive figure. There is dissension and distrust on the Trojan side: Hector is hostile to Rhesus and criticizes him at length to his face; the Charioteer supposes that Rhesus died because of Trojan treachery. Hector, Dolon and Rhesus all display exaggerated over-confidence. Alexandros (Paris) appears on stage only to be deceived without difficulty by Athena; similarly the chorus are easily duped by Odysseus. Hector is shown in conflict with Aeneas, Rhesus and the charioteer in succession. He also upbraids the chorus (with some justice) for neglecting their guard duties, and they defend themselves with obvious falsehoods. We might suspect the poet of Greek chauvinism, were it not that the presentation of Odysseus and Diomedes is scarcely favourable. When they first appear on stage they are hesitant and ready to withdraw at the first obstacle, until Athena gives them instructions. They have already killed Dolon (a disturbing scene even in the epic); they now proceed to slaughter Rhesus and his comrades while they sleep. It may be excessive to call this an anti-heroic picture, but neither side seems to come out of the episode with much credit. The combination of self-important braggadocio, divinely authorized assassination, mis-understanding, recriminations and ineptitude produces a remarkably negative interpretation of an episode which in Homer was essentially an exciting narrative of a bold expedition by two of our favourite heroes. Perhaps the most moving part of the drama is the lament by the dead Rhesus' mother, who sees clearly who was behind the events and voices her bitter hostility to Athena: the double use of opposed divinities in this play is reminiscent of the opposition of Aphrodite and Artemis in *Hippolytus*.

We can no longer avoid the question of the authorship of this curious drama. It seems more or less certain that Euripides did write a *Rhesus*, but the ancient commentators who composed the 'summaries' prefaced to the play were aware of doubts as to whether this play was actually his. There was also a mystery regarding its prologue. In our texts there is none; the play begins with the chorus hurrying in and surrounding Hector's tent. Two openings were known, however, and both are quoted by the summary: of one we have only a line, but the other, of which we have an extract running to eleven lines, evidently included a dialogue between Hera and Athena debating how to help the Greek forces.★ Whether either of these was the work of Euripides is hard to decide: what all this does suggest is that the play was of uncertain status. One theory is that the editors who collected Euripides' work in Alexandria in the third century BC may have acquired some plays by other authors, misguidedly accepting them as Euripidean in their eagerness to amass as many authentic plays as possible.

This external evidence does not add up to much. More important is the internal evidence of vocabulary, style, metre and dramatic technique. These and similar questions have been investigated with great thoroughness in a monograph by W. Ritchie. He has systematically

---

★For the reader's interest I translate these. The first is only an incomplete sentence, 'now the chariot-driven [noun lacking, probably "night"] . . . the fair moon's light': obviously someone is making explicit that night has fallen. This could be an authentically Euripidean first line, but we can hardly say. The longer passage is the opening of a speech by Hera to Athena. 'O Pallas, valiant child of all-mighty Zeus, what are we to do? We should no longer delay in giving support to the Argive host. For now they are suffering in battle, sent spinning off course by Hector's violent spear. There is no burden for me to bear more painful than this, since the time when Alexandros judged the Cyprian goddess superior in beauty to my own looks, and yours, Athena, whom I love most among the gods – if I am not to see the city of Priam demolished, uprooted by force and ground into extinction.'

This does not resemble any Euripidean prologue that survives. The closest parallel would be the dialogues between gods which occur in *Alcestis* and *Trojan Women*, but even there the standard procedure is followed whereby one speaker gives an exposition of the situation before engaging in dialogue with the other. The author of the summary in which it is quoted calls the passage 'prosaic and unworthy of Euripides'.

compared the *Rhesus* with other tragedies, especially those of Euripides, and has reached the conclusion that there is very little which cannot be paralleled in the author's certainly genuine works. In his view the *Rhesus* is probably an early work, perhaps the earliest play by Euripides that we have (earlier than *Alcestis* of 438). Not all, however, have been convinced. Ritchie has undoubtedly shown that many of the criticisms lodged against the play are unjustified, and that the poet uses a style which is (most of the time) very like that of Euripides. But in his determination to find parallels he is sometimes guilty of exaggerating similarities and minimizing peculiarities.

Different critics will of course find different points particularly convincing on one side or the other. If I were asked to say what features of the *Rhesus* seem to me to make Euripidean authorship unlikely, I would mention the following. The plot falls into two unequal parts: the Dolon-plot is dropped, almost forgotten, when the Rhesus-plot takes over. A more skilful dramatist might surely have done more to integrate the two. On the level of characterization, those of whom we see most are too similar and too monolithic. There is a marked absence of the rhetorical and philosophic generalizations that we associate with Euripides (especially in the confrontation between Hector and Rhesus, which is very unlike the typical Euripidean *agon*-scene). There are dramaturgical oddities: the handling of Athena's epiphany is unique, and the messenger speech, delivered only to the chorus in the absence of Hector, is at least unconventional. There are also anomalous features at the end of the play (nowhere else in tragedy does a *deus ex machina* sing as well as speak). The structuring of the choral interventions is abnormal in several respects. Some of these phenomena can be at least partly paralleled elsewhere, others may be defended as bold innovations (after all, what is Euripides if not unconventional?). But the overall effect of the play *feels*, to my mind, very unlike the rest of the poet's œuvre. Nevertheless, we must remember how much we have lost and bear in mind the versatility of these poets. I am content to echo the judicious words of Euripides' best modern editor, James Diggle: 'I have little confidence that Euripides did write the *Rhesus*; I would not dare say that he could not have done so.'

In any case, preoccupation with the question of authenticity risks neglecting the particular interest of the drama. If it is by another hand, and possibly from the fourth century BC, that significantly increases our knowledge of the genre – we have the work of four poets, not just three (or indeed five, assuming that the *Prometheus Bound* is not by Aeschylus). Whether the *Rhesus* is Euripidean or not, it gives us a rare opportunity to see a tragedian reshaping a particular Homeric episode, enhancing the elements of ironic deception and pathos; no less than the *Orestes* and *Iphigenia at Aulis*, it enables us to see how heroic values and traditional mythical characters were put under scrutiny in the developed tragic genre; and it sheds further light on the Greeks' perception of war and the foreign antagonist. The great sequence of dramas that begins for us with Aeschylus' *Persians* reaches a fitting conclusion with the *Rhesus*.

CHARACTERS

CHORUS *of Trojan sentries*
HECTOR, *commander of the Trojans*
AENEAS, *a Trojan captain*
DOLON, *a Trojan*
MESSENGER, *a herdsman*
RHESUS, *king of Thrace, son of Strymon, the river-god, and a Muse*
ODYSSEUS, *a Greek captain*
DIOMEDES, *a Greek captain*
ATHENA, *a goddess*
ALEXANDROS, *a Trojan prince, also known as Paris, brother of Hector*
CHARIOTEER *of Rhesus*
MUSE, *mother of Rhesus*

[*The scene is the Trojan camp close to the Greek ships, where the victorious Trojans have pitched their tents for the night, hoping to drive the enemy into the sea the next morning.*]

CHORUS:[1] *On to the tent of Hector! Which shield-bearer or armour-bearer of the king is awake? He must hear the report from the young men who for the fourth watch have been set to guard the whole army! Raise your head, Hector, lean on your elbow, shake the sleep from those eyes of yours that strike terror, and leave your bed strewn with leaves! It's time to listen!*

HECTOR [*emerging from his tent*]: *Who's there? Is that a friend's cry? What man is it? What is the watchword? Speak! What men approach my bed in the watches of the night? You must speak!*

CHORUS: *Men who guard the army.*

HECTOR: *Why such haste and disorder? Perhaps you have some news of the night? Do you not know we are next to the spears of the Greeks and keep our night's sleep in full armour?*

CHORUS [Strophe]: *Arm your hand; go to the tents of your allies, Hector, urge them to lift their spears, rouse them from sleep! Send friends to go to your own company, fit bridles on your horses!*

Who will go to the son of Panthous or of Europa, leader of Lycia's men?

Where are the overseers of sacrifice, where the kings of the light-armed fighters and the Phrygian archers? Fit the arrows bound with horn to your bowstrings!

HECTOR: *You bring news terrible to hear and yet you tell us to have*

234

confidence; this lacks all clarity. Can it be the fearful whip of Pan,[2]
*grandson of Cronus, that makes you afraid, prompting you to leave
your watch and start this commotion in the army? What are you
saying? What news should I say you bring? You have said much but
shown nothing plainly.*   40

CHORUS [Antistrophe]: *The Greek army has been kindling
watchfires*[3] *all through the night, Hector, and their ships' mooring
stations are bright with beacons. This night their entire host has
approached Agamemnon's tent with clamorous desire to hear some
fresh report. Never yet has such fear filled their seafaring ranks. I have
come to bring you this message, with doubt in my heart about the*   50
future, so that never may you have words of reproach for me.

HECTOR: You have come at the right time, though your message
is one of fear; the enemy plan to row away by night from our
land and make their escape, without my knowledge. This
night watch gives me encouragement.

O Fortune, I am like the lion whose hunting you have
blessed only to be turned away from my prey before destroying
the whole Greek army with this spear at one swoop! If only
the sun's gleaming torches had not frustrated me, I should not   60
have checked my prospering spear before firing their ships
and sweeping through their tents, killing Greeks with this
murderous hand!

Indeed I was eager to hurl my spear and to ride the swell
of fortune's favour in the night. But the wise prophets, who
know heaven's will, persuaded me to wait for the light of day
and then to leave not one Greek on dry land.

But the enemy are not waiting for the counsels of my
priests to take effect; darkness is a powerful friend to run-
aways.

No, I must lose no time in passing the instruction on to the
army: they are to shake off sleep and have their weapons   70
ready, so that one of them, even as he leaps on to a ship, may
spatter the gangway with blood from his scarred back, while

235

the enemy, bound and made captive, may learn to plough the soil of Phrygia's fields.

CHORUS-LEADER: Hector, you make haste before knowing what is happening; we do not know for sure if the enemy are in flight.

HECTOR: What reason is there, then, for the Greek army to be lighting fires?

CHORUS-LEADER: I do not know; but apprehension fills my heart.

80 HECTOR: Be assured, if you fear this, you would fear anything.

CHORUS-LEADER: Never until now have the enemy kindled so great a blaze.

HECTOR: Never before have they fallen so shamefully in the rout of battle!

CHORUS-LEADER: This was your doing; now you must consider the future.

HECTOR: In the face of the enemy the watchword is simple: 'to arms!'

CHORUS-LEADER: Here comes Aeneas in great haste, with some new matter to tell his comrades.

[AENEAS *enters with followers, including* DOLON.[4]]

AENEAS:[5] Hector, why is it that night sentries throughout the army have come to your tents to confer in fear? Why are the troops stirring?

90 HECTOR: Aeneas, arm yourself from head to foot!

AENEAS: What is it? Surely not a report that the enemy have laid some secret ambush in the darkness?

HECTOR: They are in flight and taking to their ships.

AENEAS: What sure proof of this can you give?

HECTOR: All night they have been kindling beacons of fire. I think they will not wait until tomorrow but after lighting torches on their sturdy ships will weigh anchor and sail in flight from this land for home.

AENEAS: How do you intend to combat this, now that you are fully armed?

HECTOR: As they flee and jump on to their ships I will check

them with my spear and press them hard. It will bring shame   100
on us, and, besides shame, harm, if, when a god puts the
enemy at our mercy, we allow them to flee without a fight
after all the suffering they have caused.

AENEAS: If only you were a man whose judgement matched
his deeds in battle! But it is not human nature that the same
man should know everything. Different men have different
gifts: you are a fighter, others give shrewd counsel. Hearing
that the Greeks were lighting fire-beacons, you became   110
excited and now intend to cross their trenches at the head of
our troops in the dead of night. And yet if you cross those
deep and hollow ditches and find the enemy not in flight from
Troyland but facing your spear, there will be no coming back
for you in defeat. For how will our men, running for their
lives, get over the palisades? How, too, will our charioteers
cross the causeways without smashing the hubs of their
wheels?

If the attack succeeds, the next opponent you must face is
the son of Peleus,[6] who will not let you fling brands on the   120
ships or make havoc among the Greeks as you think you can.
He is a man of fiery temper, whose fearless nature makes him
a tower of strength.

No, let us allow the troops to sleep soundly with shields
beside them after the toil of murderous war. I propose that
we send a man, whoever volunteers, to spy on the enemy. If
they are taking flight, let us go forward and attack the Greek
army. But if some trickery lies beneath this beacon-lighting,
we will learn the enemy's stratagem from the spy and take
counsel. This is my advice, my royal lord.   130

CHORUS [Strophe]: *I approve this plan, change your thoughts and
accept these words of his. A commander's power should not be exercised
perilously. There is no better course than this: a spy quick on his feet
should approach the ships and learn why the enemy have fires burning
in front of their anchored fleet.*

HECTOR: I yield to your words, as this is the view of all. Go and calm our allies; perhaps the men may be disturbed at hearing of a call to assemble by night. I shall send a man to spy on the enemy. If we discover that they are planning something, you will be present to hear and share all our counsels. And if they weigh anchor, starting to flee, expect the trumpet's voice, wait for it with open ear, for I will not wait; I'll penetrate to where their ships are moored and attack the Greek army there.

140

AENEAS: Send him without delay; now your thinking is sound. You will see me at your side unfaltering whenever the need arises.

[*Exit* AENEAS *with a few followers: a larger group of Trojan soldiers remains.*]

HECTOR: Which, then, of you Trojans who have heard my words is willing to go as a spy on the ships of the Greeks? Who will do his country this service? [*No one speaks.*] Who says 'I will'? [*Further silence.*] I alone cannot bear all the responsibilities to our home city and our allies.

150

DOLON: I am willing to run this risk for my country and go to spy on the Greek fleet. Once I have learned all the Greeks' plans, I shall return. On these conditions I undertake this task.

HECTOR: You are well named, Dolon, and a true patriot. Your father's house was glorious before this day but now you have brought it glory twice as great.

160

DOLON: As I must sweat to achieve this, is it not right that my sweat should earn a fee? A reward set for any work returns the favour rendered.

HECTOR: Yes, I see the justice in this and do not disagree. Name your reward, but let it not be my princely power!

DOLON: It is not your power as prince of Troy I desire.

HECTOR: Well then, take to wife a daughter of the royal house and become my kinsman in marriage!

DOLON: I have no wish to marry beyond my status.

HECTOR: There is gold to hand, if this is the prize you seek.

DOLON: Gold I have at home; my wealth is sufficient. 170

HECTOR: Then what do you desire among the treasures of Troy?

DOLON: When we have conquered the Greeks, grant me gifts.

HECTOR: So I shall; ask for anything but the commanders of the ships.

DOLON: Kill them, I do not ask you to spare Menelaus.

HECTOR: Surely you do not ask me to be given the son of Oileus?[7]

DOLON: Well-bred hands do not take well to the plough.

HECTOR: Then which of the Greeks do you want to hold alive to ransom?

DOLON: I said it before: I have gold at home.

HECTOR: Well then, you shall be there to have your choice in person from the spoils.

DOLON: Nail them to temple walls in honour of the gods! 180

HECTOR: Then what greater prize than these will you ask of me?

DOLON: The horses of Achilles; a man must labour for a fitting reward, if he is to risk his life in Fortune's game of dice.

HECTOR: Why, your desire for these horses matches my own;[8] they bear the furious son of Peleus as the immortal offspring of immortal sires. The Lord Poseidon, ocean's king, tamed them with his own hands, men say, before giving them to Peleus. But I will not prove false after honouring you with my praise; I will give you as the fairest of possessions in your home the steeds of Achilles. 190

DOLON: I thank you; I say that, if I won them, I would receive the noblest gift the Trojans could bestow on my courage. But you must not grudge me; there are a host of other prizes to gladden your heart when you become master of this land.

CHORUS [Antistrophe]: *Great is the contest, great the honours you intend to win; and blessed will you be, once they are attained. This is a task that brings glory; it is a great thing to become a king's kinsman in marriage.*

As to what depends on the gods, let Justice see to that, but men,
200   *I think, have striven to make your happiness complete.*

DOLON: I should be on my way; I will go to my tent and at my
own hearthside clothe myself in dress to suit my ends, then
from there set out for the ships of the Greeks.

CHORUS-LEADER: Why, what form of dress will you have
other than this?[9]

DOLON: One that suits the deed and a stealthy way of walking.

CHORUS-LEADER: From a clever man one should learn some
piece of cleverness; tell me, what dress shall cover this body
of yours?

DOLON: On my back I'll fix the pelt of a wolf and round my
face the beast's gaping jaws; I'll fasten its forepaws to my hands
210   and hind-legs to my legs, then mimic a wolf's gait with four
feet, hard for the enemy to trace, as I draw near to the trenches
and ships' defences. When I reach a quiet spot, I'll walk on
two feet; that's the scope of my crafty scheme.

CHORUS-LEADER: Well, may Hermes, the master of cheats,[10]
Maia's son, guide you safely there and back! The task lies
before you; all you need is a happy result.

DOLON: I shall get back safely, depend upon it; I'll kill Odysseus
and bring you back his head – clear proof for you to say that
220   Dolon went to the ships of the Greeks – or the son of Tydeus.
There shall be blood on my hand when I return to my tent
before light visits the earth!

[*Exit* DOLON; HECTOR *remains on stage.*]

CHORUS [Strophe]: *Lord of Thymbra and of Delos, Apollo, who
dwell in your Lycian temple, fairest son of Zeus, come with arrows
and bow, come to us this night, be saviour and guide to this man on*
230   *his mission and lend your aid to Dardanus' people, o all-powerful
one, who built the ancient walls of Troy!*[11]

[Antistrophe:] *May he reach the place where the ships are moored
and come to spy on the army of Greece, and then may he return
to the Trojan hearth of his father's home! And some day, when his*

master has routed the warriors of Greece, may he mount the chariot behind the horses of Phthia, the creatures given to Peleus, son of Aeacus, by the ocean's lord! 240

[Strophe:] *For he alone has dared for home and country's sake to go and spy on the mooring-place of the ships; I wonder at his courage; there is ever a lack of brave men, whenever it is sunless on the sea and the ship of state[12] is tossed by waves. Phrygia has yet a man of valour to call her own; there is a heart that will not flinch in battle; where is he now, the man of Mysia[13] who scorns me as his comrade-in-arms?* 250

[Antistrophe:] *Which soldier of Greece will the earth-treading assassin strike down among the tents, as he imitates a wild beast, covering the ground on all fours? May he bring down Menelaus, may he kill Agamemnon and bring his head for Helen to hold, making her weep tears of grief for her wicked brother-in-law, the man who came to the land of Troy with a host of a thousand ships!* 260

[*A man runs in from the fields.*]

MESSENGER: My lord, may any messages I bring my masters in days to come be like the one I carry now for your ears! 270

HECTOR: How dull-witted these country fellows are! Look at you – your master still wears his armour and here you are, it seems, to bring him news of his herds, at a place most unsuitable! Do you not know of my palace, of my father's throne, where you should deliver news that the cattle are prospering?

MESSENGER: I am a foolish herdsman; I don't deny it. But just the same I bring you good news!

HECTOR: Enough of your words about the fortunes of my cattle-stalls; the burden we bear with us is one of battles and spears.

MESSENGER: This is the business I, too, have come to announce! A man who commands a mighty force is coming as a staunch ally to you and this land!

HECTOR: What is his native country that he has left so desolate?

MESSENGER: Thrace; he boasts Strymon as his father.

HECTOR: You mean that Rhesus is setting foot in the Troad? 280

241

MESSENGER: You have my message and have relieved me of tidings twice as great.

HECTOR: How is it he makes his march to Ida's glens, straying from the open plain with its broad pathways for wagons?

MESSENGER: I can't say for sure; but I can guess. By night it's no easy task for an army to invade, when they know that the plains are full of enemy troops. He gave us countryfolk a fright, living as we do on Ida's rocky uplands, where our earliest ancestors dwelt, marching into our woodlands by night, home to wild beasts! For they made a mighty noise,

290 those warriors of Thrace, as they streamed onward. In some dismay we started driving our herds to the heights of the mountain, fearing that some Greek was coming to drive off the cattle and make havoc of your pens.

But then our ears took in the sound of speech that was not Greek[14] and we stopped being afraid. I went up to the scouts sent ahead by their master to explore the route and questioned them in the Thracian tongue: 'Who is your commander and whose son is he, advancing on the city as an ally to Priam's sons?'

After hearing their replies I remained where I stood; I saw

300 Rhesus standing like a god among the horses and chariots of Thrace. A yoke of gold confined the hardy necks of his horses, whose coats shone brighter than snow. A shield decorated with figures of beaten gold was gleaming on his shoulders. A Gorgon, as on the aegis of the goddess, hung in bronze from the horses' brows and with its many bells sent out a ring of terror.

The full number of the army you could not set down, even using a counting-board, so vast it was to the eye, a host of

310 horsemen, a host of slingers in their ranks, a host of archers with their quivers, a mighty host of light-armed infantry all together, wearing Thracian dress.

Such is the man who has come to stand as Troy's comrade-in-arms, one whom Peleus' son will not be able to escape, whether he takes to flight or stands his ground with the spear.

CHORUS-LEADER: Whenever the gods hold firm in defence of a city, its fortunes rise in the scale from bad to good.

HECTOR: No lack of friends shall I find, when my spear prospers and Zeus is with us. But I have no need of those who long since have refused to share our toil,[15] when war's fury with violent blast was ripping apart the sails of our ship of state. Rhesus showed what kind of friend he was to Troy; now he arrives for the feast, though he did not help the hunters as they strove to catch their prey or lend the labour of his spear. 320

CHORUS-LEADER: You are right to deny your friends honour and to take them to task; but do not turn away those who would help your city.

HECTOR: We who have saved Ilium all these years are sufficient to the task!

CHORUS-LEADER: You are confident that the enemy is already defeated? 330

HECTOR: I am; tomorrow god's sun will reveal this.

CHORUS-LEADER: Look to the future; often heaven brings change of fortune.

HECTOR: I hate the man who comes too late to help a friend in trouble. Ah well, since he did come, though not to share our fighting but our board, let him sit as a guest at our table; he has forfeited the thanks of Priam's people.

CHORUS-LEADER: My lord, it is invidious to reject an ally.

MESSENGER: If they but saw him, the enemy would know fear.

HECTOR [to the CHORUS-LEADER]: Your advice is sound. [To the MESSENGER:] And you have used your eyes to good effect. Let Rhesus the lord of the golden armour, as my 340 messenger has it, present himself as this land's ally!

[Exit MESSENGER.]

CHORUS [Strophe]: *May Adrasteia,[16] daughter of Zeus, protect my words from thoughts of ill! For I shall say all that my soul longs to tell. You have come, son of the river, you have come, most welcome you have approached the halls of Zeus the Hospitable, since at last your Pierian mother has brought you, and the fair-bridged river* 350

[Antistrophe]: *Strymon, who once, whirling in watery form*[17] *through the virgin lap of the songstress Muse, fathered your manly form. You have come to me as Zeus the Bringer of Light,*[18] *riding behind your dappled steeds! Now, my homeland, my Phrygia, now with the god's help can you name Zeus the Deliverer!*

[Strophe]: *Shall it ever come again, the time when ancient Troy* 360 *shall fill the live-long day with revelling bands of drinkers, as melodies of love resound and men compete from left to right with cups that send the wine flying, when over the sea to Sparta the sons of Atreus have left Ilium's shore? O my friend, may you enter my home having accomplished this task with the might of your spear!*

[Antistrophe:] *Come, appear, hold up your shield of gold before* 370 *the face of Peleus' son, raising it aslant along the branching chariot-rail, rousing your steeds and brandishing a two-pronged spear. For no man shall ever tread the dance in Argive Hera's temple after facing you in battle; he will be slain by a doom from Thrace and this land will bear his weight, a burden most welcome.*[19]

[RHESUS *enters.*]

All hail, mighty king! A fine lion-cub you have reared, o Thrace; 380 *his looks proclaim him royal! See his sturdy frame that gold adorns, hear, too, ringing out from the shield-straps, the bells that sound their proud challenge! As a god, a god, o Troy, as Ares himself is he here to inspire you, the lusty son of Strymon and the minstrel Muse!*

RHESUS: Greetings, Hector, worthy son of a worthy father, ruler of this land! After many a day I address you. I am pleased 390 that fortune favours you and you are encamped at the enemy's defences. Here I am to help you undermine their walls and fire their ships.

HECTOR: Son of the songstress mother,[20] one of the Muses, and of Strymon, river of Thrace, my way is to speak the truth always; I am not a man who hides his heart.

Long, long ago you should have come and shared this land's labours, and not, for your part, let Troy fall to enemy spears, levelled by the Greeks. You surely cannot say that you did not come, that you denied us your help and attention, because

your friends sent no summons. What herald or embassy of   400
Phrygian elders did not visit you with the charge to come to
Troy's defence? What kind of splendid gifts did we not send?
You are not of Greek stock, and neither are we: yet despite
our kinship, you betrayed us, as far as in you lay, to Greeks.

Indeed you were a minor princeling[21] before this hand of
mine made you the mighty ruler of Thrace, that day when at
Pangaeum's base in the land of the Paeonians I fell upon the
noblest men of Thrace. Face to face I smashed their ranks of
shield-bearers, reduced their infantry to slavery and handed
them over to you. And now, spurning the debt you owe for   410
this great service, you come running too late with help when
your friends are in distress.

As to those men who share no bond of common blood
with us and yet have long shared our fortune, some have died
and lie in tombs of heaped earth, no mean proof of loyalty to
Troy; others, standing in armour or mounted on chariots,
stoutly endure the chilly blast and parching fire of the sun-god,
not lying on couches, like you, pledging each other's health
in bottomless cups.[22] I make these accusations before you and
voice them to your face, so that you may know that Hector
always speaks his heart.   420

RHESUS: Such a man am I also in nature, cutting a direct path
of speech and laying bare my inmost thoughts. My absence
from this land vexed me; it weighed heavy on my heart and
taxed me more with grief than you. But Scythia's folk, whose
land borders on mine, made war upon me as I was about to
cross over on my journey to Ilium. I had reached the shores
of the Inhospitable Sea and was on the point of ferrying my
Thracian army across. But here my spear had to shed a pool
of Scythian blood on the earth and, mingled with it, Thracian 430
blood as well. Such was the misfortune that prevented me
from coming to the land of Troy and taking my stand in battle
at your side.

When I had defeated them and taken their children as
hostages, ordering them to bring a yearly tax in payment to

my palace, I sailed over the gulf of the Sea and now am here,
crossing the remaining borders of land on foot – not, as you
foolishly insist, downing brimming cups of wine, or taking
my ease in a golden palace; no, I know what icy blasts I
440   suffered on sleepless nights, I and this cloak of mine, the kind
that vex the Thracian Sea and Paeonia's folk.

I came late, I grant you, but not too late; this is now the
tenth year of your fighting without success, and day after day
you risk the war against the Greeks on a gambler's throw. But
a single dawning of the sun[23] will suffice for me to sack these
towers, fall upon their ships at anchor and kill the Greeks. On
the day following I will leave Troy for home, having cut short
450   your labours. Let none of you raise his shield on his arm; with
my spear I'll curb these Greeks who boast so loudly and bring
them low, for all my late arrival.

CHORUS [Strophe]: *Oh, oh, welcome are your words, welcome your
coming from Zeus! I only pray that sovereign Zeus is willing to keep
irresistible envy from your words. No man in earlier days or now have
460   Greek ships brought here to match your worth. How, I ask, could
Achilles withstand your spear, how Ajax? If only I might see the
day, my lord, when with spear you claim the reward of your murderous
hands!*

RHESUS: Such deeds I will undertake to perform for you in
return for my long absence; I call to witness Adrasteia. When
we have freed this city from its enemies and you have marked
470   out for the gods the first fruits of victory, I wish to march at
your side against the land of the Greeks and to lay waste all of
Greece with my spear, so they in turn may learn the cost of
war.

HECTOR: Were I to gain release from these our present troubles
and to dwell in Troy as once we did, free from harm, then I
would feel no small gratitude to the gods. But the region
around Argos and the land of Greece are not as easily sacked
by the spear as you claim.

RHESUS: Do they not say that these men who have come are the champions of Greece?

HECTOR: Yes, and we respect them, but it is wearisome keeping them at bay. 480

RHESUS: Then in killing them have we not achieved everything?

HECTOR: In looking to wider aims you must not ignore what is pressing now.

RHESUS: You are content, it seems, to suffer and not to act!

HECTOR: Yes, for the kingdom I rule is broad, though I remain here. You may set your light-armed troops and station your infantry on the left wing or the right, or in the centre of the allies.

RHESUS: I wish to fight the enemy unsupported, Hector. If you think it shameful not to assist in firing the ships' sterns, as one who bore the brunt of battle for many a long day before now, 490 put me where I can face Achilles and his troops.

HECTOR: You cannot point your furious spear against that man.

RHESUS: But surely the story was that he had sailed to Troy.

HECTOR: He sailed and he is here; but anger against the commanders keeps him from raising his spear.

RHESUS: What other man in the army after him enjoys renown?

HECTOR: Ajax I consider not at all inferior, and the son of Tydeus. Then there is Odysseus, a cunning piece of craftsmanship,[24] who is bold enough in spirit and has done more damage to this land than any other man; he entered Athena's temple 500 by night, stole her statue and carried it back to the Greek ships. He had already come inside the walls as a peddler wearing beggar's rags, and uttered many dire curses against the Greeks, though sent to spy on Ilium. He killed the guards and watchmen on the gates before making his escape. He is always to be found sitting in ambush at the altar of Thymbrian Apollo hard by the town. We have a deadly plague to wrestle in him.

RHESUS: No man of courage thinks it right to kill his enemy by stealth, but only in face-to-face confrontation. I'll catch 510 him alive, this fellow you describe, who skulks like a robber in his hideout hatching schemes, and then impale him on the city gates as a feast for swooping vultures. As a brigand and robber of the gods' shrines he ought to die a death like this.

HECTOR: For the present make camp; for it is night. I will show you the place where your army must pass the night, apart from my troops. Our watchword is 'Phoebus', if any need arises. Remember what you have heard and give this message to your men from Thrace. [*To the men of the* CHORUS:] You must go and keep sharp watch in front of the ranks and welcome Dolon, who has gone to spy on the ships. For, if he is unharmed, by now he will be approaching the Trojan camp.

[HECTOR *and* RHESUS *leave the stage. In the following lyrics the* CHORUS*'s song gives way twice to contributions from individual members.*]

CHORUS [Strophe]: *Whose is the watch? Who takes my watch over? The first stars are setting and the seven journeying Pleiads are in the sky; the eagle is hovering midway in the heavens. Rouse yourselves! No delaying! Leave your sleeping quarters and return to your post! Do you not see the moon's gleam? Dawn, yes, dawn is soon to break and there's one of her stars sent ahead to reconnoitre!*

Whom did the herald name as taking the first watch?

Mygdon's son, they say, Coroebus.

Who came after him?

The Paeonian troops roused the Cilicians, and the Mysians us.

Then is it not time for us to go and rouse the Lycians for the fifth watch, as the lot's division instructs?

[Antistrophe:] *Aye, and now I hear it: sitting on her bloody nest by Simois, the nightingale with voice of many tones sings her doleful song for her slaughtered brood.*[25] *Already the flocks are at their pasture on Ida; I hear the voice of the shepherd's pipe that peals through the night. Sleep casts his spell over my eyes; most welcome is his coming to men's eyes as dawn draws near.*

Why is he not back with us, the scout whom Hector urged to spy on the ships?

I am afraid; he has been gone a long time.

    Can it be he has blundered into a secret ambush and met his end?
It may be so; I fear it.   560

    I say we must go and rouse the Lycians for the fifth watch as the
lot's division instructs.

[*The* CHORUS *leave the orchestra.*²⁶ *In the darkness* ODYS-
SEUS *and* DIOMEDES *enter.*²⁷]

ODYSSEUS: Diomedes, was that a meaningless noise I heard, or
   did you just hear weapons rattling?

DIOMEDES: No, a clang of iron came from harness hung from
   chariot-rails. I, too, was afraid, until I recognized the sound
   of horses' tackle.

ODYSSEUS: Take care you don't meet any guards in the
   darkness.   570

DIOMEDES: I'll watch out, even when I'm stepping in shadow.

ODYSSEUS: Good; but if you rouse them, do you know the
   password of their army?

DIOMEDES: 'Phoebus' – I know it, having heard the word from
   Dolon.

ODYSSEUS: Look! I see these beds deserted by the enemy!

DIOMEDES: Yet Dolon said that this was where Hector takes
   his rest, for whom this sword has been unsheathed.

ODYSSEUS: What reason can there be? Surely a troop has not
   gone off somewhere?

DIOMEDES: Perhaps they mean to set some trap for us.

ODYSSEUS: Yes, for Hector is bold now, since he has the upper
   hand, bold indeed.

DIOMEDES: Well, Odysseus, what should we do? We haven't
   found our man in his bed and our hopes are dashed.   580

ODYSSEUS: Let's go as fast as we can to where our ships are
   anchored. The god who gives a man success also keeps him
   safe. We must not try to force fortune's hand.

DIOMEDES: Then aren't we to go to Aeneas or the Phrygian
   we hate the most, Paris, and cut off their heads with the
   sword?

ODYSSEUS: How, then, in the darkness will you be able to

search up and down the enemy ranks and kill them without risk to yourself?

DIOMEDES: Well, it will bring us no honour to return to the ships of the Greeks without doing some harm to the enemy.

ODYSSEUS: But you have done something! Have we not killed Dolon who came to spy on our ships at anchor? Don't we still have with us the spoils we took from him? Or do you think you will sack the whole camp?

DIOMEDES: Well said! Let's go back; may fortune be generous to us!

[*The goddess* ATHENA *suddenly speaks, appearing above the stage-building.*[28]]

ATHENA: And where are you going, leaving the Trojan lines, heartbroken with grief that a god does not allow the pair of you to kill Hector or Paris? Have you not learned that a man, Rhesus, has come to Troy in grand style to share her battles? If he lives through this night to see tomorrow,[29] not Achilles, not Ajax with his spear, would prevent him from destroying all the ships of the Greeks where they lie at anchor, once he has levelled the fortifications and is dealing havoc far and wide inside the gates with his spear. Kill this man and everything is yours; think no more of Hector's sleeping quarters or spilling blood by cutting off men's heads. That man's death will come from another hand.

ODYSSEUS: Lady Athena, I recognized the familiar sound of your voice, for in my struggles you are always there to give protection. Tell us where the man lies sleeping. In what part of the enemy host does he keep guard?

ATHENA: He is to be found near by, not quartered with the army. Hector has given him a place to sleep outside the Trojan lines, until night gives way to day. Hard by, his white horses, shining out in the night, are tethered to their Thracian chariots. They gleam like the feathers of a river swan. Kill their master and carry them off, a prize that will bring great renown to your houses; no place on earth conceals a team of horses to match these.

ODYSSEUS: Diomedes, either kill the Thracian men yourself, or leave the task to me, and you must make the horses your business.

DIOMEDES: I will do the killing, and you the horse-breaking. You are experienced in subtleties and have a quick mind. A man should be posted where he can be of greatest benefit.

[ODYSSEUS *leaves the stage.*]

ATHENA: Look, here I see Alexandros[30] coming towards us, after learning from some guard hazy reports of enemies approaching.

DIOMEDES: Does he come with others or alone? 630

ATHENA: Alone; he is coming to Hector's sleeping quarters, it seems, to tell him that men have come to spy on the army.

DIOMEDES: Should he not be the first to die?

ATHENA: You should not go beyond what fate has prescribed; it is not ordained that this man should die at your hands.[31] But hurry to the man you are after, bringing with you deadly slaughter. I shall answer this man I hate with words of deception, pretending to be his ally, the Cyprian, and to stand at his side, a helper in his troubles. I have spoken these words, yet the doomed man does not know, and did not hear my 640 words, though he is near.

[DIOMEDES *leaves to kill* RHESUS; *from the other side of the stage, enter* ALEXANDROS.]

ALEXANDROS: Hector, brother and commander, it's you I'm calling! Are you asleep? Should you not have stirred? Some of the enemy are approaching our camp, thieves, it may be, or spies!

ATHENA: Have no fear; I, the Cyprian, who wish you well, keep watch over you. I am mindful of this war of yours, and have not forgotten the honour you paid me, but am grateful for your kindness that day. And now, to crown the good fortune of the Trojan army, I come bringing a man who is a powerful friend to you, the Thracian son of the melodious 650 goddess.

ALEXANDROS: Always you have proved a true friend to my city and to me. By judging in your favour, I say that I have given this city the greatest treasure I ever bestowed on her. I am here since I have heard, not plainly – a rumour reached the watchmen – that spies have come from the Greeks. And one man talks of them, without having seen them, while another, who did see them coming, can give no account of
660   it. This is why I have come to Hector's tent.

ATHENA: No need for alarm; nothing has happened in the camp. Hector has gone to arrange sleeping quarters for the Thracian troops.

ALEXANDROS: You convince me; I will trust your words and go to guard my post, free from fear.

    [ALEXANDROS *leaves*.]

ATHENA: Do so; my wish is to take thought for all your concerns, so that I may see my comrades-in-arms prospering. You will discover for yourself how much love I bear you.

    [ODYSSEUS *hurries on stage, closely followed by the* CHORUS.]

    You two, whose eagerness has gone too far,[32] hear me!
Son of Laertes, sheathe your whetted sword! The Thracian
670   commander lies dead before us and his horses are ours, but the enemy have realized this and are advancing on you. You must lose no time but flee to the ships at anchor. Why do you hesitate to save your lives when the enemy thunderbolt is rushing down?

    [*Exit* ATHENA.]

CHORUS: *Aha! Pelt him, pelt him, pelt him! Strike, strike, strike!*
    – What man?
    – Look! It's him I mean!
    – This way, this way, everyone! [They surround the Greek
680   warriors.]
    – I have them, I've caught these thieves who were slipping through our camp in the dark!
    – [to ODYSSEUS:] *What's your company? Where have you come from? What country?*

ODYSSEUS: It's not for you to know.

CHORUS: You'll die this day for your foul deeds! Tell us the
password, before this spear goes through your chest!

ODYSSEUS: It will not cause me fear.

CHORUS: Every man, come near and strike! Were you the one
who killed Rhesus?

ODYSSEUS: No, I killed the man who would have killed you.
Hold back, all of you!

CHORUS: We will not!

ODYSSEUS: No! Do not kill a man who is your friend!

CHORUS: Then what is the password?

ODYSSEUS: Phoebus.

CHORUS: He is right; lower your spears, everyone! Do you
know where the men have gone?

ODYSSEUS [*pointing*]: That's where they were heading.

CHORUS: Every man follow their tracks! Should we raise a cry?
No, it would be unnerving to plague our allies with fear in   690
the night.

    [ODYSSEUS *slips away as the* CHORUS *circle in agitation around
the stage.*]

CHORUS [Strophe]: *Which man was it who got away? What spirit
so greatly daring shall boast he has escaped my hands? Where shall I
go to find him? To whom shall I liken him, the one who with fearless
tread came under night's cover through soldiers and sentinels at their
posts? Is he a man of Thessaly or one who inhabits the city of the*   700
*Locrians by the sea? Or is he a lonely island-dweller? Who was he?
Where did he come from? What sort of land does he come from?
What god supreme does he name in prayer?*

    *— Is this the deed of Odysseus? Or whose is it? If we are to judge
by earlier actions, then certainly it is.*

    — Do you think so?

    — Assuredly.

    — Well, he is brave enough towards us.

    — What man are you praising for his courage in war?

    — Odysseus.

    — Do not praise the treacherous spear of a thief!

[Antistrophe:] *Once before he came to our city,*[33] *with furtive eye*
710 *and clad in ragged clothes, armed with a sword concealed in his*
cloak. Begging for his livelihood, he made his way along, like some
impoverished servant, his head all rough and filthy.

And showing his hatred of the commanders, he spoke many insults,
indeed, against the royal house of Atreus' sons. Oh, ruin take him,
720 *ruin, as he deserves, before he ever sets foot in the land of the*
Phrygians!

— Whether it is Odysseus who is the cause or not, I am afraid!
For Hector shall blame us guards.

— What shall he say to us? — He will be vexed . . .

— That we did what? Why are you afraid?

— That they passed through us . . . — What men?

— The ones who came into the Phrygian camp this night.

[*The* CHARIOTEER *of Rhesus enters, wounded.*[34]]

CHARIOTEER: *Oh, oh! A cruel stroke from heaven! What sorrow!*

CHORUS: Look out! Crouch down, every man, and not a sound!
730 Someone may be entering the net!

CHARIOTEER: *Oh, oh! What a catastrophe for the Thracians!*

CHORUS: It is one of our allies who makes this lament.

CHARIOTEER: *Oh, oh! How wretched am I, and you, king of the*
Thracians! O how hateful has the sight of Troy proved to you, what
an end to life has overtaken you!

CHORUS: Which of our allies are you? The night has dimmed
my eyes and I do not recognize you plainly.

CHARIOTEER: *Where am I to find one of the Trojan princes? Where*
does Hector sleep with shield for pillow? What captain of the army
740 *should I tell of what has befallen us, what someone has done to us,*
wreaking his harm unseen and making his escape, but devising for
the men of Thrace a sorrow all too plain to view!

CHORUS-LEADER: Some disaster, it seems, has afflicted the
Thracian host, to gather from this man's words.

CHARIOTEER: *The army is no more, our king has fallen to treacherous*
blows! Ah, what pain! The agony of my bloody wound tears at my
750 *insides! Oh, give me death! Was it right that Rhesus and I should*

die without glory when we had reached Troy with our ships to bring
her aid?

CHORUS-LEADER: These woes he speaks of are not in doubt;
he says clearly that our allies have perished.

CHARIOTEER: Calamity has overtaken us, and to calamity is
added deepest shame. And such calamity is twofold indeed.
For a glorious death, if death must come, is painful to the one
who suffers it – this we must not doubt – but to the living it
brings pride and fair fame for the house. But we have perished
foolishly and without glory.   760

When Hector's hand had secured our rest, and he had given
us the password, we slept, overcome by the fatigue of our
march. Our camp was not guarded by night sentries, our
weapons were not lying ready in the lines and the goads were
not fixed to the horses' yokes, as our king had learned that
you Trojans had the upper hand and were keeping a watchful
eye on their ships at anchor. We slept without concern where
we had fallen.

But I had awoken with anxious heart, and was doling out
fodder for my horses with generous hand, expecting to yoke   770
them for battle at dawn. I saw two men making their way
through the troops in the thick darkness. When I stirred, they
crouched and began to move away. I shouted to them not to
come near the camp, thinking they were some of our allies,
bent on stealing.

They made no reply, and I certainly had no more to say to
them. Returning to my bed once more, I fell asleep. And in
my sleep a vision appeared at my side: I saw wolves sitting on   780
the backs of the mares I reared and drove, standing at the side
of Rhesus, for this is what I seemed to see in my dream. They
were lashing the hairy flanks of the mares with their tails
as they drove them on, and they were snorting from their
windpipes, breathing fury, and tossing their manes in terror. I
woke up as I was trying to keep the beasts away from the
horses; for the nightmare roused me.[35]

When I raised my head, I heard the moans of dying men,

790 and from my slaughtered master, as he died in agony, a warm
jet of newly shed blood struck me. I leaped to my feet with
no spear in my hand; and now, as I was seeing clearly and
hunting for my sword, a strong fellow stood beside me and
buried his sword in the lower part of my side. I felt the blow
of a sword and knew I had received the wound's deep furrow.
Down I fell headlong, and they, seizing the chariot-team,
whipped the horses off at a gallop.

Ah, ah! The pain tears at me! Oh, misery, I can't keep my
800 feet! I know I have witnessed a disaster but, as to how the
slain met their end, or at whose hand, I cannot tell. But I can
guess that we have been foully treated by those we trusted.

CHORUS-LEADER: Charioteer of the ill-fated Thracian, spare
yourself further distress; an enemy has done these deeds. Look,
Hector himself is coming, having learned of the disaster; he
shares your grief, it seems, at your sufferings.

[HECTOR *enters.*]

HECTOR: O you architects of greatest sorrows, you enemy
spies, how could those enemy spies come here, how could
the army be slaughtered, all shamefully unobserved by you?
810 How could you fail to drive them away, either as they entered
or as they left the camp? [*He turns from the* CHORUS *to their
leader:*] Who will answer for this if not you? You, I say, were
the guardian of the camp! They have gone without a single
wound, laughing long at Trojan cowardice and at me, your
commander!

Now know this well – I swear it by Father Zeus – either
death by scourging or the axe awaits you for such conduct, or
else you may think Hector a nonentity, a man of straw.

CHORUS [Antistrophe]: *O sovereign protector of the city, mighty,*
820 *mighty in my eyes, surely it was then they came,*[36] *the time when I
had gone to bring you news that flames were burning round the ships!
I did not let my sleepless eyes close in the night or give way to slumber,
no, by the streams of Simois! Do not be angry with me, my lord! I
am not to blame for any of these woes. If in time you learn of deed*

or word of mine not in due season, send me alive to the world below!   830
No plea shall I make.

CHARIOTEER: Why do you threaten these men, and, no subtle
Greek yourself, undermine my unsubtle words with your
clever arguments? It is you who have done this; we would
accept no other culprit, we killed or wounded. Long and
shrewd is the argument you need to persuade me that you did
not kill your friends through your desire for the horses which
led you to shed your allies' blood, while repeatedly urging
them to come. They did come and they are dead. Paris showed
more propriety in defiling the rites of hospitality than you,   840
guilty of murdering comrades-in-arms!

    Spare me any plea that some Greek came and destroyed us.
Who could have come against us, evading ambush by the
Trojans, and remain unnoticed as well? You were encamped
in front of us, you and the Phrygian army.

    Which of your own allies, then, has been wounded or killed
as a result of the enemy incursion you speak of?

    We have suffered wounds indeed, while those who met a
worse fate do not see the light of the sun. To put it plainly,
we hold no Greek to blame. What enemy making his en-   850
trance would have found the bed of Rhesus in the night,
unless some god had kept telling the killers?[37] They did not
even know that Rhesus had arrived at all; this is a plot of your
making.

HECTOR: I have dealt with allies for as long as the Greek army
has been in this land, and I know that I have not heard a harsh
word from them. I should begin with you. I pray that I may
never become so enamoured of horses as to kill friends! This   860
too is the work of Odysseus; what other man of Greece would
ever have done or devised this? I fear him; he stirs an anxious
thought in my heart that he may have met Dolon as well and
killed him. For he has been absent a long time and is not to
be seen.

CHARIOTEER: I do not know of these Odysseuses of yours in

your account; our wounds have not been inflicted by any of the enemy.

HECTOR: Well, think that, as you are determined to.

CHARIOTEER: O land of my fathers, how I wish to die in you!

870 HECTOR: Do not die; the mass of dead is enough.

CHARIOTEER: Where am I to turn now that I have lost my master?

HECTOR: My own house shall shelter you and heal your wound.

CHARIOTEER: How will I receive care from the hands of murderers?

HECTOR: Will this fellow not cease from saying the same speech?

CHARIOTEER: May he perish, the man who did the deed! This is no mere tongue directed at you, as you vainly say. [*He draws his sword and rushes at* HECTOR.] Justice knows it. [*He collapses from his wound.*]

HECTOR [*to some of the Trojan watch who had attempted to defend him*]: Put up your arms! Take him to my house and give him such care that he shall not continue in his slanders. [*To the rest of the watch:*] You must go to those on the battlements, to Priam and the elders, to get their authority for burying the

880 dead at the resting-places off the public way.

CHORUS: *Why does a hostile god remove Troy from her great prosperity and restore her to her sorrows once more? What seed is he planting?*

[THE MUSE *appears above the stage, holding the body of her son,* RHESUS.]³⁸

Ah! What god appears above your head, my king, embracing the newly dead body on a bier? I shudder as I look at this woeful sight.

THE MUSE: Be not afraid to look, you men of Troy! I who am

890 honoured among poets am here, one of the sisterhood of Muses,³⁹ seeing my beloved son here piteously slain by enemies. His murderer, the crafty Odysseus, shall at some time to come pay the penalty he deserves.

[*She sings a lament. Strophe*]: *With spontaneous dirge do I weep for you, my child – o grief to your mother – what a voyage did you make to Troy! How ill fated, how wretched it was, when you left*

behind a mother's pleas, a father's passionate entreaties! Oh, how I   900
weep for you, my dear, dear babe, my child, how I weep!

CHORUS-LEADER: So far as I may, as one not privy to your
family's sorrow, I pity your son.

THE MUSE [*continuing her sung lament. Antistrophe*]: *I curse the
grandson of Oeneus, I curse the son of Laertes, who robbed me of a
child, the finest son a mother ever bore*;[40] *her, too, I curse, who left
her home in Greece and sailed here,*[41] *taking a Phrygian for her lover,*   910
*where she brought destruction on you for Troy's sake, my dearest
child, and made cities past number bereft of their bravest sons.*

[*She reverts to spoken verse.*]

Son of Philammon,[42] much did I think of you when you
lived, and much once you had passed to the world below. For
the arrogance that was your downfall and your quarrel with
the Muses made me bear this child to wretchedness. For, as I
passed over his flowing river, I entered Strymon's potent
embrace, when we Muses came to Pangaeum's uplands fertile   920
in gold. We were bearing our instruments for the mighty
contest in song with the famous poet of Thrace, and we
blinded Thamyris, the gross reviler of our art.

And when I gave you birth, out of respect for my sisters
and their virginity I sent you to your father's lovely whirling
waters, and Strymon gave you to be reared, not into mortal
hands, but to the nymphs of the springs. There were you
raised most nobly by these maids, and became foremost of
men, my child, ruling over Thrace. I had no fears that you   930
would die in your native land, marshalling bloodthirsty battles.
But I told you never to voyage to the city of Troy, since I
knew your fate.[43] Yet Hector's endless councils of elders pre-
vailed with their embassies and you went to bring succour to
your allies.

And for this, for all this death, Athena, you are responsible
– it was not the doing of Odysseus, no, or of Tydeus' son –
do not imagine your action has gone unnoticed! And yet we
sister Muses pay the greatest honours to your city and treat   940
your land with the utmost kindness;[44] the torch-processions

of the secret mysteries were revealed by Orpheus, who was
full cousin to this dead man whom you killed; and Musaeus,
your august citizen whose achievements surpassed all men's,
received instruction from Phoebus and my sisters. And as my
reward for this I hold my son in my arms and sing his death-
song; I shall call on no other poet to assist me.

CHORUS-LEADER: Misplaced, then, Hector, were the Thracian
950   charioteer's accusations that we had plotted this man's
death.

HECTOR: This I knew; there was no need of prophets to tell us
that he died through Odysseus' stratagems. But seeing the
Greek army camped on our land, surely it was not to be
imagined that I would fail to send heralds to our friends, asking
them to come and help our country? I did send; and he did
come, as his duty prescribed, to share our toil.

Yet it gives me no joy, believe me, that he has died; indeed,
now I am ready to build a tomb for him and to burn for him
960   besides countless splendid robes; for he came in friendship and
departs in sorrow.

THE MUSE: He shall not go into the dark earth; this much shall
I ask of the maid who dwells below,[45] daughter of Demeter,
the goddess who gives fruit, that she release his soul; she owes
it to me to show that she honours the family of Orpheus.[46]
To me henceforth he shall be as one dead who sees the light
no more; for never more shall he meet me, nor look on his
970   mother's face. Yet, hidden in a cavern of the silver-veined
earth shall he lie,[47] alive, both man and god, the prophet of
Bacchus who made his dwelling in Pangaeum's rock, a god
revered by those who have knowledge. I shall bear a lighter
grief than the sea-goddess; for her son is also fated to be killed.
First in our dirge shall we sister Muses sing of you, and then,
in Thetis' time of grief, shall we sing of Achilles. Pallas who
brought death to you shall not keep it from him; such is the
arrow that Loxias' quiver keeps for him.

O what sorrows accompany child-bearing![48] How they
980   torment the hearts of mortals! For whoever considers them

rightly will pass his days without offspring and not produce children only to bury them!

[THE MUSE *withdraws, still carrying the body of* RHESUS.]

CHORUS-LEADER: This man's burial rites are now his mother's concern. But if you mean to take any further measures in the task ahead of us, Hector, now is the time; yonder rises this day's sun.

HECTOR [*to the men of the watch*]: On your way! Bid our allies quickly arm themselves and harness their horses' necks! You must wait for the voice of the Tuscan trumpet, torches in hand; for I have confidence that, forcing my way through the trench and defences of the Greeks, I will fire their ships,[49] and that the sun's rising beams are bringing the day of freedom for the Trojans.

990

CHORUS: *The king must be obeyed. Let us don our armour and go to bear these tidings to the allies. Perhaps the god who favours us may grant victory!*[50]

[*Exeunt all.*]

NOTES

PHOENICIAN WOMEN

1. JOCASTA: The prologue, as so often in Euripides, begins with a fairly detailed account of past action by an individual alone on stage: often, as in *Hippolytus, Bacchae* and others, the speaker is a god. This résumé may form the whole of the prologue, as in *Bacchae*, or a second part, more lively and varied, may intervene before the entrance of the chorus (as here and e.g. in *Electra* or *Orestes*). It became a Euripidean convention to have this first speaker trace his or her ancestry (and often outline the remote origins of the present crisis): the tendency is mocked in Aristophanes' *Frogs*. Sophocles, who normally opens his plays with dialogue, seems to have been more alert to the dangers of monotony.

Jocasta mentions a number of earlier episodes in the mythical history of Thebes, and many more are referred to later in the play. It may therefore be convenient to summarize this history, so that readers may consult this note in order to see how a particular allusion fits into the mythical chronology. Of course, the stories were variable in detail, and poets treated them freely and allusively: it was prose writers such as the mythographers who tried to systematize them in this fashion.

Io, daughter of the River Inachus, was beloved by Zeus, but in order to conceal her from Hera he turned her into cow-form with a touch of his hand; undeceived, Hera persecuted Io, driving her across the world tormented by a gadfly. Eventually she reached Egypt, was changed back into human form, and bore a son Epaphus (676–82). His descendant, Agenor, went to settle in Phoenicia. He was the father of a daughter, Europa, and a son, Cadmus. Europa, playing on the seashore with her friends, was abducted by Zeus in the form of a bull and carried overseas. Cadmus set out in quest of her, but was told by an oracle to abandon this search and instead to found a city at the spot where a cow with particular markings finally sat down (638–48). This animal led him to the site of the future Thebes.

Cadmus prepared to offer the cow as a sacrifice (662), but was barred from a spring of water by a great serpent (657ff.), which some authors called the offspring of Ares. Cadmus killed this serpent with Athena's aid, and on her advice sowed its teeth in the earth: from this spot grew up armed warriors, the so-called 'Sown Men', who immediately began fighting each other: the survivors became the original Thebans (the myth obviously implies that the Thebans are born warriors) (657–75, 818–21). Cadmus became king of Thebes and married Harmonia, daughter of Ares (822–3). Later, however, he was driven into exile. In the *Phoenician Women* the continuing anger of Ares at the slaying of his serpent is an important motif that helps explain the catastrophes afflicting Thebes: at one point (1065–6) it is suggested that Ares sent the Sphinx in retribution.

The next ruler of Thebes referred to in this play was Laius, son of Labdacus and father of Oedipus. Jocasta summarizes his story in the prologue: warned that if he fathered a son that son would kill him, he first tried to refrain from intercourse, but when a son did appear exposed him. But the child survived and eventually killed his father without recognizing him (13–45, 801–5). When Thebes was being attacked by the monstrous Sphinx, it became clear that no one could kill the beast except by solving its riddle. Oedipus did so (46–50, 806–11, 1018–50). Tragedy often refers to the riddle but never quotes it: various versions are found in prose accounts and commentators. Essentially it was 'what creature has four legs, two legs and three legs?' and the answer was 'man' (crawling on all fours as a child, walking on two legs as an adult, walking with a stick when old).

Oedipus, still unrecognized, was rewarded with the throne and Jocasta's hand in marriage. This incestuous relationship was as horrific in Greek eyes as in ours; still worse was the fact that Jocasta bore her son children: two sons, Eteocles and Polyneices, and two daughters, Ismene (mentioned but ignored in Euripides' play) and Antigone (51–8, 1047–50). The process by which his true identity was exposed after many years is dramatized in Sophocles' *Oedipus the King*. In that play Jocasta commits suicide and Oedipus seems likely to be sent into exile. Euripides allows both of them to live on in war-torn Thebes. At some point before the action of this play begins Oedipus has cursed his sons: this was a traditional part of the legend, though explanations of his motives varied. Whether their bitter enmity is a result of his curses is questionable, but it is obvious that their mutual fratricide, the climax of this play, is the final upshot of their father's anger. (Euripides, however, makes Oedipus now regret having uttered these curses.)

On the question of how and where Oedipus eventually dies, see note 83.

2. *O Sun, whirling*: The textual uncertainties of the play are well illustrated by the fact that the first two lines in the manuscripts are almost certainly spurious. The full manuscript version begins: 'O you who cut your path amid the stars of heaven, mounted in a chariot of beaten gold, o Sun, whirling . . .' The evidence that lines 1–2 are a later expansion is unusually clear-cut. Two ancient papyri of the opening of the play begin with line 3; an ancient collection of summaries of Euripidean plays quotes the same line as the 'beginning'; and various later writers, e.g. on metrical matters, quote it in contexts that suggest it was well known, probably because it was the opening line. The issue is fully discussed by M. Haslam, 'The Authenticity of Euripides, *Phoenissae* 1–2 and Sophocles, *Electra* 1', *Greek Roman and Byzantine Studies* 16 (1975), pp. 149–74.

3. *wade through blood*: The stress here on the bloody fate of the whole house, absent from the Sophoclean version of the oracle, is obviously better suited to the themes of this play, which focuses on the generation after Oedipus and culminates in the deaths of Laius' widow and grandsons.

4. *golden brooch-pins*: The detail recalls Sophocles' version, where Oedipus blinds himself with the brooches he finds on Jocasta herself after her suicide. Here, of course, Jocasta is not dead; but Euripides does not feel obliged to think of an alternative instrument.

5. *with whetted sword*: The prophecy of Apollo might be thought to have already guaranteed this; Oedipus' fury with his sons adds a further level of supernatural causation. This form of 'overdetermination' is common in tragedy. Oedipus seems to be angry because his sons have virtually imprisoned him in the palace. In the early epic tradition it was said that he was outraged at being served an inferior cut of meat: later authors probably found this motive too trivial.

6. *behind the stage-building*: The scene which follows, while not integral to the action, enlarges our sense of the drama of the war, and introduces us to Antigone, here an attractive character in her youthful enthusiasm. The episode is modelled on the scene on the walls of Troy in *Iliad* 3 known as the 'Teichoskopia' (The Viewing from the Walls) in which Priam questions Helen about the identity of the Greek warriors whom he sees moving to and fro on the battlefield below. Here the situation is reversed: a young woman questions an old man.

7. *you are royal*: In contemporary Athens well-born women, especially if unmarried, were not expected to roam freely outside the home. These values are transferred to the heroic age.

8. *from the men of Argos*: Euripides is more concerned than the earlier tragedians with realistic detail of this kind; this contrasts with Aeschylus' relative indifference to such matters. In the *Seven against Thebes* the older poet includes a lengthy scene in which a scout reports to Eteocles every detail of the accoutrements of the attacking champions, including much that he could hardly have witnessed.

9. *Amphiaraus*: The only one of the Seven who traditionally came on the expedition unwillingly. As a prophet, he foresaw the outcome without being able to avert it. See also lines 1111ff. and Aeschylus, *Seven against Thebes* 568ff.

10. *to say nothing good of each other*: The servant's comments anticipate the entry of the chorus. As at the beginning of the scene, he is anxious to protect Antigone's reputation. The disparaging remarks on women are the kind of thing that encouraged audiences to regard Euripides as a misogynist; but the opinions of a character should not be automatically ascribed to the author.

11. *from the Phoenician isle*: The reference is to Tyre, an island until it was joined to the mainland by a mole during Alexander's siege of 332 BC.

12. *serve as a slave to Phoebus*: The chorus are being sent from Phoenicia to Delphi to serve in Apollo's shrine as temple servants. En route for Delphi they have reached Thebes, and are now confined there by the siege which has just begun. Because of their Phoenician ancestry they are distantly related to the Thebans (see note 1), but their dress and probably their style of singing and dancing would mark them as foreigners. Euripides no doubt wished to use a different kind of chorus from Aeschylus in the *Seven against Thebes* (whose chorus consists of Theban women); he also often prefers to characterize the chorus as marginal (foreigners in a strange land, old men, maidens), able to comment on events from a different perspective although caught up in them. See J. Gould, 'Tragedy and Collective Experience', in *Tragedy and the Tragic*, ed. M. S. Silk (Oxford 1996), pp. 217–43 (= J. Gould, *Myth, Ritual, Memory and Exchange* (Oxford 2001), pp. 378–404); also D. J. Mastronarde, 'Knowledge and Authority in the Choral Voice of Euripidean Tragedy', *Syllecta Classica* 10 (1999), pp. 87–104.

13. *Zephyrus' chariot . . . unharvested plains*: Zephyrus is the favourable west wind, blowing across the Mediterranean from Sicily (the geography is colourful rather than precise). 'Unharvested plains' is modelled on a Homeric phrase referring to the sea.

14. *glorious sons of Agenor*: See note 1 above; Cadmus, founder of Thebes, was son of Agenor and set out on his travels from Phoenicia.

15. *O rock . . . navel*: This stanza paints a picture of the neighbourhood of Thebes, the city where Dionysus was born and where his rites continue to be celebrated on Mount Cithaeron. For the serpent of Ares see note 1 above. But the chorus would prefer to leave this city, for all its wonders, and find refuge in worship at Delphi.

16. *near by I see the altar-hearth*: This phrase hints at the possibility of taking refuge as a suppliant on sacred ground. Euripides often uses the supplication-ritual elsewhere (e.g. the openings of *Children of Heracles*, *Heracles* and *Helen* find the sympathetic characters seeking sanctuary in this way). Here Polyneices' words may lead the audience to expect a development which does not come about.

17. *sings a monody of welcome*: It is typical of Greek tragedy that emotional moments involve lyric song, particularly from female characters. Jocasta's monody may be compared with other set-piece arias in Euripides' work: Evadne in *Suppliant Women* 990ff., Cassandra in *Trojan Women* 308ff. A common pattern in the genre is for matters to be treated first in lyric, then recapitulated in calmer vein through spoken verse. So here Jocasta's song anticipates various topics subsequently handled in the dialogue.

18. *Offspring exert . . . all womankind love their children*: The choral comment is obvious and banal, as these two-line remarks after long speeches or songs often are (cf. 526–7, 586–7). They offer an opportunity for both performers and audience to draw breath; it has even been suggested that they may have been drowned by applause at the end of a virtuoso passage.

19. *what is my old father doing . . . in his eyes*: Jocasta had described Oedipus' condition in her monody, but the recapitulation is conventional (see note 17).

20. *Adrastus' daughters should wed a boar and a lion*: It is fairly obvious that Apollo meant that their husbands would be violent warriors, and the point is understood a few lines later, when Polyneices describes how he and Tydeus fought for a bed. In tragedy oracles are conventionally enigmatic and are rarely understood by the characters at first hearing, though their meaning will usually be plain to the audience.

21. *It is an old, old saying . . . counts for nothing*: Many editors have cut the comments on wealth, ending the speech at 437. It has been thought that Polyneices should not be dwelling so much on his own self-interest. But even if we accept that Euripides is treating Polyneices sympathetically, that need not exclude a desire to recover his rightful share of his inheritance. Odysseus in Homer and Orestes in Aeschylus' *Libation-Bearers* also show a natural concern for their property.

22. *Mother, here I am*: The arrival of Eteocles initiates the *agon*-scene, the rhetorical contest which is a regular part of Euripides' repertoire (see M. Lloyd, *The Agon in Euripides* (Oxford 1992)). Speeches in an *agon* are usually long, rhetorically sophisticated and highly self-conscious (the openings of both Polyneices' and Eteocles' speeches contain self-referential comments on truth and argumentation). This is also a part of the play in which 'modern' issues, topics important in Euripides' own time, regularly make their appearance – in this case, the opposition between absolute power and equality. The three-cornered debate in this scene is unusual; most *agon*-scenes involve a confrontation between two opponents, but here Jocasta tries in vain to act as peacemaker.

In tragedy the *agon* illuminates the matters at stake, but does not settle anything; normally, as here, it only intensifies conflict. The long speeches are followed by quickfire dialogue between the brothers which again heightens their antagonism: towards the end of the scene Jocasta tries to intervene in this exchange, with equal lack of success.

23. *If all men agreed . . . is not reality*: These lines are difficult and no doubt deliberately challenging for the audience. Two ideas seem to be combined: first, that no consensus can be reached among men concerning moral judgements (and therefore Eteocles cannot be expected to take the same view as Polyneices regarding the rights in this case); second, that morality is only a matter of words, without underlying reality. The two points are distinct, since it would be possible to believe that good and bad do exist even if one could not identify them to universal agreement. These ideas have the flavour of contemporary sophistic thought: Gorgias and Protagoras taught various kinds of relativism, and some of their pupils carried these arguments into the political arena.

24. *In all else should a man fear the gods*: These lines are shocking to orthodox opinion, and became notorious for their ruthless frankness. Julius Caesar is reported to have quoted them regularly (Cicero, *On Duties* 3.82, Suetonius, *Life of Caesar* 30.5).

25. *Equality*: The language is reminiscent of political debate: *isotes* ('equality') recalls *isonomia* ('equality before the law'), one of the catch-words of Athenian democracy. Here equality is personified and seen as a ruling principle of the universe. Traditional imagery of the changing cycle of nature (compare Sophocles, *Ajax* 669ff.) is combined with more modern ideological polemic.

26. *trophies of victory to Zeus*: It was standard practice for the Greeks to dedicate spoils to Zeus and other gods after success in battle, sometimes adding a commemorative inscription: for many examples see W. K. Pritchett, *The Greek State at War* ii (Berkeley and London 1974), pp. 246–75. Jocasta's point is that for Polyneices to boast in this way of sacking his own city would be disgraceful, not glorious.

27. *the contest is no longer one of words*: The futility of the debate is clearly marked, and Jocasta's intervention proves futile: neither of the brothers attempts to answer her arguments. Failure of persuasion is a common theme in Greek tragedy: see e.g. Orestes' failure to convince Tyndareus and Menelaus in the *agon*-scene of the *Orestes*. At this point the metre changes, and the remainder of this scene is in trochaic tetrameters, a longer line which seems regularly to be used by Euripides for agitated or excited dialogue. This effect is heightened from 603 onwards ('With more than your share?') as the lines are repeatedly split between the two brothers. The argument becomes more rapid and heated.

28. *riders of the white horses*: The two brothers Amphion and Zethus, in a Theban context almost equivalent to Castor and Polydeuces.

29. *Where will you take your stance before the gates?*: This exchange marks an important modification of Aeschylus' *Seven against Thebes*. In that play, Eteocles appoints a series of Theban champions to confront the leaders of the attacking forces at each of the seven gates of Thebes. Only when the scout identifies the assailant at the last gate as Polyneices does Eteocles realize that it is now inevitable that he himself must face his brother, fulfilling his undesired destiny (653ff.). In Euripides the hatred each brother feels for the other is such that both of them actually desire to have the opportunity for fratricide.

30. *your father's curses*: Again the themes of the *Seven against Thebes* are evoked. See especially lines 655 and 709, where Eteocles recognizes the fulfilment of the curses, and 677ff., where the chorus make repeated efforts to dissuade him.

31. *named you Polyneices, 'man of much strife'*: The etymology is explicit here, and alluded to later at 1494 (see also Aeschylus, *Seven against Thebes* 405, 829ff.). The name suggests that it was traditionally Polyneices who was seen as the aggressor (and Jocasta's speech still emphasizes this aspect). Euripides has modified the characterization, making Eteocles a much less sympathetic figure than his brother. Significant names (as 'expressions of destiny') are common in Greek literature, especially in epic and tragedy: compare *Bacchae* 367, 506–8, Aeschylus, *Agamemnon* 681–98, and many other cases.

32. *From Tyre to this land came Cadmus*: On the mythology of Cadmus see note 1 above. The choral ode exemplifies in an extreme form Euripides' late lyric manner, often referred to as 'dithyrambic' because the dithyramb, a type of song in honour of Dionysus, was generally regarded as wilder and less disciplined in structure and thought than other hymnic forms. D. J. Mastronarde's summary of the characteristics of Euripides' style in the odes of this play is as follows: 'short cola, an abundance of compound epithets (several unique in extant Greek or used in a uniquely eccentric sense), run-on appositions, accumulation of relative clauses and imbalance between main clauses and subordinate clauses, verbal repetitions, and the paradoxical wedding of beautiful language and sensuous description to violent content' (D. J. Mastronarde (ed.), *Phoenician Women* (Cambridge 1994), p. 331.)

33. *the Roaring One*: This translates Bromios, one of the names of Dionysus, son of Zeus and Semele, who was born at Thebes. For more detail on his birth see *Bacchae* 1ff., 88ff., 242–5, 519–29 and notes.

34. *Epaphus*: He was the son of Zeus by Io, brought to birth when she reached Egypt. See Aeschylus, *Suppliants* 291–315, *Prometheus Bound* 846–52. His grandson Agenor settled in Phoenicia; hence Io is the chorus's 'first mother'. See also note 1 above.

35. *Creon, son of Menoeceus*: Creon is a regular figure in the Theban dramas, appearing in all of Sophocles' plays on these legends (though very differently characterized in each). He is both son and father of Menoeceus: in historical Greek genealogies, names often recur every other generation. This scene contrasts Eteocles, the hot-tempered and impulsive ruler, with Creon, an older and more prudent figure. We have already seen that Eteocles is a proud and power-hungry monarch; we now see that he is no great strategist.

36. *a company to lead against our seven gates*: The traditional picture, immortalized by Aeschylus' play, was for seven champions on each side to confront one another. Euripides introduces a more realistic note (as Eteocles' preceding remark may imply) by making each of these men leader of a company of soldiers.

37. *It would be a costly waste of time . . . our very walls*: These lines are clearly a mischievous critique of the central scene of Aeschylus' *Seven against Thebes*, in which nearly 300 lines are occupied by just such a description. The allusive reference to his great predecessor can be paralleled most clearly in the *Electra* (Electra's sceptical comments on the tokens which had convinced her proto-type in Aeschylus' *Libation-Bearers*), and other cases of allusive reminiscence have been plausibly detected.

38. *But if I meet with any misfortune . . .*: The remainder of Eteocles' speech is subject to considerable critical doubt. In particular, lines 757–62 and 774–7, the passages which confirm Antigone's betrothal to Haemon and forbid the burial of Polyneices, seem clearly to be composed in order to connect this play with the plot of Sophocles' *Antigone*, in which Antigone buries her brother in defiance of Creon's edict and perishes together with her fiancé Haemon. It is undramatic for Eteocles to be so explicitly expecting to die, and these sections, with their over-precise predictions of the future (especially 777 'even if related by blood') are probably later additions to Euripides' text. If this is right, so too will be the later developments of this theme, above all the confrontation of Creon and Antigone at the end of the play (1625–82: see notes there). The interest of these sections for the subsequent reception of Euripides' play is such as to justify their inclusion here.

39. *the prophet Teiresias*: This blind seer regularly figures in tragedies set at Thebes: he appears also in the *Bacchae* and in Sophocles' *Antigone* and *Oedipus the King*. It is common for him to advise rulers and for his warnings to be rejected angrily, but in the end they are always justified. That Eteocles has alienated this authoritative prophet is another indication of his inadequacy as a ruler.

40. *Precaution*: Not a regular deity of cult. Also, calling a god 'serviceable' is virtually unparalleled, and suits Eteocles' pragmatic piety.

41. *so out of tune with the festivals of the Roaring One*: The chorus devote the first strophe of this ode to an elaborate contrast between the joyous dances and festivity of peace (presided over by Thebes' patron Dionysus) and the 'savage dance graced by no music', the warfare inspired by and welcome to Ares. Warfare is seen as a kind of caricature of festivity. This type of image, involving the hideous distortion of something normal or pleasant, is frequent in tragedy.

42. *Cithaeron*: This was the mountain on which the infant Oedipus was exposed. The chorus, having begun with the present, moves back in time, wishing Oedipus had never survived, or that the Sphinx had never threatened Thebes (for in that case Oedipus would not have had to solve her riddle and thus become king, and none of the subsequent disasters would have happened). For the sequence of events see Jocasta's account in 1–80, and note 1; for more on Oedipus and the Sphinx see the next choral ode, 1019ff., and note. The sequence of thought is loose; the connections of cause and effect, which would be familiar to the audience, are not spelt out in full.

43. *You brought to birth . . .*: The final part of the ode moves still further back in time, to describe the foundation of Thebes and the birth of the Sown Men (see note 1 above). The relevance of this will become apparent in the next scene, when Teiresias declares that one of the direct descendants of the Sown Men must die.

44. *Harmonia's nuptials*: This refers to the marriage of Cadmus to Harmonia, daughter of Ares. That the gods attended their wedding feast as a sign of special favour is mentioned in Pindar, *Pythian* 3.87ff. The prosperity and divine goodwill enjoyed by Thebes in the past is contrasted with her present misfortunes (compare the treatment of Troy's past in *Trojan Women* 820–59).

45. *Amphion's lyre-strings*: Amphion and his brother Zethus, sons of Zeus and Antiope, are figures from the early history of Thebes; their mythological relation to Cadmus and his family is somewhat ill defined. Amphion was a gifted musician, and his greatest achievement, referred to here, was to play so enchantingly that the stones moved of their own accord to form the defensive walls of Thebes. Euripides' lost play *Antiope* included a famous *agon* between the practical brother Zethus and the artistic Amphion; in the final scene Hermes predicted the building of these walls and so vindicated Amphion.

46. *where Ares' finest garlands may be gained*: I.e., where victory in war can bring glory – but for which side?

47. *from the land of Erechtheus' sons*: The ancient commentators on this passage remark that this is an anachronistic reference included to glorify Athens (Erechtheus and Cecrops are both mythical kings of Athens). The war referred to was dramatically treated by Euripides in his earlier *Erechtheus*, another lost play, but there is no particular reason to suppose that Teiresias was a character.

Apart from intertextual ingenuity, the playwright presumably means us to recall that this legend involved human sacrifice in order to save Athens; Teiresias is about to recommend the same drastic measure to aid Thebes.

48. *There is no alternative*: Teiresias turns to leave, without having divulged his secret. Creon indignantly restrains him and demands the truth. The scene is modelled on the exchange between Oedipus and Teiresias in Sophocles, *Oedipus the King* 297ff.; at line 320 there the prophet asks to be taken home, and Oedipus protests.

49. *You must sacrifice Menoeceus here . . .*: The sacrifice of a pure or virginal young man or woman is a recurrent motif in tragedy (Iphigenia is the most famous), and Euripides is particularly fond of this type of situation, in which a divine command requires that one should die so that many can be saved. The same sequence is found in his *Children of Heracles* and was evidently prominent in the lost *Erechtheus*. Such plots permit a powerful clash between the individual's desires and the public good, normally solved by the victim nobly accepting his or her death as a duty. In this play the initial reluctance of Menoeceus turns out to be feigned, a clever variation on the regular pattern. More problematic are the cases where the victim is to die in order to allow an expedition to sail (as in *Iphigenia at Aulis*), or to satisfy a dead ghost (as Polyxena is sacrificed to appease the dead Achilles in *Hecabe*). For discussions see J. Schmitt, *Freiwilliger Opfertod bei Euripides* (Giessen 1921); E. O'Connor-Visser, *Aspects of Human Sacrifice in the Tragedies of Euripides* (Amsterdam 1987); J. Wilkins, 'The State and the Individual: Euripides' Plays of Voluntary Self-sacrifice', in A. Powell (ed.), *Euripides, Women and Sexuality* (London 1990), pp. 177–94; ironic readings in H. Foley, *Ritual Irony: Poetry and Sacrifice in Euripides* (Ithaca and London 1985).

The demand for Menoeceus to die is probably a Euripidean invention. Sophocles, *Antigone* 1303 refers to the earlier death of a son of Creon, Megareus, but no circumstances are specified.

50. *I beg you by your knees*: This is a gesture of supplication, the procedure by which one person throws himself on another's mercy: physical contact establishes a bond. Creon kneels and reaches out to touch Teiresias. The appeal is ritualistic, and Zeus in his capacity as god of suppliants is thought to be concerned for their interests. Supplication thus imposes an obligation, but it can still be resisted or rejected. See further J. Gould's detailed treatment in 'Hiketeia', *Journal of Hellenic Studies* 93 (1973), pp. 74–103 (= J. Gould, *Myth, Ritual, Memory and Exchange*, pp. 22–77).

51. *Haemon's coming marriage . . . he is still betrothed*: This rather fussy explanation is probably a later addition, made at the same time as the interpolations introducing the theme of Antigone's betrothal to Haemon in the previous scene (see note 38 above). Diggle follows Willink in bracketing these lines as non-Euripidean.

52. *am ready to die to save my country*: If 944–6 are genuine (unlikely: see last note), Creon's desperate resolve would be futile, for he is himself a married man. This is a further argument for their exclusion.

53. *If only every man would take . . . bless them*: These high-minded lines (perhaps not authentic) paint an ideal vision of politics. The Athenian audience would no doubt think of ways in which their own society fell short of this ideal. This type of moralizing generality is much more common in tragedy than precise political allusion to current events.

54. *You came, you came, winged creature*: The chorus address the Sphinx, now long dead, using the rhetorical device called apostrophe. For mythical details see note 1 above. The strophe describes how Thebes suffered from the Sphinx's flying raids, the antistrophe refers to the coming of Oedipus, apparently a saviour-figure, but one who brought further misfortunes through the pollution of his crime and the curses he laid on his sons. The false saviour Oedipus is then contrasted with the true saviour Menoeceus.

55. *A* MESSENGER *enters*: Large-scale events such as battles and slaughter were not easy to present on the Greek stage: hence the frequent use of the messenger, anonymous but clearly identified as a servant or loyal supporter of the royal house. The speech developed a rhetoric of its own: vivid, detailed, often using language reminiscent of epic, frequently including quotation of direct speech, usually ending with a moralizing tag. It is conventional for the speaker to be able to tell the listeners much more than one individual could in fact have seen, though there are occasional gestures towards realism. For many aspects of the Euripidean messenger speech see I. de Jong, *Narrative in Drama: the Art of the Euripidean Messenger-speech* (*Mnemosyne* Suppl. 116, Leiden 1991). Most Greek tragedies include a messenger-speech and many have more than one. In this play there are two messengers and four speeches! Another convention is that time seems effectively to stand still while the messenger is narrating events: although in some plays there is urgent need for action, this is ignored until the narration is complete (e.g. *Iphigenia among the Taurians* 1322ff., *Helen* 1526ff., cf. 1622–3). So too here: in real life, the messenger would explain the new plan of single combat at once, but here the narrative is expounded in chronological sequence, and the need for action by Jocasta only emerges at 1259ff.

56. *When Creon's son . . . to save the land*: It is surprising that more is not made of Menoeceus' self-sacrifice; instead it is disposed of in three lines, so that the narrative of the battle can follow. Perhaps the drama of decision-making appealed more to the poet than the suicidal moment itself.

57. *And first to lead his troops . . .*: The catalogue of warriors' names and description of their shields' symbols again recalls Aeschylus' *Seven against Thebes*. The passage also adds the details of which gate most of the warriors are attacking: some of these repeat the Aeschylean version, others diverge. The inclusion of Adrastus, Polyneices' father-in-law, as one of the Seven is unusual. He replaces a hero called Eteoclus (mentioned in Aeschylus and in Euripides' own *Suppliant Women*; also in a similar list in Sophocles, *Oedipus at Colonus* 1313–25). Possibly the name was thought confusing in a play that says so much about Eteocles. Some scholars see the list of warriors as a later elaboration (Diggle brackets 1104–40). But tragic poetry often includes catalogues of this kind.

58. *the monster that sees all*: This refers to Argus, the mythical figure set to guard Io: he was suited to the task by having countless eyes, so that he was never wholly asleep. Nevertheless, Hermes lulled him to sleep and killed him.

59. *Titan Prometheus*: A difficult passage. It appears that Tydeus is being compared with Prometheus, though some editors take this to be a further symbol on his shield. Whereas Prometheus brought fire to men and helped them with this gift, Tydeus is bringing fire against Thebes in order to burn and destroy it.

60. *All this I was able to see . . . carrying the password*: The messenger gives his credentials, so to speak. Similarly the servant in the prologue explained to Antigone how he knew all the names of the warriors on the opposing side (95ff., 141ff.). The intermittent concern for realistic justification is characteristic of Euripides.

61. *the fury of Capaneus' attack*: See already 179–92. Capaneus was traditionally characterized by arrogance amounting to blasphemy: he boasted that he would burn Thebes whether Zeus willed it or not, and was punished with a thunderbolt. Cf. Aeschylus *Seven against Thebes* 423ff., Sophocles *Antigone* 127–40 (unnamed; the audience is expected to know who is meant).

62. *why would you not let me give my good news . . . tale of woe*: An almost metatextual allusion to the normal conventions, whereby the messenger gives his account and leaves at once. Here, however, a second speech follows. For good news in one speech followed by bad in another compare Aeschylus *Agamemnon* 503ff., 636ff.

63. *Priests began sacrificing sheep*: In historical times it was standard practice to test the gods' will by divination before battle, and seers (the Greek *manteis* suggests 'prophets' rather than simply 'priests') accompanied armies on their expeditions. Bad omens could sometimes be disposed of by a second attempt, or even several. See further R. Parker, 'Sacrifice and Battle' in *War and Violence in Ancient Greece*, ed. H. Van Wees (London and Swansea 2000), pp. 299–313.

64. *go, prevent your sons . . . fearful contest*: Once again Jocasta must attempt to play the peacemaker, this time with deeds as well as words; and once again she will fail.

65. *Which of her two sons shall pierce*: Typical tragic irony. The chorus assume that one of the battling brothers will die, but the audience know that both are doomed. Teiresias in fact predicts this at 880 (in a passage deleted by some editors), but an audience would not be likely to recall this; in any case, warnings of this kind are often forgotten until too late.

66. *Yet here I see Creon*: Some scholars (including Diggle in the Oxford text) believe that in Euripides' original play Creon's role was confined to the scenes with Eteocles and Teiresias, and that all parts of the text from this point on involving him are spurious. If this is right, the passage which follows must have replaced or expanded a scene in which a messenger conversed simply with the chorus. My own preference is to regard the present scene and most of the text down to 1583 as substantially authentic: see further note 75 below, and for more detailed debate Mastronarde's commentary.

67. *O house of Oedipus*: Creon addresses the palace, represented by the stage-building. The house is seen as almost a living entity, experiencing the burden of guilt and crime in Oedipus' family and sharing the pain of its inhabitants. This kind of personification of the house was brilliantly exploited by Aeschylus in the *Oresteia*; he may well have invented the concept, if as is likely the stage-building was then a recent addition to the tragic performance. See further J. Jones, *On Aristotle and Greek Tragedy* (London 1962), pp. 82–111, O. Taplin, *The Stagecraft of Aeschylus* (Oxford 1977), pp. 319–20, 458–9.

68. *Etruscan trumpet*: In the sixth and fifth centuries BC 'Tyrrhenian' (Etruscan) was used by Greek writers to refer to the non-Greek peoples of Italy, with whom Greek colonists had been acquainted since the extensive settlements in the west in the eighth century BC. The notion of metalwork being imported from Italy to Greece in the heroic age is anachronistic, but not glaringly so: Hesiod in the last section of the *Theogony* already mentions the Tyrrhenians in a heroic context.

69. *traitors to my marriage*: The meaning is that Antigone's brothers would have been expected to play a role in managing her marriage ceremony, as was normal when a father was dead or incapacitated. Some take these lines differently, dividing the speech so that part (rendered as 'supporters of your mother . . .') is spoken by Jocasta, part by Antigone.

70. *thrusting the blade straight through her neck*: The weapon is of course readily available on the battlefield. This is however an unconventional death for a woman: most tragic heroines committing suicide hang themselves (Antigone, Phaedra), and Jocasta did so in Sophocles. It is perhaps significant that Jocasta directs the blow at her *neck*. See further N. Loraux, *Tragic Ways of Killing a Woman* (Eng. tr. Cambridge, Mass., and London 1987), p. 51 on this point.

71. *the troops rushed to arms*: The madness continues; Eteocles' proposal to avoid bloodshed by single combat, belated as it was, proves ineffective. For a parallel in the historical period see Herodotus 1.82 (Sparta versus Argos).

72. *Polyneices, your name proved true*: The name means 'much strife', as already stated in 636 (see note 31 above).

73. *O house, o house*: The repetition is emotional, typical of tragic lyric at moments of intensity, not least passages of lamentation. Tragedy goes even further along this road than earlier lyric verse (see G. O. Hutchinson, *Greek Lyric Poetry* (Oxford 2001), pp. 429–32), and Euripides is notorious for repetitions of this kind (extensively parodied in Aristophanes, *Frogs*: e.g. 1137, 1352–5).

74. *No one was unaware . . . woe upon our house*: The song of Antigone concludes with a vivid picture of pathetic appeal (Jocasta bares her breast as Hecabe did in an effort to arouse pity in Hector in the *Iliad*, or as Clytemnestra does in an effort to move her son in Aeschylus, *Libation-Bearers*). Her feminine distress is juxtaposed with their male violence; the setting 'in a meadow of lotus flowers' provides a further contrast with the bloodshed. The lines, however effective, reach a level of mannerism that is extreme even for late Euripides (especially the lines on the 'libation of blood'). Diggle may well be right to doubt the authenticity of 1570–76.

75. *be blessed with happier fortune!*: Most scholars agree that the remainder of the play is not authentic, but the work of a later hand. It is not certain how the play originally ended – most probably with lamentation and perhaps with preparations for burial. The present ending is clearly composed (together, probably, with some shorter passages earlier in the play) in order to link the plot up with the stories dramatized in Sophocles' *Antigone* (Antigone buries Polyneices despite Creon's edict) and *Oedipus at Colonus* (Oedipus ends his exile and his life in Attica, accompanied by Antigone). The awkwardness of the ending as it stands is obvious. How can Antigone remain and bury Polyneices (and die for it, as the *Antigone*-plot demands) and *also* accompany her father into exile, especially if (as in Sophocles) he may have to journey for many years? Also, Antigone's challenge to Creon *before* she buries her brother is sure to make it difficult if not impossible to execute her intention; while Creon's failure to place her under some form of restraint is inexplicable. The desire for dramatic confrontation has resulted in a striking but highly implausible sequence. It appears that at the time this ending was composed (probably in the fourth century BC) the fame of the *Antigone* was such that the temptation to anticipate that plot was irresistible. A similar procedure has produced a hybrid text at the end of the *Seven against Thebes* (1005–53 are plainly intrusive, and most probably the daughters of Oedipus played no part at all in Aeschylus' original text).

The play was evidently known in its present form to the Roman poets of the first century AD: Statius in the last books of his *Thebaid* quarries the last scenes extensively. For this reason and for the general interest of the conclusion, it is rendered here in full, although it seems clear that at least large portions of it are not Euripidean.

76. *Come, take your leave*: The exchange here inverts the finale of Sophocles' *Oedipus the King*. There, Oedipus demands to be sent into exile, and Creon is hesitant, deferring decision until he has consulted Delphi.

77. *should serve Polybus as my master*: A very odd description in any version of the story. Polybus, king of Corinth, is normally said to have adopted Oedipus as his son (see Jocasta's narrative at 28ff. for a variant on this).

78. *wind my arms around your knees*: A gesture of supplication: compare 923 and note 50 above.

79. *It is to be left alone . . .*: The allusion to the plot of *Antigone* comes close to direct quotation here: compare lines 29–30 and 205 of Sophocles' play.

80. *one of the daughters of Danaus!* The fifty Danaids, forced into marriage with their cousins, killed their husbands on their wedding night (all except Hypermestra, who helped hers escape). Hence they became a proverbial example of female atrocity.

81. *Creon leaves*: The staging here is very uncertain. Now that Creon is aware of Antigone's intention, it hardly makes sense for him to leave the stage simply assuming she will depart from Thebes; but he makes no further contribution to the play. An alternative is to have him withdraw from the main acting area but remain visible with his guards as a menacing presence. The problem is bound up with the general patchwork quality of this ending.

82. *Where is Oedipus, the glorious master of riddles?*: As so often, tragedy highlights present disaster by recalling the happier or more successful times now long past (in this case, Oedipus' triumph over the Sphinx, see note 1 above). A close parallel is Theseus' effort to put heart into the despairing Heracles (Euripides, *Heracles* 1250), 'Are these the words of Heracles, the all-enduring?' Heracles replies 'Never did I know sorrow such as this.' But in the lyrics which follow the present passage the actors change their tone: Oedipus recalls his success with the riddle, Antigone warns him to accept his lot (1728ff.).

83. *Now Loxias' oracle is being fulfilled, my child . . .*: The six lines which end this dialogue allude to the events dramatized in Sophocles' *Oedipus at Colonus*, in which the aged king, after years of wandering, finds refuge in Theseus' Athens and dies in mysterious and supernatural circumstances at the rural district of

Colonus: in that play it seems to be assumed that he has joined the number of the heroes, former mortals who receive cult and worship (see esp. E. Kearns, *The Heroes of Attica* (London 1989), pp. 50–52, 208–9). Sophocles' play was produced posthumously, some years after the *Phoenician Women*. It is possible that the tradition of Oedipus' death at Athens was older than Sophocles (though we have no other evidence besides this passage; according to the *Iliad* he was buried at Thebes); but if it is right to see the end of this play as a later composition, these lines would obviously be inspired by Sophocles' classic treatment.

84. *the god of horses*: Poseidon, who is said to have offered a horse as his gift to Athens in competition with Athena to become the city's patron (she offered the olive-tree).

85. *I shall shroud him in dark earth*: After a long passage in which Antigone has assured her father of her company in his exile, we revert to her intention to bury her brother. Again we see the incompatibility of motifs. Greek tragedy often admits calculated inconsistency, but in minor matters or else scattered across widely dispersed passages (see R. Scodel, *Credible Impossibilities* (Stuttgart-Leipzig 1999)): this kind of blatant and persistent confusion is quite abnormal and betrays the hand of an inferior poet.

86. *Go to where . . . mountain slopes*: Oedipus seems to mean 'lead me to Cithaeron', where Bacchic rites were celebrated.

87. *O you citizens of a land renowned*: Unless Creon and his men are still there, no citizens are on stage (the chorus are foreign). Is Oedipus to be seen as addressing the Athenian audience? If so, this would be a further indication of late composition: explicit audience address is alien to fifth-century BC tragedy (D. Bain, 'Audience Address in Greek Tragedy', *Classical Quarterly* 25 (1975), pp. 13–25, O. Taplin, *Stagecraft of Aeschylus*, pp. 129–34 (though Taplin has since modified his position considerably, especially as regards pp. 132–4: cf. General Introduction, note 16)). The lines resemble, and are probably an imitation of, the conclusion of Sophocles' *Oedipus the King* (1524–30), where it is disputed whether they belong to Oedipus or the chorus.

88. *O Victory . . . your crown*: This short conclusion also appears in the manuscripts at the end of several other plays by Euripides, including *Orestes* (in *Hippolytus* and *Iphigenia among the Taurians* it follows an authentic tailpiece). It is obviously spurious: the invocation of victory by the dramatist through his spokesman on stage is a further breach of dramatic illusion and belongs to a later age.

ORESTES

1. ELECTRA: On the prologue-technique, see notes on the opening of *Phoenician Women*. As there, it will be convenient to give here a summary of the relevant myths concerning the family history of Orestes, and to refer back to this note when individual episodes are mentioned later in the play.

The founder of the house was Tantalus, a son of Zeus. Although favoured by the gods and permitted to share their feasts, he committed some crime which earned him eternal punishment. The poets differ on what his offence was: Euripides speaks of his ungovernable tongue, which may mean he passed on secrets of the gods to men. Others refer to his attempting to steal the divine food ambrosia, or testing the gods' wisdom by feeding them human flesh. His punishment is placed in Hades by Homer; on the novel idea that he is suspended in mid-air, see 982 ff. and note 55. In the *Odyssey* he is constantly tormented by having food and drink forever out of his reach; the notion that he has a rock suspended over him threatening to fall is perhaps a later development, found first in Archilochus.

Tantalus' son was Pelops, who gave his name to the Peloponnese. He courted Hippodameia, daughter of King Oenomaus of Sicyon. This king, being opposed to his daughter's marriage, habitually challenged her suitors to a chariot race and slew them when they were defeated. Pelops bribed his charioteer Myrtilus to sabotage the king's chariot, and thus won the race and caused Oenomaus' death. Pelops later also killed Myrtilus (988), hurling him into the sea near Geraestus in south Euboea; according to some this was because Myrtilus attempted to seduce Hippodameia. With his dying words Myrtilus cursed Pelops and his descendants.

Pelops' sons were Atreus and Thyestes, who both claimed the kingship of Mycenae-Argos. Their dispute focused on possession of a golden lamb which seems to have guaranteed right to the kingship: Atreus had it, but Thyestes stole it by seducing Atreus' wife Aerope (996 ff., 1008–10). Atreus, however, was confirmed in power by a celestial portent, the reversal of the sun in its course (1001ff.). Feigning friendship to his brother, Atreus invited him to a dinner at which he served him with the chopped-up flesh of Thyestes' own sons, whom he had just killed, mixed with other meat (1007–8). Thyestes, horror-stricken, withdrew into exile; his surviving son Aegisthus vowed revenge. (In later versions, especially in Latin writers, the reversal of the sun or other heavenly bodies takes place at the time of the Thyestean feast, marking the enormity of Atreus' crime).

As Electra explains, Agamemnon and Menelaus were the sons of Atreus:

they ruled in Mycenae-Argos and Sparta respectively, and married the two daughters of Tyndareus, Clytemnestra and Helen. Helen's abduction (or seduction) by Paris caused the Trojan War; in Agamemnon's absence Aegisthus seduced Clytemnestra, and the two of them plotted to kill him on his return. (On the sacrifice of Iphigenia as one motive for Clytemnestra's antagonism to her husband see Preface to *Iphigenia at Aulis*.) Orestes was sent away for safety (in some versions despatched by Electra or his nurse) and was brought up in Phocis, near Delphi, with his close friend Pylades, son of the local king Strophius. On coming of age he consulted the oracle of Apollo and was commanded to avenge his father by killing his mother (and of course Aegisthus, but that is treated as uncontroversial). He was successful, but the present play deals with the psychological and political consequences.

2. *Chrysothemis*: She is mentioned in the *Iliad* and in other sources, but rarely plays a part in the legend: in extant tragedy she appears only in Sophocles' *Electra*, as a more timid foil to Electra herself. She is ignored in the rest of this play.

3. *her motives*: Electra refers to Clytemnestra's adulterous affair with Aegisthus while Agamemnon was absent at Troy.

4. *There is no point in accusing Phoebus . . .*: Despite this remark, many characters, including Electra, do question or find fault with Apollo's command in the course of the play: see 76, 163–5, 191–4, 285–7, 416–17, 591–6, 956. Already in his *Electra* Euripides had allowed the god's wisdom to be challenged, even by his fellow deities (1244–7, 1302). Moral criticism of the myths, with their often bloody and barbarous deeds, was common in Euripides' time. In the end Apollo does resolve the problems of the survivors, but this does not mean that every spectator will be confident that the matricide was a good deed. Tragedy characteristically highlights deeds and choices which are morally difficult, sometimes insoluble.

5. *shared in the murder*: As also in Euripides' own *Electra*; in the versions by the other tragedians Electra only lent moral support.

6. *the Kindly Ones*: (In Greek *Eumenides*.) She means the Furies, who had been given this euphemistic title in Aeschylus' *Eumenides*. The reference to terrors that plague Orestes prepares for the madness-scene, but so far we can still assume that the Furies are real rather than the hallucinatory fears which afflict Orestes later. Even in Aeschylus, there is ambiguity: at the end of the *Libation-Bearers* the Furies are invisible to all but Orestes, whereas in the *Eumenides* they are present on stage and form the chorus.

7. *It is the decree of this city of Argos*: These lines introduce an important new element in the story. In Aeschylus' *Libation-Bearers*, the people of Argos had been oppressed by the tyrannical rule of Clytemnestra and Aegisthus, and

Orestes after their deaths is hailed as a liberator. In this play the matricidal act revolts the Argive people: besides the persecution by the Furies (even if they exist only in his mind), Orestes must cope with the political consequences of his action. Electra's comments here also make clear that events have reached a crisis ('This is the appointed day . . .' : cf. Aristotle, *Poetics* 5 on the tendency for tragedy to restrict its time frame to a single day).

8. *entrusted to my mother's fostering*: This explains the presence of Hermione, who is needed for later developments. It is almost certainly an *ad hoc* invention by Euripides, who frequently adds explanatory 'footnotes' of this type.

9. *Maiden for all too long a day*: This line plays on the etymology of the name Electra, which is often treated as equivalent to *a-lektr-*. This means 'deprived of marriage bed', and alludes to the refusal of Clytemnestra and Aegisthus to let Electra marry. Cf. Sophocles, *Electra* 963–6. In the end Electra will marry Pylades.

10. *contaminated:* Those who have committed bloodshed are thought to be 'polluted' in the religious sense, and may bring bad luck on those they touch or even speak to. For this range of ideas see W. Burkert, *Greek Religion* (Eng. tr. Oxford 1985), pp. 75–82 and especially R. Parker, *Miasma. Pollution and Purification in Greek Religion* (Oxford 1983).

11. HERMIONE *exits offstage*: Hermione is completely silent in her brief appearance. This is a consequence of the three-actor rule: Electra and Orestes, playing major speaking parts, will both be continuously on stage for some time to come, and the third actor plays Helen. Hermione here (but not when she reappears) is played by a mute player.

12. *who will sing with my lament*: The explicit anticipation of a lyric exchange is one of many self-consciously 'theatrical' or metatextual touches in this play.

13. *tread softly*: For an actor to admonish the others on stage and entreat them not to awaken a sleeping figure seems to be a 'typical scene' of tragedy. Scenes like this appear in Euripides' *Heracles*, Sophocles' *Women at Trachis* and *Philoctetes* (produced in the previous year).

14. *Oh no – your eyes are rolling, Brother*: These lines make a swift introduction to the madness-scene, one of the most famous parts of the play (alluded to by Virgil in the *Aeneid* and quoted by Longinus in *On the Sublime*). Euripides' presentation of madness is analysed in more detail by G. W. Bond in his commentary on the *Heracles* (Oxford 1981) (general note to 930–1009).

15. *Give me my horn-tipped bow . . .*: In the lyric poem entitled *Oresteia* by Stesichorus (fragment 217), Apollo had given a real bow to Orestes in order to fend off real Furies. In this scene the Furies are hallucinations, and probably no bow is physically present either. Orestes faces psychological, not supernatural, terrors.

16. *calm descending on the stormy waves*: Ancient tradition records the entertaining story that an actor called Hegelochus mispronounced the word 'calm' in this line, so that he appeared to be replacing it with the similar Greek word for 'weasel'. This seems to be an authentic anecdote deriving from the earliest production, as it is alluded to by Aristophanes (*Frogs* 303–4) only a few years later (other comedians also make fun of the occasion).

17. *would have begged me earnestly, clasping my chin*: This is a gesture of supplication. The notion of Agamemnon wanting Clytemnestra to be spared is a novel one, running completely contrary to tradition. In Homer's *Odyssey* his ghost speaks of her with bitter resentment in the underworld, and in Aeschylus Electra and Orestes try to summon their father's wrathful spirit to lend them support in the matricide.

18. *O you terrible goddesses . . .*: One cannot pray to a hallucination; in this song the chorus are assuming that the Furies are real and that Orestes' madness is the result of their persecution. Thus after the more 'psychological' presentation in the previous scene we return to a more mythological perspective. Either we can see this as preserving a significant ambiguity (cf. note 6 above) or it may be that the explanation lies in the different register: dialogue and lyric song permit different perspectives.

19. *derives from wedlock with gods*: Tantalus (note 1 above) was a son of Zeus, but sources are vague about his mother. According to the scholia he also married Dione, a daughter of Atlas.

20. *in grand luxury*: There is some similarity to the fulsome address by the chorus to Agamemnon when he appears on stage in Aeschylus' *Agamemnon*. The reference to luxury may imply that Menelaus has been corrupted by his time in the East (though the allusion to his family background, if the text is sound, would suggest that he was a ready victim to such corruption).

21. *Glaucus, son of Nereus*: In the *Odyssey* Menelaus was informed of his brother's fate by the sea-god Proteus in Egypt. Rather than simply repeating the Homeric version, Euripides plays a variation.

22. *so I wouldn't recognize him if I saw him*: We note Euripides' concern for realism and chronology. The Trojan war lasted ten years and Menelaus has been absent for a further seven (the figures go back to Homer); Orestes must therefore be at least seventeen or eighteen years old. Euripides may be consciously improving on a rather implausible passage in Homer, where Helen recognizes Telemachus, whom she has not seen for a similar length of time (*Odyssey* 4.141ff.).

23. *leafless prayers*: 'Leafless' because suppliants normally carried sacred boughs (*Iliad* 1.14, Sophocles, *Oedipus the King* 3, etc.); Orestes does not.

24. *Awareness*: The line is enigmatic, the expression abstract: Menelaus is naturally puzzled. The usual reading of this line takes it as referring to 'conscience'; for discussion of alternatives see D. H. Porter, *Studies in Euripides' Orestes* (*Mnemosyne* Suppl. 128, Leiden 1993), Appendix 1 (pp. 298–313).

25. *Pylades*: The tradition is consistent that Pylades came to Argos with Orestes and supported him at the crisis. His absence in the first part of this play is nowhere explained: in part it results from Euripides' need to use all three actors for other roles.

26. *A man does not show . . . loved ones*: The sequence of thought is unclear and the text probably corrupt.

27. *Oeax . . . what happened at Troy*: This is a typical example of Euripides' delight in connecting stories with one another or exploring the implications of relationships. Oeax was the son of Palamedes, who was one of the cleverest of the Greeks at Troy. This aroused Odysseus' jealousy, and he plotted either to murder Palamedes or to frame him and get him condemned to death by the Greeks. His treacherous behaviour became known, and Palamedes' father Nauplius in revenge lit beacons at night which lured some of the returning Greek ships on to the rocks. Euripides suggests that Oeax would have inherited the family feud.

28. *Here comes Tyndareus*: The appearance of a new character forestalls Menelaus' reply. Tyndareus, the father of Clytemnestra and Helen, is not a familiar figure in the legend, although the fifth-century BC historian Hellanicus appears to have written of the relations of Clytemnestra, presumably including her father, bringing charges against Orestes (fragment 169 in R. Fowler, *Early Greek Mythography* I (Oxford 2000)). The extreme awkwardness for Orestes of coming face to face with a grandfather whose daughter he has murdered gives spice to the scene; the audience will already be anticipating fierce exchanges of words. Tyndareus' cloak of mourning contrasts visually with Menelaus' finery (and Orestes' filthy condition).

29. *fellow husband with Zeus*: This bizarre formulation alludes to the uncertainty as to whether Helen was the daughter of Leda by her husband Tyndareus or by Zeus himself (the latter is normally assumed, and is confirmed by Apollo at the end of the play): cf. *Helen* 18–21, *Iphigenia at Aulis* 794 ff. Clytemnestra by contrast is of purely human parentage.

30. *Ah, there he stands before the palace . . .*: Tyndareus sees Orestes but for some time avoids even speaking to him, confining himself to discussion with Menelaus. This expresses his revulsion at coming into any contact with the criminal. Only at 526 does he finally address Orestes.

31. *Everything that is caused . . . wise men's eyes*: An obscure reply, probably alluding to sophistic ideas. In context it probably means that the compulsion imposed by the laws should not be slavishly accepted, i.e. that there is room for debate as to whether the laws are always right. But Menelaus may be deliberately avoiding putting his cards on the table.

32. *Now is the time to debate wisdom with this man*: The text is uncertain, but something like this seems likely to be the sense. The term *agon* ('debate' or 'contest') is used in this line, introducing the standard rhetorical conflict which we find in most Euripidean plays. (Cf. note 22 to *Phoenician Women*, and for discussion of the present debate M. Lloyd, *The Agon in Euripides* (Oxford 1992), ch. 7). This is a curious example, as the natural opponents are Tyndareus and Orestes, but Tyndareus for much of his speech speaks through Menelaus (at 526–33 he directs his attack at Orestes, but then turns back to Menelaus for the close of his speech). The response of Orestes is made directly to Tyndareus. After a further brief speech Tyndareus departs; Orestes then addresses Menelaus in an appeal which has some of the agonistic qualities (especially artificiality of argument), but also carries intense emotional appeal. Menelaus' reply does not partake of the *agon* conventions and fails to engage with any of Orestes' points.

33. *He neither showed regard for justice . . . law of the Greeks*: Tyndareus' account of what Orestes should have done has often been criticized as anachronistic: was it possible in the heroic age to oust Aegisthus and Clytemnestra by any means other than force? Did the legal system Tyndareus presupposes even exist? Was the court founded at Athens in Aeschylus' trilogy conceived as the first human court for homicide cases? Even if Tyndareus' alternative is not as far-fetched as some critics maintain, it is significant that no character in the other versions of the story ever suggests this course of action.

34. *when your mother held out her breast to you in supplication*: This was a famous climactic moment. See especially Aeschylus, *Libation-Bearers* 896ff., Euripides, *Electra* 1206ff., and in this play itself 825ff. with 841 below.

35. *My father sowed the seed of my life . . . seed from another*: The idea that the father's role is primary and the mother is merely the receptacle for his seed is used in defence of Orestes by Apollo in Aeschylus, *Eumenides* 658–9, and can be paralleled elsewhere. It was not, however, a universal view, and even in Aeschylus it hardly mitigates the horror of matricide; still less here, where Orestes is snatching at any argument he can find in his own defence.

36. *let me tell you how I have benefited all Greece by my action*: This is a paradoxical argument reminiscent of the rhetorical schools of the day. The sophist Gorgias argued that Helen was equally innocent of crime whether it was passion, persuasion, the gods or compulsion that made her go to Troy. Plato in the *Phaedrus* has Lysias argue that one should yield to the courtship of a non-lover rather than a lover. Euripides' work includes many such speeches maintaining bizarre or counter-intuitive propositions. In *Medea* Jason undertakes to prove that his abandoning Medea for another woman is wise, virtuous and beneficial for Medea; in the lost *Cretans*, Pasiphae undertook to prove that it was Minos' fault, not hers, that she had slept with a bull (F 427e).

Talk of the benefit of Orestes' deed recurs in the Argive assembly, where it forms the basis for some obviously dubious arguments. It is interesting that Iphigenia in the *Iphigenia at Aulis* declares her intention to die for the good of Greece, although others question her decision. We may suspect that Euripides had heard many high-sounding claims from orators that their policies were for the greater national good.

37. *what would the dead man have done to me?*: The question is raised also, though not answered, in the Aeschylean trilogy. Orestes lists the perils which are threatened if he disobeys Apollo's command (*Libation-Bearers* 275ff.), but these seem to be plagues sent by the god, not by Agamemnon. At the crisis Clytemnestra warns him to beware the hounds (i.e. the Furies) of his mother, but Orestes replies, 'but if I shirk this task, how can I escape the hounds of my father?' (924–5).

38. *And what of Apollo?*: This concluding passage is the most forceful passage questioning Apollo's role that we have heard so far. Orestes' almost hysterical demand that Apollo should be executed is not to be taken seriously, but a real point is being made: where is Apollo, and why is he not present to defend his agent, as in the *Eumenides*? His appearance at the end of the play does not answer all questions. See Preface.

39. *She deserves death more than you . . .* : The hostile characterization of Electra here seems quite different from the woman we have so far seen, who tends her brother with tearful sympathy. She is more like the heroine of Euripides' earlier *Electra*. Is this intertextual allusion, or Tyndareus' angry distortion of the facts? In any case, it paves the way for the later scenes in which Electra becomes more aggressive: note especially the imagery of fire, anticipating the threat to burn down the whole palace in the closing scene.

40. *I do not ask that you kill Hermione*: The sacrifice of Iphigenia is not referred to elsewhere in the play, and for Orestes to drag it in here is strangely irrelevant. The idea of a matching sacrifice by Menelaus is grotesque – nor would such an act make any difference to Orestes' own dilemma. His weak position is reinforced by weak arguments.

41. *imagine that it is he who hears this . . .*: The rhetoric continues to be extravagant. Agamemnon is imagined as performing a dual role, both speaking and listening!

42. *I will go and try to persuade . . . moderation*: Although we may sympathize with Menelaus' dilemma, he does not cut a very impressive figure here. He fails to answer any of Orestes' points or to refer to his debt to Agamemnon;

his efforts to persuade Tyndareus will obviously fail; and Orestes will have no way of telling whether Menelaus has tried at all. His prevarications suggest that he has been intimidated by Tyndareus' stern warning. Although we may allow that Menelaus is not positively portrayed, Aristotle's complaint that Euripides has made him unnecessarily wicked seems misguided (*Poetics* 1451a, 1461b).

43. *Enter* PYLADES: At this point the metre changes to trochaic tetrameters, a metre increasingly used by Euripides in later plays and very prominent in the *Orestes*. The metre is used for all of the rest of this scene. It here conveys excitement and a sense of urgency; this is increased when at 774–98 each line is divided between the two friends. Compare the same techniques in *Phoenician Women* 588–624.

44. *rather she brought him*: The idea is that Menelaus is under Helen's thumb. Cf. *Electra* 930–31, on Aegisthus as submissive to Clytemnestra. For the idea that Menelaus is not a serious fighter cf. the jibe in *Iliad* 17.588, and lines 717ff., 1201–2 here.

45. *the ancient misfortune of that house* . . .: The events referred to are explained in note 1 above. 'Tantalus' sons' is loosely used: Atreus and Thyestes were actually his grandsons. As often in tragedy, present disaster is set against past prosperity.

46. *Not noble was that noble act* . . .: Deliberately expressed in contradictory terms. Orestes' action is both honourable dealing-out of justice and horrific crime: the latter perception of his deed is highlighted here through the vivid recollection of the moment of killing, including even direct speech. In contrast with their earlier adherence to Electra's cause, the chorus now explicitly condemn Orestes' deed (though in the concluding lines they allow that he is 'wretched').

47. *A* MESSENGER . . .: On the messenger speech in tragedy see note 55 on *Phoenician Women*. As usual, the characterization is light. This man is a countryman, loyal to the family of Agamemnon, sympathetic to Orestes, honest but naive in his reactions to the rhetoric of the assembly.

The description of the assembly is one of the passages which comes closest to the fifth-century BC politics of Euripides' own day. Many lines would have evoked amused or sour recognition of the rhetorical tactics and dubious motives familiar to the Athenians from their own democratic debates. The opening formula in line 885 'Who wishes to say . . .' echoes the initial question opening a debate in Athens (cf. *Suppliant Women* 438–9). The complaints about demagogues and slick speakers recall contemporary discussions of the weaknesses of the assembly (see especially Thucydides' Mytilene debate, 3.38ff.). Possibly the speech has been supplemented to enhance these 'modern' notes (Diggle follows earlier scholars in deleting 895–7 (on heralds) and 904–

13 (on demagogues), but if so the interpolator was following Euripides' clear lead.

On the contrast between the Athenian court of the Areopagus in Aeschylus' *Eumenides*, which finally acquits Orestes, and the Argive court here, which condemns him to death, see C. B. R. Pelling, *Literary Texts and the Greek Historian* (London 1999), pp. 164–88.

48. *where men say Danaus . . . Aegyptus*: This refers to the legend of Danaus and his daughters, but seemingly not the version dramatized by Aeschylus. After the Danaids had slain their husbands, the father of the dead men, Aegyptus, came to Argos demanding reparation. Danaus at first thought of giving battle, but was persuaded to summon (or go before) an Argive court for arbitration. This version is summarized by the ancient scholia on this passage.

49. *Talthybius*: He was the herald of Agamemnon in the *Iliad*, where he is mentioned at various points but has no significant part to play. He figures in Euripides' *Hecabe* and *Trojan Women*, in both of which he is a relatively sympathetic figure, compassionate towards Hecabe although forced to carry out his own orders. Here the characterization is negative, reinforcing Orestes' isolation. For Euripides' tendency to present heralds in a bad light compare *Suppliant Women* 399ff., 426ff.

50. *an Argive and yet no true Argive*: This line is reminiscent of the various attacks on politicians accusing them of foreign birth (thus Aeschines calls Demosthenes 'son of the Scythian'). Ancient scholars detected a sneer at the contemporary politician Cleophon, who suffered from similar slanders; but it is unlikely that the poet intended a specific allegory. The man is an archetypal demagogue (the next line reminds us of descriptions in Aristophanes and Thucydides of the more famous Cleon, by now dead).

51. *it is ruin they have brought*: In conjunction with the name Phoebus, it is clear that this is a play on the resemblance between his other name, Apollo, and the Greek verb used here, *apôlesen*, 'brought ruin, destroyed'. Again the questioning of Apollo's role and reliability is given prominence (in Aeschylus he appears and speaks for Orestes at his trial).

52. *share the lament that follows*: Who sings what in the following passage has been much discussed (the manuscripts have no authority in such matters). The arrangement here follows Diggle. Others have given the whole sung interlude to Electra or (less plausibly) to the chorus. For discussion and bibliography see M. Damen, 'Electra's Monody and the Role of the Chorus in Euripides' *Orestes*', *Transactions of the American Philological Association* 120 (1990), pp. 133–45. Cf. note 55.

53. *Cyclopean land*: Mycenae, whose massive walls were thought to have been constructed by Cyclopes.

54. *setting shearing steel to the head*: The reference is to cutting one's hair in mourning. The 'land', personified, is urged to do what its womenfolk will do.

55. *O that I might come to the rock . . . necessity of this house*: After two stanzas of lamentation from the chorus, the singing role passes to Electra, who sings of the sorrows of her family in more detail. Whereas the chorus's contribution formed a strophic pair, Electra's lament is 'astrophic', a single aria without stanzaic structure. This seems to reflect her greater involvement and deeper distress.

On the myths referred to here (the punishment of Tantalus; Pelops, Oenomaus and Myrtilus; the golden lamb; the Thyestean feast and Aerope's adultery), see note 1 above.

The punishment of Tantalus is here described in a novel way (developing the hint of an unusual version in 7: 'hovers in the air'). Traditionally the stone hangs or hovers over his head in Hades; here it is hung between heaven and earth and he in some way whirls or orbits with it. The 'golden chains' allude to passages spoken by Zeus in Homer, in which he threatens to suspend Hera or the other gods by them: these were interpreted allegorically by some later readers (*Iliad* 8.19ff., 15.19–20). Astronomical theories such as those of Anaxagoras are also clearly in the poet's mind (especially 'the rock . . . a lump from Olympus' mass', an expression which suggests that the heavenly bodies are solid objects, not divine powers).

For Euripides' fondness for 'escape-lyric' see *Bacchae* 402ff. and note 39.

56. *Why should I any longer feel shame at this . . .*: The true hero does not weep or indulge in sentimental protestations. Having first contrasted Electra's distress with Orestes' sternness, Euripides now allows a moment of tenderness and shared emotion.

57. *You have a city*: This neglects Pylades' explanation at 765 that he has been exiled. The inconsistency is trivial, and easily explained: Pylades' devotion will be greater if he has something to sacrifice by dying with his friends.

58. *let us consider together how Menelaus should share our misery*: This line and Orestes' enthusiastic response marks the transition from one plot-line (means of escape sought but not found) to another (plotting and revenge). Euripides in his later plays makes a habit of combining story-patterns which could be used separately, creating more complex plots and enhancing the emotional range. See F. Solmsen, *Kleine Schriften* (Hildesheim 1968), pp. 141ff.; P. Burian, 'Myth into *Muthos*: the Shaping of the Tragic Plot' in P. E. Easterling (ed.), *Cambridge Companion to Greek Tragedy* (Cambridge 1997), pp. 186–90. The effect of this transition on the audience's moral assessment of the characters is disorienting: from being helpless and distressed victims Orestes and (shortly) Electra are swiftly transformed into merciless conspirators. The desire to hurt

Menelaus is understandable; to kill Helen is extreme, despite the regular hostility toward her in tragedy; to contemplate killing Hermione too is shocking. See further Preface.

59. *they are here as our friends*: The presence of the chorus is often awkward for intrigues, but the convention that they keep secrets is so well established that the matter is disposed of in two lines (earlier in the century they would no doubt have been asked to swear an oath, as e.g. in *Medea* and *Ion*).

60. *I understand the sign*: An obscure line, but seemingly spelling out what Pylades evasively implied in 'the deed'. 'I understand the clue you are giving me.' Others render 'watchword' rather than 'sign'.

61. *But as it is . . .*: Pylades' stirring summons to take proper revenge for all the dead at Troy echoes some features of the anti-Helen tradition (in Aeschylus' *Agamemnon* the people of Argos are said to be resentful of the many deaths 'for the sake of another man's wife'; cf. in this play 57ff., 98ff.). But Pylades exaggerates this hatred of Helen to fantastic heights, imagining that their deed will make them into national heroes. There are hints of delusion, even of fanaticism, in the latter part of this scene.

62. *Brother, I think I see a way to achieve this very thing . . .*: The increasingly negative presentation of the trio extends now to Electra. Her hatred of Menelaus and Helen makes her indifferent to the innocent Hermione.

63. *O Father, who dwell . . . helper*: The invocation of Agamemnon's ghost recalls the scene at his tomb in Aeschylus' *Libation-Bearers*, where Orestes, Electra and the chorus call on him for aid in the task of revenge. There the scene extends through nearly 200 lines of lyrics and concludes with a shorter sequence of trimeters (306ff., 479ff.). Here the invocation is confined to spoken verse and is a perfunctory effort. The task for which they seek his aid is also strongly contrasted.

64. *Have their swords lost their edge in the face of beauty?*: This recalls the story in the Epic Cycle (echoed also in Aristophanes, *Lysistrata* 155–6), that during the sack of Troy Menelaus was ready to kill Helen, but she bared her breasts and he, spellbound, lowered his sword. The same episode underlies the scene involving Menelaus and Helen in *Trojan Women* 860ff.

65. *[screaming from inside]*: The cry of the victim from within is a typical feature of the intrigue-plot: the audience would have been waiting as eagerly as Electra. The archetypal example is the crying out of Agamemnon as he is murdered (Aeschylus, *Agamemnon* 1343ff.)

66. *Stab her, kill her, strike her, destroy her*: This is a chilling moment, even if the audience still believes that Euripides cannot allow the conspirators' plot to succeed. The vicious note of lust for revenge makes it hard to continue sympathizing with Electra. (Whether she or the chorus or both chant these lines is disputed, but it seems unlikely that she is excluded.)

67. *here comes Hermione . . .*: The scene which follows is a typical 'entrapment' sequence, another recurrent feature of the intrigue-plot. The ambiguities in Electra's replies are characteristic of such scenes.

68. *But there is a rumbling . . .* Lines 1366–8 are deleted by some editors, on the basis of a comment in the scholia ascribing them to actors in a post-Euripidean production. This issue is connected with the question of how the Phrygian's entry was staged. It would be simpler if he simply ran out the door (through which Orestes certainly emerges later), but more spectacular if he climbed out of the roof of the stage-building and jumped or let himself down on a rope from that high point. (For use of the stage roof by actors compare *Phoenician Women* 88ff.) The latter staging may be implied by his opening words ('climbing over the cedar rafters . . . down the Dorian triglyphs'). If the chorus's lines are authentic, they could be misdirection, encouraging the audience to expect an entry from the doorway – but they would only be deceived for a moment. The matter will remain controversial: for a recent discussion see T. Falkner, 'Scholars Versus Actors: Text and Performance in the Greek Tragic Scholia', in P. E. Easterling and E. Hall (eds.), *Greek and Roman Actors: Aspects of an Ancient Profession* (Cambridge 2002), pp. 342–61.

The Phrygian himself is one of the boldest surprises Euripides has for his audience. In effect he is a messenger, but of a unique type: a singing messenger, and one who gives his account of events in a highly colourful, exotic and often opaque style far removed from the customary clear exposition of such figures. Also, those messengers are normally given full knowledge of events: but the Phrygian leaves it quite unclear what has happened to Helen, an important ambiguity. He is also the only anonymous singing slave in tragedy (apart from choruses). That he is represented as a eunuch is likely (see 1528); that he is dressed in Eastern style is certain. He sings throughout (up to the point where Orestes enters); the chorus responds in spoken verse. The metres are astrophic and bewilderingly diverse. Although there is some difficulty in understanding exactly what has happened in the house, this is more because of the Phrygian's own agitation and uncertainties, not from any incoherence on his part: despite the impression given by some translations (notably that of W. Arrowsmith in the *Complete Greek Tragedies* series), he is not speaking pidgin-Greek but uses highly sophisticated diction and imagery. We see the influence of the 'new music' fashionable in Athens at this time (though Euripides' closeness to the work of Timotheus, of whose work most survives, has perhaps been exaggerated).

69. *beauty bird-born, Leda's swan-winged chick*: Zeus came to Leda, Helen's mother, in the form of a swan (as in Yeats's magnificent poem): hence it was sometimes illogically supposed that she was born of an egg, an idea treated with reserve by Helen herself (*Helen* 18ff., 256ff.). If the text can be credited, swan-form is figuratively ascribed here even to Helen.

70. *Ganymede*: A beautiful boy of the Trojan royal family, abducted by Zeus to act as his wine-waiter by day and to share his bed by night. Cf. *Trojan Women* 820ff.

71. *a cunning net . . . that serpent who killed his mother*: The imagery is strongly reminiscent of Aeschylus' *Oresteia*, and the associations of treachery, trapping and snake-like poison cannot but have a negative effect on our view of Orestes.

72. *In the Phrygian fashion . . . the Phrygian . . . stirring the air, the air*: The lyric repetitiousness of style is parodied by Aristophanes, *Frogs* 1352ff.

73. *how much we Phrygians are inferior . . . martial process*: The national chauvinism of Greek thinking about East and West was given added impetus by their success in resisting the Persian invasions earlier in the fifth century BC. See esp. E. Hall, *Inventing the Barbarian: Greek Self-definition through Tragedy* (Oxford 1989). Needless to say, this crudity of outlook need not be Euripides' own opinion, but he is prepared to use the 'stock' assumptions where it suits him. A far more complex spectrum of attitudes is visible in Herodotus' great History.

74. ORESTES *enters from the palace doorway*: The scene between Orestes and the Phrygian (1506–31) is in trochaic tetrameters (cf. note 43); this seems to suit the lively and fast-moving exchange. The tone of the scene is hard to catch. The scholia already complain (on 1512) 'what is said here is unworthy both of tragedy and of Orestes' unhappy situation'. Orestes is in a position of superior power and enjoys it; the Phrygian is a comical and untragic figure (still more so to many Athenians, no doubt; see last note), and in the end he does get safely away. But Orestes' taunts and threats leave an unpleasant taste in the mouth. They also make clear that Hermione can expect no mercy.

75. *Tyndareus' daughter perished*: Orestes here and in 1533, 1536, assumes Helen is in fact dead; the audience, having heard the Phrygian's account, is not so sure. At 1580 and subsequent lines Orestes has changed his tune (we can assume, if we like, that he has found no corpse indoors; but such filling-in of detail is hardly necessary in such a fast-moving play).

76. *fallen, fallen . . . because Myrtilus fell*: The use of the same verb is also present in the Greek and clearly deliberate. On Pelops' killing of Myrtilus see note 1 above; also 992.

77. *His silence proclaims he does*: This is an in-joke alluding to theatrical convention: Orestes and Menelaus are already onstage, Apollo is about to appear (the audience do not know this, but they may have guessed a *deus ex machina* is imminent); hence three actors are already needed for this scene, and Pylades must be played by a mute extra. Moroever, there is an ingenious reversal of the climactic scene in Aeschylus' *Libation-Bearers*. There, Orestes along with a so-far silent Pylades confronts his mother: she appeals to him for pity, and he falters, asking Pylades what he should do; and Pylades responds by reminding him of the command of Apollo. There an apparently mute actor suddenly spoke; here a previously vocal actor is silent. Orestes needs no encouragement on his destructive course.

78. *Oh, take your sword away from my daughter*: The following section of dialogue (down to 1617 'You have trapped yourself . . .') involves division of each line between speakers, and in each line Orestes caps Menelaus: he has the upper hand. (There has been some reordering of the lines in order to produce a more plausible sequence: C. W. Willink (*Orestes*, Oxford 1986), followed by Diggle, places 1608–12 after 1599. Hence the odd appearance of the marginal line-numbers.)

79. *Apollo appears on high*: Orestes, Pylades and Hermione certainly, and Electra very probably, are already on the roof of the stage-building. Apollo must appear on a still higher level, probably on the 'crane' (Greek *mechane*, Latin *machina*; hence '*deus ex machina*') which was regularly used to bring flying figures into view. This device was certainly used in some famous scenes, e.g. for Medea's departure in the chariot of the sun at the end of *Medea*, or for Bellerophon flying on Pegasus in the lost play *Bellerophon* (parodied in the first scene of Aristophanes' *Peace*). It is not certain that Helen appears with Apollo, but it seems desirable that Menelaus and Orestes should both be shown her true state (if 1631–2, deleted by Murray and Diggle and omitted in our version, were genuine that would make her presence certain, but they are probably spurious). Some doubt that the crane could support both characters' weight. Others hold that there may have been a still higher platform above the stage-building, reserved for the gods. For discussion see D. J. Mastronarde, 'Actors on High: the Skene-Roof, the Crane and the Gods in Attic Drama', *Classical Antiquity* 9 (1990), pp. 247–94.

On the role of Apollo see Preface to this play.

80. *bringing safety to mariners*: The role of Castor and Polydeuces, Helen's brothers, as protectors of seafarers is well known. Helen was worshipped as a deity at Sparta and shared cult with her brothers, but her role as a sea-goddess seems to be Euripides' invention. Indeed, this whole section of the play involves innovation on his part. In Homer Helen returns to Sparta with Menelaus and they live in harmony together, but it is foretold that when they die they will both dwell in Elysium, the home of a few privileged heroes in the afterlife. This future is also predicted for them at the end of Euripides' *Helen*. For her life to be cut short and her divinity established almost immediately after her return to Greece is unprecedented; but it provides a way to end the conflict and gives clearer justification for her miraculous disappearance from the palace.

81. *to rid the earth of its complement of mortals*: This explanation for the Trojan war, absent from Homer, was found in the early epic poem called the *Cypria*, and is also mentioned in the prologue to the *Helen*. It reinforces our sense of the gods as remote from mankind and little concerned with their interests.

82. *You, Orestes . . . destined to prevail*: Orestes will spend a year in exile, in line with Athenian law on an *involuntary* homicide. He will give his name to a town in Arcadia (aetiology): cf. *Electra* 1272–3, where the Dioscuri make a similar prediction, but apparently predicting lifelong exile. After that he will undergo trial at Athens, but this is to be a very different trial from that in Aeschylus (and still more from the assembly-scene in this play, whose decision it overturns). In the *Eumenides* he was tried by men, but Apollo predicts a trial by gods, and assures him of the favourable verdict. Any potential tragic tension is dissipated.

83. *Neoptolemus*: Son of Achilles. This alludes to a different strand of legend, dramatized in rather different terms by Euripides in *Andromache*. There Hermione is discontented with her marriage; here she will not have to endure it. The death of Neoptolemus at Delphi further suggests the power of the gods to help and harm. Apollo raises up the son of Agamemnon, but will strike down the son of Achilles.

84. *some spirit of vengeance*: Orestes uses the word *alastor*, denoting a supernatural power that afflicts a family or household with punishment for past crimes, often by misleading or tricking individuals. Cf. Aeschylus, *Persians* 354, *Agamemnon* 1501, 1508, Euripides, *Hippolytus* 820, etc.

85. *O Victory . . . giving me your crown*: These lines also appear at the end of the *Phoenician Women*: see note there. They are certainly spurious in both places. Probably they replaced an authentic choral tailpiece in some later production.

BACCHAE

Bacchae: 'Bacchae', women of Dionysus-Bacchus, are synonymous with Bacchants and maenads; many other names are used for them in Greek, though not in this play. On worship of Dionysus in classical times see Preface to the play. In mythology and art there are recurring features, some but not all of which may have been reflected in actual ritual: the wearing of fawnskins, often loosely worn; bare arms and feet; the carrying of the thyrsus, a staff or wand of fennel adorned with vine-leaves, which are also often worn in the hair; agitated dancing and shaking of the head back and forth; playing of musical instruments, especially drums and tambourines; handling of wild creatures, notably snakes. For illustrations in art see T. Carpenter, *Dionysiac Imagery in Archaic Art* (Oxford 1986); H. A. Shapiro, *Myth into Art: Poet and Painter in Classical Greece* (London and New York 1994), pp. 171–6; and the plates illustrating R. Osborne's essay in C. B. R. Pelling (ed.), *Greek Tragedy and the Historian* (Oxford 1997), following p. 212.

1. *delivered by the lightning-flame*: Semele was another of Zeus' many mortal lovers. Hera, as usual jealous and vindictive about her rival, disguised herself as an old woman who befriended Semele and cast doubt on the divinity of her lover. She advised her to make this alleged Zeus swear an oath by Styx to grant her any request. Zeus was sufficiently infatuated to do so. Semele then (still acting on Hera's malicious advice) asked him to appear to her in his divine glory as he appeared on Olympus. Zeus regretted his promise but was bound by it. The unfortunate Semele was engulfed by divine flame (the glory of the epiphany involved the bolts of lightning which were Zeus' characteristic weapon). Semele died, but Zeus rescued the unborn Dionysus from her womb: see further note 9 below.

2. *from a god's to a man's*: This point is repeatedly stressed in the prologue, as if to ensure that the audience is not in doubt. The repetition points to the unusual technique: see Preface. We know of no other drama in which a disguised god played a leading role and remained in disguise almost throughout.

3. *I come from Lydia's fields*: Although Dionysus by birth belongs to Thebes, he is also seen as a foreign god arriving from the exotic east: this helps to explain his androgynous appearance, the wildness of his rites, and the Greeks' unfamiliarity with him. At one time scholars believed that he was indeed a god imported from further east, but the discovery of his name in Mycenaean texts, centuries before Euripides' time, makes this less plausible (see e.g. W. Burkert, *Greek Religion* (Eng. tr. Oxford 1985), pp. 162, with pp. 357 n. 71 and 364 n.24). The story of his arrival from foreign lands may best be seen as a suitable framework for the god's epiphany (cf. 22, 47, 50).

4. *leading my maenads into battle*: This is typical Euripidean false preparation. Although Pentheus several times announces his intention to use military force (784, 809, 845), and Dionysus is prepared to meet him on these terms, it is on the level of the king's individual psyche that the god will win his triumph. The conflict in battle was probably traditional; Euripides may even have invented the version in which Pentheus dresses as a woman and goes to spy on them, but if so he is using a recurrent story-pattern (parodied in Aristophanes' *Women at the Thesmophoria*): cf. note 71 below.

5. *Mother Rhea and myself*: Rhea is the wife of Zeus' father and predecessor, the Titan Cronos. She is identified with the Great Mother or Mountain

Mother, Cybele, an Asiatic deity worshipped with dances and noisy processions on various mountains. Because of the affinity between her rites and those of Dionysus they were often associated.

6. *as they enter*: The entry-song of the chorus forms a glorification of the god. The language reflects religious ritual (especially the summons 'On you Bacchants' and the call for pious silence; the repeated 'to the mountain' at 116, 165, may also echo authentic Bacchic celebrations); the words translated here 'hymns ever honoured by custom' function as a generic marker: the song is a hymn, and like most Greek hymns includes a narrative portion. This ode, like most of the songs in the *Bacchae*, is composed mainly in ionic metre (the basic rhythm is *u u - -*), which has associations elsewhere with cult hymns to Dionysus (especially Aristophanes, *Frogs* 324ff.).

7. *the Roaring One*: One of the titles of Dionysus, reminding us of his bestial aspect: he can take the form of lion, bull or snake. The emphasis on *noise* in this ode is noteworthy (cf. the colourful scene of Dionysus' arrival in Catullus 64), and doubtless reflects the musical accompaniment of the chorus's entry.

8. *crying 'Evoe'*: Evoe or Eu(h)oi is an untranslatable cry of exultant celebration, associated with Dionysus, to whom the word in adjectival form is sometimes applied (157, 413, 566, 579).

9. *While his mother was carrying him . . .*: The birth-myth, a common feature of hymnic poetry. When Semele perished, Zeus rescued the half-grown foetus from her womb and stitched the child magically within his own thigh, where he grew to maturity then emerged. Miraculous births are common in divine myth: cf. especially Athena, born from Zeus's head. For further lyric narrative of the same event see 519ff.; for Teiresias' version see 286ff. and note 30. As there is a parallel Indian myth of a god (Soma) being inserted in the thigh of the sky-god, this may be a very old Indo-European tale inherited by the Greeks. The idea that Zeus was hiding the child from Hera would then be Greek embroidery, fitting in with much later stories of the enmity between Hera and Zeus's bastard children (cf. her persecution of Heracles).

10. *a child with bull horns*: On Dionysus as bull see 66 and note 7; also 922, 1017–9. As a god of nature and of the wild, he can readily shift into bestial forms.

11. *whence it is . . . serpents they have caught*: An aetiology, i.e. a tale that explains why things are as they are – in this case, why maenads are (at least in art) regularly believed to handle snakes. The explanation given is that they are mimicking the appearance of the new-born Dionysus.

12. *O secret chamber of the Curetes . . .*: A complex stanza. We have here another aetiology, for the kettledrum. The chorus go back to an earlier divine birth, that of Zeus, who was hidden away in 'sacred haunts of Crete' to protect him from his cannibal father Cronos. There is a clear analogy with Zeus hiding Dionysus from the wrath of Hera. In the story of Zeus' childhood, the Curetes or Corybantes were his protectors on Crete, and devised the kettledrum to drown the infant's wails and prevent Cronos from hearing him. Later the drum was presented to Rhea to be used in her rites. The satyrs, attendants of Dionysus, obtained it from her and introduced it into Dionysus' rites. The last point looks like a later elaboration to 'explain' why such drums are also used in Bacchic worship.

13. *the second-year feast that delights Dionysus*: In historic times the Dionysiac festivals involving maenadic rituals took place every second year in midwinter (though other celebrations of the god, including the Athenian dramatic festivals, were organized on an annual basis).

14. *He is a delight to see*: 'He' is Dionysus, participating in and leading his own worshippers. A. Henrichs, 'Male Intruders among the Maenads: The So-called Male Celebrant', in *Mnemai: Classical Studies in Memory of Karl K. Hulley*, ed. H. D. Evjen (Chico 1984), pp. 69–91 and elsewhere, has shown that there are no grounds for Dodds's belief that the rites were led by a male celebrant in whom the god was thought to be incarnate.

15. *the slaughtered goat, carnivorous delight*: This clearly implies that the god or his worshippers will hunt down and tear to pieces a goat (a beast regularly sacrificed to Dionysus) and devour its raw flesh. The tearing of animals limb from limb by the Theban Bacchants is described later in the play, and eventually Pentheus suffers the same fate. The poet does not describe any kind of meal being made on either occasion; but Agaue does invite the chorus to join her in a feast (1184), a suggestion from which they recoil. All this has suggested to some critics that tearing and eating of raw flesh may have formed a part of the god's festival even in historic times; but the evidence is not at all strong (cf. A. Henrichs, 'Greek Maenadism from Olympias to Messalina', *Harvard Studies in Classical Philology* 82 (1978), pp. 150–52.

16. *Enter* TEIRESIAS: On Teiresias, a regular character in Theban plays, see note 39 to *Phoenician Women*. Here he enters alone, without his usual attendant. The transition from the chorus's vision of a youthful worshipper 'gambolling on swift feet' to the slow entry of the blind old man is telling. Teiresias is anxious to participate in the worship of the new god, but he and Cadmus make ungainly and uncertain Bacchants. Although they speak of being rejuvenated, the burst of energy is short-lived (364–5). There is surely some humour in the sequence that follows, but it is important not to overstate this: Cadmus and Teiresias are right, and the main point of the scene is to show Pentheus in the wrong, rejecting the advice of two men he has good reason to listen to, his grandfather and a seer with a proven record of prophetic power.

Scenes involving the repudiation of warnings from a 'wise adviser' are common in Greek literature: cf. Teiresias to Oedipus in Sophocles, *Oedipus the King* and to Creon in *Antigone*, the servant to Hippolytus in *Hippolytus* 88ff., or Solon to Croesus in Herodotus book 1. However, this is not a conventional 'wise adviser' scene: Teiresias' warnings in his main speech are combined with peculiar arguments derived from 'modern' sophistic theorizing (note 30 below), and his own words strongly imply that Pentheus is not far wrong in thinking that he wishes to exploit the arrival of the new divinity for his own advantage (255–7, with 306–9). Cadmus' motives too are partly self-interested (note 34 below)

17. *Agenor's son . . . towered city of the Thebans*: On the myths concerning Cadmus, see note 1 to *Phoenician Women*.

18. *Shall we not go to the mountain by carriage?*: A humorous touch. Cadmus is not confident that he is as tireless as he just declared himself.

19. *We do not chop logic when speaking of divinity*: The details of text and translation are disputed. Another possible sense is 'we have no wisdom in the gods' eyes'. Lines 199–203 are rejected by Diggle, but they seem defensible and interesting (though it is possible that there has been something lost after 200). One objection is the fact that Teiresias describes Dionysiac worship as if it were old and well established, when in the play the god has only just arrived in Greece. But Teiresias is concerned to establish him as a respected figure as swiftly as possible; also, there is a 'time-shift' effect on the part of the poet, momentarily altering the perspective to that of his own time. (A similar effect at lines 71–2 'hymns ever honoured by custom'.)

20. *How excited he is*: This strikes the keynote of Pentheus' character: hot-tempered, lacking in self-discipline, unwilling to listen to anyone else or alter his own narrow views.

21. *He is at first unaware of* CADMUS *and* TEIRESIAS: To the modern reader it is much odder that Pentheus pays no attention to the presence of the chorus, a band of foreign women in weird dress at large in his city without supervision. But it is conventional for the chorus to be ignored when necessary, and for Pentheus to start questioning them before turning to the old men would be distracting, and would delay the true point of this scene. When Pentheus does come to ask questions about Dionysiac practice, it will be face to face with the disguised god.

22. *strange goings-on in Thebes*: E. Hall, in P. E. Easterling (ed.), *The Cambridge Companion to Greek Tragedy* (Cambridge 1997), pp. 106–9, points out a recurrent situation in tragedy: when the ruler is away, women get up to mischief (Agamemnon's absence at Troy, Theseus' in *Hippolytus*). This echoes Athenian misogynistic assumptions. But here the situation is more complex, as the god is behind the disruption of Theban life, and the women's behaviour is no mere pretence.

23. *to serve the lusts of men*: Even Pentheus' most fervent defenders can hardly deny that he is obsessed with sexual motives: cf. 225, 237ff., 260ff., 353ff., 487, 812ff., 957ff., 1062. He is himself unmarried; he makes a point of mocking the stranger's beauty and long hair when he has him in his power; some passages suggest a particular closeness to his mother. Psychological criticism has not resisted these alluring details. Cf. E. R. Dodds, *Bacchae* (2nd edn Oxford 1960), pp. xliii, 97ff., 172; C. Segal, 'Pentheus and Hippolytus on the Couch and on the Grid: Psychoanalytic and Structuralist Readings of Greek Tragedy', in E. Segal, *Interpreting Greek Tragedy* (Ithaca and London 1986), pp. 268–93.

24. *in the public gaol*: Cf. 259. Soon they will be released miraculously (443ff.), as will Dionysus himself when Pentheus attempts to imprison him (497ff., 545ff.). Yet later Pentheus still threatens the god with prison (793). Language of binding and constraint also appears in his hopeless effort to tie up the bull in the stables: see note 56 below.

25. *I'll cut his head off his shoulders*: Obviously there is irony here, perhaps already apparent to the audience who know the legend. It is Pentheus who will be finally decapitated.

26. *falsely named Zeus as her lover*: Pentheus adopts the mistaken version circulated by his mother and aunts (26ff.). They are already being punished for this slander of Semele, and so will he be.

27. *fees for burned sacrifices*: Teiresias is attacked in these terms elsewhere in tragedy (Sophocles, *Oedipus the King* 388, *Antigone* 1050), but he is able to treat those accusations with contempt. In this scene we may suspect there is rather more justification in Pentheus' suspicions, but he is still wrong to ignore the prophet's advice.

28. *who sowed the earth-born crop?*: On the legend of the Sown Men, of whom Echion was one, see note 1 to *Phoenician Women*.

29. *When a clever man . . . intelligence*: Reflections on rhetorical technique and the dangers of fair-seeming speech are frequent in Euripides, and reflect Athenian interest in and suspicion of the arts of persuasion. See S. Halliwell, 'Between Public and Private: Tragedy and Athenian Experience of Rhetoric', in *Greek Tragedy and the Historian*, ed. C. B. R. Pelling (Oxford 1997), pp. 121–41 (references in tragedy at 131 n.34). Often such sentiments are found in the *agon*-scene. This is not properly an *agon* (Teiresias and Cadmus are speaking on the same side, and Pentheus says too little in response to either man's arguments), but it has something of the same self-conscious qualities.

30. *This new god . . .*: Teiresias embarks on a full defence of Dionysus, which has several curious feaures. One is the medley of different, even incompatible, types of argument (at one point Dionysus is equivalent to wine, at another he is a highly anthropomorphic god who desires honour); another is the way in which they are juxtaposed rather than combined in an effective structure. We may suspect that Euripides is parodying a 'sophistic' lecturing style.

The equation Demeter = earth, Dionysus = wine is unmistakably alluding to the teaching of the sophist Prodicus (fragment B5). The 'rationalizing' of the story of Zeus' thigh, a thoroughly inadequate attempt to make the story more credible, uses similarities of words (*meros* = thigh, *homeros* = hostage) in a way reminiscent of etymological explanations in Herodotus and (later) Plato's *Cratylus*. The reference to 'ether', a buzz word of intellectuals, also points to a sophistic source or inspiration.

31. *He, a god himself, is poured out . . . man's blessings*: This peculiar formulation is hardly likely to persuade Pentheus to worship the new deity. Even the slow-witted Cyclops laughs at the idea of a god living inside a bottle (*Cyclops* 525–7).

32. *You shall yet see him on Delphi's rocky summit*: Teiresias predicts here the importance of Dionysus at Apollo's shrine in historical times. Apollo held sway there in nine months of the year, but during the winter Dionysus was thought to be in residence, and the oracle was closed for the season.

33. *takes pleasure in receiving honour*: Gods, like men, expect and demand recognition of their true status. Cf. Aphrodite in the *Hippolytus* (7–8), or the Furies in Aeschylus' *Eumenides*.

34. *Even if, as you say . . . say that he does*: Cadmus wants the distinction of having a god in the family, even if Dionysus turns out not to be one. The characterization is humorous but devastating. For Cadmus' concern with the family and its interests see 1250, 1304ff.; in the end all his relatives, and he himself, are involved in its downfall.

35. *the pitiful end of Actaeon*: The example of Actaeon, Pentheus' cousin, is invoked as a warning; in fact it is also terrible foreshadowing of events. Pentheus too will be torn apart on Cithaeron (and by women compared with hounds). The more familiar version of his offence, popularized by Ovid, is that he chanced upon Artemis (Diana) bathing while he was out hunting. That is possibly a later variant.

36. *asking the god to do nothing untoward*: The servant in Hippolytus similarly prays to Aphrodite on his master's behalf, and with as little effect. Note in what follows Teiresias' despondency and diminished energy. The old men are no longer joyously young. The mood of the scene has darkened; whereas at first they were amusing, now the old men, as they leave with faltering steps, seem pathetic figures.

37. *bring sorrow*: The line alludes to the resemblance between Pentheus' name and *penthos* ('grief'). See further 507–8. On name-etymologies see note 31 to *Phoenician Women*.

38. *To be clever is not to be wise*: The expression is sharper in Greek, using two cognate forms (*to sophon* is not *sophia*). The distinction is significant, and will recur later in the play; the actual terms appear frequently. Fundamental is the contrast between human (imperfect or deluded) 'cleverness' and divine (superior) wisdom. There is also a contrast between excessively subtle or ambitious ways of thinking and the simplicity of accepting what the gods send and enjoying their gifts (cf. the end of this ode). The chorus reject not only the overconfident assurance of Pentheus but also, probably, the hypersophisticated theorizing of Teiresias (and by implication other, modern thinkers?). But the terms become elusive: Pentheus accuses the stranger of being too clever, Dionysus insists that he is wise in the way he should be; in a later ode, wisdom is shockingly defined as triumphal revenge over enemies. See further lines 200ff., 332, 480, 490, 506, 641, 655, 824ff., 877ff., 1005, 1190.

39. *Oh, that I might come to Cyprus*: Euripidean characters and choruses often express the desire to fly far away to some place of refuge from present misfortunes ('escape-lyric'): e.g. *Hippolytus* 742ff., *Heracles* 1157ff. Paphos is a town on the south-west coast of Cyprus. The 'barbarian river' with a hundred mouths is the Nile, which was believed in antiquity to flow underground beneath the Mediterranean and so to fertilize Cyprus.

40. *we've caught the prey you sent us after*: The language of hunting – both imagery and reality – will be prominent in the play henceforth. At present the god is ensnared, 'a tame beast'; but the hunter Pentheus will become the hunted, and the tame, courteous captive will unleash savage violence (cf. 1192 'our lord is a hunter'). See further lines 618ff., 848, 861ff., 977ff., 1017–23, 1108.

The apparently helpless captive recalls the disguised Dionysus in the Homeric hymn to Dionysus. There pirates abduct a young man who is similarly compliant and unresisting. He is of course the god himself, and once they have shown their callous intentions, he assumes the form of a lion and they end up in the sea, transformed into dolphins.

41. *with a smile*: It is widely held that the actor playing Dionysus wore a smiling mask throughout (cf. 1021). On masks see A. W. Pickard-Cambridge, *The Dramatic Festivals of Athens*, 2nd edn revised by J. Gould and D. M. Lewis (Oxford 1968; reissued 1988), pp. 192ff. (with illustrations); for a sceptical treatment see S. Halliwell, 'The Function and Aesthetics of the Greek Tragic Mask', in *Drama* 2 (1993), pp. 195–211 = *Intertextualität in der griechisch-römischen Komödie*, ed. N. W. Slater and B. Zimmermann (Stuttgart 1993) 195ff.

42. *Well, stranger, your body is not without beauty*: This scene in which Pentheus taunts Dionysus is one of the passages which clearly imitates Aeschylus' lost Dionysiac plays. The parody of an Aeschylean scene in Aristophanes, combined with the ancient comments on that scene, makes plain that Dionysus was taken captive, interrogated and mocked for his feminine looks and costume (Aristophanes, *Women at the Thesmophoria* 134ff., with scholia; Aeschylus, *Edonoi* fragment 61, perhaps also 59, 60, 62). In Aeschylus it is likely that Lycurgus, another standard opponent of Dionysus, was the questioner.

43. *Dionysus himself initiated me*: Dionysiac mysteries certainly existed in antiquity (cf. W. Burkert, *Greek Religion*, pp. 290–5). R. Seaford in a series of papers, and in his commentary, has made a case for their being important as background for the *Bacchae*. In his view much that is said to or by Pentheus, and much that he does, corresponds to aspects of the initiation process as performed in classical times. The evidence is uneven and scattered in place and date; the case is not proven (though that is not to say that Seaford is definitely wrong). It must be stressed, however, that normal initiation would be a path to happiness and fulfilment, whereas for Pentheus the end is delusion and death. The sequence in the play, therefore (as Seaford himself says), would be a caricature or negative image of true initiation.

44. *Is there a Zeus there who fathers new gods?*: Cf. Menelaus' bewildered puzzlings over a 'daughter of Zeus' called Helen in Egypt (*Helen* 489ff.).

45. *much less sense than Greeks*: Pentheus' cocky reply is in context deeply misguided, but no doubt reflects Greek chauvinism (cf. Hermione's attitude in the *Andromache* or the slogans bandied in the *Iphigenia at Aulis*; also Herodotus 1.60.3). Dionysus' response echoes the more enlightened attitude of more sophisticated thinkers. Cf. W. K. C. Guthrie, *History of Greek Philosophy* iii (Cambridge 1969), pp. 160–3. See also notes 65 and 67 to *Iphigenia at Aulis*.

46. *a name that makes you ripe for disaster*: The banality of Pentheus' superficial reply is obvious: he answers only the last question, and on a crudely literal level. The god replies with an ominous prediction, alluding to the meaning of the king's name (see note 37 above). Teiresias had made a similar point, but to Cadmus behind Pentheus' back; now it is put to him face to face.

47. *off to prison*: The location of the prison is unclear. Is it within the precincts of Pentheus' palace, or further off? Since after the next ode his cries come from behind the stage-building, and he surely emerges from the central door, it is probably best to assume that he is taken into the palace at this point.

48. *Daughter of Achelous, sovereign Dirce*: The chorus address the river Dirce, one of the two rivers of Thebes, as though she were a deity, then the reference to 'your springs' makes her physical reality more prominent; but a moment later she is representative of the people of Thebes ('you . . . are thrusting me away . . . Why do you reject me?').

49. *the infant son of Zeus . . . by this name*: A further recounting of the myth of Dionysus' preservation and birth (note 9), made more vivid by the use of direct speech. 'Dithyrambus' is a further title of Dionysus, connected with the dithyramb, a type of song performed in his honour. Its significance is unclear: perhaps 'triumphant'.

50. *sprung from the dragon of old*: The serpent that Cadmus slew and from whose teeth grew the Sown Men: see note 1 to *Phoenician Women*. Creatures born of the earth ('chthonic') often have a sinister or malignant aspect (cf. the Giants, Typhon). This image of Pentheus as a dark and monstrous figure appears several times in the chorus's songs, but seems inappropriate to the king we have seen on stage. Perhaps we are meant to see the chorus as demonizing Pentheus: if so, this has its implications for our sympathies later on.

51. *Come down from Olympus, lord*: Summoning a god to appear and give aid is a regular feature of hymns (hence the expression 'kletic hymn', i.e. one which calls upon or summons). Of course, Dionysus is much closer than the chorus think.

52. *Axius' swift-flowing stream . . . father Lydias*: The Axius and the Lydias are rivers in Macedonia which the god will cross in his journey (apparently from Thrace or Lydia) to Pieria, birthplace and home of the Muses. There may be a compliment here to Euripides' Macedonian hosts (see General Introduction, p. xxxvi).

53. *The voice of* DIONYSUS *suddenly rings out from inside the palace*: This scene, often referred to as the 'Palace Miracles', has been much discussed. The god cries out from within; the chorus seem to recognize him as Dionysus and anticipate an epiphany. He calls for the spirit of the earthquake to 'shake the earth's floor', and the chorus describe the palace as collapsing; fire and lightning are also mentioned. How much of this was dramatized in visible form in the Athenian theatre is doubtful: very probably the words (and the agitated song and rhythms) were judged sufficient to stimulate the audience's imagination. Parallel scenes elsewhere in tragedy where again there can be no question of fully realistic production include the final scene of the *Prometheus Bound* (where Prometheus and the chorus are engulfed by an earthquake); Euripides, *Heracles* 904ff. (the destruction of parts of Heracles' house); *Erechtheus* fragment 370 (an earthquake caused by Poseidon).

When the stranger emerges, he continues to play his part even with the chorus, and they show no suspicion that he may in fact be the god. See S. Goldhill, *Reading Greek Tragedy* (Cambridge 1986), pp. 276–83, for discussion of ways in which Euripides seems to play with theatrical illusion in this sequence.

54. *Women of Asia . . .*: From this point to the end of his narrative of events offstage Dionysus and the chorus leader speak in trochaic tetrameters, the alternative dialogue metre revived by Euripides in his later plays. It occurs only here in this play. The effect is more rapid and perhaps less dignified than the normal iambic trimeter: it seems to be meant to convey the god's amusement with his game, though it is also typically associated with swift or violent action.

55. *easily and without effort*: This contrasts with the emphasis in his next speech on Pentheus' violent and futile activity. Gods do all things 'with ease', a point made often in Homer (e.g. *Iliad* 3.381, 15.356ff.).

56. *while sweat dripped from his body*: R. P. Winnington-Ingram, *Euripides and Dionysus* (Cambridge 1948), p. 84 offers a subtle reading: 'in binding it with effort and strain Pentheus is performing the futile task of constraining the animal Dionysus within himself'. Some critics find this excessively Freudian, but whatever we think about this specific scene, the poet has made it hard for us to ignore Pentheus' psychology.

57. *grow for mortals*: There is clearly something lost after these words, and the line printed in square brackets in the translation is an attempt to supply the likely sense.

58. *you are clever, clever . . . cleverness is needed*: The theme of wisdom and cleverness (both expressed in the Greek *sophos*) recurs: see note 38.

59. *A* MESSENGER *enters*: On the convention of the messenger-speech, see note 55 to *Phoenician Women*. In this play there are two examples, related in a number of ways. Both describe an expedition to the mountain and an attempt to spy on or get the better of the maenads; in both, the women are at first calm and at peace in their mountain refuge, but once provoked turn to violence and display supernatural strength. This speech should provide a warning for Pentheus; instead he persists in his defiance of the god and becomes the victim whose death is described in the later speech. Dismemberment and tearing of flesh figure in both – of animals in this speech but of Pentheus himself later on.

The speech evokes complicated responses from the audience. On the one hand the beauty and the wonder of Dionysiac worship is described (the miracles performed by the women, and their gracefulness); on the other, the swiftness with which the bacchants become aggressive is alarming (still more disturbing their raids on the villages and abduction of children). The account of how they were pursued but proved immune to men's weapons should also warn Pentheus against any idea of military action against them; but here again he fails to heed the lessons he might learn from the messenger.

60. *I fear your quick temper . . . kingly manner*: It is a natural technique in drama, which lacks an authorial voice, to characterize people through the comments of others.

61. *three bands of female worshippers*: Not just because there were three daughters of Cadmus to account for: it appears that triple division into 'companies' of maenads persisted in historical Thebes and elsewhere (Rhodes, Magnesia).

62. *they weren't, as you say . . . wood*: This explicit contradiction of Pentheus' assumptions by an eye-witness is clearly important; but the king chooses to ignore it (814, etc.).

63. *one fellow who hung about in town . . . ready tongue*: Obviously negative characterization, though perhaps more to show the messenger's retrospective disapproval than to damn the 'townish' type as a whole. But such characters often do receive criticism in Euripides (cf. the contrast between the city demagogue and the naively virtuous farmer in the messenger speech of the *Orestes*, 902ff.).

64. *were possessed by the god*: An echo of Aeschylus' trilogy on Lycurgus, 'the house is inspired, the palace is possessed' (fragment 58). Both lines are quoted by Longinus, *On the Sublime* 15, who considers that Euripides has moderated the boldness of Aeschylus' conception.

65. *So welcome this god . . . pleasure left to man*: The messenger draws the right conclusion but his final reasoning is naive and simple-minded, hardly doing justice to the eerie and disturbing sequence of events he has described. His mention of wine and Aphrodite ('the Cyprian') is also ill judged, given the prejudices of his ruler.

66. *tell them to assemble . . .*: Pentheus begins to muster his army. For the expectation of an armed attack on the Bacchants see note 4 above.

67. *You hear my words, Pentheus*: This is the first time Dionysus has used any form of address to Pentheus; it adds emphasis to his warning. The god gives the man one last chance to alter his course; but he surely knows, as we do, that Pentheus will not take that chance.

68. *Spare me your lectures*: Formally the scene now gathers pace: distichomythia (two lines from each speaker in turn) in 792–801, then stichomythia (one line from each in turn) in 802–44.

69. *My good fellow*: The expression used is a difficult one, rare in tragedy and probably colloquial. While there is some variation according to context, it seems to have a rather superior and patronizing or ironic tinge. See E. Dickey, *Greek Forms of Address* (Oxford 1996), pp. 158–60.

70. *Ah*: This enigmatic exclamation by Dionysus is the turning point of the play. From this point on he proceeds remorselessly to arrange Pentheus' death. The importance of the moment is marked by the exclamation being extra-metrical, interrupting the sequence of stichomythia. What is the tone? Gloating, disappointed, resigned, pitying, dismissive? Each director will have her own ideas. The ambiguity of tone is discussed by O. Taplin, *Greek Tragedy in Action* (London 1978), pp. 120–21 and S. Goldhill, *Reading Greek Tragedy*, pp. 284–5.

71. *Do you want to see them*: A new motif is introduced: instead of making war on the maenads, Pentheus will have the chance to spy on them. For the notion of observing forbidden rituals compare the stories of intruders at the Thesmophoria, a festival reserved for women: in one account King Battos of Cyrene came to spy on the rites and was caught and castrated (Aelian fragment 44); in another Aristomenes of Messenia made a similar attempt and was overpowered by women with sacrificing knives and torches, and taken captive (Pausanias 4.17.1). The plot of Aristophanes' *Women at the Thesmophoria* is a parodic version of this story-pattern.

Pentheus' reaction to Dionysus' question is hard to assess. His eagerness to see the maenads is extraordinary, and his loss of self-control in the rest of this scene seems to suggest that he is already falling under the god's power (though Dionysus only calls down madness upon him at 850ff.). Greek myth is full of stories in which divinities send mortals mad (cf. the proverbial 'quem deus vult perdere, prius dementat'). In Homer, though perhaps less often in other authors, divine intervention normally works on impulses already present in the mortal concerned. On the same model it is suggested, especially by E. R. Dodds and R. P. Winnington-Ingram, that something in Pentheus (repressed desires?) motivates his replies. The god sees the weaknesses that will enable him to destroy his opponent. For criticism of this psychic reading see Seaford's introduction to his commentary, in *Bacchae* (Warminster 1996), pp. 33–5.

72. *Am I to give up . . . and rank as a woman?*: Pentheus is still sufficiently in control to rebel at this suggestion. Joining in Bacchic worship, as Teiresias and Cadmus did, does not involve dressing in women's clothes: this transvestism is a fresh element. Obviously it provides a further means to humiliate Pentheus; it can also be seen in terms of his own psychology (cf. previous note). On another level it *may* have some ritual significance (Seaford, *Bacchae*, introduction p. 33 and note on 912–76), perhaps associated with initiation or '*rites de passage*'; but this hypothesis needs to be treated with great caution. There is no clear evidence for ritual transvestism in Dionysiac religion.

73. *Let us go into the palace*: There is something wrong with the text here: most probably a line has been lost and two separate speakers' lines merged. The translation offered seeks to restore the sense required, following the suggestions of Jackson (see Diggle's apparatus).

74. *either I'll set out with my army or I'll take your advice*: Pentheus as he goes inside maintains that he is still considering the alternatives. This is clearly self-deception, and we hear no more about armed assaults in the next scene, where he is totally in the power of Dionysus.

75. *is by turns*: This translates Diggle's emendation *en merei* for the manuscript's *en telei*. The transmitted text is difficult, but is normally taken as meaning 'a god in authority' or 'a god in all fulness' (Kirk translates 'he shall recognize the son of Zeus, Dionysus, as a god in perfect essence – a terrible one, but to men most gentle': *The Bacchae by Euripides* (Englewood Cliffs and Bristol 1970)). This may be thought preferable to the rather banal idea that he is terrible on some days, gentle on others; but we continue our policy of rendering the text as printed by Diggle.

76. *What is wisdom? . . . ever cherished*: These lines form a refrain (877–81 = 896–901). A refrain is also found in 991–6 = 1012–16 (elsewhere in Euripides only at *Ion* 125–9 = 141–3, a hymn to Apollo). Refrains are more frequent in Aeschylus, and seem to be especially associated with ritual or ceremonial contexts.

There is cause to doubt the text here (Diggle obelizes the opening of the refrain), but we translate the traditional readings (except that in 876 the second *to* must be deleted (Paley)). The reference to wisdom (thematic in the play) presumably implies that what follows is wise as well as honourable. The principle of helping your friends and harming your enemies (and indeed enjoying their distress), while resisted by Socrates in Plato and repugnant to many later thinkers, is well established in Greek popular ethics (see K. J. Dover, *Greek Popular Morality* (Oxford 1974), pp. 180–84, and M. Whitlock Blundell, *Helping Friends and Harming Enemies* (Cambridge 1989), ch. 1), and the increasing bloodthirstiness of the chorus's sentiments suits the pattern of the play: they will go further still in the next ode.

77. *what custom has prescribed*: As before, the chorus advocate a simple and unreflecting acceptance of traditional practice, including religious devotion (Dionysiac worship being included). The passage hints at the currents of scepticism and questioning of old values which we can discern in other texts of the late fifth century BC. Even the chorus's own language is affected by these ideas: 'whatever the divine may be' is on the one hand an admission of human ignorance, but also reminds us of the agnosticism of sophists such as Protagoras. The final sentence of the antistrophe also alludes to contemporary debates, especially the opposition of *nomos* (law, custom or tradition) and *phusis* (human nature): see W. K. C. Guthrie, *History of Greek Philosophy* iii, ch. 4, esp. pp. 55–60, 113–16, 129–31. A common approach among intellectuals was to say that custom had no real justification, and that human nature, sometimes construed as appetite or selfish ambition, should take priority (e.g. Callicles in Plato, *Gorgias* 482–6). The chorus prefer the view that *nomos* ('what has become accepted . . .') is itself rooted in and justified by 'nature'.

78. *I think I see two suns . . . bull now*: Pentheus' delusion partly involves seeing falsely but also gives him a kind of muddled insight. The vision of Dionysus as a bull is a kind of truth: the savage, bestial side of the god is being revealed. The hallucinations of Pentheus are alluded to in a famous passage of Virgil (*Aeneid* 4), quoted on p. xlv above.

79. *now you see what you should see*: The first of a series of sinister ambiguities in this scene, relished by the audience but missed by the bemused Pentheus.

80. *I am completely in your hands*: The phrase can also be understood as 'I am dedicated/committed to you', and may imply ritual dedication to the god. For an essay analysing this aspect see B. Seidensticker, 'Sacrificial Ritual in the *Bacchae*', in *Arktouros* (Festschrift B. Knox), ed. G. W. Bowersock et al. (Berlin and New York 1979), pp. 181–90.

81. *through the midst of the land of Thebes*: In his altered state of mind, Pentheus no longer feels any misgivings about being seen by the citizens.

82. *bears the burden for this city*: Again the phrase seems to evoke religious ideas, this time of the scapegoat who suffers punishment for the sins of the community. See R. Parker, *Miasma. Pollution and Purification in Early Greek Religion* (Oxford 1983), pp. 257–71; J. Bremmer, 'Scapegoat Rituals in Ancient Greece', *Harvard Studies in Classical Philology* 87 (1983), pp. 299–320.

83. *renown that towers to heaven*: Up to this point Pentheus can be supposed to hear Dionysus' words, though not fully grasping their meaning. The 'renown' he will gain will not be the glory of the victor but the notoriety of being made a lasting example of the folly of offending the god.

84. *On, swift hounds of Madness . . .*: The ode is composed mainly in the metre known as dochmiacs, virtually confined to tragedy and associated with moods of intense excitement and emotion. The chorus anticipate with fierce delight the downfall of their persecutor. 'Madness' is personified, but the focus is on her agents or 'hounds', the hunting Bacchants. By contrast, in Aeschylus' Bacchic play *Xantriae* it appears that Madness appeared in person (as in Euripides' *Heracles*).

85. *First his mother will see him . . .*: Vivid visualization of the scene which is imagined to be happening or about to happen as they sing. The use of direct speech makes the scene even more immediate (see V. Bers, *Speech within Speech* (Lanham, Maryland, and London 1997), pp. 91–2, 112–13). The irony of Agaue's second question is patent. In the lines which follow we see again the building-up of Pentheus as a monstrous or demonic figure, in contrast with the pathetic pawn we have witnessed in the previous scene.

86. *Death will discipline his purpose*: The passage extending from this phrase to the end of 1007 is the most difficult in the play, because the transmitted text is clearly corrupt in several places. To restore precisely what Euripides wrote is hopeless; we provide here a possible version incorporating emendations by various scholars, mostly printed in Diggle's apparatus.

87. *Come, Bacchus, beast-god . . . net of death*: The hunter of Bacchants, Pentheus, becomes the hunted: on the motif, cf. note 40. On 'smiling face', cf. note 41 above.

88. *A* MESSENGER *enters*: The exchange between the messenger and the chorus is striking formally, as the messenger speaks, but the chorus sing in response. His sombre comments contrast with their exultant tone of celebration. We should contrast the opening of the next scene, in which Agaue and the chorus combine in sung exchange.

89. *When we had left behind . . .*: For comparison of the earlier messenger speech with this one see note 59 above. Some of the details were rather speculatively connected with ritual e.g. by E. R. Dodds (the placing of Pentheus in the tree, the pelting of the victim with stones). There is little justification for this.

90. *capture this climbing beast*: Dionysus had referred to Pentheus as a man, and only a man, not a beast, can tell tales about the Bacchants' activities. We see the beginning of Agaue's delusion (cf. 1123): see further the ambiguous phrase in 1141–2 'as if it were a mountain lion's', which could be either a simile or Agaue's own perspective: in the next scene we see it is the latter.

91. *because of my offences*: In a notorious passage of his commentary (p. 217), Dodds commented: 'Pentheus dies sane and repentant: along with the ritual *mitra* ("headband") he has discarded the madness which he acquired when he put it on. His repentance must be taken as sincere, and is fatal to the view which sees in him a blameless victim of religious fanaticism.' This surely goes too far. Pentheus regains his sanity and realizes that he was a fool to intrude on the bacchants' dances, but there is no reason to suppose that in this moment of panic he suddenly sees that he should have revered Dionysus as a god all along. More important is the need for the poet to show him fully aware of what is happening to him: the quotation of his actual words enhances the horror.

92. *in sport like a ball*: A brilliant metaphor, bringing to a close perhaps the most horrific passage in Greek tragedy. As often, the tragic poet increases the terror and pathos of a key moment by contrasting it with some normal, positive or innocent pastime.

93. *Let us dance for the Bacchic god . . . drips with his blood*: A short but important song, involving a significant shift of tone. At the start the emphasis is on celebrating Pentheus' downfall, but at the end the chorus's thoughts turn to what this means for those who killed him ('lamentation and tears'), and above all for his mother ('to clasp a child . . .'). This sympathy for Agaue is vital for the next scene.

94. *Agaue enters*: It is not certain whether the wand or pole with her son's head on it is actually used on stage. It would be easier to carry the head (represented, of course, by Pentheus' mask) cradled in her arms, and she is certainly holding it by line 1277.

95. *Share now in the feast*: Another moment of supreme horror, as Agaue can only be suggesting feeding on her spoils (probably also implied at 1241–2). Cannibalism does occasionally feature in tragedy (always involuntary, as in the feasting of Thyestes), and the idea of *omophagia* (eating raw flesh) was part of the Dionysiac experience at least in myth (cf. note 15); but for it to be enacted on stage would be bold even for Euripides. At any rate, the chorus recoil.

96. *a skilful huntsman, skilfully*: This rendering obscures the recurrence of the word *sophos* ('clever, wise': see note 38), here reused in a different sense. Dionysus is wise not only in his divine foreknowledge and ability to outwit Pentheus, but also in his skilful direction of his hunting 'hounds'.

97. *Cadmus now enters*: Cadmus himself says that his search was endless, and he only began it once he heard what had happened. Meanwhile Agaue raced to the city 'on frenzied feet'. The time-scheme is impossible in realistic terms, but tragedy often manipulates time in this fashion (choral odes, moreover, regularly indicate the passage of an unspecific period of time).

98. *justly, but excessively, though he is our own kin*: Important lines. Cadmus earlier emphasized the need for family solidarity: it will be good for the prestige of the royal house to have a god in it (even if he is not one). Now it adds bitterness to his loss that Dionysus has treated them in this way despite being a relation. We soon learn that his kinship with Agaue and Pentheus will condemn Cadmus to exile as well (see note 104 below). Cadmus admits that the punishment of his daughter and grandson is just, but claims it was excessive (cf. 1346). Some ancient and modern defenders of the gods may argue the power of the gods cannot be regulated by human ideas of what is and is not enough: indeed, in myth it is typical of them to retaliate with revenge far sterner than the original offence, and extending more widely (e.g. all of Troy must be destroyed for Paris' crime and/or because of the judgement of Paris). But Cadmus' response cannot but strike a chord in a sympathetic theatrical audience.

99. *What cause for shame is here?*: The dialogue shifts to stichomythia (one-line exchange), in a moving scene of question and answer as Cadmus tries to calm his daughter and draw her back to reality. The episode has been described as the 'psychotherapy scene' (G. Devereux, 'The Psychotherapy Scene in Euripides'

Bacchae', *Journal of Hellenic Studies* 93 (1973), pp. 36–49; see already E. R. Dodds, *Bacchae*, on the lines). It is closely comparable with the scene in the *Heracles* where Amphitryon (again a father) helps Heracles towards realization of what he has done (1109 ff.).

100. *decently arranged, limb to limb*: The single manuscript which preserves this play goes straight on to the next line ('What part . . . ?'), but this leaves Agaue's first question unanswered. It is clear that something has been lost here, though how much is disputed. The decision depends on what we suppose originally stood in this gap ('lacuna' is the technical term) and what in the (surely very considerable) gap after 1329. It seems from later sources that the scene originally included the revelation and piecing together of the fragments of Pentheus' body, and a lament over her son by Agaue including much self-reproach. Many scholars put this in the later lacuna, but I am inclined to agree with those who would put it here. If so, we may assume that at least twenty lines are lost at this point.

101. *O my child . . . believe in the gods*: If the reconstruction in the previous note is correct, Agaue has lamented her son and now Cadmus follows suit, in a pathetic eulogy which melds grief and self-pity. What he remembers of Pentheus is the readiness of the young king to protect his grandfather. The cameo is touching, and the characterization of Pentheus, hot-tempered and quick to deal out punishments, rings wonderfully true.

102. *Your lot is painful . . . brings you pain*: This, the last significant comment by the chorus in the surviving text, shows a judicious balance of tone: they feel for Cadmus but do not regret Pentheus' death. The audience may by now feel a good deal more compassion for the dead man and the survivors. This chorus at least is hardly a moral guide for the spectator.

103. *the change in my fortunes . . .*: Agaue's sentence is incomplete. Here there is a second and probably a longer lacuna. In the lost portion there may have been further dialogue; possibly the piecing-together of the body (though this should, I believe, take place in the earlier lacuna, see note 100 above). Some evidence has been assembled which may help in reconstructing the missing part: a single line in which a speaker (Agaue, we assume) says, 'For if I had not taken this pollution upon my own hands'; fragments of a papyrus which may preserve part of Dionysus' speech (little is clear, but the name of Zeus figures, also references to 'learning' and 'impious' or 'impiety'); help has also been sought from the curious work known as the *Christus Patiens* ('Suffering Christ'), a Byzantine dramatization of the Passion which adapts a good deal of Euripidean material and may well have made use of lines which we have now lost. But the arguments here are tenuous, and cannot carry us as far as a total reconstruction.

During the lacuna Dionysus appears above the stage-building. (There would be no need in this case for the crane to be used: on the various means of dramatizing scenes on a higher level, see D. J. Mastronarde 'Actors on High: the Skene-Roof, the Crane and the Gods in Attic Drama', *Classical Antiquity* 9 (1990), pp. 247–94). Probably he was attired in more majestic fashion; those who suppose that he wore a smiling mask earlier must assume that he now wore a more austere one.

When the text resumes he is in mid-speech. The ancient hypothesis to the play says that he declared the establishment of his rites, and it is clear that he must also specify exile as punishment for Agaue and her sisters (see 1363). In the text that survives he addresses Cadmus.

104. *You will be transformed . . . land of the blessed*: This extraordinary speech combines a variety of traditions concerning Cadmus, not all of which are attested before Euripides. We may distinguish the following elements: (a) he is punished by being transformed into a snake (a creature like the serpent he slew when young); (b) he will lead a barbarian army against cities of Greece, winning many successes but eventually being repulsed at Delphi ('the oracle of Loxias'); (c) after death he and his wife will dwell in the isles of the blessed (this is already referred to in Pindar). These are clearly three distinct versions, and the first two are hardly compatible (is Cadmus to act as leader while in snake form?). Some scholars believe that (b) reflects Greek knowledge of the destruction of major Greek cities at the time of the Dorian invasion. Herodotus also knows of an oracle that barbarians would sack Delphi and be destroyed as a result: the Persians in 480–479 BC believed this referred to themselves, wrongly according to Herodotus (9.42 ff., 5.61). Euripides has evidently created a compound version which seems bizarre to the modern reader and perhaps struck an odd note even to the ancients: but it does provide a longer perspective and quasi-aetiological elements of the kind familiar in other speeches by gods at the end of plays.

Metamorphosis is predicted also at the end of the *Hecabe* (Hecabe is to become a wild bitch), but there it can be argued that the change reflects her vicious personality.

Agaue and her sisters are exiled because they are polluted by blood-guilt: this is the normal treatment of such offenders in mythology. Why is Cadmus punished? Some critics believe it is because his worship of Dionysus was inadequate or insincere (cf. 333 and note 34 above). This is unlikely: although intellectuals might worry about purity of heart and mind, the general assumption in Greek religion was that the ritual act was the crucial thing, rather than the beliefs of the worshipper (a strong statement to this effect by S. Price, *Religions of the Ancient Greeks* (Cambridge 1999), pp. 3, 183). It is more probable that Cadmus is so treated as head of the offending household: family solidarity again.

'The land of the blessed' is Elysium, the remote mythical region (usually thought of as an island) where some of the heroes were destined to go after death – a privileged few who were spared the horrors of Hades. The notion is first found in the *Odyssey*. But Cadmus views the prospect of eternal life with despondency.

105. *Dionysus, we beseech you, we have done wrong*: This exchange highlights some of the central issues of debate concerning Euripides' treatment of the gods. Humans naturally protest (and the audience, being human, should pity them and share some of their concern); but despite human hopes (1348) gods are *not* like men, and are not answerable to them. The will of Zeus is impenetrable. Yet divine retribution frequently seems cruel and excessive to the victim and the onlooker. Tragedy may dramatize divine justice, but it is a harsh justice. These dilemmas were particularly prominent in Euripides' work: 1348 is close to the famous line in a much earlier play, *Hippolytus*, 'gods ought to be wiser than men' (120). For discussion of Euripides' gods, see General Introduction, pp. xxxiii–xxxv; for a different view see e.g. M. Lefkowitz, ' "Impiety" and " Atheism" in Euripides' Dramas' in J. Mossman (ed.), *Euripides* (Oxford 2003), pp. 102–21 (arguing that they are more just, and more traditional, than most scholars think). More generally see R. Parker 'Gods Cruel and Kind: Tragic and Civic Theology', in C. B. R. Pelling (ed.), *Greek Tragedy and the Historian*, pp. 143–60.

106. DIONYSUS *leaves the stage*: This is controversial. There are no stage directions in our manuscript; all such additions are based on the judgement of editors and commentators in modern times. The sole manuscript which preserves this part of the play does ascribe one more speech to Dionysus, namely 1377–8: 'Yes, for terrible was my treatment at your hands, having my name go without honour in Thebes.' The nineteenth-century scholars E. Bothe and G. Hermann decided that Cadmus should be the speaker and made the tiny changes which adjust the grammar (in the Greek this amounts to altering only two letters). In the text as printed by Diggle these emendations are incorporated, so that Dionysus says no more. Our practice is to translate Diggle's text, and I believe the ascription to Cadmus is correct, but it has not convinced all scholars: D. J. Mastronarde, *Contact and Discontinuity* (Berkeley 1979), p. 96 argues strongly that it would be unparalleled for a god to withdraw so unobtrusively from a *deus ex machina* scene. (The compromise that Dionysus remains but says no more is conceivable, and could make a powerful contrast with the human plane, but is again atypical.)

107. *Father, I must go . . . share my path*: The scene recalls the parting of Electra and Orestes at the end of Euripides' *Electra* (1308 ff.); perhaps that had been particularly successful in performance.

108. *to the house of Aristaeus*: Aristaeus was the father of Actaeon (cf. 1227). There is a very short gap here. No doubt the original text would have made clear the point of this instruction (perhaps Dionysus told Agaue to meet her sisters there).

109. *Yes, for terrible was his treatment*: On the manuscript reading 'was my treatment', implying that these lines belong to Dionysus, see note 106 above.

110. *And so it has turned out here today*: These closing choral lines also appear in identical or closely similar form at the end of *Alcestis, Medea, Andromache* and *Helen*. It has often been suggested that they are editorial insertions in some places, but a choral comment is normal at the end of a Greek tragedy, and the sentiments, though conventional, are appropriate enough in each case. For discussion, see D. H. Roberts, 'Parting Words: Final Lines in Sophocles and Euripides', *Classical Quarterly* 37 (1987), pp. 51–64.

IPHIGENIA AT AULIS

1. AGAMEMNON'*s tent*: 'Tent' may be a misleading term. The army has been based at Aulis for weeks, if not months: it is likely enough that the commander-in-chief has requisitioned a local house, and later scenes seem to require something more substantial than a canvas door to separate inside from out.

2. *Old man, come out here in front of the tent . . .*: The prologue of this play, as it stands in our manuscripts, is highly unusual in form. It begins (lines 1–48) with a passage of dialogue between Agamemnon and his old servant, a figure who will be important later in the play: this is composed in anapaests, a metre often employed for the entry of choruses in other dramas, or for greetings by the chorus to new arrivals, but never used by Euripides in his surviving plays for an opening dialogue (there is however testimony that this metre was used in the prologue of the lost *Andromeda*). Next, after the slave's request to be enlightened about his master's anxieties, there follows an expository passage by Agamemnon (49–114), composed in iambic trimeters and similar in style to many other expository prologues by Euripides: however, it restates some things the old man has long known. Third comes another set of exchanges in anapaests (115–62), in which the old man receives instructions and exhortations before setting out on his mission. At the end of this Agamemnon voices a brief moralizing comment and re-enters his shelter.

Critics differ strongly as to which parts of this opening (if any) should be seen as genuine. Some think the iambics authentic, the anapaests a later addition (England, Page, Kovacs); others declare the anapaests Euripidean, the iambics spurious (Fraenkel); others again suppose both to be genuine (Knox); while some declare the whole prologue post-Euripidean (e.g. Diggle). Murray attempted to improve matters by placing the iambic passage before both sets of anapaests. The reader will probably find the opening effective enough, if somewhat repetitive; in my view it clearly derives from two different drafts imperfectly combined, but whether either was partly or wholly by Euripides is hard to determine. It must be borne in mind that 'non-Euripidean poetry' does not necessarily mean 'bad poetry'.

For further discussion see B. M. W. Knox, *Word and Action: Essays on the Ancient Theater* (Baltimore 1979), pp. 275–94; C. W. Willink, 'The Prologue of *Iphigenia at Aulis*', *Classical Quarterly* 21 (1971), pp. 343–64; D. Bain, 'The Prologues of *Iphigenia at Aulis*', *Classical Quarterly* 27 (1977), pp. 10–26; D. Kovacs, 'Towards a Reconstruction of *Iphigenia Aulidensis*', *Journal of Hellenic Studies* 123 (2003), pp. 77–103, where references to more detailed discussions can be found.

3. *you keep writing*: In epic the heroes appear to be illiterate. Only in one passage in Homer is writing alluded to, and this is in a separate narrative, in which it is treated as something mysterious and sinister (*Iliad* 6.168 ff.). But tragedy, composed in a period where writing was much more common, includes a number of scenes in which it is used. In the *Hippolytus*, Phaedra leaves a suicide note accusing Hippolytus of raping her; in the *Iphigenia among the Taurians*, Iphigenia proposes to send a letter to her brother.

4. *that man who judged the goddesses*: The reference is to Paris, also often called Alexander or Alexandros, who decided that the prize for beauty, a golden apple, should go to Aphrodite. (She bribed the young man with the promise of Helen as his bride.) The hatred of Hera and Athena for Troy originated with this episode. The contest is described in more detail at 572ff. and 1283–1311. It is a favourite theme in Euripides, especially in lyrics: for a detailed study see T. C. W. Stinton, *Collected Papers on Greek Tragedy* (Oxford 1990), pp. 17–75.

5. *as the story goes*: Euripides frequently allows his characters to draw attention to the 'traditional' nature of the mythic background. Sometimes this is done in order to cast doubt on the tradition or at least to highlight its implausibility (as at 794–800), but this seems to be a relatively neutral case.

6. *Of the Greeks only we four . . . Menelaus and I*: This translation renders an emended version of the line: the manuscripts have 'Of the Greeks we alone know the true situation – Calchas, Odysseus and Menelaus.' Although Diggle prints the manuscript reading, some alteration seems inevitable. The difficulties are more wide-ranging, however: how much is known to the army at large? Do they know of the pretence of a false marriage, but believe it to be true? That seems hard to maintain, given the account of the soldiers' curiosity and questioning on Iphigenia's arrival, as narrated by the messenger (425ff.); moreover, even Achilles himself later proves ignorant of the alleged offer (801ff., esp. 835–43). But when the army is later baying for blood, it is clear that they know that Artemis demands the girl's sacrifice: so when did they learn this? Are we to assume that Calchas has told them (as Agamemnon fears will happen, 518ff., 528ff.)? D. Kovacs ('Towards a Reconstruction') regards this as a key element in testing the authenticity of different parts of the play. The discrepancies are real, but it is not altogether plain that Euripides had made up his mind on the exact sequence of revelation.

7. AGAMEMNON *and the* OLD MAN *now sing in a lyric exchange*: The metre shifts back from iambics to anapaests. These were sometimes chanted, and elsewhere we normally do not italicize such passages, but we do so here to emphasize the different quality of the separate parts of the prologue. Also, this section, unlike the first, includes some sequences in Agamemnon's speech which are in 'melic' anapaests and were evidently sung: for the distinction see A. M. Dale, *The Lyric Metres of Greek Drama* (2nd edn Cambridge 1968) ch. 4, esp. pp. 50ff.; M. L. West, *Greek Metre* (1982), p. 122. B. M. W. Knox, *Word and Action*, pp. 288–9, sees characterization in the metrical shifts; D. Kovacs, 'Towards a Reconstruction', pp. 82–3, sees the inconsistency as a sign of later composition.

8. *It is the name and nothing else that Achilles provides*: Euripides is fond of distinctions of this kind, making explicit the gap between appearance and reality: in this play cf. 910, 938–9. These ideas are especially prominent in the *Helen*: see note 6 on *Helen* in volume 3 of this translation.

9. *dwellings raised by the Cyclopes*: The majestic strongholds of Mycenae and other ancient cities were often said to have been built with aid from the Cyclopes, one-eyed giants of superhuman strength.

10. *The* CHORUS *enters*: The chorus of this play, as in most of Euripides' extant dramas, is female. They are from Chalcis, a town directly opposite Aulis on the island of Euboea; the Euripus is the channel that separates the two. The decision of the poet to make the chorus a group of females with no direct involvement in the action, as opposed to the more obvious alternative of a chorus of Greek soldiers, is an important one. It means that they have no stake in the expedition, and that they are ready to empathize with Clytemnestra and Iphigenia. See further Gould and Mastronarde as cited in note 12 to *Phoenician Women*.

The structure of the opening song casts doubt on the authenticity of the latter part. The first section (164–230) is triadic (strophe and matching anti-strophe, then a concluding stanza known as an epode); after that there are only matching strophic pairs. The second section (231–302) is also inferior in sense and style, and includes numerous heroes of inferior rank. It is especially suspicious that Ajax reappears in the second part after being mentioned more briefly in the first. Most probably the original song ended at 230, having reached a climax with the crucial figure of Achilles. The remainder is a pastiche inspired partly by the catalogue of ships in book 2 of the *Iliad*.

For a discussion of the role of the choral songs in this play see H. Foley, *Ritual Irony* (Ithaca 1985), pp. 78–84, who argues that they present a more positive and romantic image of the Greeks and the war than the dialogue sections of the play.

For information on individual heroes mentioned see the Glossary: some are of very minor importance.

11. *Palamedes*: For this clever and inventive hero see note 27 to *Orestes*. In the several plays featuring him, he regularly gave a catalogue of the benefits he had devised for the Greeks: the diversion of board-games was among them.

12. *from the land of Phocis*: Something appears to have dropped out of the text here and at the corresponding point in the antistrophe. The sense is not significantly affected.

13. *That's a reproach that brings me honour*: The virtuous slave is a recurrent figure in Euripides. See further K. Synodinou, *On the Concept of Slavery in Euripides* (Ioannina 1977); also E. Hall, in P. Easterling (ed.), *The Cambridge Companion to Greek Tragedy* (Cambridge 1997), pp. 93–126, esp. pp. 110–18, 123–4.

14. *What is this disturbance outside my tent*: The metre shifts into trochaic tetrameters, and this is sustained through the argument that follows until the end of Agamemnon's response (401), except that the chorus's intervening comment, in itself a standard feature, is in iambic trimeters (an unparalleled breach of such a trochaic sequence). On the mood of these trochaic passages see note 27 to *Phoenician Women*. They are more numerous in this play than in any other.

With the slave's hasty disappearance, the *agon* begins. This is an unusual version of that 'typical' form. After an exchange of one-liners, Menelaus makes a long speech, Agamemnon replies with a significantly shorter one, and a few more stichomythic jibes follow. The usual expectation would be that the opponents would separate, further apart than ever; but here the messenger arrives with fresh news, and Agamemnon's deep distress at the news of his family's arrival prompts a change of heart from Menelaus. On the sequel see note 23 below. This *agon* is also abnormal in that the main speeches are in tetrameters: that metre had been used for follow-up dialogue in *agon*-scenes in *Phoenician Women* and *Orestes*, but not for the long speeches by the antagonists.

Despite a number of oddities, there can be little doubt that this scene is substantially Euripidean: the sharp-edged rhetoric and the 'unpacking' of the seamier side of the heroic age are entirely characteristic. For a useful discussion of the scene see S. Halliwell in *Greek Tragedy and the Historian*, ed. C. B. R. Pelling (Oxford 1997) at pp. 135–7 (note esp. p. 137 on alternative versions of events).

15. *You remember the time . . .*: Menelaus on Agamemnon's electioneering strikes an entertainingly anachronistic note: it surely owes much to Euripides' experience of Athenian political activity. (Cf. e.g. Aristotle, *Constitution of Athens* 27.3; Plutarch, *Themistocles* 5.6; *Nicias* 9.5; P. J. Rhodes, 'Political Activity in Classical Athens', *Journal of Hellenic Studies* 106 (1986), pp. 132–44) This first part of the speech also redeploys the motif of inconsistency and change of mind (cf. Agamemnon's change of mind in the prologue, alluded to at 363ff.; and see note 23 below).

16. *you and the army of all Greece*: The word used here, *Panhellenes*, is the first indication that some at least of the characters view this campaign as a pan-hellenic expedition, and this strikes a note of patriotic fanfare which becomes more strident later in the play: cf. 370 in this speech, and 1264ff., 1271–5, 1379ff. (esp. 1384, 1386, 1400–1401), 1446, 1456, 1474. See further Introduction to this play, and note 65 below.

17. *Do you yearn to have a good wife?*: Cf. 389, 'the man who lost a bad wife and now wants to get her back'. In Homer Helen is a fascinating and attractive figure, but even in the *Iliad* the elders of Troy, while admiring her beauty, feel that she should be sent home to her own country, and Achilles allows himself a jibe or two at the devotion of the sons of Atreus to their wives (*Iliad* 3.156–60; 9.337–43). In tragedy hostility towards Helen is normal: Aeschylus set the pattern (*Agamemnon* 62, 225, 686ff. etc.), and negative comment is frequent in Euripides. Hence the recovery of Helen is a dubious gain; this theme is developed further by Menelaus at 485ff. (after his change of heart) and by Clytemnestra at 1166ff.

18. *some heaven-sent affliction*: For the idea that the whole of the army, or of Greece, is suffering from some delusion or mad desire for the campaign, compare 807, 1264. For comparable language in historical narration see Thucydides 6.24.2–4.

19. *The army has heard . . .*: On the problems of who among the army knows how much about Agamemnon's intentions, see note 6 above. The case of the messenger, however, is straightforward: as the servant of Clytemnestra, he knows only what she knows, that her daughter has been summoned to Aulis for a distinguished marriage. Hence his cheerful but misguided eagerness to proceed with the celebrations (435ff.)

20. *Oh, what pain . . .*: Agamemnon's speech is treated as almost a monologue, despite the presence of both Menelaus and the chorus. True soliloquy in the Shakespearian style is rare in Greek tragedy. See W. Schadewaldt, *Monolog und Selbstgespräch* (Berlin 1926) (pp. 232ff. on this speech).

21. *Hades, it seems, will be her bridegroom soon*: The same motif is found at 540, 1278. The macabre idea of 'marriage' to Hades is quite frequent in tragedy, especially in the context of virgin sacrifice or execution. See further H. Foley, *Ritual Irony: Poetry and Sacrifice in Euripides* (Ithaca 1985), pp. 84–92 (some wild points); R. Seaford, 'The Tragic Wedding', *Journal of Hellenic Studies* 107 (1987), pp. 106–30; R. Rehm, *Marriage to Death: the Conflation of Wedding and Funeral Rituals in Greek Tragedy* (Princeton 1994).

22. *He is still a baby*: Orestes, the future murderer of Clytemnestra, is only an infant here. He would probably have been represented by a dummy wrapped in swaddling clothes. Some editors are sceptical about the appearance of Orestes in Euripides' version, and regard all references to him as later additions, but this is to cast doubt on an improbably large number of passages. Children are introduced elsewhere in Euripides for pathetic effect (*Alcestis, Medea, Andromache, Trojan Women*).

23. *Brother, give me your right hand to clasp*: In response to his brother's misery Menelaus undergoes an unexpected change of heart. This is a characteristic feature of the play: in the prologue Agamemnon has thought better of his original intention and is sending a second message; in this scene, now that Menelaus has changed his mind, Agamemnon will change his. Later in the play we have the crucial change of mind when Iphigenia declares her willingness to be sacrificed. Changes of mind are much more frequent (and often more puzzling in motivation) in Euripides than in his predecessors. See esp. B. M. W. Knox, 'Second Thoughts in Greek Tragedy', *Word and Action*, pp. 231–49; also J. Griffin, 'Characterization in Euripides', in *Characterization and Individuality in Greek Literature*, ed. C. B. R. Pelling (Oxford 1990), pp. 128–49, esp. pp. 140–49; J. Gibert, *Change of Mind in Greek Tragedy* (Hypomnemata vol. 108, Göttingen 1995).

24. *worthy of Tantalus, son of Zeus*: Tantalus was Menelaus' great-grandfather: see note 1 to *Orestes* above. Since he was chiefly famous as one of the great sinners, we must suspect a mischievous touch of humour by the poet.

25. *The whole gathering of the Greek army*: A very important line. In earlier versions we have no reason to suppose that the army put pressure on Agamemnon to kill his daughter (though in Aeschylus the king dreads the thought of being seen to abandon the expedition). In this play the army, frequently mentioned and described as an unruly mob, is a sinister presence offstage, and in the second scene with Achilles almost bursts into the action (1338ff.). Racine developed this motif further in his play on the same theme.

26. *The whole breed of prophets*: Euripidean characters often express hostility toward prophets: e.g. *Helen* 744–60, *Bacchae* 255–7, fragment 795. For their role and status in Greek society in general see W. Burkert, *Greek Religion* (Eng. tr. Oxford 1985), pp. 111–14; J. D. Mikalson, *Athenian Popular Religion* (Chapel Hill 1983), ch. 6.

27. *Sisyphus*: In the *Odyssey* and most other sources, Odysseus is the son of Laertes, but there was an alternative tradition that Laertes' wife Anticleia was already pregnant by the crafty Corinthian Sisyphus when he married her. In tragedy this accusation often goes with a negative portrayal of Odysseus as a villain (e.g. Sophocles, *Philoctetes* 417).

28. *Cyclopean walls*: See note 9 above.

29. *keep silence*: The familiar convention of choral discretion is once more taken for granted: compare *Orestes* 1103–4.

30. *among women . . . countless forms*: The sense is obscure here, but the translation we offer seems the most convincing in this context.

31. *You came, Paris . . .*: This passage refers to the 'Judgement of Paris' (see note 4 above). Paris, while minding herds on Mount Ida near Troy, was visited by the three goddesses Hera, Athena and Aphrodite, escorted by the messenger-god Hermes. He was asked to decide which of them was the most beautiful; each goddess promised different rewards. Paris chose Aphrodite as the winner, and his reward was the beautiful Helen.

The myth described Paris as living on the hillside tending herds. At some stage it was evidently felt that this was an unworthy occupation for a Trojan prince, and an elaborate story was devised in which Paris was exposed at birth on Mount Ida, because of fears arising from a sinister dream that his mother Hecabe had, in which she bore a firebrand which consumed all of Troy. Paris survived, grew up as a shepherd, and only in adulthood came to be recognized as a son of Priam. The story was dramatized by Euripides in the *Alexandros* (see Preface to *Trojan Women* in *Electra and Other Plays*, volume 2 of this translation).

32. *Clytemnestra . . . another carriage*: Some editors argue that the spectacle of a series of carriages has been added to a Euripidean version in which Clytemnestra and Iphigenia arrived with less pomp and circumstance. For discussion see D. L. Page, *Actors' Interpolations in Greek Tragedy* (Oxford 1934), pp. 166–8; O. Taplin, *The Stagecraft of Aeschylus* (Oxford 1977), p. 77. In that case some of the choral welcome and parts of Clytemnestra's speech would need to be cut. It is true that the scene of arrival is unduly protracted, but the issue is not as important as some of the other controversies concerning this play.

33. *I don't understand . . . understand*: This very weak line (there is nothing obscure about Agamemnon's apparent meaning, though of course the real import of his words is hidden) interrupts the regularity of the stichomythia and is certainly an intrusion.

34. *You will come to the same place as your father, daughter*: This probably means Hades, but again the stichomythia is disrupted and the authenticity of this line is very doubtful.

35. *You aren't finding . . . father?*: Oddly, Iphigenia seems ignorant in this context of the wedding supposedly arranged. Perhaps part of this scene is spurious; it can only be defended by assuming that she is pretending ignorance, teasing her father.

36. *Kiss me and let me take your hand . . .*: Physical contact generates emotion, and Agamemnon almost breaks down. Cf. the famous moment when Medea prepares to kill her children, but is distracted by the sight of their hands, faces and soft skin (*Medea* 1069ff.).

37. *Aegina was the daughter of Asopus . . .*: This gradual release of information through stichomythia seems highly artificial to modern taste, but scenes of this kind seem to have appealed to the Athenian audience, many of whom were no doubt pleased to be able to answer the questions before the actor did (cf. Aristophanes, *Frogs* 1109–18 on the sophistication of the theatre-going public). For somewhat similar exchanges see *Iphigenia among the Taurians* 515ff., Sophocles *Philoctetes* 410ff. On stichomythia generally see C. Collard, 'On Stichomythia', *Liverpool Classical Monthly* 5 (1980), pp. 77–85.

38. *Peleus won the hand of Nereus' daughter*: On the wedding of Peleus and Thetis see the extended description in 1036–79: see note 52 below.

39. *Cheiron*: Cheiron, the most famous of the Centaurs, traditionally wise and well disposed to mankind. That he was Achilles' tutor is already mentioned in the *Iliad* (11.831ff.).

40. *Have you already performed . . . fine prows*: This passage in particular includes a number of details about the wedding rituals of ancient Greece. For fuller accounts and ancient illustrations see R. Garland, *The Greek Way of Life* (London 1990), pp. 219–25; J. Oakley and R. Sinos, *The Wedding in Ancient Athens* (Wisconsin 1993).

41. *Queen of Argos*: This refers to Hera, who not only holds Argos in special esteem (*Iliad* 4.52) but oversees marriage.

42. *where Phoebus toiled*: Apollo and Poseidon spent a year in service to the Trojan King Laomedon (who then foolishly cheated them of their payment).

See *Iliad* 21.441–9, where it is said that Poseidon built the walls and Apollo looked after the herds.

43. *Cassandra*: She was a daughter of Priam, and was beloved by Apollo, who gave her the power of prophecy; but when she refused to sleep with him, being unable to take back the gift, he made it useless by decreeing that none would ever believe her predictions. Her ecstatic state when inspired by the god's power is dramatized in famous scenes of Aeschylus' *Agamemnon* and Euripides' *Trojan Women*.

44. *offspring of the long-necked swan*: Helen is the daughter of Leda, who was married to Tyndareus, but she is normally said to be the child of Zeus, who seduced or raped Leda in the form of a swan (see also *Orestes* 1385–6 and note 69). As in the case of Heracles, who can be described as son of Zeus or of Amphitryon, she has two fathers. But in the *Helen* (lines 17–21) she herself adopts a sceptical attitude to the myth of her own birth, and the chorus take the same line here. In the late fifth century BC rationalizing or demystifying mythology was a common practice among intellectuals (compare e.g. *Trojan Women* 988–90, and Plato, *Phaedrus* 229c–30a).

45. *enter* CLYTEMNESTRA *from the door of the tent*: To appreciate the scene which follows we need to be conscious of Athenian conventions regarding the behaviour of women, which were extremely strict. A well-born woman married to one man should not be found speaking in public (or at all) with another man; and Achilles' anxiety reflects his awareness that even an innocent conversation might be misconstrued. When Clytemnestra even goes so far as to initiate physical contact he is shocked. For the social comedy here compare *Ion* 517ff., another scene which depends on a misunderstanding of two parties' relationship.

46. *Stranger, born of Aeacus' line, wait . . .*: The whole passage which follows, from 855 to 916 (the next intervention of the chorus), is in the lively longer lines called trochaic tetrameters, regularly used in scenes of agitation and excitement. The same metre is used elsewhere in the play (see note 14 above; see esp. 1338–1401, the moment of crisis). It was also used in the similar scene in *Ion* (see previous note).

47. *to fall at your knees*: On the ritual of supplication see note 50 to *Phoenician Women*.

48. *can be of service when they will . . .*: Clytemnestra hints that the army may, with Achilles' aid, follow his lead and help them prevent Iphigenia's sacrifice. But her hopes are deluded, as a later scene shows (1344ff.).

49. *My anger rises . . .*: For a discussion of the problems of this speech (919–74) see W. Ritchie, 'Euripides, *Iphigenia at Aulis*, 919–74' in *Dionysiaca* (Festschrift D. L. Page), ed. R. D. Dawe et al. (Cambridge 1978), pp. 179–203.

50. *It is not for the sake of marriage that I have said this* . . .: This slightly comic passage includes some reminiscences of Homer ('anticipations', in the sense that the plot of the *Iliad* is chronologically in the future). The motifs of a quarrel with Agamemnon, and the issue of keeping a woman who is in a sense his, recur in the first book of the *Iliad*; also, in book 9 the hero declares that he has no need to marry a daughter of Agamemnon, as there are plenty of possible wives for him at home. But the subsequent lines here are bizarre: Achilles appears to say that he would have been perfectly happy to go ahead with the deception for the public good, if only Agamemnon had consulted him about it! Sly characterization by Euripides here seems a better explanation than bungling by an interpolator (for the latter view see e.g. D. Kovacs, 'Towards a Reconstruction', p. 92.

51. *If the gods are intelligent*: Typically provocative Euripidean speculative comment, effectively placed as the coda to a speech and scene.

52. *Hymenaeus*: A deity presiding over and symbolizing marriage; wedding-songs frequently invoke him, and his name itself can refer to such a song. The wedding of Peleus and Thetis was famous in mythology as an occasion in which the whole company of the gods attended the marital feast and brought gifts for the distinguished couple. Pindar, in *Pythian Odes* 3.85ff., treats the wedding feasts of Cadmus and Peleus as moments of supreme human felicity. But the happiness of this festive occasion is flawed in several ways: Peleus and Thetis were subsequently to part (already they live apart in the *Iliad*, and Achilles anticipates a wretched old age for his father); their only son Achilles is to die young; and the celebration was marred by the unexpected appearance of Eris (Discord), who cast a golden apple into their midst and declared that it belonged to the most beautiful one present: this led to the dispute among the goddesses which the Judgement of Paris was meant to solve (see 71 and 573 and notes 4 and 31 above).

53. *Ganymede*: A beautiful Trojan prince abducted by Zeus to serve as his lover and also to act as cupbearer at the feast of the gods. His presence at the wedding-feast of Peleus and Thetis is not a stock detail, but serves as a contrast with Iphigenia in the epode of this song. Whereas Ganymede is favoured by the gods, Iphigenia seems destined to die at their command; but the audience may be meant to recall that she too in some versions is translated to divinity.

54. *shall be furnished with a suit of armour for his body* . . .: Cheiron foresees the events of the *Iliad*, in which divine armour is forged by Hephaestus and brought to Achilles by Thetis: see *Iliad* 18.368–617, 19.1–22.

55. *The lustral water* . . . *dark blood for Artemis*: The religious rituals in preparation for a sacrifice are described: Agamemnon mentions heifers as victims, but has of course another victim in mind. For extended ancient descriptions of sacrificial ritual see Homer, *Odyssey* 3.404–63, Euripides, *Electra* 791–839; for a modern summary, W. Burkert, *Greek Religion*, pp. 55–9.

56. *let me make this my first charge against you . . .*: The quasi-legal language is a regular feature of an *agon*-scene (though this scene does not develop into a full *agon*). Clytemnestra's denunciation of Agamemnon's past misdemeanours recalls the Athenian orators' practice of recapitulating their opponents' careers. In Euripides, compare esp. the speech of Electra addressing the dead Aegisthus (*Electra* 907ff.). The present speech includes some mythical novelties: Clytemnestra's previous marriage and Agamemnon's murder of her child are surely Euripidean inventions. Tantalus must be a different figure from the ancestor of Agamemnon and Menelaus.

57. *Come, if you go to war . . .*: This ingenious passage exploits the audience's knowledge of the mythical 'future', in which Clytemnestra avenges Iphigenia by killing Agamemnon on his return from Troy (for this motive see Pindar, *Pythian Odes* 11.22ff.; Aeschylus, *Agamemnon* 1412–19). Other motives are ignored. The same effect is achieved in a later passage (1454–5).

58. *and no one else the killer . . . to her home*: The text is doubtful here. It is possible that a line has been lost, and we translate on that assumption, attempting to fill the gap with a plausible line of thought.

59. *If I had the eloquence of Orpheus . . .*: Iphigenia's plea was notoriously contrasted with her later speech by Aristotle (*Poetics* 15); we can be confident that both these scenes were already there in his text. On the interpretation of her change of attitude see note 65 below.

Orpheus was the archetypal poet, a mythical singer who was capable of beguiling wild beasts and even of attracting natural objects such as rocks and trees.

On the formal aspects of this scene (what appeared to begin as an *agon* modulates into a supplication-sequence) see M. Lloyd, *The Agon in Euripides* (Oxford, 1992), p. 9

60. *It is a terrible thing . . . and terrible if I do not*: For Agamemnon's statement of his dilemma cf. Aeschylus *Agamemnon* 206ff. (a chorus quoting the king's actual words); but the role of the threatening army here is a Euripidean innovation.

61. *Ah, ah, snow-clad glen of Phrygia*: Iphigenia launches on an extended monody, the first example of this favourite Euripidean form in the play. Like Electra's lament in *Orestes* 982ff., the song is astrophic, lacking stanza form (the same aplies to the shorter song which precedes her final exit, 1475ff.). For a sensitive analysis see T. C. W. Stinton, *Collected Papers*, pp. 40–44.

62. *where Priam once cast . . . city of the Phrygians*: On the exposure of Paris as an infant see note 31. Mount Ida was where he was abandoned but grew up as a shepherd. His double name was thought to derive from his foster-parents having given him a different name: usually Alexander is the name bestowed by Priam and Hecabe, Paris the name he bears among the herdsmen. The following passage reverts to the theme of the Judgement (cf. note 4 above).

63. *Would that he had never been raised as a herdsman among cattle*: Cf. 1319: 'I wish that Aulis had never . . .' For 'counterfactual' prayers cf. *Medea* 1ff.

64. *O Mother, my Mother . . .*: Formal features of this scene (effaced in a prose version) demand some attention. In 1338–401 we have the rapid, excited trochaic tetrameters again; from Achilles' entrance at 1345 there is constant use of *antilabe* (division of line between speakers), with lines divided between Achilles and Clytemnestra until 1368, where Iphigenia breaks silence, interrupting their dialogue in mid-line, with her crucial speech. At the end of the speech the normal iambic trimeters resume with the chorus's comment (1402).

65. *Mother, you must hear what I have to say*: Iphigenia's speech is the crux of the play (see also pp. 173–4). In some sense the audience 'knows' that it is coming: she must be sacrificed if the war of Troy is to take place, and no Greek poet, not even Euripides, would be capable of revising the myths to that extent. In voluntarily accepting the necessity of self-sacrifice she resembles Heracles' daughter in the *Children of Heracles* and Menoeceus in the *Phoenician Women* (see note 49 to that play above); similar also is the scene in the fragmentary *Erechtheus* in which a mother offers up her daughter to save Athens (fragment 360: C. Collard et al., *Euripides: the Fragmentary Plays* i (Warminster 1995), pp. 148–94, at pp. 158ff.). There are two problems here: the characterization of Iphigenia and the nature of the cause for which she is to die. Aristotle in the *Poetics* regards consistency as one of the qualities needed in a dramatic character: 'For even if the person being imitated is of an inconsistent sort and that kind of character has been posited, still he should be consistently inconsistent. An example . . . of inconsistency is the *Iphigenia at Aulis*, for the girl who makes the speech of supplication bears no resemblance to the later one' (15.1454a26ff.). As we have seen, however, change of mind is thematic in this play, and even if Iphigenia's new mood is not expected (arguably it would be, given the conventional pattern of this plot: Menoeceus too at first seems reluctant, and so was the mother in the *Erechtheus*), it is not inexplicable: after at first naturally recoiling from the prospect of death, she in the end rises to the occasion and accepts her heroic duty in a great cause.

But is the cause in fact so great? We may accept that most Athenians would feel that Greek interests should be preferred to barbarians' (Persia's involvement in the latter part of the Peloponnesian war is hardly irrelevant), and that the language of panhellenic unity might strike a chord in some of those who sympathized with the sentiments expressed by Lysistrata a few years earlier in

Aristophanes (*Lysistrata* 1123–56, esp. 1128–34): talk of alliance among Greeks, aggression towards 'barbarians' played a significant part in the rhetoric of the fifth century BC (Thucydides 4.20.4, 5.29.3, Xenophon, *Hellenica* 1.6.7, and later 6.5.33ff.). Gorgias in an oration at the Olympic games (probably of 408 BC) had called for 'unanimity' among the warring Greeks; Lysias echoed these sentiments in 388 BC. But in Euripides' drama the Greeks are not resolving on unity but bent on retribution; they are in the grip of a heaven-sent affliction (411), a god-inspired passion (807, cf. 1264). The panhellenic enterprise of the Trojan war has been shown in such a poor light earlier in the play (Agamemnon's careerism, Menelaus' lustfulness), and the potential danger of further foreign wife-stealing seems so implausible that the speech must, I believe, be read as noble but deluded. If Iphigenia had to die, it should have been for a better cause.

For a valuable statement of the contrary position, see B. M. W. Knox, *Word and Action*, pp. 343–54, esp. pp. 348–9. On ideas of panhellenism see further F. W. Walbank, 'The Problem of Greek Nationality', *Phoenix* 5 (1981), pp. 31–60 = *Selected Papers* (Cambridge 1985), pp. 1–19; also K. J. Dover, *Greek Popular Morality* (Oxford 1974), pp. 83–5, 279ff.; E. Hall, *Inventing the Barbarian: Greek Self-definition through Tragedy* (Oxford 1989), pp. 160–5, 190–200.

66. *You bore me to be the child of all Greeks, not yours alone*: This line is especially close to the patriotic sentiments of Euripides' *Erechtheus* F 360 (where it is the mother who declares herself ready to surrender her daughter for sacrifice). The difference in situation is important, however: there the girl dies to save Athens. In Euripides' own *Electra* Clytemnestra explicitly contrasts the hypothetical need for a child to die for the sake of the city with the actual situation facing Agamemnon (1020–29, a passage often neglected in discussion of the *Iphigenia at Aulis*).

67. *One man . . . ten thousand women*: The difficulties of interpreting this speech are increased by the fact that most modern audiences will rebel against such sentiments as this one and the statement of the Greeks' right to rule over barbarians (see next note). We naturally prefer to read such passages in an ironic sense, as overstated or absurd. Before moving too swiftly to an ironic reading we should bear in mind how many people might have found such statements perfectly reasonable even a century ago. However, it is perhaps possible to draw a distinction between the views of Iphigenia (young, enthusiastic, idealistic) and those of Euripides. The playwright's own opinions are of course irrecoverable, but we can at least note that many women and some foreigners are painted in positive or at least sympathetic lights in his plays (e.g. E. Hall, *Inventing the Barbarian*, ch. 5; also her essay in P. Easterling (ed.), *The Cambridge Companion to Greek Tragedy*, pp. 118–24).

68. *It is natural that Greeks rule barbarians, Mother, not barbarians Greeks*: Cf. Aristotle, *Politics* 1.2.1252b, who quotes this line. Aristotle discusses the whole topic in *Politics* 1.2–7, 3.14, and is an important source for educated Greek opinion. For a helpful account drawing on his work and other sources, see P. Cartledge, *The Greeks* (Oxford 1993), ch. 3 on Greeks versus barbarians (also ch. 6, on the related topic of 'free versus slave').

69. *Ah, noble spirit*: Achilles' admiring words are followed by a restatement of his willingness to help her if she (again!) changes her mind. There is a puzzling clash between Achilles' statement of his intentions and what he actually does: at 1568ff. we see him actually assisting in the sacrificial ritual. That later passage, however, is almost certainly a spurious addition.

70. *Do not hate my father . . .*: As in 1171ff., the words of the characters clearly foreshadow Clytemnestra's revenge and Agamemnon's death ten years hence.

71. *sing . . . the paean to Artemis*: The paean is a form of hymn, particularly associated with Apollo but sometimes with other gods: as his sister, Artemis is suited to receive such a tribute. But the paean usually has positive associations (or at least expresses a hope that misfortune will be averted); in this context it must be a distorted version, replacing lamentation. On all aspects of the paean see Ian Rutherford, *Pindar's Paeans* (Oxford and New York 2002), part I, esp. pp. 108–26 on the tragic paean (p. 115 on this passage).

72. *Hail her . . .*: The extensive echoes of Iphigenia's song in this choral passage make it probable that lines 1510–31 are a later pastiche composed in imitation of 1475ff.

73. *a fame that will never die*: Even if the preceding section is genuine, the remaining part of the play is generally regarded as spurious. It is not clear whether Euripides himself composed a conclusion, or whether it followed or would have followed the same lines (see pp. 174–5). Some parts of the existing ending display such linguistic and metrical weaknesses that they must have been composed at a very late date (Byzantine times?). See further M. L. West, 'Tragica V', *Bulletin of the Institute of Classical Studies* 28 (1981), pp. 61–78, esp. pp. 73–6, who sets out the faulty details (pp. 74–5) and argues that 1546–77 are a passable imitation of Euripides, based on the description of Polyxena's sacrifice in *Hecabe* 521–64, while 1578–1629 are inadequate in so many ways that they must have been composed at some point between the fourth and seventh centuries AD. The motive for the addition of this material may well have been that the play came at the end of a codex in which the final pages were lost or damaged.

74. *unless my memory stumbles . . . tongue in the telling*: The messenger's uncertainty can be paralleled in other dramas: see I. J. F. de Jong, *Narrative in Drama:*

the Art of the Euripidean Messenger-speech (*Mnemosyne* Suppl. 116, Leiden 1991), pp. 9–14 on limitations on the messenger's knowledge or understanding.

75. *spinner of your shining beams by kindly night*: Artemis is here treated as a moon goddess. D. Kovacs, 'Towards a Reconstruction', p. 98 n. 73 regards this as a further sign of the late date of this section.

76. *Bitter anguish was filling my heart*: For the messenger's personal emotion see I. J. F. de Jong, *Narrative in Drama*, pp. 106–16.

77. *a deer was lying on the ground*: The substitution of a deer for the human victim is a traditional part of the legend: it figures already in the epic *Cypria* and in Hesiod fragment 23. On the similarity to the tale of Abraham and Isaac see A. Henrichs, in *Le Sacrifice dans l'antiquité*, Fondation Hardt Entretiens 27 (Vandoeuvres-Geneva 1981), pp. 195–242. The Greek version is more sombre, as the human disappears anyway: although Calchas and the messenger may declare that she has joined the gods, Clytemnestra does not seem convinced. There will be no doubt, however, that Agamemnon's behaviour has left lasting resentment that will bear bitter fruit on his eventual return.

As explained above, this is not the authentic Euripidean ending. It is likely that the original finished with a *deus ex machina* appearance by Artemis, from which a few lines are quoted by the late author Aelian (*On the nature of animals* 7.39, printed as fragment i on p. 422 of Diggle's Oxford text). The quoted words are: 'I shall place a horned deer in the Greeks' own hands; sacrificing it they will boast that they are sacrificing your daughter.' The speech must have been addressed to Clytemnestra.

The authenticity of the fragment has been questioned, but on no very solid grounds. The argument of D. Kovacs ('Towards a Reconstruction', p. 98) that in Euripides' play Iphigenia did truly die at the altar is not persuasive.

78. *My child . . .*: Lines 1615–20 are a poor effort at anapaests, lines 1627–9 (the closing choral tag) an 'unconvincing snatch of "lyric"' (M. L. West, 'Tragica V'; his article gives more detail).

79. *new-born calf of ours*: This refers to the infant Orestes.

RHESUS

1. CHORUS: The text of the play begins with the entry of the chorus. This is not unparalleled in tragedy (especially in the early period), but it is unusual in Euripides (to judge from the surviving works) and unlikely in an imitator of his style. Ancient scholars knew of more than one prologue in iambic trimeters which they associated with this play. It is at least possible that an authentic prologue has been lost (as argued by W. Ritchie, *The Authenticity* *of the Rhesus of Euripides* (Cambridge 1964), pp. 104–13 (henceforth cited as 'Ritchie')).

2. *the fearful whip of Pan*: Sudden alarm and unexplained excitement were sometimes associated with divine intervention and particularly that of Pan (hence 'panic'). Cf. *Medea* 1171–3. Pan is in fact Cronos' great-grandson (being son of Hermes, son of Zeus, son of Cronos).

3. *The Greek army has been kindling watchfires*: In Homer it is the Trojans who kindle fires on the plain and cause dismay among the Greeks.

4. *including Dolon*: It is not certain how many people come on with Aeneas, and whether Dolon is among them, but this seems a plausible reconstruction. It would be unusual in tragedy for a named character to enter as part of an anonymous group (here a company of soldiers) and only later to emerge as an individual; but there are so many unique features to this play that we can hardly rule it out. The alternative is to have him appear from the wings at Hector's call for volunteers. See Ritchie, pp. 113–15.

5. AENEAS: Aeneas, most famous in later times for his role in the Roman foundation-legends, is already a figure of considerable stature in the *Iliad*. There he is a reliable fighter but not up to Hector's standard. In this scene he acts as a foil to Hector: his prudent counsel balances Hector's rash optimism. The poet is imitating the scenes in the *Iliad* in which the more pessimistic Polydamas acts as 'wise adviser', urging caution on Hector (see especially *Iliad* 18.243–313). See Ritchie, pp. 66ff.

6. *son of Peleus*: This of course means Achilles, the most dangerous fighter on the Greek side, who will eventually kill Hector. According to the plot of the *Iliad* he has withdrawn from the battle at this stage, furious with the treatment he has received from Agamemnon. This is mentioned later in the play (491–5) but ignored here. Perhaps the audience is meant to recall Achilles' declaration in Homer that he will resume fighting only when the fire reaches his own ships (9.650–5).

7. *the son of Oileus*: The lesser Ajax, one of the Greek warriors of the second rank. It is not clear why Hector mentions him as opposed to any other leader. Indeed, the previous exchange might have been thought to have disposed of this topic. Perhaps 175–6 should be deleted.

8. *your desire for these horses matches my own*: In the *Iliad* Dolon makes the same request, which is overconfident in two ways: he assumes that he will survive the expedition, and that the Trojans will win the war. Both hopes are misguided. The horses of Achilles figure several times in Homer, in memorable scenes (especially *Iliad* 17.426–56, 19.392–424). The idea that Hector himself covets this prize is the dramatist's invention: Hector's willingness to forgo it in the public interest shows his nobility.

9. *Why, what form of dress will you have other than this?*: In Homer Dolon puts on a wolf-skin cloak; here the disguise is taken further, as he envisages creeping around the Greek camp disguised as a wolf. The notion of a full wolf-costume is earlier than Euripides, as can be seen from an Attic red-figure vase-painting now in the Louvre (*Lexicon Iconographicum Mythologiae Classicae* 3.660ff., plates vol. p. 525, no. 2: early fifth century). For a complex but suggestive argument that the wolf-disguise is a relic of primeval magical rituals whereby confraternities don animal disguises, perhaps as a form of initiation, see L. Gernet, *The Anthropology of Ancient Greece* (Eng. tr. Baltimore and London 1981), pp. 125–39, 'Dolon the Wolf' (originally published 1936).

10. *Hermes, master of cheats*: Hermes is notoriously a trickster: already in his infancy he stole Apollo's cattle (see the account in the *Homeric Hymn to Hermes*). He is thus a suitable patron for those undertaking deception. The name 'Dolon' means 'trick' or 'guile'.

11. *who built the ancient walls of Troy*: Apollo and Poseidon built the walls of Troy for King Laomedon, though he then defrauded them of their reward (*Iliad* 21.436–57).

12. *the ship of state*: The image is used in early lyric poetry (notably by Alcaeus, e.g. fragment 326) and is frequent in tragedy: it is extensively deployed in Aeschylus' *Seven against Thebes*.

13. *where is he now, the man of Mysia*: 'Mysia' refers to the coastal region of Asia Minor lying between Phrygia to the north and Lydia to the south. The idea is that none of their neighbours should now scorn Trojan valour.

14. *speech that was not Greek*: An interesting modification of the Homeric picture, where there is no linguistic differentiation between Greeks and Trojans (at *Iliad* 2.803ff. there is a reference to the multiple languages of the Trojan allies, but this never causes any failure of communication in the poem as a whole). Cf. E. Hall, *Inventing the Barbarian: Greek Self-definition through Tragedy* (Oxford 1989), pp. 13–17, 19–55. Athens had settlements and a continuing interest in the Thracian region, so that the theatrical audience might well be conscious of the fact that there was a 'Thracian tongue'.

15. *But I have no need . . . share our toil*: This is a new element to the story, introduced as a source of antagonism between Hector and Rhesus. But the hostility is handled rather unsatisfactorily: in the present scene Hector is calmed down by the chorus-leader, and in the next the conflict between the two men evaporates as soon as Rhesus has defended himself. This is not the familiar agonistic style of Euripides.

16. *Adrasteia*: Another name for the goddess Nemesis, a deity who is thought to observe and punish overconfidence and excessive success.

17. *Strymon, who once, whirling in watery form*: In a manner frequent in Greek and Latin mythology, the river is treated as both a watery force of nature and an anthropomorphic god. Cf. e.g. *Odyssey* 11.241ff., where Poseidon 'lay in the springs of the eddying river', then engulfs the maiden Tyro in his/its waters and makes love to her.

The run-over of the sentence from strophe to antistrophe is highly unusual in tragedy, and contrary to the practice of Euripides elsewhere: in almost all cases stanzas of odes are syntactically self-contained. This is one of the strongest arguments for non-Euripidean authorship.

18. *You have come to me as Zeus the bringer of light*: This highly honorific language seems to anticipate the reverential treatment of living mortals in ruler-cult (first clearly attested for the Spartan Lysander in the late fifth century BC). Cf. 385ff. below. In the world of tragedy this hyperbolic style would probably suggest to the audience that the addressee is rising too high and likely to meet with disaster (cf. the acclamation of Heracles' triumph in Euripides' *Heracles*).

19. *a burden most welcome*: The meaning is that the opponents of Rhesus will be buried in Trojan soil.

20. *Son of the songstress mother*: In the *Iliad* allies of the Trojans sometimes find fault with Hector (5.471ff., 17.140ff.). Here the reverse is the case.

21. *Indeed you were a minor princeling*: The poet adds colourful background and introduces a debt of gratitude which Rhesus should have kept in mind: we cannot prove that the details of Hector's aid to Rhesus were novel in this play, but it seems probable. This kind of elaboration of the bare mythical record is very much in the Euripidean manner.

22. *in bottomless cups*: Greeks regarded Thracians as excessively heavy drinkers. Cf. Xenophon, *Anabasis* 7.31.21−33, Plato, *Laws* 637d.

23. *a single dawning of the sun*: The version recounted by Pindar (see Preface to this play) allowed Rhesus one day of fighting on which he swept all before him; it was on the following night that he was killed by the Greek spies. This version may be in the dramatist's mind at this point. But it also characterizes Rhesus as bold to the point of overconfidence (like Dolon, and indeed Hector himself).

24. *Then there is Odysseus, a cunning piece of craftsmanship . . .*: On the negative portrayal of Odysseus in most tragedies, see W. B. Stanford, *The Ulysses Theme* (2nd edn Oxford 1963), pp. 102ff. Obviously this account prepares for his appearance a little later in the play, which the audience familiar with *Iliad* 10 will already be anticipating.

Hector refers to the following deeds of Odysseus. (1) He sneaked into Troy and managed to steal the Palladion, a cult image of Pallas Athena, doing so because the Greeks had learned of a prophecy that Troy could not fall as long as this object remained within her walls. Diomedes was his companion in this exploit too. The episode was included in the lost early epic poem known as the *Little Iliad*. (2) On another occasion Odysseus entered Troy disguised as a beggar, on a spying mission, and left after killing many Trojans. This is mentioned in the *Odyssey* (4.242ff.). (3) For the reference to staging an ambush, compare *Odyssey* 14.468ff. (a narrative of Odysseus about a night expedition during the war).

25. *the nightingale . . . slaughtered brood*: A particularly grim and horrific myth, often referred to in poetry and dramatized by Sophocles in his lost *Tereus*. Tereus married Procne, but lusted after her sister Philomela. He cunningly trapped Philomela and raped her, then cut out her tongue to protect himself; but she wove her experience as an image in an embroidery and so revealed the truth to her sister. In revenge Procne killed and chopped up her son by Tereus, Itys, and fed him to her husband (a variant on the Thyestean feast). All three were eventually turned into birds, Procne becoming the nightingale, whose song is regarded as a perpetual lament for her son (cf. Aeschylus, *Suppliants* 60ff., and often elsewhere). The canonical narrative version is that of Ovid, *Metamorphoses* 6.426–674 (which strongly influenced Shakespeare's *Titus Andronicus*). The Latin poets tend to identify the nightingale with Philomela – oddly, since in human form she had lost her power of speech.

26. *The* CHORUS *leave the orchestra*: For the chorus to depart in mid-play is unusual but not unparalleled: it occurs also in Aeschylus' *Eumenides*, Sophocles' *Ajax* and Euripides' *Alcestis* and *Helen*. For discussion see O. Taplin, *The Stagecraft of Aeschylus* (Oxford 1977), pp. 375–81, 384–7.

27. ODYSSEUS *and* DIOMEDES *enter*: Obviously the chorus go out along one exit from the theatrical space, the two Greeks enter by another. It appears from 591–3 that they have spoils from Dolon with them, probably including the wolf-skin (but it is unlikely that Odysseus is actually wearing it, as Ritchie suggests). The characterization of the Greeks as hyper-cautious and timid until egged on by Athena provides a contrast not only with their efficient energy in the *Iliad* but also with the overconfidence of the Trojans and Rhesus.

28. *The goddess* ATHENA *suddenly speaks . . . stage-building*: On how scenes of this kind were staged, see D. J. Mastronarde, 'Actors on High: the Skene-Roof, the Crane and the Gods in Attic Drama', *Classical Antiquity* 9 (1990), pp. 247–94. The appearance of a deity in mid-play is unusual, though Euripides' *Heracles* offers a parallel (Madness and Iris), and Sophocles' *Niobe* seems to have involved a mid-play epiphany of Apollo and Artemis. The present scene has a number of oddities, however: it seems that the humans can only hear Athena, not see her (because it is night?). It is sometimes said that this is also the case in the prologue to Sophocles' *Ajax*, but this is not a plausible interpretation of that scene. Furthermore, she later assumes the role (and voice?) of Aphrodite in order to deceive Paris (a superfluous sequence, since Paris has no other part to play in the story). In the *Iliad* Dolon, not Athena, told the Greek spies about Rhesus.

29. *If he lives through this night to see tomorrow*: The ancient scholia (commentaries) on Homer report a version according to which Rhesus would be invincible once he spent a night in Troy and once his horses had fed on the Trojan plain and drunk of the rivers of Troy. The story is alluded to by Virgil (*Aeneid* 1.472–3). B. Fenik, *Iliad 10 and the Rhesus: the Myth* (Brussels 1964), has argued that this version was earlier than the *Rhesus* and that these lines reveal knowledge of it. Alternatively they have been seen as giving rise to the story (so Ritchie, p. 64).

30. *Alexandros*: Alexandros is another name for Paris, who abducted Helen and caused the war. Athena refers below to her hatred of Paris: this is because he adjudicated in the beauty-contest among the three goddesses, the 'Judgement of Paris', and chose Aphrodite ('the Cyprian'): see 647–8, and notes 31 and 62 to *Iphigenia at Aulis*. Hence Paris is befriended by Aphrodite, and will naturally trust a voice he supposes to be hers. This gives the poet the opportunity to introduce ironic ambiguities (see 665–7).

31. *it is not ordained . . . die at your hands*: Paris will eventually be killed by Philoctetes, using the bow of Heracles.

32. *You two, whose eagerness has gone too far . . .*: The staging of this sequence is not clear. Either Odysseus (and Diomedes?) reappear on stage in time to hear Athena's words, or, more probably, they are still offstage, engaged in slaughtering Rhesus' men, and she is to be thought of as projecting a warning to them, since a god's voice can be heard from afar by supernatural means (cf. *Iphigeneia among the Taurians* 1385ff. and 1446ff.). If the latter is right, Odysseus will dash on stage as soon as Athena has withdrawn, with the chorus in hot pursuit. Whether Diomedes reappears or not is uncertain; at any rate, he says nothing. Possibly he is to be thought of as minding Rhesus' horses some distance away. The horses will surely not have been brought on stage, and they can hardly have been abandoned temporarily.

The rapid entry of the chorus in pursuit and shouting 'Pelt him, pelt him!' resembles comedy rather than tragedy: compare especially Aristophanes, *Acharnians* 204ff.

33. *Once before he came to our city*: On this episode see note 24 above.

34. *The* CHARIOTEER *of Rhesus enters, wounded*: This is a kind of messenger-scene, but unusual in concept and construction. Normally a messenger, however moved or grief-stricken by events, is not personally involved, whereas here the man who brings the news is himself among the wounded. Moreover, the charioteer sings on first entry (this is of course expressive of his grief and pain); only at 756 does he revert to trimeters. Second, although he gives an accurate account, as far as he is able, of what has happened, the charioteer places a completely false interpretation on the events: he supposes that Rhesus has been the victim of Hector's treachery. It is presumably for this reason that he does not wait for Hector to arrive before giving his report.

The narrative is an elaborated version of the scene in the *Doloneia*. See *Iliad* 10.471ff. The ominous dream that disturbs the charioteer is much more briefly referred to there, and is given to Rhesus (497ff.).

35. *for the nightmare roused me*: Cf. *Iliad* 10.514ff., where Apollo, indignant at the killings prompted by Athena, causes Rhesus' cousin Hippocoon to awaken: 'and on emerging from sleep, when he saw the deserted space where the swift horses had stood, and the men gasping amid cruel bloodshed, he groaned aloud and called out the name of his dear comrade'.

36. *surely it was then they came*: This is not the case, and seems to be an effort on the chorus's part to protect themselves by misleading or misrepresenting the facts to Hector. Choral deception of a character is paralleled e.g. in Euripides' *Helen* 1619ff., where the chorus-leader tries to pull the wool over Theoclymenus' eyes.

37. *unless some god had kept telling the killers?*: The charioteer puts this explanation forward with dismissive scorn, but the audience recognizes the unconscious description of Athena's role in the action.

38. THE MUSE *appears* ... RHESUS: A *deus ex machina* ends the majority of Euripides' authentic plays. Often the god's intervention is necessary because the action has become so tangled or the conflicts so acute that they cannot be resolved on the human plane: a god is needed to 'cut the knot'. This is not the case here: all that the Muse does is make clear that the charioteer's accusations were unjustified (and he is no longer present to learn this). Much more important is the pathetic impact of the divine parent mourning her dead son. The miniature monody from a divinity is unparalleled, though it may have had precedent in some earlier tragic representation of Thetis, Achilles' mother (Aeschylus, fragment 350, preserves part of a spoken lament by Thetis). Her lamentation for her son played a major part in some of the early epics and is reflected even in the *Iliad*, where Achilles still lives (see especially 18.50–64). The model of Thetis is an important influence on the portrayal of the Muse here (as 976ff. effectively acknowledge). For the presentation above the stage of mother and dead child cf. and contrast *Medea* 1317ff., where Medea plays the *deus* role.

It is noteworthy that the two divinities, the Muse and Athena, are the only female characters in the play. Athena's martial support for the Greeks and its destructive effect are contrasted with the Muse's maternal love and (below) her cultural gifts. Athena of course is a virgin goddess and has no children. This opposition is one of the most effective features of the play.

On the questions of staging see Mastronarde, 'Actors on High' (note 28); on the question which actors sing and why, see E. Hall, 'Actor's Song in Greek Tragedy', in S. Goldhill and R. Osborne (eds.), *Performance Culture and Athenian Democracy* (Cambridge 1999), pp. 96–122 at 97, 108, 111.

39. *one of the sisterhood of Muses*: The Homeric commentator who summarizes Pindar's poem (see Preface to this play) says that Rhesus' mother was the Muse Euterpe; in this play she is unnamed.

40. *the finest son a mother ever bore*: Here too the poet pays tribute to the *Iliad*'s presentation of Thetis (at 18.54 she describes herself in closely similar language as 'unhappy mother of the finest of sons').

41. *her too, I curse, who left her home in Greece and sailed here*: The Muse refers to Helen. Condemnation of Helen's selfish infidelity is a cliché of tragedy, e.g. Aeschylus, *Agamemnon* 62, 225, 448, 681ff., Euripides *Andromache* 590–69, *Iphigenia among the Taurians* 356, 438ff., or *Orestes* 126ff. and often later in that play. The more compassionate note which we find in Homer is rare in later literature (though Sappho, fragment 16, is a significant exception).

42. *Son of Philammon*: The son of Philammon is Thamyris, a Thracian poet who was foolish enough to challenge the Muses to a singing contest. Such ambitious challenges by mortals inevitably end in disaster: the Muses not only emerged as victors but punished him with blindness. The story is briefly related in the *Iliad* (2.594–600); Homer does not mention Philammon, and we may assume that other poets had developed the theme. For Strymon's 'potent embrace' see 348–54.

43. *since I knew your fate*: Again the parallel with Thetis and Achilles is evident (see e.g. *Iliad* 1.414ff., 18.436ff.).

44. *And yet we sister Muses . . . utmost kindness*: Indirect compliments to Athens are often introduced in tragedy (e.g. in the *Trojan Women* the captives hope that they will be sent in slavery to Athens, not Sparta!). This is a particularly ingenious example. For Athens as a land favoured by the Muses see *Medea* 824ff. Orpheus, the mythical singer, was the son of either Apollo or Oeagrus and one of the Muses (Calliope according to Apollonius); hence he is Rhesus' cousin. As one who had journeyed to the underworld and returned, Orpheus was thought to have special knowledge of life and death, and so he was thought to have founded 'mysteries' which were often associated with those of Dionysus and Demeter. For other references see Aristophanes, *Frogs* 1032, Plato, *Republic* 2.365–6. Musaeus, another early culture-hero, has a name that suggests a connection with the Muses, and is often paired with Orpheus: Aristophanes in the same passage of *Frogs* describes him as bringing medical cures and oracles

to mankind. He was said to have been the father of Eumolpus, the first priest
of the mysteries of Demeter and Persephone at Eleusis. Thus Athens is glorified
firstly as a city of culture, but still more as a centre of religion. On mystery-
religions see W. Burkert, *Greek Religion* (Eng. tr. Oxford 1985), pp. 296–301,
and the same author's *Ancient Mystery Cults* (Oxford 1987).

45. *this much shall I ask of the maid who dwells below*: She means Persephone,
consort of Hades and queen of the dead. There was a general inhibition about
naming her: hence 'the maid'.

46. *she owes it to me to show that she honours the family of Orpheus*: Presumably
because Orpheus is thought to have instructed mankind in the mysteries of
Demeter and Persephone.

47. *Yet, hidden in a cavern of the silver-veined earth shall he lie . . .*: A remarkable
passage. As in many of the authentic plays, the god proclaims a cult for which
the events of the drama provide an aetiology (narrative of origin). The Muse
seems to be predicting that Rhesus will attain 'heroic' status, less than divine
but receiving worship and possessing supernatural powers, like Oedipus at the
end of the *Oedipus at Colonus*. On hero-cult see further W. Burkert, *Greek
Religion*, pp. 199–208. Mount Pangaeum was a site of Bacchic worship (Hero-
dotus 7.111–12), but there is no other reference to Rhesus being honoured
there alongside Dionysus. The only other notable reference to Rhesus, in the
much later author Polyaenus, refers to the Athenian general Hagnon bringing
his bones from Troy to Amphipolis in 437/6 BC and burying them near the
Strymon, an act which may imply he regarded the bones as having some
symbolic or talismanic power (compare the recovery by the Spartans of the
bones of Orestes, Herodotus 1.67–8). The Strymon runs down from Mount
Pangaeum past Amphipolis (cf. 916–22). The poet may have modified a
traditional aetiology; he is most unlikely to have invented it.

48. *O what sorrows accompany child-bearing*: Another tragic commonplace. Cf.
Medea 1090ff.

49. *forcing my way through the trench . . . I will fire their ships*: After the wholly
unhomeric scene with the Muse, the plot-line of the *Iliad* is resumed: Hector
and the Trojans breach the Greeks' defensive trench and wall in book 12, and
are fighting by the ships at the end of book 15; the first of the ships is set on
fire at 16.112ff. It is at that point that Patroclus, dressed in Achilles' armour,
enters the battle and turns the tide.

50. *may grant victory*: There is presumably an ambiguity here: within the play
the soldiers hope for military success; in the world of the theatre, the chorus
hope for success in the dramatic contest. This kind of double meaning is more
effective than the spurious endings of *Phoenician Women* and *Orestes*, where the
dramatic illusion is broken completely.

BIBLIOGRAPHY

Texts

The standard Greek text, which forms the basis for this translation, is the new Oxford Classical Text edited by J. Diggle (3 volumes, 1981–94); this supersedes the much-used edition by G. Murray in the same series. The edition is arranged chronologically. All the plays translated in the present volume are in volume 3 of this text.

Those wishing to consult the plays in Greek will find the best guidance in the following annotated editions:

Phoenician Women: D. J. Mastronarde (Cambridge 1994): authoritative, detailed, indispensable. See also the edition by E. Craik (Warminster 1988), including translation: more accessible than Mastronarde, but less reliable.

Orestes: C. W. Willink (Oxford 1986: detailed); M. L. West (Warminster 1987: includes translation).

Bacchae: E. R. Dodds (2nd edn Oxford 1960: a classic work); R. Seaford Warminster 1996: includes translation).

Iphigenia at Aulis: no modern commentary in English: one is imminent from C. Collard. In German note W. Stockert (Vienna 1992); in Italian F. Turato (Venice 2001).

Rhesus: no modern commentary in English (the old school edition by W. H. Porter (Cambridge 1916) is better than nothing). M. Fantuzzi is preparing a commentary for Cambridge.

Other translations

The Loeb Classical Library, which publishes bilingual editions of most classical authors, has recently published a complete edition of Euripides by David Kovacs in six volumes (1994–2002), arranged chronologically: this edition replaces an older and wholly unsatisfactory edition by A. S. Way. Those who need to consider the detail of the Greek text should note that Kovacs presents his own text, which often differs from Diggle's. Kovacs explains his textual choices in the companion volumes *Euripidea, Euripidea Altera* and *Euripidea Tertia*.

Other translations available include those by various hands in the series edited by D. Grene and R. Lattimore, *The Complete Greek Tragedies* (Chicago 1941–58). Otherwise, complete versions of Euripides are hard to find, though the major plays are often translated individually or in smaller selections. The series *Greek Tragedy in New Translations* published by Oxford University Press (USA) now covers most of the canon, each volume involving collaboration between a poet and a scholar. Other notable individual versions include G. S. Kirk, *The Bacchae by Euripides* (Englewood Cliffs and Bristol 1970;) K. Cavander, *Iphigeneia at Aulis* (Englewood Cliffs 1973).

A parallel enterprise to our own is the series published by Oxford University Press, with translations (prose) by James Morwood and introductions by Edith Hall. These are grouped thematically rather than chronologically; the emphasis in the introductions is on reception and performance history.

General works on Greek tragedy

Goldhill, S., *Reading Greek Tragedy* (Cambridge 1986).

Hall, E., *Inventing the Barbarian: Greek Self-definition through Tragedy* (Oxford 1989).

Heath, M., *The Poetics of Greek Tragedy* (London 1987).

Jones, J., *On Aristotle and Greek Tragedy* (London 1962).

Knox, B. M. W., *Word and Action: Essays on the Ancient Theater* (Baltimore 1979).

Lesky, A., *Greek Tragedy* (Eng. tr. London 1954).

Taplin, O., *The Stagecraft of Aeschylus* (Oxford 1977): despite the title, relevant to all the tragedians.

Taplin, O., *Greek Tragedy in Action* (London 1978).

Vernant, J.-P. and Vidal-Naquet, P., *Myth and Tragedy in Ancient Greece* (New York 1988): amalgamates two earlier collections of essays.

Vickers, B., *Towards Greek Tragedy* (London 1973).

Easterling, P. E. and Knox, B. M. W. (eds.), *The Cambridge History of Classical Literature*, vol. 1 (Cambridge 1985), includes expert essays on the Greek theatre and on each of the three tragedians (Knox covers Euripides); these chapters, together with those on satyric drama and comedy, are reissued in paperback as *Greek Drama*, ed. Easterling and Knox (Cambridge 1989).

Useful collections of work include:

Cropp, M., Lee, K. and Sansone, D. (eds.), *Euripides and Tragic Theatre in the Late Fifth Century* (Illinois 2000) (= *Illinois Classical Studies*, vols. 24–5).

Easterling, P. E. (ed.), *The Cambridge Companion to Greek Tragedy* (Cambridge 1997).

McAuslan, I. and Walcot, P. (eds.), *Greek Tragedy* (*Greece and Rome Studies* 2, Oxford 1993).

Mossman, J. (ed.), *Euripides* (Oxford Readings in Classical Studies) (Oxford 2003).

Pelling, C. B. R. (ed.), *Greek Tragedy and the Historian* (Oxford 1997).

Segal, E. (ed.), *Oxford Readings in Greek Tragedy* (Oxford 1983).

Silk, M. (ed.), *Tragedy and the Tragic* (Oxford 1996).

Sommerstein, A., Halliwell, S., Henderson, J. and Zimmermann, B. (eds.), *Tragedy, Comedy and the Polis* (Bari 1993).

The Greek theatre

Csapo, E. and Slater, W. J., *The Context of Ancient Drama* (Michigan 1995): this excellent source-book translates and discusses many ancient texts relevant to theatrical conditions in the Greek and Roman world.

Easterling, P. E. and Hall, E. (eds.), *Greek and Roman Actors: Aspects of an Ancient Profession* (Cambridge 2002).

Green, J. R., *Theatre in Ancient Greek Society* (London 1994).

Green, R. and Handley, E., *Images of the Greek Theatre* (London 1995).

Pickard-Cambridge, A. W., *The Dramatic Festivals of Athens* (2nd edn revised by J. Gould and D. M. Lewis, Oxford 1968; reissued 1988): an outstanding work, but requires considerable knowledge of Greek.

Simon, E., *The Ancient Theatre* (Eng. tr. London and New York 1982).

Historical and cultural background

Andrewes, A., *Greek Society* (London 1971); originally published as *The Greeks* (London 1967).

Davies, J. K., *Democracy and Classical Greece* (London 1978; revised and expanded 1993).

Hornblower, S., *The Greek World 479–323 BC* (3rd edn London 2002).
Osborne, R. (ed.), *Classical Greece* (Oxford 2000).

Religion and thought

Bremmer, J. N., *Greek Religion* (*Greece and Rome New Surveys* 24, Oxford 1994).
Burkert, W., *Greek Religion* (Eng. tr. Oxford 1985).
Dodds, E. R., *The Greeks and the Irrational* (Berkeley 1951).
Mikalson, J., *Athenian Popular Religion* (Chapel Hill 1983).
Mikalson, J., *Honor thy Gods: Popular Religion in Greek Tragedy* (Chapel Hill and London 1991): helpful, but perhaps emphasizes too strongly the gap between literature and the realities of cult and worship.
Parker, R. *Miasma. Pollution and Purification in Early Greek Religion* (Oxford 1983).
Parker, R., 'Gods Cruel and Kind: Tragic and Civic Religion', in C. B. R. Pelling (ed.), *Greek Tragedy and the Historian* (see above), pp. 143–60.
Parker, R., *Polytheism and Society at Athens* (Oxford forthcoming 2005), ch. 7, 'Religion in the Theatre'.
Sourvinou-Inwood, C., *Tragedy and Athenian Religion* (Lanham and Oxford 2003): advanced and specialized, but important.

Studies of Euripides in general

Collard, C., *Euripides* (*Greece and Rome New Surveys* 14, Oxford 1981): an excellent short account with many examples and full bibliographical guidance.
Conacher, D. J., *Euripidean Drama: Myth, Theme and Structure* (Toronto and London 1967).
Grube, G. M. A., *The Drama of Euripides* (2nd edn London 1961): sensible, but dated in approach.
Mastronarde, D. J., *Euripides and his Art* (forthcoming): a general study.
Matthiessen, K., *Die Tragoedien des Euripides* (Wiesbaden 2002).
Michelini, A. N., *Euripides and the Tragic Tradition* (Madison and London 1987): valuable chapters on the history of interpretation.
Murray, G., *Euripides and his Age* (London 1913): influential, but now very dated.

Discussions of plays in this volume

PHOENICIAN WOMEN

Arthur, M. B., 'The Curse of Civilisation: the Choral Odes of the *Phoenissae*', *Harvard Studies in Classical Philology* 81 (1977), pp. 163–85.

Foley, H., *Ritual Irony: Poetry and Sacrifice in Euripides* (Ithaca 1985), ch. 3.

Mastronarde, D. J., 'The Optimistic Rationalist in Euripides', in *Greek Tragedy and its Legacy* (Festschrift D. J. Conacher), ed. M. Cropp, E. Fantham, S. E. Scully (Calgary 1986), pp. 201–11.

Mueller-Goldingen, C., *Untersuchungen zu den Phönissen des Euripides* (Stuttgart 1985).

Podlecki, A. J., 'Some Themes in Euripides' *Phoenissae*', *Phoenix* 21 (1967), pp. 20–26.

Rawson, E., 'Family and Fatherland in Euripides' *Phoenissae*', *Greek Roman and Byzantine Studies* 11 (1970), pp. 109–27.

ORESTES

Burkert, W., 'Die Absurdität der Gewalt und das Ende der Tragödie: Euripides' *Orestes*', *Antike und Abendland* 20 (1974), pp. 97–109.

Hall, E., 'Political and Cosmic Turbulence in Euripides' *Orestes*', in A. Sommerstein et al. (eds.), *Tragedy, Comedy and the Polis* (see above), pp. 263–85.

Pelling, C. B. R., *Greek Literary Texts and the Historian* (London 1999), pp. 164–88.

Porter, D. H., *Studies in Euripides' Orestes* (*Mnemosyne* Suppl. 128, Leiden 1993).

Reinhardt, K., 'Die Sinneskrise bei Euripides', originally published 1957; Eng. tr. in J. Mossman (ed.), *Euripides* (see above), pp. 16–46.

Schein, S. L., 'Mythical Allusion and Historical Reality in Euripides' *Orestes*', *Wiener Studien* 9 (1975), pp. 49–66.

Zeitlin, F., 'The Closet of Masks: Role-playing and Myth-making in the *Orestes* of Euripides', *Ramus* 9 (1980), pp. 51–77, reprinted in J. Mossman (ed.), *Euripides* (see above), pp. 309–41.

BACCHAE

(a) Studies of the play

Arthur, M. B., 'The Choral Odes of the *Bacchae* of Euripides', *Yale Classical Studies* 22 (1972), pp. 145–79.

Burnett, A. P., 'Pentheus and Dionysus: Host and Guest', *Classical Philology* 65 (1970), pp. 15–29.

Foley, H. P., 'The Masque of Dionysus', *Transactions of the American Philological Association* 110 (1980), pp. 107–33, reprinted in J. Mossman (ed.), *Euripides* (see above).

March, J., 'Euripides' *Bacchae*: a Reconsideration in the Light of the Vase-Paintings', *Bulletin of the Institute of Classical Studies* 36 (1989), pp. 33–65.

Mills, S., *Euripides: Bacchae* (London 2005).

Oranje, H., *Euripides' Bacchae. The Play and its Audience* (Leiden 1984).

Rijksbaron, A., *Grammatical Observations on Euripides' Bacchae* (Amsterdam 1991).

Segal, C., *Dionysiac Poetics and Euripides' Bacchae* (Princeton 1982; reprint with important Afterword 1997).

Seidensticker, B. 'Comic Elements in Euripides' *Bacchae*', *American Journal of Philology* 99 (1978), pp. 303–20.

Seidensticker, B., 'Sacrificial Ritual in the *Bacchae*', in *Arktouros: Hellenic Studies Presented to Bernard M. W. Knox on the Occasion of His 65th Birthday*, ed. G. W. Bowersock and others (Berlin and New York 1979), pp. 181–96.

Winnington-Ingram, R. P., *Euripides and Dionysus* (Cambridge 1948; reprint with foreword by P. E. Easterling, Bristol 1997).

(b) Studies of Dionysiac religion and related issues

Bremmer, J. N., 'Greek Maenadism Reconsidered', *Zeitschrift für Papyrologie und Epigraphik* 55 (1984), pp. 267–86.

Carpenter, T. H. and Faraone, C. A., *Masks of Dionysus* (Cornell 1993).

Henrichs, A., 'Loss of Self, Suffering, Violence: the Modern View of Dionysus from Nietzsche to Girard', *Harvard Studies in Classical Philology* 88 (1984), pp. 205–40: perhaps the most accessible of an important series of papers on Dionysiac religion by this scholar: most of the others are listed in Segal (see *Dionysiac Poetics* above), pp. 398, 407–8.

Seaford, R., 'Dionysiac Drama and the Dionysian Mysteries', *Classical Quarterly* 31 (1981), pp. 252–75.

IPHIGENIA AT AULIS

Foley, H., *Ritual Irony: Poetry and Sacrifice in Euripides* (Ithaca, 1985), ch.2.

Knox, B., 'Euripides' *Iphigenia in Aulide* 1–163 (in that order)', *Yale Classical Studies* 22 (1972), pp. 239–61 = Knox, *Word and Action* (see above), pp. 275–94.

Knox, B., 'Review: Iphigenia at Aulis', in Knox, *Word and Action* (see above), pp. 343–54.

Kovacs, D., 'Towards a Reconstruction of *Iphigenia Aulidensis*', *Journal of Hellenic Studies* 123 (2003), pp. 77–103.

Michelakis, P., *Achilles in Greek Tragedy* (Cambridge 2002) ch. 4.

341

Michelakis, P., *Euripides: Iphigenia at Aulis* (London 2005).

Michelini, A. N., 'The Expansion of Myth in Late Euripides: *Iphigeneia at Aulis*', in Cropp et al. (eds.), *Euripides and Tragic Theatre* (see above), pp. 41–57.

Page, D. L., *Actors' Interpolations in Greek Tragedy* (Oxford 1934).

RHESUS

Burnett, A. P., '*Rhesus*: Are Smiles Allowed?', in P. Burian (ed.), *Directions in Euripidean Criticism* (Durham, N. C. 1985), pp. 13–51.

Fenik, B., *Iliad 10 and the Rhesus: the Myth* (Brussels 1964): mainly concerned with the original mythical background.

Kitto, H. D. F., 'The *Rhesus* and Related Matters', *Yale Classical Studies* 25 (1977), pp. 317–50.

Ritchie, W., *The Authenticity of the Rhesus of Euripides* (Cambridge 1964): the most detailed investigation, which argues for its being an authentic early work of the poet. (For the other side see E. Fraenkel's review-discussion of Ritchie, in *Gnomon* 37 (1965), pp. 228–41 (in German)).

Special aspects

Barlow, S. A., *The Imagery of Euripides* (London 1971).

de Jong, I. J. F., *Narrative in Drama: the Art of the Euripidean Messenger-speech* (*Mnemosyne Suppl.* 116, Leiden 1991).

Diggle, J., *Studies in the Text of Euripides* (Oxford 1982) and *Euripidea* (Oxford 1994): detailed discussions of many textual problems by the editor of the standard text.

Foley, H., *Female Acts in Greek Tragedy* (Princeton 2001).

Halleran, M. R., *Stagecraft in Euripides* (London and Sydney 1985).

Kovacs, D., *Euripidea* (*Mnemosyne Suppl.* 132, Leiden 1994): includes detailed collection and translations of ancient texts which refer to Euripides.

Kovacs, D., *Euripidea Tertia* (*Mnemosyne Suppl.* 240, Leiden 2003): includes discussion of textual problems in the plays in this volume, defending the text printed in the author's Loeb edition.

Lloyd, M., *The Agon in Euripides* (Oxford 1992).

Stinton, T. C. W., 'Euripides and the Judgement of Paris', *Journal of Hellenic Studies: Supplementary Paper* 11 (1965); reprinted in Stinton, *Collected Papers on Greek Tragedy* (Oxford 1990), pp. 17–75.

General reference works

Hornblower, S. and Spawforth, A. (eds.), *The Oxford Classical Dictionary* (3rd edn Oxford 1996): detailed and authoritative; for some users the abridged and illustrated version, *The Oxford Companion to Classical Civilisation* (1998), will be more suitable.

Howatson, M., *The Oxford Companion to Classical Literature* (Oxford 1989): useful particularly for summaries of myths.

Gantz, T. N., *Early Greek Myth: a Guide to Literary and Artistic Sources* (Baltimore 1993). This work is greatly superior to the undeservedly popular account by R. Graves, *The Greek Myths* (Penguin 1955), which is full of highly fanciful interpretations.

GLOSSARY OF MYTHOLOGICAL
AND GEOGRAPHICAL NAMES

ACHAEANS often used simply to mean 'Greeks'; more specifically, an ethnic group of the northern Peloponnese.

ACHELOUS one of the rivers of Thebes.

ACHERON one of the rivers of the Underworld. Its name signifies grief and lamentation.

ACHILLES son of the hero Peleus and the sea-nymph Thetis; greatest of the Greek heroes who fought at Troy; clad in armour forged by Hephaestus, he killed the Trojan champion Hector, but died in battle later, slain by Paris' arrow.

ACTAEON one of the royal family of Thebes; after boasting that his prowess as a hunter exceeded that of Artemis, he was torn apart by his own hounds as punishment.

ADRASTEIA another name for Nemesis, the divine personification of retribution.

ADRASTUS king of Argos; married his daughters to Tydeus and Polyneices; misguidedly undertook to assist the latter in the expedition against Thebes. He is merely mentioned in the *Phoenician Women*; he plays a more significant part in the *Suppliant Women*.

AEACUS father of Peleus and grandfather of Achilles.

AEGEAN SEA the part of the Mediterranean Sea separating Greece from Asia Minor.

AEGINA a nymph, who married Aeacus, grandfather of Achilles; the island Aegina was named after her.

AEGISTHUS son of Thyestes and lover of Clytemnestra, with whom he conspired to murder Agamemnon. Killed by Orestes.

AEGYPTUS descendant of Io, brother of Danaus. His fifty sons pursued their cousins, Danaus' fifty daughters, and insisted on marrying them despite the girls' reluctance. On the wedding night all but one of the wives assassinated their husbands. The mass murder and earlier matters of dispute were debated in an Argive court.

AENEAS a Trojan leader, already prominent in the *Iliad*, regularly represented as prudent and pious.

AENIANS a people who contributed a force to the Trojan War, under the command of their king Gouneus.

AEROPE in the genealogy used by Euripides, the wife of Atreus and mother of Agamemnon and Menelaus.

AETOLIA a large region in central Greece, north of the Gulf of Corinth.

AGAMEMNON king of Argos and Mycenae, leader of the Greek expedition against Troy. Son of Atreus, brother of Menelaus. Father of Iphigenia, Orestes and Electra (also, in some versions, of Chrysothemis). Killed by his wife Clytemnestra.

AGAUE daughter of Cadmus, mother of Pentheus, king of Thebes; under the influence of Dionysiac madness she and her sisters tear her son limb from limb.

AGENOR king of Tyre, father of Cadmus.

AJAX (the greater) son of Telamon, from Salamis; one of the major Greek heroes at Troy.

AJAX (the lesser) son of Oileus; a less significant Greek hero at Troy.

ALEXANDER or ALEXANDROS see PARIS.

ALPHEUS a river originating in Arcadia in the Peloponnese and passing by the great cult-site of Zeus at Olympia; flows into the Ionian Sea.

AMPHIARAUS one of the Seven against Thebes, and the only one who, being a prophet, foresaw the failure of the expedition and argued against it. He was forced to join it by a promise to his wife. In the end he was miraculously swallowed up by the earth.

AMPHION son of Zeus and Antiope; a marvellous singer and player of music, whose songs enchanted wild beasts and even moved the stones forming the walls of Thebes, which he ruled jointly with his twin brother Zethus.

AMYMONE one of the fifty daughters of Danaus. A spring was named after her.

ANTIGONE daughter of Oedipus and Jocasta; her most famous action, dramatized by Sophocles, was to bury her brother Polyneices despite the edict forbidding this action.

APHRODITE daughter of Zeus; goddess of love and desire.

APIDANUS a river in Thessaly, in northern Greece.

APOLLO son of Zeus and Leto, brother of Artemis; one of the most powerful and dignified of the Olympian gods. He was famous for his good looks, his prowess as an archer, his musical gifts and above all his power of prophesying the future through his oracles, of which that at Delphi was the most famous.

ARABIA as in modern times, a region bordering the extreme south-eastern Mediterranean, east of Egypt.

ARCADIA a mountainous region in the central Peloponnese.

ARES son of Zeus and Hera; god of war, usually regarded as a cruel and threatening figure.

ARES' HILL (AREOPAGUS) the location of Athens' most prestigious lawcourt, particularly concerned with homicide. From at least the time of Aeschylus, this was identified as the place where Orestes was tried for matricide.

ARETHUSA name of a spring or stream. The most famous spring of that name was in Sicily, but the name is found in other locations: an Arethusa apparently located near Chalcis in Euboea is mentioned in the *Iphigenia at Aulis*.

ARGOS city in the northern Peloponnese, often conflated in tragedy with the older site near by, Mycenae.

ARISTAEUS husband of the Theban princess Autonoe, and father of Actaeon.

ARTEMIS daughter of Zeus and Leto; sister of Apollo, and like him an archer; virgin goddess, associated with hunting and wild animals.

ASIA in Euripides a fairly vague term for the lands east of Greece, from the Hellespont as far as India. More specifically, Asia Minor, what is now mostly Turkey.

ASOPUS a river near the border between Attica and Boeotia, running south of Thebes.

ATALANTA a beautiful young woman who resisted marriage until won by Hippomenes, who defeated her in a race. Their son was the attractive Parthenopaeus, one of the Seven against Thebes.

ATHENA daughter of Zeus; virginal goddess of wisdom and patroness of Athens.

ATHENS the main settlement in Attica, in central Greece. See further General Introduction.

ATREUS former king of Argos and Mycenae, father of Agamemnon and Menelaus.

ATTICA the country around Athens and controlled by her, in central Greece.

AULIS a Greek town in Boeotia, opposite Euboea; the place where the great fleet of Greek forces assembled to set out for Troy. Because of unfavourable winds, Agamemnon was forced to sacrifice his daughter Iphigenia before they could leave there.

AUTONOE one of the daughters of Cadmus, mother of Actaeon.

AXIUS a river in Macedonia.

BACCHANT a follower (usually female) of Bacchus, inspired with irrational ecstasy, often wild and violent in action.

BACCHUS see DIONYSUS.

BACTRIA an extensive region in eastern Asia, between the River Oxus and the Hindu Kush; in classical times at least partly under the control of the Persian empire, and little known to Greeks.

BOEOTIA a state in Greece, north of Attica; Thebes was its chief city.

BROMIUS a cult-title of Dionysus, meaning 'the roaring one'.

CADMEANS the Thebans, so called because Cadmus founded Thebes and brought their race into being.

CADMUS son of Agenor from Tyre; founder of Thebes after he had slain a monstrous dragon guarding the site. He sowed the dragon's teeth, from which sprang forth warriors, the first men of Thebes.

CALCHAS the prophet and adviser of the Greek army during the Trojan war. Although sympathetically presented in Homer, he gains a more sinister reputation in later times.

CAPANEUS one of the Seven against Thebes, famous for his sacrilegious boasting, for which he was struck down by Zeus' thunderbolt.

CASSANDRA Trojan princess, daughter of Priam and Hecabe; priestess of Apollo, who attempted to seduce or rape her, but she resisted. He had given her the power of prophecy, but in anger at her rejection of him, he negated it by declaring that her predictions would never be believed.

CASTALIA a sacred spring on Mount Parnassus, near Delphi. Those who wished to consult the Delphic oracle were required to purify themselves in this spring first.

CASTOR like his brother Pollux (or Polydeuces), a son of Zeus by Leda; brother of Helen and Clytemnestra. In some stories only one of them was immortal, but they are normally paired as the Dioscuri or Heavenly Twins, elevated after death to divine status and placed among the stars (the constellation Gemini, 'the Twins'). They were thought to watch over sailors at sea.

CECROPS early mythical king of Athens, allegedly half man, half snake, and said to have been born from the earth itself.

CENTAURS mythical creatures, half horse, half man. They were ambiguous in other ways: some (particularly the wise Cheiron, tutor of Achilles) were kind and benevolent to men, while others were dangerous or potentially violent. This violent side was notoriously revealed when the Centaurs got drunk at the marriage of Pirithous and Hippodamia; a pitched battle ensued (the battle of the Lapiths and Centaurs).

CHALCIS a town on the island of Euboea.

CHEIRON a wise and virtuous Centaur, who educated a number of heroes, notably Achilles.

CHRYSOTHEMIS daughter of Agamemnon and Clytemnestra; a less important figure than her sisters Electra and Iphigenia and her brother Orestes.

CILICIA a country on the eastern part of the southern coast of Asia Minor. In Homer the Cilicians inhabit the southern Troad.

CITHAERON, MOUNT, western part of the mountain range separating northern Attica from Boeotia. Here Oedipus was exposed as an infant.

CLYTEMNESTRA wife of Agamemnon, whom she murdered on his return from Troy, partly because of his treatment of Iphigenia, her daughter. Also mother of Orestes, Electra and Chrysothemis.

COLONUS a small village-community in Attica. In Sophocles' *Oedipus at Colonus* and related texts Oedipus finds refuge from his wanderings there.

COROEBUS son of Mygdon; in the *Rhesus*, one of the sentries on watch in the Trojan camp. A Trojan ally of this name figures in Virgil's *Aeneid* as a suitor of Cassandra; possibly he figured in the early Greek epics now lost.

CORYBANTES male priests, part of the entourage of Cybele, the Great Mother Goddess.

CORYCIA the 'Corycian heights' mentioned in the *Bacchae* as a haunt of Dionysus were on the ridges of Parnassus.

CREON one of the royal family of Thebes, brother of Jocasta. After the deaths of Oedipus' sons, he assumed the kingship.

CRONUS father of Zeus and mightiest of the previous generation of immortal Titans, whom Zeus and other gods overthrew.

CURETES mythical attendants on the goddess Rhea.

CYBELE a great goddess of nature and fertility, worshipped in Phrygia and absorbed into Greek myth, where she was sometimes identified with Demeter, sometimes with Rhea. Her genealogical relation to the Olympians is left vague. A major cult-centre was at Mount Dindyma.

CYCLOPS (plural CYCLOPES) a one-eyed giant, hostile to men. The most famous Cyclops was Polyphemus in Homer's *Odyssey*, who trapped Odysseus and his men on their wanderings, and ate many of them before the hero managed to devise an escape. Cyclopes were thought to have helped in the building of some of the most ancient Greek cities, including Mycenae and Tiryns.

CYPRIS, or the CYPRIAN Aphrodite, who was born from the sea off Cyprus, and who was held in special honour there.

CYPRUS large island in the eastern Mediterranean.

DANAANS see DANAUS.

DANAUS father of the fifty girls known as the Danaids, and more generally conceived as the ancestor of the Danaans (which is sometimes a general title for Greeks but often more specifically means Argives).

DANAUS' SONS the Argives (see DANAUS).

DARDANUS first founder and king of Troy; hence the Trojans are sometimes called 'Dardanians'.

DELOS an island (one of the Cyclades), in the middle of the Aegean sea; birthplace of Apollo and Artemis and a major cult-centre.

DELPHI a town in the mountainous region of Phocis in central Greece, location of the temple and oracular shrine of Apollo.

DEMETER goddess of fertility in nature, presiding over the crops and other products of the earth; mother of Persephone.

DIOMEDES son of Tydeus; one of the most successful Greek heroes at Troy.

DIONYSUS son of Zeus by Semele; god of wine and other natural forces; often seen as a wild and irrational deity, bringer of madness.

DIOSCURI ('sons of Zeus') Castor and Polydeuces, the Heavenly Twins; see CASTOR.

DIRCE a wicked queen of Thebes, killed by Amphion and Zethus. After her death her name was associated with a stream near Thebes.

DITHYRAMBUS a title of Dionysus, alluding to a type of lyric song (usually associated with excited emotion) performed in his honour, the dithyramb.

DODONA a sanctuary of Zeus in Epirus in north-western Greece; one of the oldest Greek oracular shrines.

DOLON a Trojan who undertakes a spying mission for Hector, but is killed for his pains.

DORIAN the Dorians were one of the major ethnic groups of the Greeks, often contrasted with the Ionians. Athens was of Ionian descent, Sparta Dorian. Forms of dress and architectural styles were named after these groups: 'Dorian' regularly suggests something austere and dignified.

ECHIDNA the name means snake. A monster of the underworld, half woman and half serpent.

ECHINAE a group of islands off Acarnania (western Greece), near Ithaca.

ECHION one of the 'Sown Men' of Thebes, father of Pentheus.

ELECTRA daughter of Agamemnon and Clytemnestra; sister of Orestes, whom she supports in the murder of their mother. She subsequently married Orestes' friend Pylades.

ELECTRAN GATE one of the seven gates of Thebes. There is no connection with the Electra who belongs to Agamemnon's family.

ELIS a Greek state in the north-western Peloponnese. Olympia, where the Olympic games took place, was located there.

EPAPHUS son of Zeus and Io, begotten not by intercourse but with a single touch of the god's hand (the name means 'he of the touch'). Ancestor of Danaus and Aegyptus.

349

EPEIANS a force from Elis, part of the expedition against Troy; also mentioned in the catalogue of ships in Homer.

EREBUS 'Darkness'. One of the gods sprung from Chaos; also commonly used as a name for the underworld.

ERECHTHEUS an early king of Athens, father of Creusa. Hence the Athenians are sometimes called Erechtheids or 'sons of Erechtheus'.

EROS 'Love', personified as a boy with a bow and arrows; son of Aphrodite and like her responsible for afflicting mortals with passion. The more familiar name of Cupid is Latin in origin.

ETEOCLES son of Oedipus, and ruling after his father in Thebes. The war of the Seven against Thebes arose because he failed to honour the agreement he had made to share power with his brother Polyneices. The two eventually killed each other in combat.

ETRUSCAN a general ethnic name referring to a people of Italy; Etruscan metalwork was famous, and they were often said to have invented the trumpet.

EUBOEA a large island off the coast of Attica and Boeotia.

EUMELUS son of Admetus and Alcestis, grandson of Pheres; in the catalogue of ships in Homer, his mares are described as being the swiftest in the Greek host.

EUMENIDES 'the Kindly Ones', a euphemistic way of referring to the Furies.

EUMOLPUS king of a Thracian people who assisted the Eleusinians in a war against Athens in the time of King Erechtheus.

EURIPUS, RIVER the narrow strait separating Euboea from Boeotia.

EUROPA beloved of Zeus, and by him mother of the Lycian hero Sarpedon (referred to as 'son of Europa', but not named, in the *Rhesus*).

EUROTAS a major river in the southern Peloponnese, running through Spartan territory.

EURYTUS in the *Iphigenia at Aulis* leader of the Epeians from Elis. In the *Iliad* it is Eurytus' son, Thalpius, who goes to Troy.

EVIUS a cult-title of Dionysus, associated with the cry of 'evoe', an expression of joy and ecstasy.

FURIES a Fury is a daemonic and dangerous creature who was thought to persecute evil-doers in life and after death; hence any horrific and avenging figure, especially female. The Furies' most famous role in mythology is as pursuers of Orestes, whom they hounded after he had killed his mother.

GANYMEDE a beautiful Trojan boy who was carried away by Zeus because of his beauty; he became the cup-bearer of Zeus on Olympus as well as sharing his bed.

GERAESTUS a promontory at the southern tip of the island of Euboea.

GERENIAN from the *Iliad* onwards, a title attached to Nestor, of uncertain meaning.

GLAUCUS son of Nereus, and like him a prophetic sea-divinity.

GORGON a type of hideous female monster with snakes for hair, so horrible that to look at one outright would turn a man to stone. The most famous Gorgon, Medusa, was slain by Perseus, who chopped off her head by looking not at her, but at her reflection in his shield. A Gorgon's head adorned the shield of Athena.

GOUNEUS king of the Aenians; mentioned in Homer's catalogue of ships.

GRACES minor goddesses who embody the graceful beauty and pleasure of life, often associated with the Muses and represented singing or dancing.

HADES (a) one of the three most powerful Olympians, the others being Zeus and Poseidon. They divided up the universe, and Hades drew the underworld as his domain; (b) the underworld itself.

HAEMON son of Creon of Thebes, betrothed to Antigone.

HARMONIA daughter of Ares and Aphrodite; wife of Cadmus of Thebes.

HEBE 'youth'. Consort of Heracles; divine personification of youthful beauty.

HECATE a sinister goddess associated with darkness, witchcraft and ghosts. Sometimes, however, she is identified with Artemis and viewed more positively.

HECTOR son of Priam and Hecabe, and prince of Troy; the most valiant of the Trojan warriors. Eventually killed by Achilles, after which Troy was doomed.

HELEN daughter of Zeus and the mortal woman Leda; wife of Menelaus and mother of Hermione. According to the usual legend, she was carried away or seduced by the Trojan Paris. The Trojan war was fought to get her back. She eventually returned to Sparta and lived with her husband (though in the *Orestes* this ending is modified).

HELIOS the sun, personified as a god. He is sometimes associated with or even identified with Apollo, who was also often regarded as a god of light (and whose sister Artemis presided over the moon).

HEPHAESTUS son of Zeus and Hera; god of fire and of the arts of craftsman-ship, especially metalwork, but lame and often treated disparagingly by his fellow divinities. His forges were thought to be located under Mount Etna.

HERA queen of the gods and consort of Zeus; presides over marriage; often associated with Argos, one of her favourite cities.

HERACLES son of Zeus and Alcmene; greatest of the Greek heroes, famous for his many victories over monsters and barbaric peoples; enslaved by Eurystheus and compelled to perform twelve labours. Eventually deified and married to Hebe.

HERMES son of Zeus and the nymph Maia; messenger of the gods.

HERMIONE daughter of Helen and Menelaus; she remained in Greece while Helen went with Paris to Troy.

HIPPOMEDON an Argive, one of the Seven against Thebes.

HOMOLOIDAN GATE one of the seven gates of Thebes

HYMEN or HYMENAEUS perhaps originally a celebratory cry at wedding ceremonies, but often taken as name of a god presiding over such events.

IDA a mountain range in the Troad, where the young Paris was exposed as a child and grew up.

ILIUM another name for Troy.

INACHUS mythical first king of Argos, usually regarded as divine embodiment of the river that bears his name. Father of Io.

INO one of the daughters of Cadmus; sister of Agaue.

IO daughter of Inachus; beloved by Zeus; ancestress of Agenor and the Tyrian people; also of Danaus and his daughters. See further note 1 to *Phoenician Women*.

IONIA, IONIAN SEAS 'Ionia' refers to the region inhabited by Greeks of that ethnic group in Asia Minor; but the 'Ionian seas' referred to in the *Phoenician Women* mean the sea to the west of central Greece, separating Corcyra and the mouth of the Corinthian gulf from Italy and Sicily.

IPHIGENIA daughter of Agamemnon and Clytemnestra. Her father was forced to sacrifice her in order to gain favourable winds for the Greek fleet; according to the version followed in *Iphigenia among the Taurians*, she was rescued by Artemis and carried off to the remote land of the Tauri.

ISMENUS a river in Theban territory.

IXION king of the Lapiths; one of the great sinners of myth, traditionally the first Greek to kill a kinsman. He also attempted to rape Hera, and was punished in the underworld by being bound for ever to a rotating wheel of fire.

JOCASTA wife of Laius and mother of Oedipus, whom she later married without knowing his true identity. By Oedipus she had four children; see further initial note to *Phoenician Women*.

KINDLY ONES see EUMENIDES.

LABDACUS king of Thebes and father of Laius.

LAERTES former king of Ithaca and father of Odysseus.

LAITUS according to the *Iphigenia at Aulis*, one of the Sown Men of Thebes and a captain of the Theban contingent to Troy. He is briefly mentioned in the *Iliad*'s catalogue of ships.

LAIUS king of Thebes; husband of Jocasta and father of Oedipus, who inadvertently killed his father.

LEDA wife of the Spartan Tyndareus, mother of Helen, Clytemnestra, Castor and Pollux.

LERNA a marshy area near Argos, chiefly famous as the abode of the monstrous Hydra.

LETO a goddess or Titaness who bore Apollo and Artemis to Zeus on the island of Delos.

LIBYA part of North Africa, sometimes loosely used to refer to the whole continent other than Egypt.

LINUS a shadowy figure. The refrain *ailinon* in songs of lamentation was thought to mean 'alas for Linus', and so stories about Linus were devised, e.g. that he was a music teacher of Heracles, slain by his pupil in a fit of anger.

LOCRIS a region north of the Gulf of Corinth; the domain of the lesser Ajax.

LOXIAS a title of Apollo, perhaps meaning 'crooked' or 'slanting', with reference to his ambiguous oracles.

LYCIA a region in southern Asia Minor.

LYDIA a region in the centre of west Asia Minor, bounded by Mysia in the north, Phrygia in the east and Caria in the south.

LYDIAS a river in Macedonia.

MAENADS another name for the Bacchants, followers of Dionysus. The name means 'mad ones'.

MAENALUS, MOUNT a mountain in Arcadia in southern Greece; the 'maid of Maenalus' is Atalanta, mother of Parthenopaea, because she was exposed there at birth.

MAIA one of the Pleiads, daughters of Atlas; mother of Hermes by Zeus.

MALEA, CAPE a promontory at the south-easternmost point of the Peloponnese. It was a region notorious for unsettled weather, and many sailors in legend, as no doubt in life, were driven off course near Malea.

MECISTEUS a Greek whose son Euryalus is mentioned as going to Troy in the Homeric catalogue of ships. 'The son of Mecisteus' is similarly referred to in the catalogue of the *Iphigenia at Aulis*, but without his name being given.

MEDES the inhabitants of Media, an Asian empire which preceded that of the Persians.

MEGES son of Phyleus; according to the catalogue in the *Iphigenia at Aulis*, king of the Taphians in the expeditionary force against Troy, but apparently subordinate to Eurytus.

MENELAUS son of Atreus and younger brother of Agamemnon; king of Sparta; husband of Helen. The Trojan war was fought by the Greeks on his behalf, to recover her.

MENOECEUS(1) a Theban, father of Creon and of Jocasta.

MENOECEUS(2) son of Creon.

MERIONES a Greek hero in the expedition against Troy; in the *Iliad* closely associated with Idomeneus.

MUSAEUS a poet-prophet and bringer of culture and mysteries; closely associated with Orpheus. See *Rhesus* 945–7 and note 44.

MUSES nine in number, goddesses of the arts and especially poetry; daughters of Memory.

MYCENAE in very ancient times, a great centre of power and wealth in the Peloponnese. By Euripides' time it was eclipsed and indeed destroyed by Argos, with which in many passages it is virtually identified.

MYGDON father of Coroebus, a Trojan warrior.

MYRMIDONS followers of Achilles in the expedition against Troy.

MYRTILUS charioteer of King Oenomaus, suborned and subsequently murdered by Pelops.

MYSIA a region of Asia Minor, north of Lydia and to the east of the Troad.

NAUPLION or NAUPLIA a town in the Peloponnese near Argos, serving as its port.

NEISTIAN GATE one of the seven gates of Thebes.

NEMESIS personification of the power of retribution for crimes.

NEOPTOLEMUS son of Achilles, brought up in Scyros while his father was in Troy. After Achilles' death he joined the expedition and played a part in the final sack of Troy.

NEREIDS sea-nymphs, daughters of Nereus. The best known was Thetis, mother of Achilles.

NEREUS a sea-divinity, often conceived as part man and part fish. He had the gift of prophecy.

NESTOR king of Pylos; one of the oldest Greeks to go to Troy, and because of his age and wisdom highly respected by Agamemnon and the other leaders.

NIOBE Theban princess, wife of Amphion; her children were killed by Apollo and Artemis because she had boasted that she was more successful at child-bearing than their mother Leto.

NIREUS already referred to in Homer as the most beautiful of the Greek heroes in the expedition against Troy.

NYSA a mountain of uncertain location, usually referred to as a place where Dionysus is celebrated.

OCEAN or OCEANUS in early Greek thought, conceived as a vast river circling the known world, and often personified as the greatest of river gods.

ODYSSEUS one of the chief leaders of the Greeks at Troy; son of Laertes, king of Ithaca, husband of Penelope. He was the favourite of Athena, and a cunning deviser of plans; often he was represented as too clever for his own good, and even as an immoral schemer.

OEAX brother of Palamedes.

OEDIPUS son of Laius and Jocasta; becomes king of Thebes but is dethroned when the truth about his past is discovered; curses his sons Eteocles and Polyneices, who in the end kill one another. See further Preface and note I to *Phoenician Women*.

OENEUS father of Tydeus, one of the Seven against Thebes.

OENONE an island south of Attica ruled by Aeacus, subsequently renamed after his wife Aegina.

OGYGIAN GATE one of the seven gates of Thebes.

OILEUS father of the lesser Ajax.

OLYMPUS a legendary figure from Phrygia or Mysia who was said to have invented the Phrygian flute or pipe. He is briefly alluded to in the *Iphigenia at Aulis*.

OLYMPUS, MOUNT a mountain in northern Greece, on the borders of Macedonia and Thessaly. Because of its majestic height, it was considered the home of the gods, though the name is sometimes used more loosely, to describe a remote heavenly realm.

ORESTES son of Agamemnon and Clytemnestra, brother of Electra. After growing up in Phocis near Delphi, he returned to Argos to avenge his father's death.

ORPHEUS a gifted poet and musician whose singing could spellbind even wild beasts and who endeavoured to charm the powers of the underworld into releasing his dead wife – in some versions successfully.

PAEONIA part of Rhesus' domain, in northwestern Thrace.

PALAMEDES a clever and inventive Greek on the expedition against Troy. Odysseus, jealous of his gifts, framed him and brought about his death.

PALLAS = ATHENA.

PAN son of Hermes; half goat, half man, this lesser deity is a figure of the wild and is often thought to induce frenzy and fits of madness (hence 'panic').

PANGAION a mountain range in Thrace, where the river-god Strymon waylaid and made love to the Muse, Rhesus' mother.

PANTHOUS a Trojan leader, probably the same as the Panthus who appears in book 2 of Virgil's *Aeneid*.

PAPHOS a city in Cyprus, and site of a famous temple to Aphrodite, near the place where she was said to have arisen from the sea.

PARIS Alexander or Alexandros, son of Priam and prince of Troy. Paris was the name given to him by the shepherds who rescued him when he was exposed in infancy. He judged Aphrodite the most beautiful of all goddesses, and was rewarded with Helen; but the consequence was the Trojan war.

PARNASSUS a mountain north of Delphi, sacred to Apollo and the Muses.

PARRHASIA a small locality in Arcadia, in the Peloponnese, where Orestes is to undergo a brief period of exile as a result of his matricide.

PARTHENOPAEUS handsome son of Atalanta, a member of the Seven against Thebes.

PELASGIA a term loosely used to refer to the area occupied by the original pre-Greek inhabitants of the Greek mainland; hence 'Greece' generally.

PELEUS son of Aeacus, king of Phthia, in Thessaly; a hero of the generation before the Trojan war; married to the sea-nymph Thetis, he became the father of Achilles.

PELION, MOUNT a mountain in Thessaly, in north-eastern Greece, inhabited by Cheiron and the Centaurs.

PELOPS son of Tantalus and early king of Pisa, father of Atreus and Thyestes. He gave his name to the Peloponnese, the massive southern part of Greece.

PENTHEUS son of Agaue and Echion, grandson of Cadmus; king of Thebes and opponent of Dionysus.

PERGAMUM or PERGAMA a name given to the inner citadel of Troy; also, more generally, used to refer to Troy itself.

PERICLYMENUS son of Poseidon and one of the defenders of Thebes against the Argive assault.

PERSEPHONE daughter of Demeter, and often associated with her in cult. Abducted by Hades, she was eventually obliged to spend part of the year on earth and part in the underworld with her husband.

PERSEUS one of the great heroes of Greek myth, slayer of the Gorgon, Medusa. He was a forebear of the even greater hero Heracles.

PERSIA in historical times, the most powerful eastern kingdom known to the Greeks. In the prologue to the *Bacchae* Dionysus describes his eastern conquests, and anachronistically refers to his journeys across 'Persia's sunny uplands'.

PHARSALUS town in southern Thessaly, part of the domain of Achilles' father Peleus.

PHERES father of Admetus and former ruler of Pherae in north-eastern Greece; grandfather of Eumelus.

PHILAMMON father of the poet Thamyris.

PHOCIS the larger territory surrounding Delphi, to the west of Boeotia.

PHOEBE a daughter of Tyndareus and Leda, hence sister to Helen and Clytemnestra; mentioned in the *Iphigenia at Aulis*, but mythologically unimportant.

PHOEBUS another name for Apollo.

PHOENICIA the territory at the easternmost part of the Mediterranean: its chief ancient cities were Sidon and Tyre.

PHRYGIA area in western Asia Minor; often used more loosely to refer to Asia and the 'barbarian' territories generally. Hence 'Phrygians' often = 'Trojans'.

PHTHIA a region in Thessaly, the kingdom of Achilles' father Peleus and subsequently of his son Neoptolemus.

PHYLEUS father of Meges, one of the Greek heroes who went to Troy.

PIERIA a district in Macedonia, on the northern slopes of Mount Olympus, a place associated with the Muses; hence they are referred to as 'Pierian maids' or 'daughters of Pieria'.

PLEIAD (plural PLEIADES) seven daughters of the Titan Atlas and of Pleione. They were pursued by Orion and turned into a constellation. They are associated with the marking of the seasons for farming activity.

POLYBUS king of Corinth; he and his wife, being childless, adopted the foundling Oedipus when he was discovered exposed on the mountain side.

POLYDEUCES Latinized as 'Pollux'; one of the Dioscuri or Heavenly Twins; see CASTOR.

POLYDORUS son of Cadmus and Harmonia; father of Labdacus.

POLYNEICES son of Oedipus and Jocasta, brother of Eteocles, whom he challenges in war for the throne of Thebes. In the end the two brothers kill each other.

POSEIDON god of the sea and also of other threatening natural forces such as earthquakes.

PRIAM king of Troy, husband of Hecabe. He was the father of many children, especially Hector, Alexander (also called Alexandros or Paris), Polyxena, Cassandra. At the sack of Troy he was killed by Neoptolemus.

PROETEAN GATE one of the seven gates of Thebes.

PROMETHEUS a Titan, who assisted Zeus in seizing power on Olympus and helped him in other ways (including enabling him to give birth to Athena); in some myths the creator of mankind, whom he befriended and to whom he gave the gift of fire. He was famous for his wisdom and ingenuity.

PROTESILAUS one of the Greek warriors on the expedition against Troy; traditionally he was the first to die when the army first entered battle.

PYLADES son of Strophius, king of Phocis, and close friend of Orestes, who was brought up in Strophius' court. He accompanied Orestes in disguise to Argos, joined him in the killing of Aegisthus and Clytemnestra, and subsequently married Electra.

PYLOS a city on the western coast of the Peloponnese, ruled by Nestor.

PYTHIAN a title of Apollo, commemorating his slaying of the snake Python, which previously guarded the oracle at Delphi; hence also an adjective meaning 'to do with Apollo, or Delphi'.

PYTHO another name for Delphi. The story was that Apollo had killed a huge snake (python), who had possessed the shrine before him. Hence Apollo bore the title 'Pythian'. The Pythian Games were held at Delphi.

RHEA mother of Zeus, Hera and other Olympian gods; consort of Cronus; often regarded as mother of all gods, and later treated as equivalent to Cybele.

RHESUS a Thracian warrior, allied to the Trojans. He figures already in book 10 of the *Iliad*; see further Preface to *Rhesus*.

ROARING ONE, THE see DIONYSUS.

SALAMIS an island off the coast of Attica, home of Telamon and his sons Ajax and Teucer.

SARDIS a major city of Lydia in Asia Minor.

SATYRS hybrid creatures, half man, half beast (often goat-like); followers of Dionysus; boisterous and lustful in their habits.

SCYTHIA a rather vague term used by the Greeks to refer to the lands to the north and east of the eastern Mediterranean, often regarded as wild, uncivilized and inhabited by nomadic tribes. Herodotus (book 4) discusses the Scythians at length.

SELENE the moon-goddess; in Hesiod she is sister to Helios (the sun) and Eos (dawn), but genealogies vary.

SEMELE mother of Dionysus by Zeus. For the details see notes 1 and 9 to the *Bacchae*.

SIDON like Tyre, a major city of Phoenicia.

SIMOIS a river of the plain of Troy.

SIPYLUS, MOUNT a mountain in Lydia in Asia Minor. In an angry speech in the *Iphigenia at Aulis* Achilles oddly refers to it as the place of origin of the Atridae, presumably because their ancestor Tantalus was also father of Niobe, who was preserved there in rock-form.

SISYPHUS a king of Corinth with a reputation for cleverness and unscrupulousness. He was sometimes said to be the real father of Odysseus. He was said even to have tried to cheat death itself. In the end he was imprisoned in the underworld and set the perpetual task of pushing a gigantic boulder up a hill; the reason for his punishment is variously reported.

SOWN MEN OF THEBES the original citizen warriors of Thebes, who sprang up from the earth when Cadmus sowed the dragon's teeth (see note 1 to *Phoenician Women*). The myth symbolizes the ferocity of the Thebans.

SPARTA chief city of Laconia, kingdom of Menelaus and Helen; in historical times one of the dominant cities of the Peloponnese and regularly opposed to Athens. This antagonism is often projected back into the mythical period.

SPHINX a monstrous female creature that threatened Thebes and devoured her citizens until Oedipus, by solving her riddle, brought about her death.

STHENELUS son of Capaneus; one of the Greek leaders in the Trojan war; friend of Diomedes.

STROPHIUS king of Phocis and ally of Agamemnon; father of Pylades.

STRYMON a river in Thrace; as a personified river-god, father of Rhesus.

TALAUS (1) grandfather of Euryalus, a member of the Greek expedition to Troy.

TALAUS (2) father of Adrastus, king of Argos.

TALTHYBIUS herald of the Greek army at Troy and particularly of Agamemnon.

TANTALUS (1) ancestor of Agamemnon and his family.

TANTALUS (2) according to the *Iphigenia at Aulis*, the name of Clytemnestra's first husband. This is probably a Euripidean invention.

TAPHOS one of the larger of the group of islands known as the Echinae, off western Greece.

TARTARUS one of the deepest regions of the underworld, where the wicked are condemned to suffer punishment.

TEIRESIAS blind prophet of Thebes, who appears frequently in tragedy, usually in order to give advice to rulers who are reluctant to accept it.

TELAMON son of Aeacus, brother of Peleus and father of the greater Ajax and of Teucer; king of the island of Salamis, and one of the heroes of the generation before the Trojan war.

TEUMESSUS a town in Boeotia, east of Thebes.

THAMYRIS legendary Thracian poet and musician, who was blinded by the Muses when he foolishly dared to compete with them.

THEBES chief city of Boeotia, north of Athens.

THEMIS an ancient goddess, daughter of Earth and Sky, and protectress of justice. Her name means 'order, law, propriety'. In early times she presided over the Delphic oracle.

THESEUS son of Aegeus and Aethra; most famous of the mythical kings of Athens.

THESPROTIA a region in Epirus in north-western Greece, notable for being the location of the great oracle of Dodona.

THESSALY a region of north-eastern Greece.

THESTIUS father of Leda, the mother of Helen and Clytemnestra.

THETIS a goddess of the sea, who married Peleus and bore him the hero Achilles. She abandoned Peleus and returned to the sea, but never entirely forgot her mortal connections.

THRACE a region to the extreme north-east of the Greek mainland, beyond Macedonia; southern Greeks regarded it as primitive and savage.

THRONIUM a city which formed part of the domain of the lesser Ajax, in Ozolian Locris; mentioned in the list of his territories in Homer's catalogue, and also referred to in the *Iphigenia at Aulis*.

THYESTES son of Pelops and brother of Atreus; father of Aegisthus, whose usurpation of Agamemnon's throne was partly a form of revenge for the crime of Atreus, who had killed Thyestes' other sons and served them up to their unsuspecting father for dinner.

THYMBRA a town close to Troy. It supplied contingents for the Trojan defence forces.

TMOLUS a large mountain in Lydia overshadowing the city of Sardis; associated with Bacchic worship.

TROJANS the people of Troy, defeated by the Greeks in the Trojan war. Most famous are their king Priam and his sons Hector, the outstanding warrior killed by Achilles, and Paris, who started the war by abducting Helen.

TROY a city in Asia Minor, ruled by Priam and his family. In earlier times its kings included Dardanus and Laomedon. Its citadel was known as Pergama or Pergamon. The Greeks destroyed it at the end of the ten-year Trojan war.

TYDEUS one of the Seven against Thebes; father of Diomedes.

TYNDAREUS father of Helen and Clytemnestra, Castor and Pollux (some of these had Zeus as their real father, particularly Helen, but terms such as 'daughter of Tyndareus' are still used in a loose way).

TYRE a city of Phoenicia, supposedly founded by Agenor, father of Cadmus.

ZEPHYRUS the west wind, usually gentle and favourable.

ZETHUS see AMPHION.

ZEUS the most powerful of the Olympian gods and head of the family of immortals; father of Apollo, Athena, Artemis and many other lesser gods, as well as of mortals such as Heracles.

PENGUIN CLASSICS

THE BIRDS AND OTHER PLAYS
ARISTOPHANES

The Knights/Peace/The Birds/The Assemblywomen/Wealth

'Oh wings are splendid things, make no mistake:
they really help you rise in the world'

The plays collected in this volume, written at different times in Aristophanes'
forty-year career as a dramatist, all contain his trademark bawdy comedy and
dazzling verbal agility. In *The Birds*, two frustrated Athenians join with the birds to
build the utopian city of 'Much Cuckoo in the Clouds'. *The Knights* is a venomous
satire on Cleon, the prominent Athenian demagogue, while *The Assemblywomen*
considers the war of the sexes, as the women of Athens infiltrate the all-male
Assembly in disguise. The lengthy conflict with Sparta is the subject of *Peace*,
inspired by the hope of a settlement in 421 BC, and *Wealth* reflects the economic
catastrophe that hit Athens after the war, as the god of riches is depicted as a
ragged, blind old man.

The lively translations by David Barrett and Alan H. Sommerstein capture the full
humour of the plays. The introduction examines Aristophanes' life and times, and
the comedy and poetry of his works. This volume also includes an introductory
note for each play.

Translated with an introduction by David Barrett and Alan H. Sommerstein

---

PENGUIN CLASSICS

MEDEA AND OTHER PLAYS
EURIPIDES

Medea/Alcestis/The Children of Heracles/Hippolytus

'That proud, impassioned soul,
so ungovernable now that she has felt the sting of injustice'

Medea, in which a spurned woman takes revenge upon her lover by killing her
children, is one of the most shocking and horrific of all the Greek tragedies.
Dominating the play is Medea herself, a towering and powerful figure who
demonstrates Euripides' unusual willingness to give voice to a woman's case.
Alcestis, a tragicomedy, is based on a magical myth in which Death is overcome,
and *The Children of Heracles* examines the conflict between might and right,
while *Hippolytus* deals with self-destructive integrity and moral dilemmas. These
plays show Euripides transforming the awesome figures of Greek mythology into
recognizable, fallible human beings.

John Davie's accessible prose translation is accompanied by a general introduction
and individual prefaces to each play.

'John Davie's translations are outstanding ... the tone throughout is refreshingly
modern yet dignified' William Allan, *Classical Review*

Previously published as *Alcestis and Other Plays*.

Translated by John Davie, with an introduction and notes by Richard Rutherford

PENGUIN CLASSICS

ELECTRA AND OTHER PLAYS
SOPHOCLES

Ajax/Electra/Women of Trachis/Philoctetes

> 'Now that he is dead,
> I turn to you; will you be brave enough
> To help me kill the man who killed our father?'

Sophocles' innovative plays transformed Greek myths into dramas featuring complex human characters, through which he explored profound moral issues. *Electra* portrays the grief of a young woman for her father Agamemnon, who has been killed by her mother's lover. Aeschylus and Euripides also dramatized this story, but the objectivity and humanity of Sophocles' version provided a new perspective. Depicting the fall of a great hero, *Ajax* examines the enigma of power and weakness combined in one being, while the *Women of Trachis* portrays the tragic love and error of Heracles' deserted wife Deianeira, and *Philoctetes* deals with the conflict between physical force and moral strength.

E. F. Watling's vivid translation is accompanied by an introduction in which he discusses Sophocles' use of a third actor to create new dramatic situations and compares the different treatments of the Electra myth by the three great tragic poets of classical Athens.

Translated with an introduction by E. F. Watling

PENGUIN CLASSICS

LYSISTRATA AND OTHER PLAYS
ARISTOPHANES

Lysistrata/The Acharnians/The Clouds

> 'But he who would provoke me should remember
> That those who rifle wasps' nests will be stung!'

Writing at a time of political and social crisis in Athens, Aristophanes (*c.* 447–*c.* 385 BC) was an eloquent, yet bawdy, challenger to the demagogue and the sophist. In *Lysistrata* and *The Acharnians*, two pleas for an end to the long war between Athens and Sparta, a band of women and a lone peasant respectively defeat the political establishment. The darker comedy of *The Clouds* satirizes Athenian philosophers, Socrates in particular, and reflects the uncertainties of a generation in which all traditional religious and ethical beliefs were being challenged.

For this edition Alan H. Sommerstein has completely revised his translation of these three plays, bringing out the full nuances of Aristophanes' ribald humour and intricate word play, with a new introduction explaining the historical and cultural background to the plays.

Translated with an introduction by Alan H. Sommerstein

PENGUIN CLASSICS

THE REPUBLIC
PLATO

> 'We are concerned with the most important of issues,
> the choice between a good and an evil life'

Plato's *Republic* is widely acknowledged as the cornerstone of Western philosophy. Presented in the form of a dialogue between Socrates and three different interlocutors, it is an inquiry into the notion of a perfect community and the ideal individual within it. During the conversation other questions are raised: what is goodness; what is reality; what is knowledge? *The Republic* also addresses the purpose of education and the roles of both women and men as 'guardians' of the people. With remarkable lucidity and deft use of allegory, Plato arrives at a depiction of a state bound by harmony and ruled by 'philosopher kings'.

Desmond Lee's translation of *The Republic* has come to be regarded as a classic in its own right. His introduction discusses contextual themes such as Plato's disillusionment with Athenian politics and the trial of Socrates. This new edition also features a revised bibliography.

Translated with an introduction by Desmond Lee

PENGUIN CLASSICS

PROMETHEUS BOUND AND OTHER PLAYS
AESCHYLUS

Prometheus Bound/The Suppliants/Seven Against Thebes/The Persians

> 'Your kindness to the human race has earned you this.
> A god who would not bow to the gods' anger – you
> Transgressing right, gave privileges to mortal men'

Aeschylus (525–456 BC) brought a new grandeur and epic sweep to the drama of classical Athens, raising it to the status of high art. In *Prometheus Bound* the defiant Titan Prometheus is brutally punished by Zeus for daring to improve the state of wretchedness and servitude in which mankind is kept. *The Suppliants* tells the story of the fifty daughters of Danaus who must flee to escape enforced marriages, while *Seven Against Thebes* shows the inexorable downfall of the last members of the cursed family of Oedipus. And *The Persians*, the only Greek tragedy to deal with events from recent Athenian history, depicts the aftermath of the defeat of Persia in the battle of Salamis, with a sympathetic portrayal of its disgraced King Xerxes.

Philip Vellacott's evocative translation is accompanied by an introduction, with individual discussions of the plays, and their sources in history and mythology.

Translated with an introduction by Philip Vellacott

THE STORY OF PENGUIN CLASSICS

Before 1946 ...'Classics' are mainly the domain of academics and students, without readable editions for everyone else. This all changes when a little-known classicist, E. V. Rieu, presents Penguin founder Allen Lane with the translation of Homer's *Odyssey* that he has been working on and reading to his wife Nelly in his spare time.

1946 *The Odyssey* becomes the first Penguin Classic published, and promptly sells three million copies. Suddenly, classic books are no longer for the privileged few.

1950s Rieu, now series editor, turns to professional writers for the best modern, readable translations, including Dorothy L. Sayers's *Inferno* and Robert Graves's *The Twelve Caesars*, which revives the salacious original.

1960s The Classics are given the distinctive black jackets that have remained a constant throughout the series's various looks. Rieu retires in 1964, hailing the Penguin Classics list as 'the greatest educative force of the 20th century'.

1970s A new generation of translators arrives to swell the Penguin Classics ranks, and the list grows to encompass more philosophy, religion, science, history and politics.

1980s The Penguin American Library joins the Classics stable, with titles such as *The Last of the Mohicans* safeguarded. Penguin Classics now offers the most comprehensive library of world literature available.

1990s The launch of Penguin Audiobooks brings the classics to a listening audience for the first time, and in 1999 the launch of the Penguin Classics website takes them online to a larger global readership than ever before.

The 21st Century Penguin Classics are rejacketed for the first time in nearly twenty years. This world famous series now consists of more than 1300 titles, making the widest range of the best books ever written available to millions – and constantly redefining the meaning of what makes a 'classic'.

The Odyssey continues ...

The best books ever written

PENGUIN 🐧 CLASSICS

SINCE 1946

Find out more at www.penguinclassics.com